Environmental Management - Pollution, Habitat, Ecology, and Sustainability

Edited by John P. Tiefenbacher

Published in London, United Kingdom

IntechOpen

Supporting open minds since 2005

Environmental Management - Pollution, Habitat, Ecology, and Sustainability
http://dx.doi.org/10.5772/intechopen.94788
Edited by John P. Tiefenbacher

Contributors
Lameed Gbolagade Akeem, Lateef Funmilayo Lewiska, Yogranjan Singh, Sarthak Pandey, Amit Kumar Goswami, Percy Jinga, Gerard Rushingabigwi, Celestin Twizere, Jean De Dieu Ntawangaheza, Liguo Sun, Philibert Nsengiyumva, Michael Thomas Aide, Indi Braden, Christine Aide, Rodrigue Constant Sandjong Sani, Mama Ntoupka, Toua Vroumsia, Adamou Ibrahima, Muniyandi Balasubramanian, Rabindra Kumar Mishra, Barun Kumar Behera, Anita Dash, Bidyut Kumar Patra, Andy Vinten, Iain D.M. Gunn, Tabbsum Hanif Mujawar, Lalasaheb Deshmukh, P. Prabhakar, Vijendra Chaudhari, Abdelkader Anouzla, Mlika Kastali, Latifa Mouhir, Abdelaziz Madinzi, Salah Souabi, Abdeslam Taleb, Neha Agarwal, Shubhagato Dasgupta, Latief Mahir Rachman, Michel Soto Chalhoub, Farida Hanna Campbell, Enes Yasa, Kadir Özdemir

First published in London, United Kingdom, 2022 by IntechOpen
IntechOpen is the global imprint of INTECHOPEN LIMITED, registered in England and Wales, registration number: 11086078, 5 Princes Gate Court, London, SW7 2QJ, United Kingdom
Printed in Croatia

British Library Cataloguing-in-Publication Data
A catalogue record for this book is available from the British Library

Additional hard and PDF copies can be obtained from orders@intechopen.com

Environmental Management - Pollution, Habitat, Ecology, and Sustainability
Edited by John P. Tiefenbacher
p. cm.
Print ISBN 978-1-83962-546-6
Online ISBN 978-1-83962-547-3
eBook (PDF) ISBN 978-1-83962-548-0

Meet the editor

Dr. John P. Tiefenbacher, Ph.D., is a Professor of Geography and Environmental Studies at Texas State University. His research has focused on various aspects of hazards and environmental management. Dr. Tiefenbacher has published on a diverse array of topics that examine perception and behaviors with regards to the application of pesticides, releases of toxic chemicals, environments of the US–Mexico borderlands, wildlife hazards, and the geography of wine. More recently his work pertains to adaptation to climate change, spatial responses of wine growing to climate change, the geographies of viticulture and wine, artificial intelligence and machine learning to predict patterns of natural processes, and disability as vulnerability to global warming-induced hazards in the Arctic.

Contents

Preface

Environmental management is a term that is very broad in scope and has many definitions. This volume regards management (recognition, analysis, assessments, and actions) taken in response to adverse circumstances with consequences for humans and the things we value. The environmental manager may be any layperson who is negatively affected by environmental degradation or disturbance, or may be the professional scientist, decisionmaker, or agent tasked with solving environmental problems for communities or societies at large. The geographical scale of environmental problems and their management may range from local to regional to global. The temporal nature of the problems may be immediate or long term, or they may be matters that will be of great importance in the future (as are the projected consequences of global warming, such as changing climates; rising seas; reorganized terrestrial, oceanic, and atmospheric circulations; disturbed, degraded, and dying ecosystems; and new patterns of hazards). So, broadly speaking, everyone is an environmental manager at some point in their lives and environmental management is usually an intentional action motivated by self-preservation or personal and collective gains.

The chapters in this book cover an array of contemporary environmental issues. They have been organized in somewhat general categories based on the foci of the issues: pollution, habitat, ecology, and sustainability. The chapters in the "Pollution" section regard studies and discussions of air pollution monitoring and assessment, groundwater pollution caused by sanitation problems with sewage and landfills, and ocean contamination due to mismanagement of plastic waste. The three chapters included in the "Habitat" section concern challenges posed to habitats of several types of organisms: people (housing comfort based on atmospheric conditions), viruses (mutation in response to habitat stresses), and monkeys (habitat loss due to hunting and deforestation). The chapters grouped under "Ecology" apply ecological analyses to several challenges: sustainable management in a national park, restoration of mining-degraded landscapes, discernment and mapping of soil types, and the economics of cultural ecosystem services. The "Sustainability" section includes chapters that pose questions about sustainability and, ultimately, survival in the contexts of complex landscapes, social systems, and extensive regions: water management for wetlands, flood mitigation, and agriculture in an arable catchment; improvement of the sustainability of water supplies by resurrecting traditional approaches; the implications of plantation agriculture on ecosystem sustainability; and recognition of the roles of environment, society, and governance in the need for countering global warming and investing in mitigation of climate change impacts.

While the chapters contained in this volume touch on only a few of the pressing matters that are important to environmental managers, they individually provide interesting insights into the problems experienced in diverse settings. From tropical to temperate regions, forests to deserts, wilderness to urbanized landscapes, and Europe (Montenegro and Scotland) and the Mediterranean Sea to Africa (Cameroon, Morocco, and Niger) and Asia (India and Indonesia), this assortment provides glimpses into topics that are the focus of scholars from these regions.

John P. Tiefenbacher
Department of Geography and Environmental Studies,
Texas State University,
San Marcos, Texas, USA

Section 1

Pollution

Chapter 1

Design and Development of Air Quality Monitoring System for Solapur City Using Smart Technologies: WSN and IoT

Tabbsum Hanif Mujawar, P. Prabhkar, Vijendra Chaudhary and Lalasaheb Deshmukh

Abstract

Owing to enhancement in technology there is inclination in miniaturization of devices which demands to build up stumpy expensive sensor, least powered and hardy devices. Accordingly, Wireless Sensor Networks (WSN) has gained significance in diverse applications: Farming, household, industries and environmental monitoring. Wireless sensor network system worn to monitor and control the air quality of an environment is developed. The air pollution monitoring system that measures temperature, humidity, SPM (Suspended Particulate Matter), NOx and CO are proposed. The conventional air quality monitoring system, prescribed by the Pollution Control Department, is tremendously pricey. Analytical measuring paraphernalia is lavish, time and power overriding, and can seldom be used for air quality exposure in real time. Endeavor has been completed to develop state of art monitoring system using commercially available standard pollutant gas sensors incorporated into a mote. An exact program made with LabVIEW is formed to constitute the measurements of sensing used in the established network. Remote monitoring of the system is made possible using IoT.

Keywords: WSN, XBee, Sensor Node, Gateway Node, IoT, Blynk Platform

1. Introduction

Fading air quality in India has moved towards malnutrition, for the past few decades. India remain one of the countries where 1.9 million untimely deaths take place due to worsening ambient air quality. The estimated financial losses caused due to air pollution in India are placed at 885 billion rupees [1, 2]. Revelation to outside air pollutants will enlarge the menace of Arrhythmia, Ischemia, Cardiac Failure and Stroke. Air quality data in Solapur has been analyzed to scrutinize its condition and to recognize its health situation.

The goal of this chapter is to tale on the development of a cost effective air quality monitoring system using wireless sensor network (WSN) and IoT, deployed in polluted areas of Solapur. The air quality in Solapur had been a tight rope walk for its citizens over the past decades [3]. Growth of Solapur had lead to rise in number of vehicles on the roads, creating supplementary pollution predicament with smoke emanation and other pollutants. Apart from the increase in vehicles, other reasons for escalating vehicular contamination are the varieties of engines used, crowded traffic, pitiable road conditions and dry climatic conditions. Solapur Municipal Corporation in alliance with Central Pollution Control Board and State Pollution Control Board has installed air quality monitoring system as an attempt of Swacch Bharat Abhiyan Project.

As data logger and hardware mechanism are not used, the present system is more superficial and user friendly. It was resolved to bail out air pollution monitoring in high traffic zones of Solapur city where pollutants exceeded the ambient air quality values as proposed by Central Pollution Control Board (CPCB). The system uses Wireless Sensor Network and IoT technology for air quality monitoring. Hitherto, the predictable monitoring system is massive, luxurious and power consuming. Therefore, incompatibility associated using wired monitoring system is replaced with a new wireless air monitoring system which is cost-effective and competent with stumpy power spending [4]. Wireless sensor networks (WSNs) are paying attention in the industry also in academia because of their significant relevance and associated security challenges. The utility of this network is to collect the data from the environment and fling it to the sink node. The present system consists of the five sensor nodes and one sink node. The chic sensor nodes are least-power gadgets outfitted with one or more sensors, microcontroller, a power supply and radio. An array of different sensors can be allied to the mote to determine environment parameters. With the establishment of 'Solapur' as smart city it becomes pertinent to employ the WSN for monitoring AAQ protocols. The smart city projects in Solapur is obligatory to put up a superior air quality monitoring system in terms of rate, power competence, ability by using contemptible handy ambient sensors. The use of IoT (Internet of Things) provides the remote monitoring of our system [5]. Internet of Things has a backbone of diverse technologies- Wireless Sensor Networks, Embedded Systems, Security Protocols and Architectures,

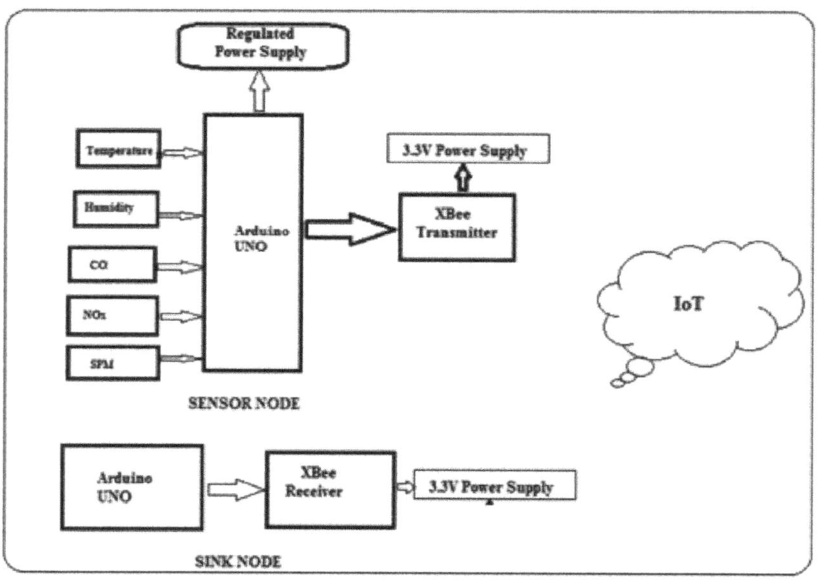

Figure 1.
Block diagram of a proposed system.

network services, Internet and Search Engines and Cloud Computing. The internet of things (IoT) is a system of unified computing gadgets, automatic and digital tackle, items, group that are provided with unique identifiers and the capability to convey data in excess of a network with no requiring user-to-user or user-to-computer dealings. Devices that work on IoT, distribute the sensor information; they amass by linking to an IoT gateway where data is sent to the cloud to be analyzed. The block diagram, **Figure 1** represents the proposed system. The use of open source IoT web server platform, to ensure an enduring storage as well as real time monitoring of air quality monitoring data makes the system more superior than the traditional data logger system. Use of flawless incorporation of smart mobile standards, WSN, and several other sensing technologies makes this system more scalable and smart. Uses of XBee wireless protocol make the system least power consumable.

2. Wireless sensor network setup for air quality monitoring system

A wireless sensor network is compacted in behavior. Generally, it provides thousands of irrelevant devices, called as sensor nodes and are incorporated to gather the data from assorted assets. The sink node collects the data from sensor node and provides necessary action on it.

2.1 Sensor node (mote)

The motes are constructed with four components (**Figure 1**), 1. Processing part made up of controller (Arduino UNO) 2. Wireless element for presuming wireless communication amid nodes (XBee) 3. Sensor to convert environment data into electrical quantity and 4. Batteries to offer power supply to the network [6]. Every constituent plays an important task in the operation of motes. Radio subsystem uses various techniques such as Bluetooth, XBee and UWB that operates at ISM band frequency of 2.4 GHz for wireless transmission. Microprocessor or microcontroller subsystem is used to offer logical decision regarding controlling of air quality monitoring system. To save energy, controller works in off, sleep, idle and active modes depending on the condition of the sensor nodes.

An array of sensors at the motes is as follows:

2.1.1 CO sensor (MQ-7)

MQ-7 Carbon monoxide sensor can sense CO gas and sends both digital and analog signals to Arduino. According to its datasheet, the MQ-7 sensor detects 20 to 2000 ppm of CO in air [7]. Its standard circuit represented in **Figure 2**. The interfacing of sensor to the arduino uno is shown in **Figure 3**.

The sensor has to be calibrated at 200 ppm of CO with R_L at 10KΩ. The load resistance R_L vary from 5KΩ to 47 KΩ. Its operating temperature range is from 20^{oc} to 50^{oc}. The surface resistance R_s varies from 2KΩ to 20KΩ. R_s can be calculated by the following formula.

$$\frac{\mathrm{Rs}}{\mathrm{Rl}} = (\mathrm{Vc} - \mathrm{VRl})/\mathrm{VRl}$$

From the datasheets, calibration of sensor in terms of ppm is done as follows.

$$\text{Concentration of gas(ppm)} = 3.027 * e^{\left(\left(\frac{3}{2.85}\right) * V - RL\right)\right)}$$

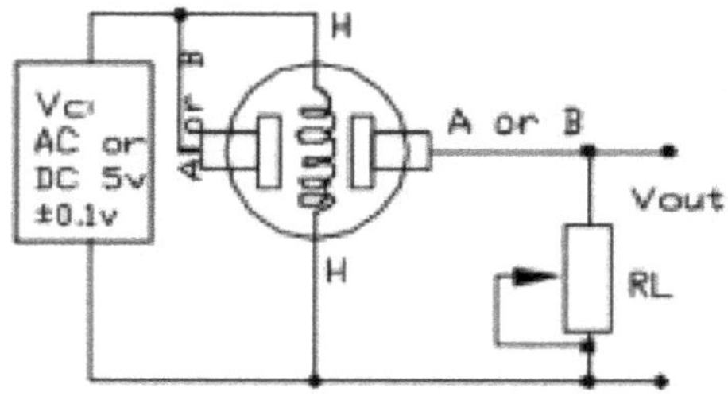

Figure 2.
Standard circuit.

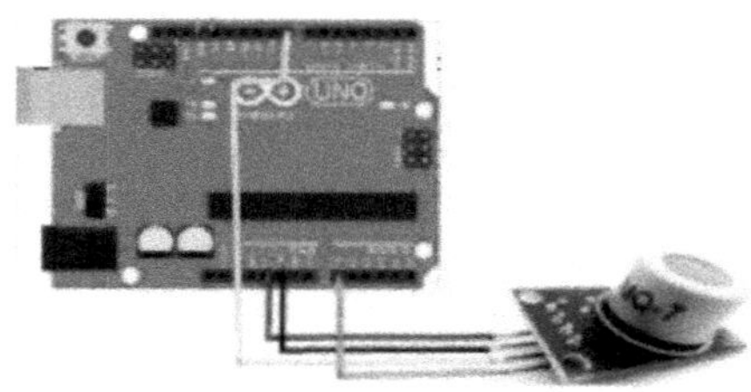

Figure 3.
Arduino interfacing of sensor.

Figure 4.
Lm-35.

2.1.2 Temperature sensor (LM-35)

LM-35 is an analog temperature sensor. It is connected to A1 of arduino UNO microcontroller at sensor node. It is shown in **Figure 4**.

Vitally, LM-35 is pre-calibrated in degree celsius to be used for temperature sensor IC. It is linear in characteristics. It does not require any external calibration and gives +10-mV/°C scale facet [8]. Accordingly, the arduino encoding is carried out and its outcomes are displayed on arduino serial monitor window. The characteristic curve and arduino interfacing of LM-35 is displayed in **Figures 5** and **6**, respectively.

2.1.3 MQ-135(NO_x and SPM sensor)

The calibrated MQ-135 air quality sensor is used for detecting an extensive series of parameters, including NH_3, NOx, alcohol, benzene, SPM and CO_2. But, it shows high sensitivity for NOx and SPM [9]. Its characteristics curve is shown in **Figures** 7 and **8**.

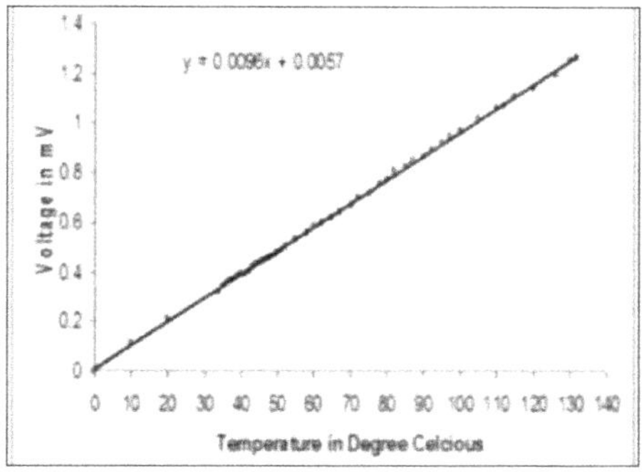

Figure 5.
LM-35 characteristics curve.

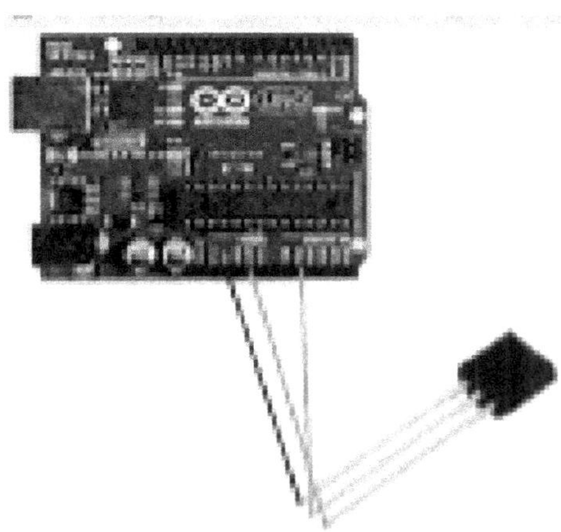

Figure 6.
Arduino interfacing.

2.1.4 Atmega 328 (controlling unit)

The Atmega 328 is an entrenched board having inbuilt USB proficiency. The minuscule and user approachable temperament makes it finer than other sophisticated microcontrollers. These microcontrollers encompass additional inbuilt amenities like +5 V, analog and digital pins. It does not comprise on board power jack. Owing to the auto switching potential of the microcontroller, no exterior power jumper is necessary [10]. It posses assorted on board pins and have advanced features as follows:

i. An automatic reset

ii. On chip broadcast and reception LED's

iii. Automatic switching to input power.

iv. Inbuilt USB flair for serial communication

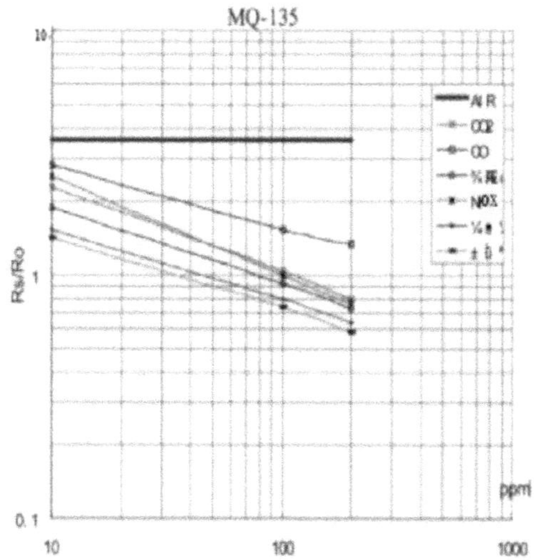

Figure 7.
Characteristics curve of MQ-135.

Figure 8.
MQ-135.

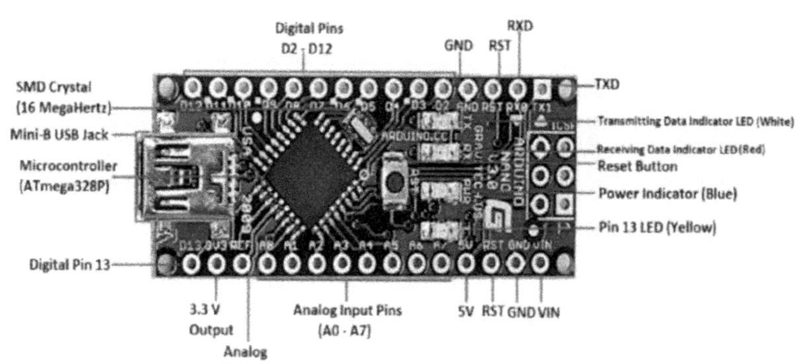

Figure 9.
Arduino nano pin configurations.

Consequently, the WSN nodes are premeditated using arduino nano-microcontroller. An actual pin specification of arduino nano is depicted in **Figure 9**.

2.1.5 XBee protocol

XBee is perched to suit the comprehensive control/sensor network standard. Usually, this module consists of a 16-bit microcontroller amid all parts as some 16 – bit microcontroller might have (ADC, timer, watchdog, sleep timer, UART, general-purpose I/O port… .etc.). The schematic representation of XBee is shown in **Figure 10**.

Figure 10.
XBee.

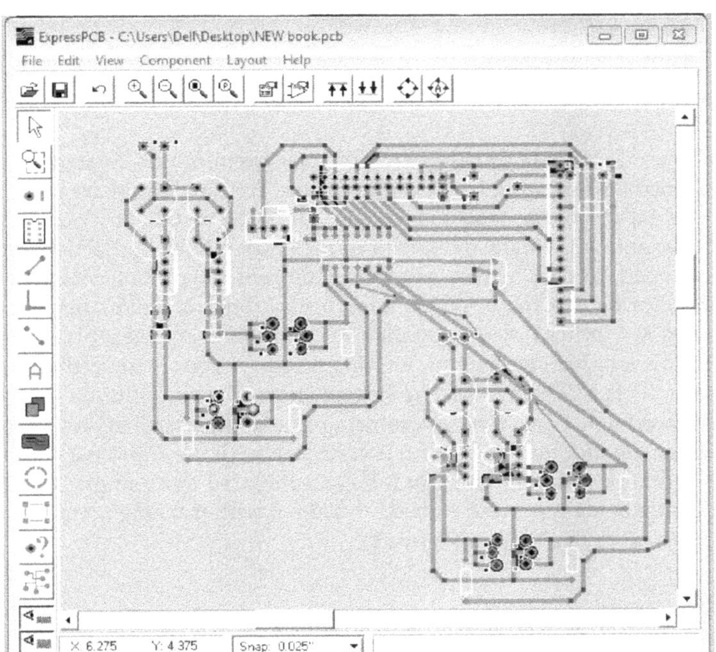

Figure 11.
PCB layout of the sensor node.

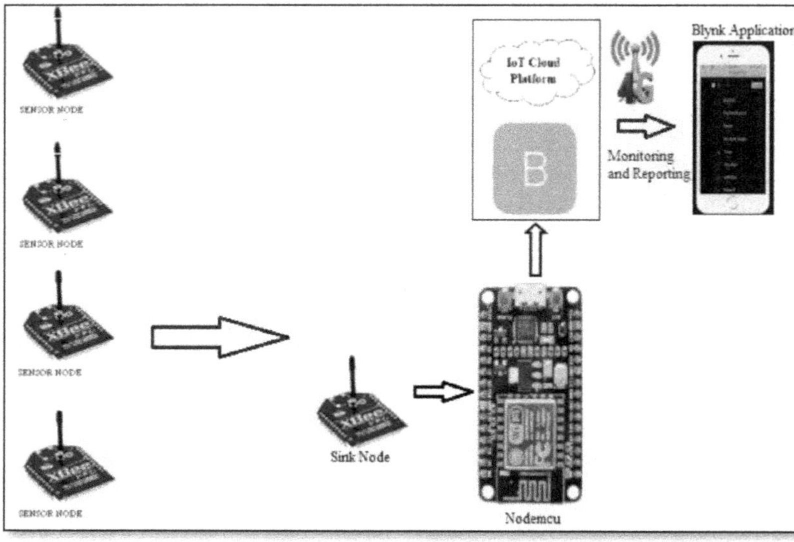

Figure 12.
Sink node setup of the present system.

Owing to the compensation of XBee technology like squat rate and stumpy power working modes and its topologies, this diminutive range communication technology is most excellent, suitable for numerous applications compared to other communications technologies such as Bluetooth, WI-FI, [11] etc. The PCB layout of sensor node drawn is shown in **Figure 11**.

The sink node of air pollution monitoring system is shown in **Figure 12**.

3. IoT (internet of things)

The IoT based air contamination monitoring system can be created via sensors and microcontrollers existing in the marketplace. The sink nodes are programmed to collect the data from the mote and transmit it to the cloud. An algorithm is proposed to examine the data and hurl it to the smart phone app. Smartphone app will be developed for user to access the air quality information in real-time [12, 13]. The IoT monitoring is scamper on the communication protocol maneuver. Internet of Things is now verdict reflective exploit in each and every area, plays an important role in this monitoring system too. This system monitors the effluence source from anywhere via PC or mobile. The system shows the air pollution in ppm on webpage, accordingly continuous monitoring can be done. IoT makes almost all "smart" which ameliorate aspects of our existence with the supremacy of data collection and networks. The thing in IoT can compared to be similar to a human being amid a diabetes supervise embed, an animal with tracking plans, etc. The basic block of IoT is depicted in **Figure 13**.

3.1 Blynk platform

Blynk is a podium with iOS and Android apps to control Arduino over the internet and is shown in **Figure 14**. It is a digital control panel where we can construct a advantage for our system by just dragging and dropping gadget. Blynk

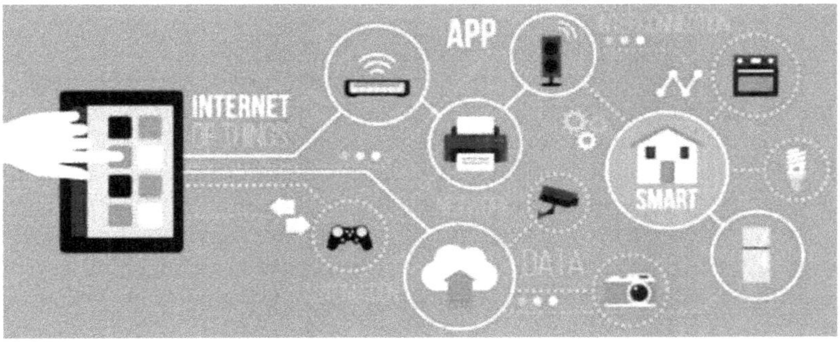

Figure 13.
Basic blocks of IoT.

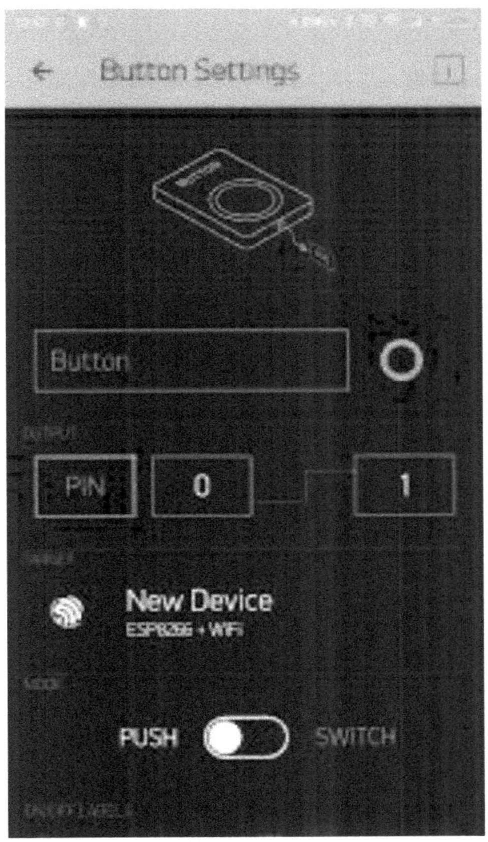

Figure 14.
Blynk platform.

can manage hardware distantly. Blynk server provides control over communication among the smartphone and hardware. It is an open source platform and be able to lever thousands of devices. Blynk Libraries are accessible and designed for almost all hardware platforms. These libraries help to communicate with the server and operate all inward and extrovert commands [14]. By pressing any key on Blynk app on the smartphone, the signal moves to the Blynk Cloud.

4. LabVIEW

LabVIEW is a software improvement environment produced by National Instruments. In order to recognize a real time data acquisition, LabVIEW is introduced. LabVIEW is worned to execute the system. The system investigates level of the entire connected sensor. At first, it was attentive on intriguing measurements from assorted lab instruments; however it has extended significantly from its initiation. LabVIEW is not a coding language, it is a graphical environment. The coding is actually called "G" code. It is a graphical indoctrination language that uses icons as a substitute of lines of text to build applications; it uses a dataflow encoding to resolve recital [15]. This software is straight forward to handle as it does not require an immense programming skills. The benefit of LabVIEW is prompt and uncomplicated erection of the graphical user interface (GUI) that process the refurbishing of parameters (without interfering with the code) and well-designed appearance of results. Tools used in LabVIEW is illustrated in **Figure 15**.

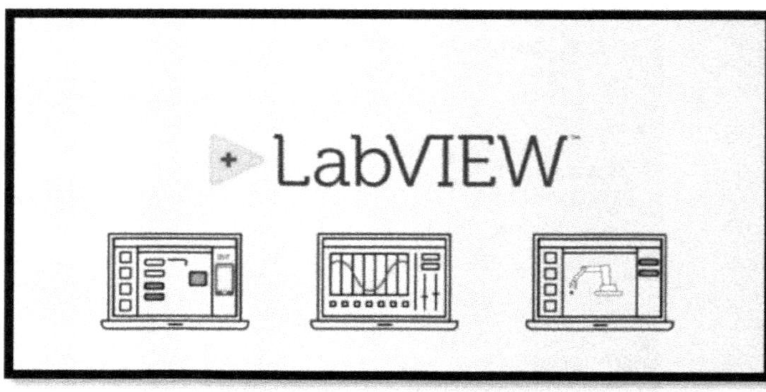

Figure 15.
Toolkits in LabVIEW.

5. Working of the system

The system proposes a design to fit monitoring applications on smartphones. Wireless sensors positioned at planned locations sense the level of carbon monoxide, nitrous oxide, humidity and temperature in the air. It provides simple access to the users to supervise real time air quality in their vicinity. It uses cost-effective and readily accessible devices such as an air quality sensor, carbon monoxide gas sensor, nitrous oxide gas sensor and SY-HS220 sensor. Microcontrollers are used at the sensor node for supervising these sensors. The sink node collects the data from sensor node and transfers it to the cloud database through wi-fi module. In the cloud, the data analysis is done so that the society takes measures to mitigate air pollution.

5.1 Accomplishment of a system to attain a data from sensor node(mote)

The air quality monitoring technique involves an interface among Arduino and LabVIEW software. The received values are keep in an Excel sheet and plotted on a chart. The LabVIEW programming for partition of data from each mote would be executed. The co-ordinator node is interfaced with LabVIEW through VISA

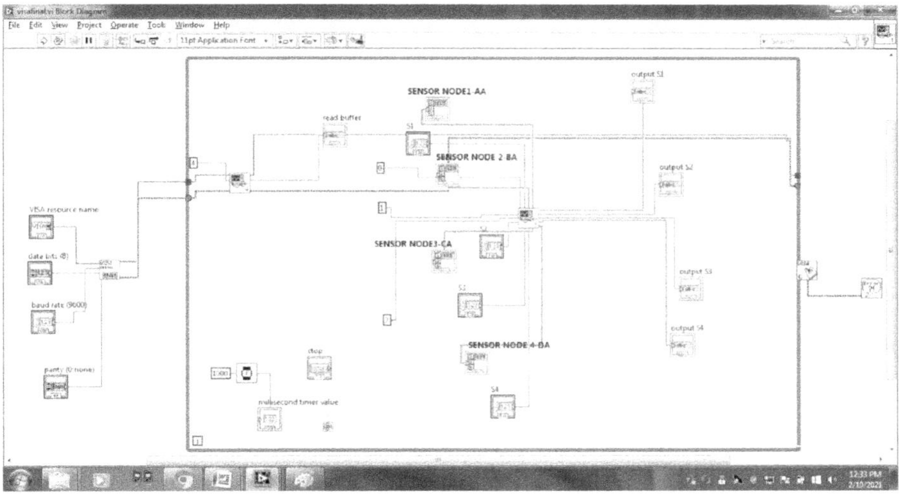

Figure 16.
LabVIEW mote data management.

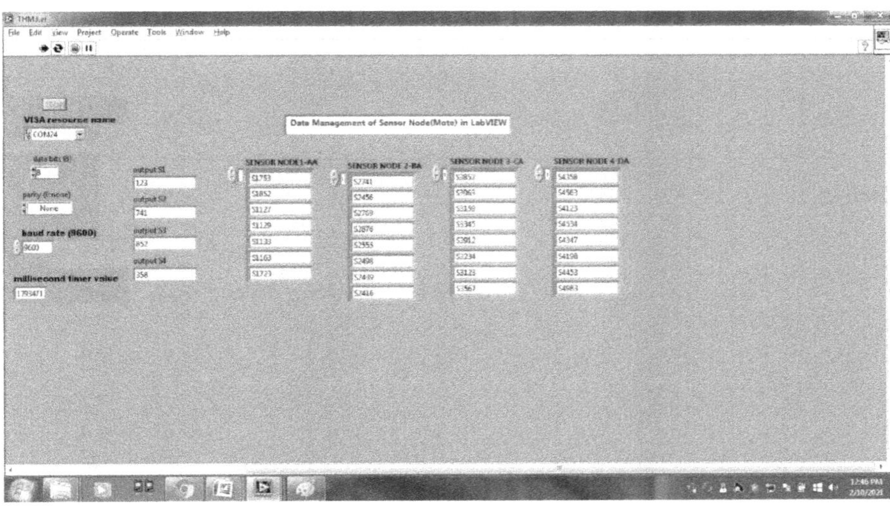

Figure 17.
GUI developed in LabVIEW for mote separation.

function tool [16]. The co-ordinator node collects the data from each mote and separated in LabVIEW and is shown in **Figures 16** and **17**.

6. Comparative analysis of current system with air quality status of Maharashtra 2019–2020 for Solapur City

For comparative study of the current system with traditional system, it has been envisaged one of the regions of Solapur city. Solapur is the fourth major city in the state of Maharashtra which has been racing simultaneously with first, second and third stages of industrial development. Solapur had hit the national headlines for being the most polluted city in India next to surat during 2001.As national ambient air quality standards the solapur municipal corporation has installed electronic sensors to detect SPM-10, SPM-2.5, NOx, SO2, CO apart from temperature, humidity, rainfall etc. Various studies titled "An insight into the unseen: A case study of AAQ in Solapur city [17]", "Air affair in the proposed smart city of Solapur [18]". The finding indicates SPM-10 to be causing worry for the citizen and is largely on the higher side of tolerance limit during the dry months. Various mitigation measures such as plantation, golf courses etc. were proposed. The present

Station name	Year	Month	Average of SO_2	Average of NOx	Average of RSPM
WIT campus	2019	Apr	18	36	82
		May	18	37	86
		Jun	19	38	81
		Jul	19	37	79
		Aug	17	35	75
		Sep	14	33	69
		Oct	13	32	68
		Nov	13	33	67
		Dec	12	32	69
	2020	Jan	12	32	68
		Feb	12	32	71
		Mar	12	32	71

Table 1.
Statistics for monthly average interpretation recorded at WIT campus.

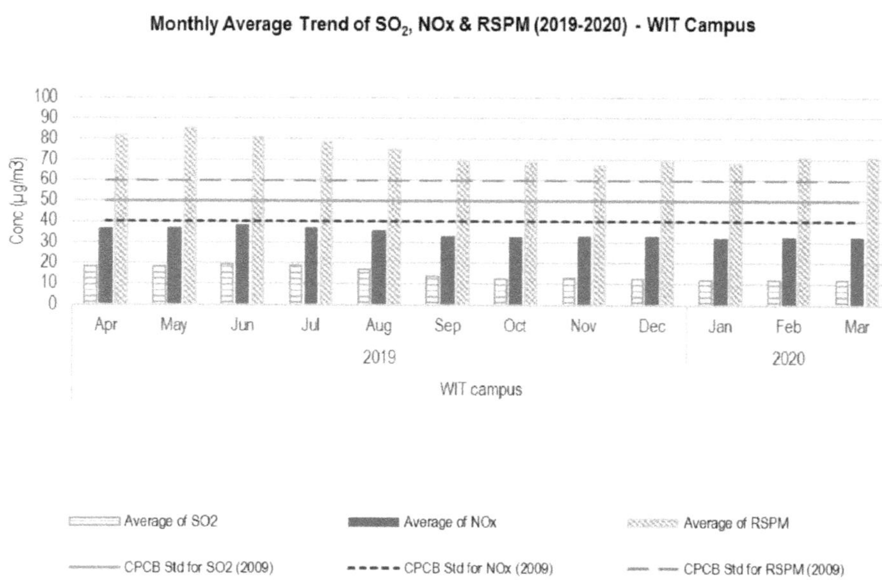

Figure 18.
Monthly standard analysis recorded at WIT campus.

smart WSN and IoT based system be installed at various stations of WIT campus area, collected data and were displayed on Android App developed on users mobile phone, on Blynk Platform, on LabVIEW Front Panel and Arduino serial monitor window. The prime advantage of developed system is that remote monitoring and controlling of air quality has been initiated. The monthly average reading recorded at WIT Campus, Solapur by CPCB (Central Pollution Control Board) is shown in **Table 1**. Its graphical representation is shown in **Figure 18**.

After deploying the sensor nodes at different locations of WIT campus, the data gathered at co-ordinator node is presented in **Table 2**. The proposed system measures the various air quality parameters such as NOx, RSPM, Temperature,

Station name	Year	Month	Average of NOx	Average of RSPM	Average of temp.	Average of humidity	Average of CO
WIT Campus	2019	Apr	38	100	44	28	120
		May	35	95	43	30	118
		Jun	38	88	40	33	115
		Jul	33	78	38	36	140
		Aug	34	72	33	40	100
		Sep	38	70	33	40	90
		Oct	31	69	32	39	88
		Nov	30	63	32	39	83
		Dec	31	68	34	32	79
	2020	Jan	32	69	33	29	78
		Feb	31	69	32	29	75
		Mar	31	69	32	30	75

Table 2.
Statistics for monthly average recorded at WIT campus by co-ordinator node.

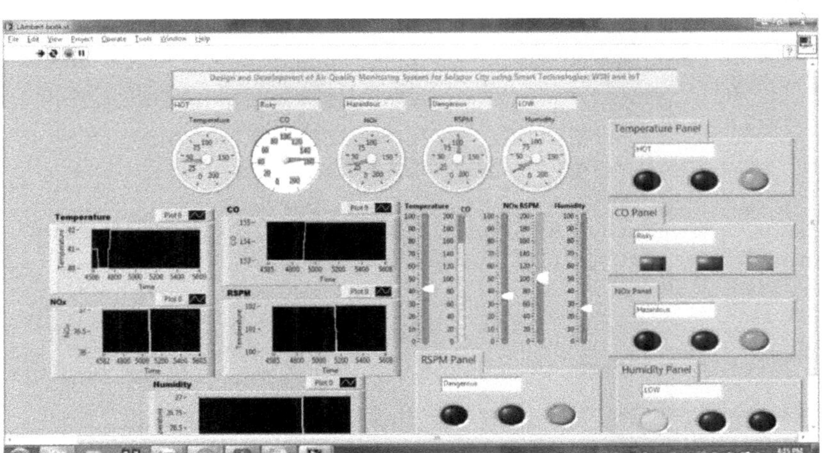

Figure 19.
Graphical user Interface on LabVIEW.

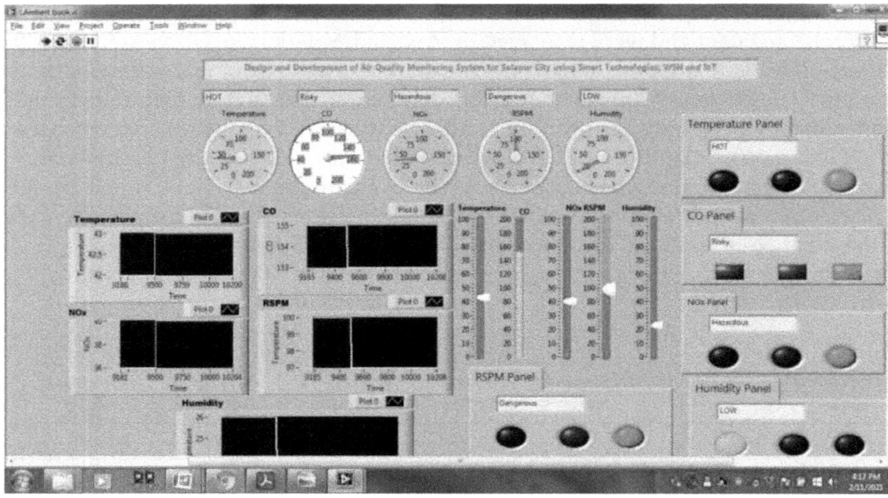

Figure 20.
Graphical user Interface on LabVIEW showing different levels of sensors.

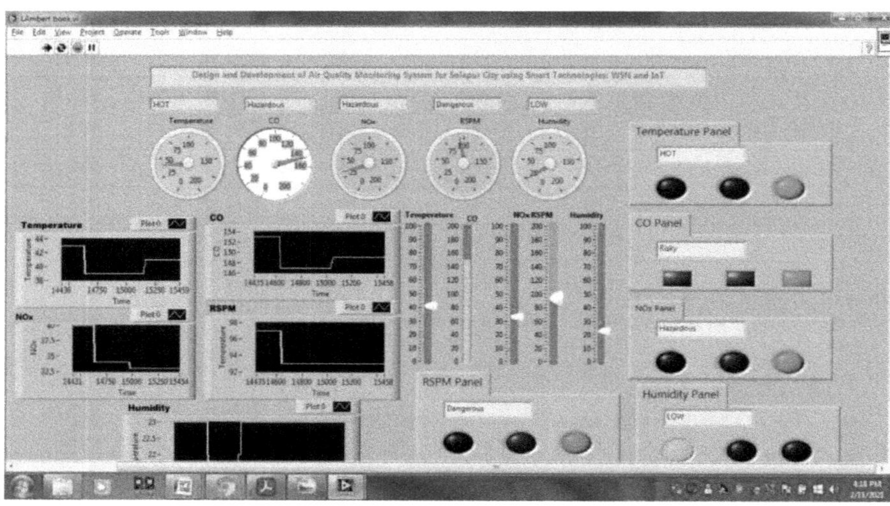

Figure 21.
Graphical user Interface on LabVIEW showing various levels of air quality.

Humidity, CO etc. Their GUI (Graphical User Interface) on LabVIEW is shown in **Figures 19–21**, respectively.

7. Results

7.1 Arduino based results

The results of air quality monitoring system are displayed on arduino serial monitor window of co-ordinator node, Front Panel of LabVIEW and on Blynk platform through the Android app developed by user's mobile phone. Arduino based results of air quality monitoring system are as follows. The sensors calibration and its coding are done in arduino IDE. This is shown in **Figure 22**.

7.2 LabVIEW based results

The LabVIEW front panel will exhibit the responses when the sensor incorporated within the sensor node collects the data within the environment. The threshold frontiers specified for this sensor are according to the OSHA standard. According to the threshold limit, different levels are displayed on the LabVIEW.

The sensors three levels are displayed on the front panel of LabVIEW. These levels are different for different sensors. For temperature sensor, cool level is displayed using green colored LED. Normal level of temperature is displayed using yellow colored LED, while red colored LED shows hot level of temperature. A voltmeter and pollution level meter is given, for easiness of users, to monitor the different pollution level. For CO sensor, Normal level is displayed using green color square LED. Hazardous level of CO is displayed using yellow color square LED, while red color square LED shows risky level of CO. For NOx sensor, normal level is displayed using green colored LED, unhealthy level of NOx is displayed using yellow colored LED, while red colored LED shows hazardous level of NOx. Low level of humidity is displayed using green colored LED. Normal level of humidity is displayed using yellow colored LED, while red colored LED shows high level of humidity. The RSPM levels such as normal, unhealthy and hazardous are displayed using green, yellow and red oval LED's respectively. The rationale of GUI is to erect the system extra interactive and superficial. The programming structure is shown in **Figure 23**. The real execution of wireless air quality monitoring system is shown in **Figure 24**.

7.3 IoT based result

Internet of things (IoT) based system helps to detect the existing level of perilous gases in the environment. The system assists to obtain the data from any locality where the mechanism is installed. All the data can be perceived in the smartphone app. The present system uses the Blynk app. The relevance for the IoT-based air

Figure 22.
Arduino coding for air quality monitoring system.

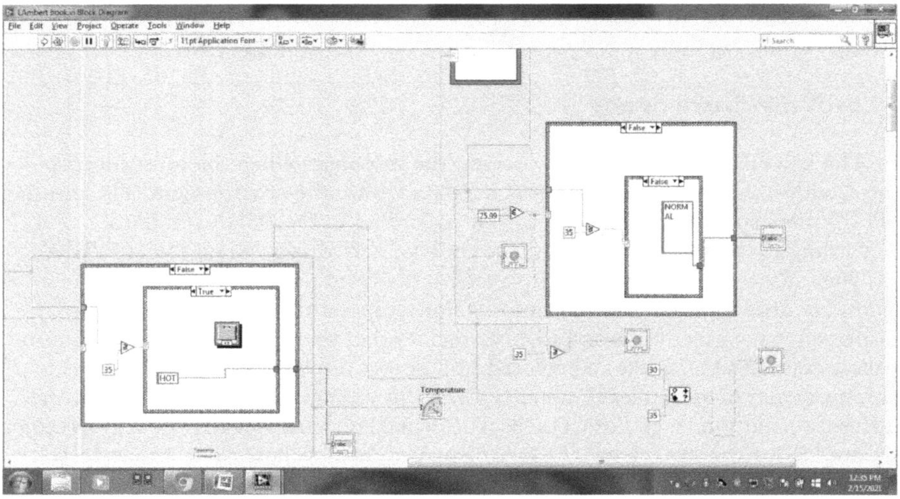

Figure 23.
LabVIEW programming structure of air quality monitoring system.

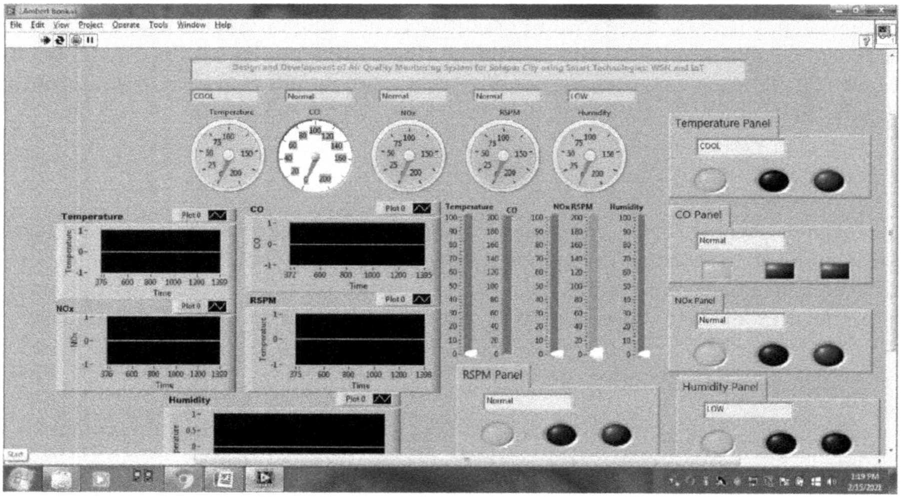

Figure 24.
Actual LabVIEW G-code for air quality monitoring system.

quality monitoring was evolved to observe the data and be vigilant users. Air quality can be scrutinized together with the web server and with linked smart devices via the application. Monitoring of air quality is effortless and competent using the Blynk App as it provides admittance anytime using smart devices. For IoT enabled system, the user obtains a notice through the Blynk Application on the mobile phone about the detection level of CO, NOx, RSPM, humidity and temperature for the area where the sensor nodes were deployed. An experimental set up for the IoT testing of air quality shown in **Figure 25**.

In **Figure 26**, the Blynk application on a mobile phone shows humidity as 20.9%, temperature as 34.17°C, CO as 44 ppm, NOx as 22 ppm and RSPM as 512 μg/m^3.

Figure 25.
Experimental set-up for the IoT testing of air quality.

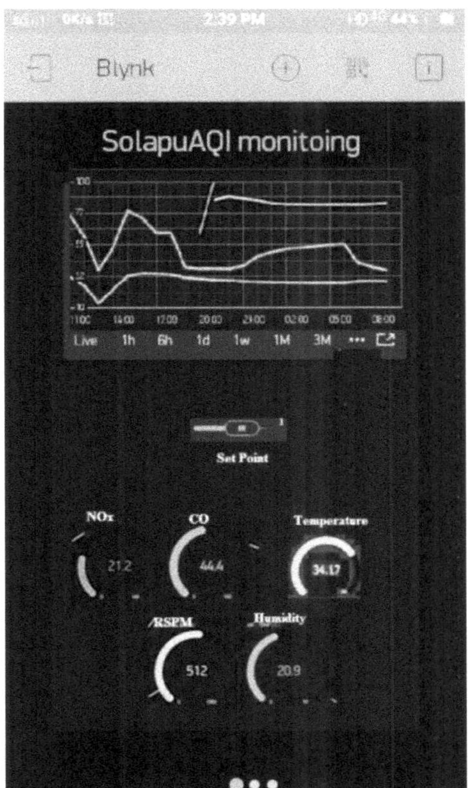

Figure 26.
Blynk app for air quality monitoring.

These real-time values are sent to the app using internet. A warning is sent to the App for alerting the user that the contamination in air is beyond which can be detrimental for human health. Alerting the users is mandatory to avert an environmental impairment and users can take instantaneously remedial measures.

8. Conclusions

This chapter describes a Wireless Sensor Network (WSN) based air quality monitoring system for Solapur city using IoT and LabVIEW. An amalgamation of WSN and IoT makes the system more reliable, smart and scalable than the traditional data logger system. A cost-effective, least power and efficient wireless star network based online air quality monitoring scheme is developed that includes temperature, humidity, RSPM, carbon monoxide and nitrous oxide measurements. The system evaluates the contamination level in the public areas. IoT accredits the users to observe the contamination levels of the region where the system is installed. Moreover, LabVIEW diminish the hardware necessity through visual coding. The real-time data on user's mobile phone can examine to recognize the air quality in the installed area of the system. Due to the use of IoT web platform and XBee wireless protocol, the developed system is less time consuming and less power consuming over to the traditional system.

Author details

Tabbsum Hanif Mujawar[1*], P. Prabhkar[2], Vijendra Chaudhary[3] and Lalasaheb Deshmukh[4]

1 School of Physical Sciences, P.A.H. Solapur University, Solapur, Maharashtra, India

2 School of Earth Sciences, P.A.H. Solapur University, Solapur, Maharashtra, India

3 Dayanand Science College, Latur, India

4 Department of Electronic Science, Savitribai Phule Pune University, Pune, Maharashtra, India

*Address all correspondence to: thmujawar@sus.ac.in

References

[1] R.K. Pachauri, P.V. Sridharan, "Looking Back to Think Ahead, Green India 2047: Growth with Resource Enhancement of Environment and Nature", Energy and Resources Institute, 1998, pp.1-368.

[2] Sengupta R, Madal S, "Health damage cost of automotive air pollution: Cost benefit analysis of fuel quality upgradation for Indian cities", eSocial Sciences, 2005.

[3] Gajul M.D. and Mujawar.K.C Prabhakar. P., "Ambient Air Quality in Solapur; A tight rope walk for Solapur citizens", Indian Society of Geochemistry, 56(2013), pp.1-6.

[4] Muthu Bharathi. M, Rajasekaran. M, "Air Quality Monitoring System Using Wireless Sensor Networks", International Journal of Engineering Research & Technology (IJERT), 6 (2018), pp. 1-6.

[5] Harsh N. Shah, Zishan Khan, Abbas Ali Merchant, Moin Moghal, Aamir Shaikh, Priti Rane , "IOT Based Air Pollution Monitoring System", International Journal of Scientific & Engineering Research, 9(2018), pp. 62-66.

[6] K. Maraiya, K. Kant and N. Gupta, "Application based Study on Wireless Sensor Network", International Journal of Computer Applications, 21(2011),pp. 9-15.

[7] https://www.sparkfun.com/datasheets/Sensors/Biometric/MQ-7

[8] https://www.ti.com/lit/ds/symlink/lm35

[9] http://china-total.com/Product/meter/gas-sensor/MQ135

[10] Margolis, Michael, Arduino Cookbook, Ed. 1, O'REILLY® Media, Inc., March 2011, pp. 81-213.

[11] XBee/XBee-Pro OEM RF Modules, Maxstream, Inc., Lindon, UT, 2007.

[12] M. Benammar, A. Abdaoui, S. Ahmad, F. Touati, and A. Kadri, "A modular IoT platform for real-time indoor air quality monitoring," Sensors, 18 (2018), pp. 581.

[13] Y. J. Fan, Y. H. Yin, L. D. Xu, Y. Zeng, and F. Wu, "IoT-based smart rehabilitation system," IEEE Transactions on Industrial Informatics, 10 (2014) , pp. 1568–1577.

[14] Rucha Golwalkar*1*, Kajal Shivgan*2*, Parul Sindhwad*3**," Pollution Monitoring System Using IoT and LabVIEW", International Journal for Research in Engineering Application & Management, 06(2020), pp.184-188.

[15] Bitter, Rick, T. Mohiuddin and M. Narocki "LabVIEW Advanced Programming Techniques "Boca Raton: CRC Press LLC, 2001

[16] T.H. Mujawar, V.D. Bachuwar, M.S. Kasbe, A. D. Shaligram, L.P. Deshmukh "Development of wireless sensor network system for LPG gas leakage detection system", International Journal of Scientific & Engineering Research, 6 (2015) 558-563.

[17] Bansode. P. B Mujawar. K. C Prabhakar. P.," An Insight into the Unseen: A Case Study of Ambient Air Quality in Solapur City, Maharashtra, India", Jour. Of Environ. Geochem.,15 (2012), pp.43-46.

[18] P Prabhakar, MD Gajul, NT Chavan, "Air affair in the proposed smart city of Solapur–a case study", Journal of Applied Geochemistry, 20(2018), pp.466-473.

Chapter 2

An Analysis of Remote Sensing Data to Evaluate the Problem of Atmospheric Aerosol Pollution in Africa

Gerard Rushingabigwi, Celestin Twizere,
Philibert Nsengiyumva, Jean De Dieu Ntawangaheza
and Liguo Sun

Abstract

The particulate matter (PM) directly endangers the human health. Remotely sensed tiny atmospheric particles, aerosols, are presented in this research as atmospheric air pollutants. Globally overviewed for the first instances, and then a focus put on Africa and Asia, the selected aerosols are fine particulates ($PM_{2.5}$), black carbon (BC), and Sulfate (SO_4). According to the existing literature, the motivation to research on air pollutants came from the fact that the polluted air globally kills many people, by attacking cardiovascular system. The online accessible remote sensing's data has been mostly collected from the second version of modern era retrospective analysis for research and applications (MERRA-2), a model selected for its update as well as the fact that its data are directly assimilated from the most renown remote sensors: Moderate resolution Imaging Spectroradiometer (MODIS) and the advanced very high-resolution radiometer (AVHRR). MERRA-2 also compiles data from different aerosol robotic networks (AERONETs). With a vast region of interest, and considering the big temporal resolution, reduced spatio-temporal resolutions facilitated the focused research. Goddard interactive online visualization and analysis infrastructure (GIOVANNI) bridged our research objectives with the data; Geographical Information Systems (Arc GIS) is a main software tool. Map-based as well as time series results for $PM_{2.5}$ and other atmospheric air pollutants are presented; health dangers associated with the dust from erstwhile research highlighted. Finding that the annually-averaged mass concentration of the dust's PM2.5 is significantly greater than the mean recommended concentration, 25 $\mu g/m^3$, in all the seasons of the center of the research region of interest (Africa), this research recommends further research on dust aerosols mitigation strategies, during the seasons of heaviest air pollutants in particular.

Keywords: Africa, aerosols health effects, atmospheric air pollutants, dust's particulate matter

1. Introduction

1.1 Understanding aerosols and their sources

Aerosols, sometimes referred to as the dust clouds, if not the airborne tiny particles, are hazardously toxic to health: human, animals and plants, especially if uncontrolled.

The dust storm (dust and sand carried away by the wind from the very dry grounds) has too many effects. For example, anthropogenic dust storm, as illustrated in **Figure 1**, directly pollutes the breathable air, food and water. If the storm is naturally caused by the desert's dust, it causes the drought [1].

As presented in **Figure 1(a)**, most of sub-Saharan inhabitants unavoidably live with anthropogenic aerosols; the most remarkable are the dust and smoke aerosols, and sometimes do not worry about the associated dangers. **Figure 1(b)** shows the smoke of the accidentally burnt house, its equipment and furniture. Hazards caused by the smoke from biomass burning's fire, volcanic eruptions, home and industrial chimneys, road vehicles exhausts, etc., is very dangerous to both health and climate uncertainties, and that's where most constituents of the fine particulate matter ($PM_{2.5}$) come from.

In **Figure 2**, the primary sources of particulate matter as aerosols are deserts, erupting volcanoes and of course some human (anthropogenic) activities, it's a matter of the dust and many other aerosol particles that are windblown over either the sea, ocean or earth surface. The aerosol particles such as Soot, fly ash, black carbon (BC) and smoke are primarily produced during different combustion activities.

The secondary sources can otherwise be generically referred to as atmospheric chemistry source where gas-phase species can chemically transform before they condense, and they are technically referred to as aerosol precursor gases [2].

Aerosol science, however, is a sub-branch of physics or physical-chemistry which, until 1980s, has been so neglected that most people did not worry about aerosols dangers to the human breathing and blood circulation. The industrial revolution in the 19th century brought high-speed machinery; dust exposure increased dramatically, for instance dust from mines, which caused more cases of lung diseases. Thus, since then onwards, it's a very hot research topic to study the physicochemical properties of aerosol: how to sample (clustering), to control and avoid them. For instance, aerosols can play a role of polluting gases removal from the atmosphere, either by absorbing them on existing ones or launching new particles. The study of aerosols, however, is not easy because airborne particles behave very differently than the air in which they are suspended and also behave very differently among themselves depending on their sizes, shape and composition [3].

The atmosphere is such a complex dynamic natural system that sustaining life on earth is very essential as the atmospheric air interacts with water and land. Acidic rain is a result of air pollution. Therefore, it's very important for an air quality engineer to understand water pollution: air normally contains water vapor (varying from one to four per cent at surface), dust pollen, sea spray, volcanic ash and various industrial pollutants [3, 4].

1.2 Significance: direct and indirect aerosols effects on health

The aerosols transported by wind over a long distance directly pollute the quality of breathable air. For instance, the windblown dust from deserts entrains particulates which are hazardous to human health [5–7]. Particularly, the diseases such as pneumonia are attributed to that type of aerosol [8, 9].

(a)

(b)

Figure 1.
Anthropogenic Aerosols (a) dust storm in the inhabited village's road (source: Original photos taken on the road under construction in June 2020); (b) smoke due to the burning (source: Original photo of the building that was accidentally burnt on 06 September, 2020).

It has been ascertained that the dust endangers the respiratory, cardiovascular and nervous systems [10].

Referring to Pope et al., as cited by Dianat et al. ([11], p. 5155), "the prolonged health exposure to $PM_{2.5}$ was most strongly associated with mortality attributable to cardiac dysrhythmias, ischemic heart diseases, cardiac arrest, and heart failure."

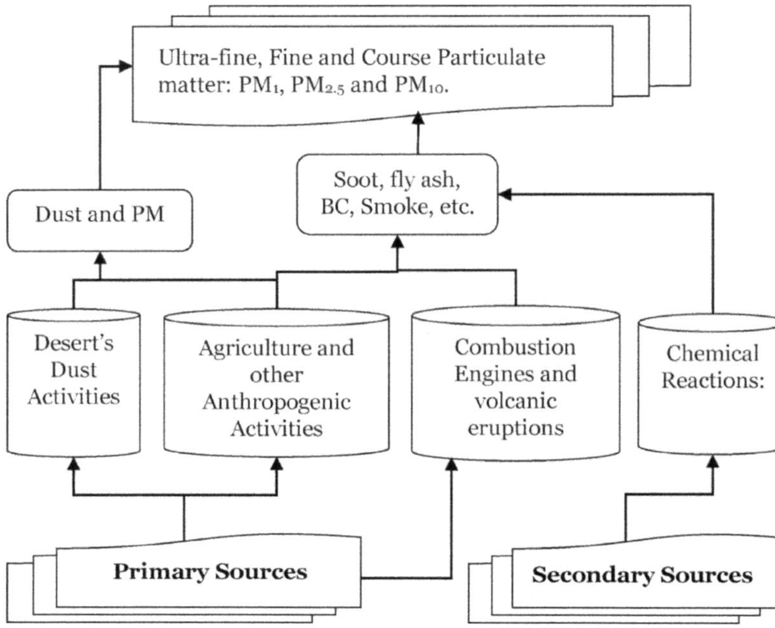

Figure 2.
Primary and secondary sources of particulate matter (PM).

Besides, an aerosol is collectively known as solid, gaseous or/and liquid particles suspended in the atmosphere, except all the hydrometeors which include the cloud droplets, ice crystals, raindrops, snowflakes, and the alike particles [12]; smoke is the famously known gaseous aerosol. Therefore, apart from the direct health effects (learned from erstwhile works in the same research field), the aerosol in general can also change the clouds properties: thus, they indirectly affect the lives on earth in causing drought, acidic rain, etc.

A research question: "how can results from the remote sensing data analysis instruct the community about the tropospheric aerosols hazards?"

1.3 Objectives

Africa and Asia are the global source of the Desert's Dust Aerosols; therefore, the main target is to continue the research works which will alert the world and inhabitants about the updates in aerosols which can endanger the earth.

Considering the formation, correlation, health effects; assessing the on-site (in situ) versus remote sensing data collection, the in-field collected data is reliable for research related with physical, biological, and social sciences. However, studying aerosols and air pollution by targeting very big areas, remote sensing data is better than in situ data [13].

The research objectives are:

- to limit the scope of research on the troposphere of African and Asian continents in different scenarios, and to study the air quality based on selected measurements under aerosols such as sulfates (SO_4), black carbon (BC), and the fine particulate matter ($PM_{2.5}$).

- to track the long-term emission of the selected remote sensing measurements over different seasons and sub-temporal resolutions in the years 1980–2020;

- to discuss the inherent health hazards that link the existing research works with findings of this research.

2. The research trends in aerosols as air pollutants

Particulate matter (PM), a type of aerosol, is a complex mixture of molecules differing in chemical composition, shape and size; PM can come from natural sources such as the wind erosion of rocks and soil, sea sprays, volcanic dust, etc. PM also come from anthropogenic sources, noting the fossil fuels combustion, industrial processes, and traffic emission [12, 14, 15].

Airborne particles can change their size and composition by condensation of vapor species or by evaporation, by coagulation with other particles, by chemical reaction, or by activation in the presence of water super-saturation to become fog and cloud droplets. Particulates are eventually removed from the atmosphere by two mechanisms: deposition at the Earth's surface (dry deposition) and incorporation into cloud droplets (wet deposition) during the precipitation in the form of rain [16].

2.1 Dust, particulate matter, black carbon

Dust, particulate matter (PM) and Black Carbon aerosols have the common characteristics, especially when it comes to polluting the atmospheric breathable air.

The heavy contribution of the deserts' dust to the global airborne particulates as well as numerous other effects of dust aerosol are very well documentable [17–19]; the effects become very dangerous to human health when the dust is characterized to the PM size [19].

The smoke as a gaseous aerosol broadly links with ecosystem, to mean the living organisms and non-living entities like atmospheric air as well as cloud and climate.

The literature reiterates that the global air polluting particles come from both the discipline of aerosols and atmospheric chemistry; in this research, the selected aerosol particles are the dust's fine particulate matter ($PM_{2.5}$), sulfates, as well as Black Carbon (BC). Cardiovascular problems and death caused by air pollution are globally reported, and air pollution kills more people than they die of viral diseases.

Due to the dust belt [17] as well as meningitis belt [20] which keep expanding, Africa is one of the best research areas, while targeting the source of different sized particulate matter, PM (PM_1, $PM_{2.5}$, PM_{10}), which are classified under solid aerosols, and breathable air pollutants in particular [21].

2.2 Sulfur dioxide

The sulfur Dioxide (SO_2) is produced from anthropogenic burning activities, and erupting volcanoes activities [22], and is recognized as a potential air pollutant; importantly, through chemical reaction, SO_2 plays a considerable role in the formation of sulfate aerosols. The role that sulfate aerosols may play in ambient particulate matter (PM) chemistry is so meaningful that the possible effects might be the product of acidic component formed by sulfur dioxide [23, 24]. Acid rain, for example, is one of main reasons why atmospheric sulfur dioxide and nitrogen oxides can be of interesting focus among the air pollutants [25–27].

For instance, it was found that rain in northwestern Europe was measured with the most increased acidity; the tendency appeared linked with certain gaseous pollutants, like SO_2, which chemically convert into strong acids in the atmosphere. Nonetheless, the trend seems to directly cause very little threat to human health.

Rather, the acidic rain can considerably damage some artificial architects, and seriously implicates to the ecosystem [25].

3. The data source, methodology, and roadmap

The collected data from multiple remote sensing instruments is trustworthy; this way of the data collection has challenged the existing methods (according to the published research works), especially when it comes to the data reliability.

Throughout the research, GIOVANNI is the core of research data collection; relying on MERRA-2 (in most cases). MERRA-2 is a remote sensing model which assimilates data from various remote sensors as well different ground aerosol robotic networks (AERONETs).

Additional software tools, such as Arc GIS, have been utilized to scientifically present the results, but the statistics was done at the level of GIOVANNI web browsing [28–31].

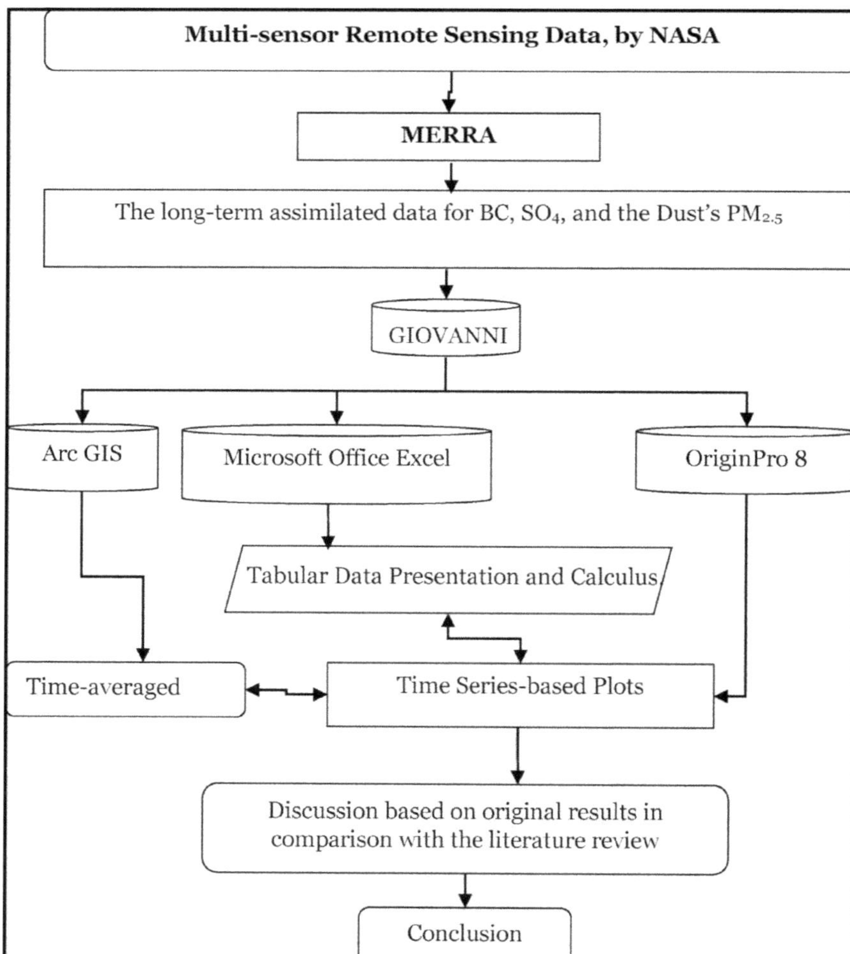

Figure 3.
The research roadmap.

3.1 The research data source and roadmap

The rough roadmap that was utilized to collect data and generate the results presented in this research is generalized and shown in **Figure 3**.

Different data types are available in various forms and formats: time averaged maps, scatter plots, time series, etc. In this research, both time averaged map based and time series data has been collected from GIOVANNI platform.

The collected data is then input to the analysis by the help of the software tools: ArcGIS/Arc Map to get the presentable map-based results; Origins, to generate different plots of results as functions of time.

That means that even though some results can directly be visualized online by the help of GIOVANNI, all the results presented in this research article have been further handled by additional software tools such as Arch GIS and Origins.

Microsoft Excel helps the research to do some necessary calculations, and elaborate the table-based results. Finally, a discussion is made on basis of the original results, in comparison with the existing literature review.

Thus, as seen in **Figures 3** and **4**, GIOVANNI is a bridge as an online platform designed by NASA Goddard Space Flight Center, to collect raw data from different satellites and remote sensors, the most notable are illustrated in **Figure 4**.

Though the remote sensed data can be collected from the most documentable remote sensors such as the Moderate-resolution Imaging Spectro-radiometer (MODIS), it has been challenging to directly detect dust from MODIS [32]. Therefore, the remote sensing model MERRA-2, an online model which directly assimilates the remote sensing data from the AERONETS, the MODIS and the advanced very high-resolution radiometer, AVHRR [32].

For the quality of data collected via GIOVANNI, data from different sources can be a good solution to the data reliability. For example, MERRA-2 is a model which treats the data from different sources, as earlier mentioned in this sub-section.

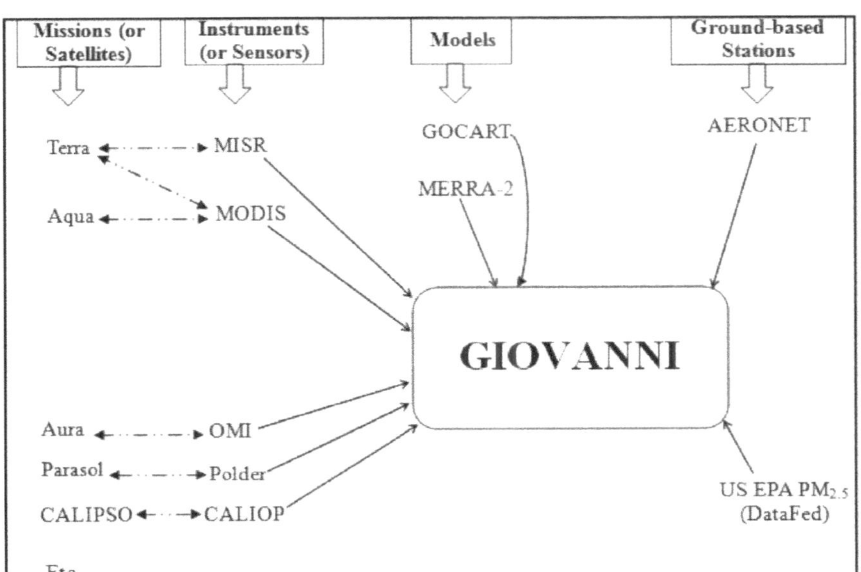

Figure 4.
A multi-sensor aerosol data bridge: GIOVANNI.

4. Analysis of remote sensing data: Air polluting aerosols effects on health

4.1 An overview for the big picture

The desert's dust together with anthropogenic biomass burning's black carbon in the tropical regions are associated with many effects to climate and air quality.

Globally overviewed in **Figure 5(a)** and **(b)**, respectively, the dust as an air polluting aerosol expands all over the world from the world's dust belt that stretches from the Atlantic Ocean in the neighborhood of West-Northern Africa to the East and Middle Asia, and the atmospheric black carbon is abundantly stretched all over the mid-latitudes of the earth.

The Global overview of these selected aerosols and air pollutants, is an important input to research contents in the subsequent sections.

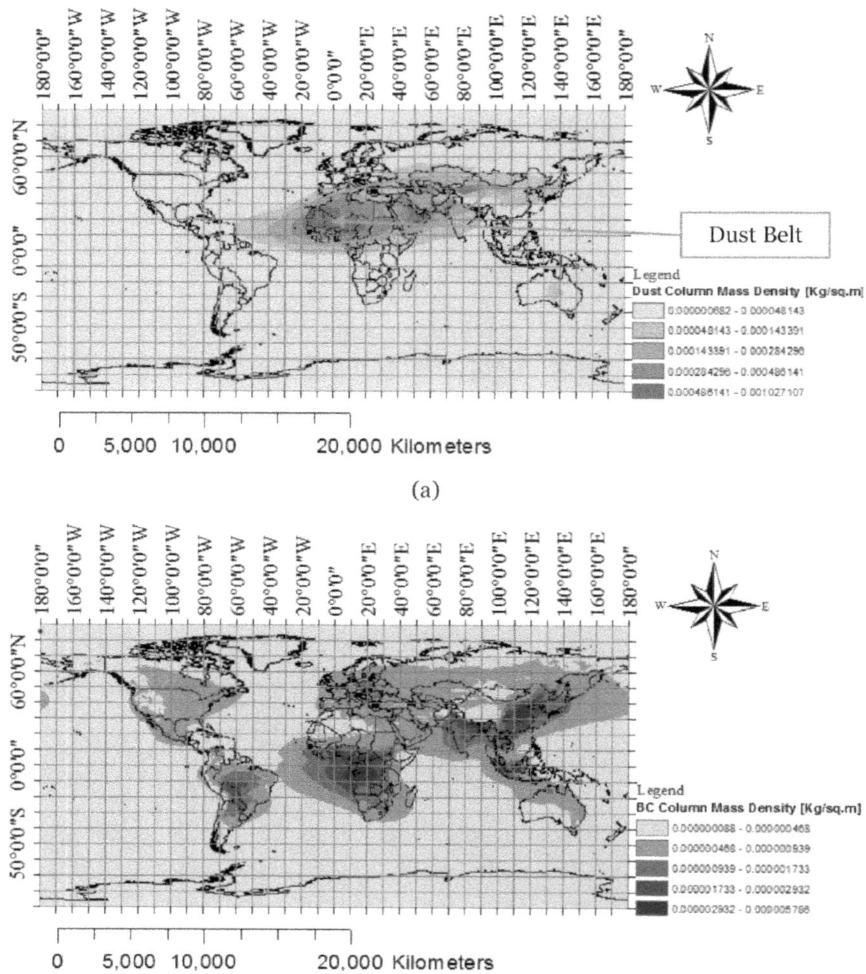

Figure 5.
The global overview of selected Aerosols and Air pollutants' column mass density: (a) dust, aerosol and air pollutant; (b) black carbon aerosol and air pollutant.

4.2 The results

The desert's dust together with anthropogenic biomass burning's black carbon in the tropical regions associate with both climate changes and air quality problems.

For example, the aerosol optical thickness (AOT), known as an extent to which aerosols obstruct the light energy transmission, via absorption or/and scattering of that light, AOT is distributed within a column of air to the top of the atmosphere [15]. The process of absorption and scattering makes up the extinction process, which means the loosing of the photon incoming energy [33].

It is according to the knowledge of the African Physical Geography as well as climates that five sub-regions had been created and those are described as region 1, 2, 3, 4 and 5.

- Region 1: 15°W, 9.5°E, (4–14) °N for the West Africa;
- Region 2: 10°W, 52°E, (24–40) °N for the North Africa and neighborhoods;
- Region 3: (9.5–30) °E, 10°S, 14°N for Central Africa;
- Region 4: (11–35) °E, (10–35) °S for the South Africa;
- Region 5: (30–52) °E, 28°S, 12°N for East Africa.

The purpose of those five subdivisions is to obtain most reliable remote sensing results, and the focus was put in the most central part of Africa.

The findings are presented in **Figure 5**.

In this research, four seasons are shortened as:

- DJF, for December, January, and February or the northern hemisphere's winter;
- MAM is standing for March, April, and May or the northern hemisphere's spring;
- JJA represents June, July, and August or the northern hemisphere's summer;
- SON for September, October, and November or the northern hemisphere's autumn.

From the existing research, the dust's particulates are one of the causes of pulmonary tuberculosis [34]; dry desert's dust in particular is one of the causes to Meningococcal meningitis ([35], p. 108–109).

In the research, **Table 1** reports the results for $PM_{2.5}$, in the 5 sub-regions of Africa, and it's found that the averaged mass concentration is very high as compared to 25 $\mu g/m^3$, the recommendable concentration [14].

Looking at the table, the vastest global Desert, Sahara, which keeps expanding [1] might be the reason for the increase of the global dust aerosol since the year 2000 onwards, most notably in the seasons of DJF and MAM, during the whole time series from the year 2000 to date.

Besides, the African Sahara Desert being the biggest contributors to global atmospheric particulate matter (PM) and air pollutants in particular, **Table 1** demonstrates the concentration of $PM_{2.5}$ in Africa.

	West-Africa				North-Africa				Central-Africa			
	DJF	**MAM**	**DJF**	**MAM**	**JJA**	**SON**	**JJA**	**SON**	**JJA**	**SON**	**JJA**	**SON**
2000	66.8	54	25.3	40.9	39.1	33.3	39.1	33.3	34.4	24.6	6.1	11.3
2001	69	38.8	29.1	39.8	39.1	33.4	39.1	33.4	31.6	21.1	5.9	12.0
2002	67.2	46.0	28.9	43.3	38.9	33.3	38.9	33.3	32.7	23.8	6.4	11.9
2003	45.1	43.2	31.3	42.8	37.6	35.5	37.6	35.5	23.3	25.9	6.2	11.2
2004	74.2	60.7	34.2	46.5	36.6	34.1	36.6	34.1	35.6	36.3	6.6	14.4
2005	75.6	44.8	36.4	43.9	38.6	33	38.6	33	34.2	26.2	6.7	12.5
2006	36.9	47.9	33.5	40	40.4	30.3	40.4	30.3	26.3	26.1	6.9	12.2
2007	84.6	54.1	31.6	44	39.4	32.3	39.4	32.3	35.4	27.7	5.7	13.4
2008	85.2	44.9	32.3	47.8	40.7	37.4	40.7	37.4	38.4	22.7	5.0	12.8
2009	59.1	42.2	39.1	42.3	37.3	31.6	37.3	31.6	29.9	27.9	6.1	12.7
2010	37.2	56	38.6	47.8	38.3	33.6	38.3	33.6	22.1	26.1	6.3	9.0
2011	58.8	37.8	34.4	42.9	40.3	31.5	40.3	31.5	28.7	25.5	12.2	12.7
2012	77.1	53.9	34.7	43.2	36.8	28.3	36.8	28.3	40.0	30.0	6.2	9.6
2013	57	25.4	33.2	46.1	38.9	30.3	38.9	30.3	32.0	20.1	5.6	10.5
2014	52.3	29.5	31.6	36.8	37.5	31.6	37.5	31.6	27.0	19.4	5.4	10.3
2015	62.9	54.5	34.3	38.7	37.8	30.3	37.8	30.3	33.6	33.7	6.5	11.0
2016	108.3	29	28	40.2	36.2	31.4	36.2	31.4	46.1	21.8	5.2	13.0
2017	67.2	41.3	30.8	41.8	36.3	30.5	36.3	30.5	36.8	27.1	9.4	17.5
2018	85.1	39.7	37	46.4	37.8	32	37.8	32	36.4	26.0	7.1	11.4
2019	63.6	41.3	10.9	N/A	32.4	39	35.1	N/A	37.0	25.5	6.1	N/A

	East-Africa				South-Africa			
	JJA	**SON**	**JJA**	**SON**	**JJA**	**SON**	**JJA**	**SON**
2000	4.5	4.6	3.7	2.5	1.6	1.8	2.1	2.1
2001	5.1	4.0	3.5	2.6	2.4	1.5	1.8	1.7
2002	5.1	3.8	4.0	2.7	2.2	1.3	1.8	1.8
2003	3.7	4.6	3.8	2.7	1.6	1.5	1.8	2.0
2004	5.2	5.1	3.7	2.7	2.7	2.4	1.9	1.8
2005	4.6	3.7	3.9	2.8	2.2	1.7	1.6	1.9
2006	4.3	4.4	3.8	2.6	2.0	1.6	1.9	1.8
2007	5.8	4.3	3.5	3.3	2.6	1.8	1.9	2.2
2008	7.3	4.6	4.0	3.6	2.2	1.3	1.6	2.1
2009	5.4	5.0	3.9	2.9	2.2	1.5	1.9	1.8
2010	4.5	4.5	3.8	3.2	2.0	1.5	1.9	2.0
2011	5.6	4.3	6.3	3.5	2.0	1.3	1.9	2.1
2012	7.8	6.6	4.5	3.0	2.7	1.8	1.9	2.0
2013	5.6	4.1	4.3	2.9	2.6	1.7	1.8	2.0
2014	5.7	3.3	3.9	2.8	2.1	1.6	1.9	1.9
2015	5.8	4.8	4.1	2.7	2.7	1.6	1.6	2.0
2016	6.5	3.8	3.8	3.2	2.7	1.7	1.7	1.9
2017	5.5	4.5	4.9	3.4	2.3	1.5	1.5	1.7
2018	6.8	4.9	5.3	2.9	2.4	1.8	2.1	1.9
2019	5.2	4.3	3.9	N/A	2.5	1.8	1.7	N/A

Table 1.
The dust's $PM_{2.5}$ mass concentration in $\mu g/m^3$ in five African sub-regions of interest [36].

Looking at some existing research works, "exposure to common air pollutants like fine and coarse particulate matter (PM2.5 and PM10), Nitrogen dioxide (NO2), and sulfur dioxide (SO2) were closely associated with asthma patients who visited Shanghai from January 22, 2014 to October 31, 2015 [37];" generally, the portion of nearly 90% of BC belongs to PM2.5 [38].

5. Discussion

It's expected that both the inhabitants of the region of interest (RoI), and visitors will understand furthermore the dangers of particulate matter, and will take precautions to comfortably live on earth because the atmosphere is shared resource: the dust belt's $PM_{2.5}$ unlimitedly spreads to the sub-Saharan, European, Asian, and Atlantic Ocean regions.

Most specifically, in this research, the direct effects of aerosols on heath are presented by results in **Table 1**, speaking of the central African focal region of interest: the dust's PM2.5 mass concentration is mostly above the highest recommended value for health which is 25 $\mu g/m^3$.

With a reference to the World's Dust Belt [17], the heavily concentrated particulate matter in the west, north and central African sub-regions is attributed to the Sahara Desert, and this has nothing to do with the population.

Apart from the world's dust belt which is due to deserts, the nature source of dust aerosols and linked air pollutant groups is also from volcanic eruption activities, and anthropogenic activities.

Therefore, inhabitants of arid regions are recommended to learn from China's policy, which turned a desert into crop and forestland, cited by Rushingabigwi et al. ([39], p. 1958), which would reduce the dust aerosols which are windblown all over the world.

6. Conclusions

Aerosol science, a sub-branch of physics or physical-chemistry which, until 1980s, has been so neglected that most people have not cared about the aerosols dangers to the human breathing and blood circulation. In this research, a quick overview of aerosols and air pollutants (solid and gaseous) has been made; the research has resulted in finding more about air polluting aerosols such as the dust's fine particulate matter, $PM_{2.5}$, an agent to many diseases leading to the mortality due to cardiac dysrhythmias, cardiac arrest, etc.

In this research, the west and north African sub-regions are characterized by the concentrations of PM2.5 above the standard, 25 $\mu g/m^3$, in all the seasons; the same thing applies to the Central African JJA season.

In any case, the atmosphere is such a complex dynamic natural system that sustaining life on earth is very essential since the atmospheric air interacts with water and land. Acidic rain due to atmospheric chemistry of sulfate aerosols reacting with the clouds Hydrogen, for instance, is a result of air pollution.

Black carbon (abundant in the African mid-latitude and the global mid-latitudes), together with dust aerosols (from deserts, volcanic activities, and anthropogenic activities), windblown from their sources to surrounding regions are certainly hazardous to the global ecosystem, especially when in the precipitation's clouds.

Therefore, for sustainability of the life on earth, this research can help policy makers to plan for the community welfare: it is expected that by publishing different research works in this area, more scholars will furthermore understand the real problem, and if supported by policy makers, smart systems will be developed for the welfare of end users.

Acknowledgements

The East Africa's Regional Centre of Excellence in Biomedical Engineering and E-health (CEBE), operating under the University of Rwanda College of Science and Technology (UR CST), is highly acknowledged for some financial support to this research.

We are very grateful with the University of Science and Technology of China (USTC), for the involvement of the University's Academic Staff Members in this research.

Last but foremost, the efforts made by all the team members of GES DISC, who contributed to enrich GIOVANNI with the useful and resourceful research tools are highly acknowledged: many thanks are addressed to NASA and fellow scientists for the supportive data that are made available online.

Conflict of interest

There exist no 'conflict of interest' in this manuscript.

Author details

Gerard Rushingabigwi[1*], Celestin Twizere[1], Philibert Nsengiyumva[1], Jean De Dieu Ntawangaheza[2] and Liguo Sun[2]

1 University of Rwanda College of Science and Technology, East Africa's Regional Centre of Excellence in Biomedical Engineering and E-Health (CEBE), Kigali, Rwanda

2 Department of Electrical Engineering and Information Science, School of Information Science and Technology, University of Science and Technology of China, Hefei, China

*Address all correspondence to: gerardrushingabigwi@yahoo.com; g.rushingabigwi@ur.ac.rw

References

[1] Thomas N., Nigam S. Twentieth-century climate change over Africa: Seasonal hydroclimate trends and sahara desert expansion. Journal of Climate, 31 (9), 3349–3370, 2018. DOI: 10.1175/JCLI-D-17-0187.1

[2] Ciarelli G., Theobald M. R., Vivanco M. G., et al. Trends of inorganic and organic aerosols and precursor gases in Europe: Insights from the EURODELTA multi-model experiment over the 1990–2010 period," Geosci. Model Dev., 12, 4923–4954, 2019. DOI: 10.5194/gmd-12-4923-2019

[3] Reist P. C. Introduction to Aerosol Science. Macmillan Publishing Company, New York, 1984.

[4] Han D. Air Pollution. Concise Environmental Engineering, ch. 9, 109-120, Booboon.com, 2012

[5] Díaz J., Linares C, Carmona R., et al., Saharan dust intrusions in Spain: Health impacts and associated synoptic conditions," Environmental Research, 156 (April), 455–467, 2017. DOI: 10.1016/j.envres.2017.03.047

[6] Middleton N. J. Desert dust hazards: A global review. Aeolian Research, 24, 53–63, 2017. DOI:10.1016/j.aeolia.2016.12.001

[7] Aili A., Oanh N. T. K. Effects of a dust storm on public health in the desert fringe area: A case study of the northeast edge of Taklimakan Desert, China. Atmospheric Pollution Research, vol. 6, issue 5, 805-814, 2015. DOI:10.5094/APR.2015.089

[8] Kang J. H., Keller J. J., Chen C. S., et al. Asian dust storm events are associated with an acute increase in pneumonia hospitalization. Annals of Epidemiology, 22(4), 257–263, 2012. DOI:10.1016/j.annepidem.2012.02.008

[9] Goudie A. S. Desert dust and human health disorders. Environment International, 63, 101–113, 2014. DOI: 10.1016/j.envint.2013.10.011

[10] Christopher S. A., and Jones T. A. Satellite and surface-based remote sensing of Saharan dust aerosols. Remote Sensing of Environment, 114 (5), 1002–1007. DOI:10.1016/j.rse.2009.12.007

[11] Dianat M., Radmanesh E., Badavi M., Mard S. A., Goudarzi, G. (2016). Disturbance effects of PM10 on iNOS and eNOS mRNA expression levels and antioxidant activity induced by ischemia-reperfusion injury in isolated rat heart: Protectiverole of vanillic acid. Environ Sci Pollut Res (2016) 23, 5154–5165. DOI:10.1007/s11356-015-5759-x

[12] Gebicki J., Szymańska K. Comparative field test for measurement of PM10 dust in atmospheric air using gravimetric (reference) method and β-absorption method (Eberline FH 62-1)," Atmospheric Environment, 54, 18–24, 2012. DOI:10.1016/j.atmosenv.2012.02.068

[13] Jensen J. R. Remote Sensing of the Environment: An Earth Resource Perspective, 2nd Edition. Pearson Education, Inc; Copyright to Science Press, Beijing, 2011

[14] Chen J., Li C., Ristovski Z., et al. A review of biomass burning: Emissions and impacts on air quality, health and climate in China," Science of the Total Environment, 579 (November 2016), 1000–1034, 2017. DOI:10.1016/j.scitotenv.2016.11.025

[15] Boucher O. Atmospheric Aerosols. In: Atmospheric Aerosols. Springer, Dordrecht, 9-24, 2015. doi:10.1007/978-94-017-9649-1_2

[16] Reche I., D'Orta G., Mladenov N., et al. Deposition rates of viruses and bacteria above the atmospheric boundary layer. The ISME Journal, 1154–1162, 2018. DOI:10.1038/s41396-017-0042-4

[17] Varga G. Spatio-temporal distribution of dust storms – a global coverage using NASA TOMS aerosol measurements. Hungarian Geographical Bulletin 61 (4), 275–298, 2012. Online, last accessed on 25 April, 2020 at http://www.mtafki.hu/konyvtar/kiadv/HunGeoBull2012/HunGeoBull_2012_4_275-298.pdf

[18] Osada K., Ura S., Kagawa M., et al. Wet and dry deposition of mineral dust particles in Japan: Factors related to temporal variation and spatial distribution. Atmospheric Chemistry and Physics, 14(2), 1107–1121, 2014. DOI:10.5194/acp-14-1107-2014

[19] Hamdan N. M., Alawadhi H., Jisrawi N., et al. Characterization of fine particulate matter in Sharjah, United Arab Emirates using complementary experimental techniques. Sustainability (Switzerland), 10(4), 1-17, 2018. DOI: 10.3390/su10041088

[20] Thomson M. C., Jancloes M., Foundation C., et al. A Climate and Health Partnership to Inform the Prevention and Control of Meningoccocal Meningitis in Sub-Saharan Africa: The MERIT Initiative. In: Asrar G., Hurrell J. (eds), Climate Science for Serving Society. Springer, Dordrecht, 459-484, 2013. DOI:10.1007/978-94-007-6692-1_17

[21] Goix S., Uzu G., Oliva P., et al. Metal concentration and bioaccessibility in different particle sizes of dust and aerosols to refine metal exposure assessmen. Journal of Hazardous Materials, 317, 552–562, 2016. doi: 10.1016/j.jhazmat.2016.05.083

[22] Graf H. E., Feichter J., Langmann B. Volcanic sulfur emissions – Estimates of source strength and its contribution to the global sulfate distribution. J. Geophysical Research, vol. 102, no. d9, 10727–10738, 1997. DOI:10.1029/96JD03265

[23] Azhari A., Latif M.T., Mohamed A. F. Road traffic as an air pollutant contributor within an industrial park environment, Atmospheric Pollution Research 2018, 9(4), 680–687, 2018. DOI:10.1016/j.apr.2018.01.007

[24] Grahame T. J., Schlesinger R. B. Evaluating the health risk from secondary sulfates in eastern north American regional ambient air particulate matter. Inhalation Toxicology, 17 (1), 15–27, 2005. DOI: 10.1080/08958370590885672

[25] Likens G. E., Bormann F. H., Johnson N. M. Acid rain. Environment, 14(2), 33–40, 1972. DOI:10.1080/00139157.1972.9933001

[26] Likens G. E., Driscoll C. T., Buso D. C., et al. The biogeochemistry of sulfur at Hubbard Brook. Biogeochemistry, 60 (3), 235–316, 2002. DOI:10.1023/A:1020972100496

[27] Unger N., Shindell D. T., Koch D. M., et al. Cross influences of ozone and sulfate precursor emissions changes on air quality and climate," Proceedings of the National Academy of Sciences, 103 (12), 4377–4380, 2006. DOI:10.1073/pnas.0508769103

[28] Prados A. I., Leptoukh G., Gopalan A. Visualization, Exploration, and model comparison of Nasa Air quality remote sensing data via Giovanni. 7th annual CMAS conference, Chapel Hill, NC, October 6-8, 2008, 7–9.

[29] GES DISC. Giovanni, the Bridge between Data and Science, version 4.28 [text]. [Internet]. 2021. Available from: https://giovanni.gsfc.nasa.gov/giovanni/

[30] Acker J., Soebiyanto R., Kiang R., et al. Use of the NASA Giovanni data system for geospatial public Health Research: Example of weather-influenza connection. ISPRS International Journal of Geo-Information, 3(4), 1372–1386, 2014. DOI:10.3390/ijgi3041372

[31] Madhavan S., Qu J. J., X., Hao. Saharan dust detection using multi-sensor satellite measurements. Heliyon, 3(2), e00241, 1-13, 2017. DOI:10.1016/j.heliyon.2017.e00241

[32] Rienecker M. M., Suarez M. J., Gelaro R., et al. MERRA: NASA's modern-era retrospective analysis for research and applications. Journal of Climate, 24(14), 3624–3648, 2011. DOI: 10.1175/JCLI-D-11-00015.1

[33] Shine K. P. Radiative forcing of climate change. Space Science Reviews, 94(1–2), 363–373, 2000. DOI:10.1023/A:1026752230256

[34] Wang Y., Wang R., Ming J., et al. Effects of dust storm events on weekly clinic visits related to pulmonary tuberculosis disease in Minqin, China. Atmospheric Environment, 127, 205–212, 2016. DOI:10.1016/j.atmosenv.2015.12.041

[35] Agier L., Martiny N., Thiongane O., et al. Towards understanding the epidemiology of Neisseria meningitidis in the African meningitis belt: A multi-disciplinary overview. International Journal of Infectious Diseases, 54, 103–112, 2017. DOI:10.1016/j.ijid.2016.10.032

[36] Rushingabigwi G, Kalisa W., Nsengiyumva P., Zimulinda F., Mukanyiligira D., Sibomana L. Analysis of effects of selected aerosol particles to the global climate change and health using remote sensing data: The focus on Africa. Rwanda Journal of Engineering, Science, Technology and Environment, Volume 3, Special Issue, June 2020, 69-80. DOI:10.4314/rjeste.v3i1.5S

[37] Guo H., Huang S., Chen M. Air pollutants and asthma patient visits: Indication of source influence. Science of the Total Environment, 625, 355–362, 2018. DOI:10.1016/j.scitotenv.2017.12.298

[38] Doumbia E. H. T., Liousse C., Galy-Lacaux C. et al., "Real time black carbon measurements in west and Central Africa urban sites," Atmospheric Environment, 54, 529–537, 2012. DOI: 10.1016/j.atmosenv.2012.02.005

[39] Rushingabigwi G., Nsengiyumva P., Twizere C., et al. Remote sensing data analysis for the effects of three selected Aerosols on both energy budgets and health: A case of south-West Asia. 2019 Photonics & Electromagnetics Research Symposium (PIERS)-fall, Xiamen, China, 17–20 Dec. 2019. DOI: 10.1109/PIERS-Fall48861.2019.9021726

Chapter 3

Managing Non-Sewered Sanitation for Achieving Sustainable Development Goal 6 in India

Shubhagato Dasgupta and Neha Agarwal

Abstract

The challenge of ensuring clean water and safely managed sanitation towards meeting the Sustainable Development Goal 6 is made more complex by unplanned urbanisation in South Asia. Nearly 50% of all toilet-owning households globally and 83% in South Asia depend on non-networked sanitation, with a multi-step service chain comprising containment, collection, conveyance, and treatment of faecal waste. Over the last few years, South Asian governments have begun to eschew the long-enduring preference for centralised sewerage infrastructure in favour of better management of non-networked sanitation as part of city-level wastewater management systems. However, these interventions have largely excluded the household-level containment systems that hold the potential to create both adverse localised and diffuse public health and environmental outcomes if dysfunctional. The present Chapter discusses evidence from a multi-state household survey in India to assess the nature and quality of containment systems in use by urban Indian households. Secondly, it reviews approaches to their governance under more evolved paradigms to inform an ecosystem-wide strategy for managing these systems in India and countries with similar contexts.

Keywords: sustainable sanitation, urban sanitation, on-site sanitation, non-networked sanitation, septic tanks, public health, prefabricated septic tanks, water pollution

1. Introduction: importance of non-networked sanitation to environmental and public health management

An extensive body of research underscores the importance of safe sanitation in reducing the incidence of waterborne diseases, maternal mortality rates, infant mortality rates, malnutrition, as well as, engendering individual well-being, productivity, and dignity. A lack of contextually designed and well-maintained sanitation systems at the level of the individual, settlements, and region, contribute to pollution of groundwater, waterways, soil, and lead to adverse public health outcomes [1, 2]. Yet, up until the last decade, the Global South has had to contend with a complete absence of basic sanitation facilities among large segments of the population leading to the practice of open defecation. At the turn of the millennium,

2.36 billion people globally practised open defecation or had access to an unimproved toilet facility, with a stark disparity in levels of sanitation between low and high income countries. As per the WHO-UNICEF Joint Monitoring Programme (JMP), seven out of every ten individuals in low-income countries lacked even basic sanitation in 2000. More broadly, 70% of the global population without access to basic sanitation resided in low- and lower-middle income countries.

The push to increase 'improved sanitation' at the level of the household under the Millennium Development Goals (MDGs) has since transformed to the Sustainable Development Goals' (SDG) focus on 'ensuring availability and sustainable management of water and sanitation for all'. While the former targeted the elimination of open defecation and the use of primitive facilities like bucket latrines, hanging toilets, pit latrines without slabs, latrines flowing into drains or the open environment, the latter reinstated the goal with the additional aims of increasing levels of wastewater management and reducing water pollution.

The increased attention to wastewater management in the wake of the SDG era has led to an improved understanding of the different approaches urban and rural households across the world adopt to manage faecal waste. In the preceding decades, vast sewerage networks conveying wastewater from the source to a centralised Sewage Treatment Plant (STP) had dominated the imagination of the city, state, and national governments alike. The last few years have witnessed an enduring recognition of how the sewerage system is unsuited to provide citywide sanitation as a universal gold standard [3]. Though the high population densities of bigger cities and metropolitans justify the cost of the networked solution to sanitation, given how fast many of the cities in the Global South have been growing, service delivery systems tend to fail in keeping pace and are left to play catch-up. Secondly, the low population densities of smaller cities, peri-urban areas, and rural settlements often do not justify the creation of sewerage systems, which are not only resource-intensive to construct, but also to operate and maintain.

By default, in the continuing absence of the networked sewerage system, improved and safe sanitation beyond the toilet takes the form of 'non-networked sanitation'. In its simplest definition, as per the International Organisation for Standardisation (ISO), non-networked sanitation comprises any sanitation system treating human excreta that operates without connection to any sewer or drainage network. According to the WHO-UNICEF JMP, in 2017, the number of people depending on non-networked sanitation is just as many as those served by sewerage systems at an approximate 3.1 billion. Unpacking the reliance on the two different types of systems across developmental regions shows that while the reliance on non-networked sanitation (in the form of septic tank, improved pit and other such systems) is much higher in low- and lower middle- income countries, it is not insignificant in upper middle- and high- income countries (**Figure 1**).

Non-networked systems take the form of septic tank systems, single pits, twin pits, composting toilets, container-based toilets, and newer varieties that convert faecal waste into fully treated liquid and solid end-products on site. Interestingly, both the conventional form of the septic tank system and the sewerage system emerged during the same period – the late 19th century - as alternatives to privies, cesspools and cesspits, that had led to disease outbreaks in rapidly-densifying European cities. The septic tank system, comprised of a watertight septic tank and a porous soak pit in series, was patented by John Mouras as the 'Mouras Automatic Scavenger' in France in 1881. The septic tank system soon landed on American shores, from where it spread widely as a low-cost technology for newly urbanising and low-density areas. Within decades, the failing systems spurred improvements in design and standardisation throughout the twentieth century. Guidance on best practices in the design of a septic tank system, known at the time as 'Typical Farm

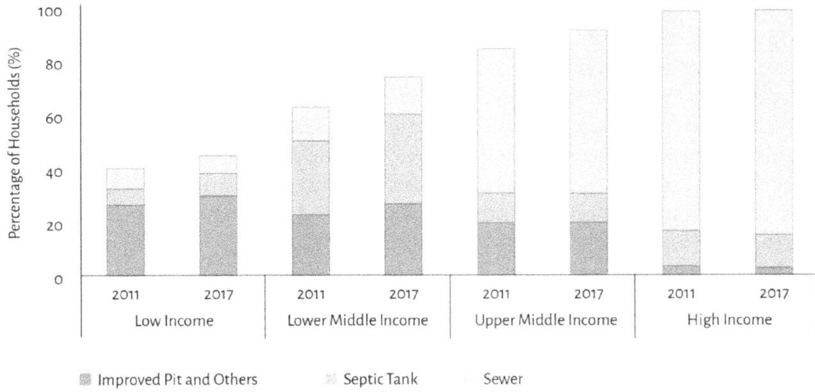

Figure 1.
Dependence on different types of sanitation systems.

Sewage Disposal System' was available in the 1920s in the USA. Formal standards also begin to emerge during this period, with the British Code of Practice first coming out in 1956 [4].

With the proliferation of the sewerage system across Europe, it began to grow in popularity as the standard model for sanitation in cities of the Global South as a result of colonial influence. As a counterpoint, the attempts to mainstream sewerage alternatives started in the 1970s with a World Bank research project that established that non-networked sanitation, or on-site sanitation, could offer a service to public health equivalent to the sewerage systems and at a lower cost. John Kalbermatten, leading the World Bank research, emphasised the importance of adopting a multi-technology strategy (sewered and non-sewered/on-site) in Urban Sanitation Planning to ensure universal coverage of adequate sanitation services [5].

Furthering this emerging unified discourse on sanitation, the United Nations declared the 1980s to be the 'International Water Supply and Sanitation Decade'. The declaration led to the formation of a Technical Advisory Group (TAG), comprised of the United Nations Development Programme (UNDP), World Bank, UNICEF, and members from the Government of India, in 1983, which recommended the 'twin-pit pour-flush latrine' as an appropriate low-cost sanitation solution for both rural and urban areas. Accordingly, the first Indian programme focused on sanitation, the Centrally Sponsored Rural Sanitation Programme (CSRSP), adopted the twin-pit system, a preference that continues in the latest national programme, the Swachh Bharat Mission (the Clean India Mission) [6].

The Group's 'Report of the Committee on Design Criteria for Pour-Flush Waterseal Latrines in Rural Communities of India' directly assisted the Bureau of Indian Standards (the national standard-setting body) in issuing the 'Code of Practice for Sanitation with Leaching Pits for Rural Communities' in 1988. The Code discusses various technical aspects of construction and maintenance of leaching pits and allows for both twin pits and the 'single pit', provided the latter is 'desludged by a vacuum tanker since its contents contain pathogen'. The Indian Code of Practice for Installation of Septic Tanks similarly discusses the design and construction criteria for septic tanks and subsoil dispersion systems in two separate parts first issued in 1963 and 1964 respectively, and significantly and substantively revised in 1985.

In the present time in India, as in other developing countries of the Global South, households construct the sanitation system, whether septic tanks or leaching pits, in situ. In contrast, developed countries that had targeted the issue of basic sanitation much earlier have created more mature ecosystems for non-networked sanitation. From the in situ construction of the systems driven by households, they have advanced to greater dependence on industrially manufactured and standardised on-site systems in a variety of materials like polyethylene and fibre-reinforced plastics, eschewing the traditional brick-and-mortar. Secondly, research and industrial innovation have led to newer on-site 'packaged' systems that perform the function of primary, secondary, and tertiary treatment in one compact unit. Thirdly, more than the unit itself, the regulatory and operative models governing non-networked sanitation and these systems have similarly evolved.

With the flagship governmental programme, Swachh Bharat Mission (SBM), segueing into its new phase, the national focus has shifted to challenges of managing faecal waste beyond the toilet. Both the urban and rural versions of SBM Phase II, announced in 2021 and 2020, respectively, mainstream Faecal Sludge Management (FSM), or the safe management of faecal sludge and septage evacuated from on-site systems as they fill up over time at an off-site facility, or a Faecal Sludge Treatment Plant (FSTP). While FSM solves the gaps in achieving safe and sustainable sanitation beyond the individual premises and is critical, a sole focus on FSM often excludes the discussion on the quality of on-site systems and its improvement from the agenda. With investments in sanitation continuing to intensify as we enter the last decade of the SDG era, it is important to evaluate the need for systematic improvement in the on-site infrastructure for ensuring that the entire service chain of sanitation is secure. The issue is only underscored by a growing institutional acceptance of the on-ground common knowledge that on-site systems do not comply with basic safety standards [6, 7].

The present paper reviews the findings of a novel sample survey focused on on-site systems administered to 3,000 households across urban India. It offers insights on the typology and compliance status of these systems and how learning from advanced contexts, the whole ecosystem for non-networked sanitation can evolve in India and similar contexts across the Global South.

2. Unearthing facts of On-Site Systems (OSS) in urban India

The global sanitation agenda has mainstreamed the importance of on-site systems and FSM in achieving safely managed sanitation in urban and rural areas alike in the Global South. The newfound recognition of non-networked sanitation as a viable and necessary alternative to sewerage systems led the Ministry of Housing and Urban Affairs (MoHUA), Government of India, to issue the National Policy on Faecal Sludge and Septage Management, 2017. The Policy has created an imperative at the national level for the implementation of FSM and set out the necessary priorities and directions for the states. It introduces the sanitation service chain as a framework for understanding the issues of non-networked sanitation, and while it does go over the importance of ensuring that on-site systems are compliant, no governmental programme for their improvement has stemmed from it so far.

Without detailed data on the exact nature of deviations and what requirements households are trying to solve for in adopting certain preferences in design, a responsive and comprehensive strategy for improving the quality of on-site systems cannot emerge. The general view of non-compliance of on-site systems derives directly from the poor application of building regulations overall in Indian cities [8]. Building regulations despite their stringent provisions for enforcement are violated in India due to low awareness of households regarding their importance, a laggard upgradation of rules and systems when compared to the ever-evolving ground realities, and perhaps most critically, the weak capacity of local authorities in enforcing the regulations.

The National Sample Survey 76th Round (administered by the Ministry of Statistics and Programme Implementation), 2018, asked households how often they desludge their on-site systems and for related details viz. service provider, place of disposal, service charges. It was the first time that recurring nation data collection efforts had articulated such questions, with the Census of India and the preceding rounds of the National Sample Survey only asking about which type of on-site system the toilet has. Still, the framing of these questions is rooted more in understanding the need for FSM than in defining the attributes of on-site systems in and of themselves. As the following sections will show, the timely desludging of faecal sludge and septage from these systems and its safe management downstream is critical, but it is a recurring event that does not inherently fix all the issues in the system's day-to-day and year-round performance.

To plug the gap in the data available on on-site systems and the agenda for their improvement, the authors' conducted a novel multi-state survey of 3,000 households across urban India. The survey focused its attention on cities and towns with a population of less than 1,000,000, given that these are the ones that, given the trajectory of sewerage system development, would continue to depend on non-networked sanitation in the medium to long term. Since typically hydrogeological factors such as the depth to the groundwater table, terrain, and soil type are contributing factors in determining the most suitable design of an on-site system, the 3,000 households were spread out over the four hydrogeologically diverse states of Madhya Pradesh (plains, moderate water table), Rajasthan (desert soils, low water table) Odisha (coastal, high water table), and Uttarakhand (hilly, moderate to low water table). The sampling design ultimately selected a total of ten cities in these four states as sites of enquiry. Structured interviews with masons, public health engineers/sanitation inspectors, and desludging service providers accompanied the household survey to allow for the triangulation and better contextualisation of the survey findings [9].

The following sub-sections discuss the main findings of the survey and their implications.

2.1 Higher dependence on septic tanks compared to leaching pits

As seen earlier, the need for the invention of the septic tank system was rooted in a desire for improving the cesspits, cesspools, and privies prevalent during the latter half of the nineteenth century. The leaching of contaminants to the subsurface in the high-density areas typical of burgeoning cities and a limited network of piped water supply combine to create disease outbreaks like the Broad Street Cholera Outbreak of 1854 in London [10]. While the unimproved systems of the time were eschewed for sewerage systems and septic tank systems in the Global North the discourse in the Global South stayed stagnated on (a) sewerage systems as the sanitation standard to aspire to and (b) twin pits as the government's preferred low-cost technological options in its absence, the latter as recently as the ongoing SBM Phase II.

Nonetheless, the data notes that nine out of ten toilet-owning households in these cities depend on a septic tank. It is important to note at this juncture that the authors' use of the phrase 'septic tank' is intentional since the majority of households construct the septic tank system only partially, i.e. construct the septic tank, which serves as the primary treatment unit, without constructing second component for secondary treatment or safe disposal of the tank effluent. The clear preference for septic tanks in urban areas is evinced by the fact that leaching pits are significantly associated ($p < 0.01$) with a lower standard of living, a lower monthly per capita expenditure, semi-permanent or temporary housing, and smaller plot sizes on average. In other words, between septic tanks and leaching pits, urban households view the former as the better option, and the construction of the latter is more a function of capital constraints than an informed preference. Another way the phenomenon manifests is when the prevalence of the two main types of on-site systems is disaggregated by whether the households constructed the toilet on their own ('privately constructed') or under a government programme ('subsidy led'). The share of leaching pits rises a little over three times among toilets constructed under the government programme (**Figure 2**).

The de facto and widespread preference for septic tanks, emerging without a governmental boost, already means that urban India is at an intermediate point in the trajectory towards mature ecosystems for non-networked sanitation. The relatively low prevalence of leaching pits at the city level may have staved off acute incidences of waterborne diseases, but as the following sections show, more ground needs covering before Indian cities have well-functioning sanitation service chains from the toilet to treatment.

2.2 Critical absence of secondary treatment of effluent and poor primary treatment to begin with

Many factors influence the performance of a septic tank as a primary treatment unit, and none of them preclude the necessity of a secondary component for the management of the effluent that a septic tank releases. The septic tank does not act on pathogens and stabilises the settled solids, or sludge, to an extent (a reduction of 30–50% in the Biochemical Oxygen Demand (BOD) and up to 50% in that of Total Suspended Solids (TSS) can be expected). Tweaking the design of the basic septic tank – whether big or small, with or without partitions, with wide or narrow channels, shallow or deep, can increase or decrease the primary treatment efficiency, i.e. the ability to separate liquids and solids and effect partial digestion of stored solids over time. But, no matter how perfect the primary treatment, the effluent from a septic tank needs further treatment due to the significant remnant pollution load (**Table 1**).

The Indian Code of Practice recognises the distinction between a 'septic tank' and a 'septic tank system' too and declares that 'under no circumstances should effluent from a septic tank be allowed into an open channel drain or body of water without adequate treatment'. The survey data shows that 72% of septic tanks discharge the tank effluent into drains designed for stormwater management. In 60% of the cases, the drains are uncovered and exposed to the environment, while in 12%, the drains have a covering. Related research investigating

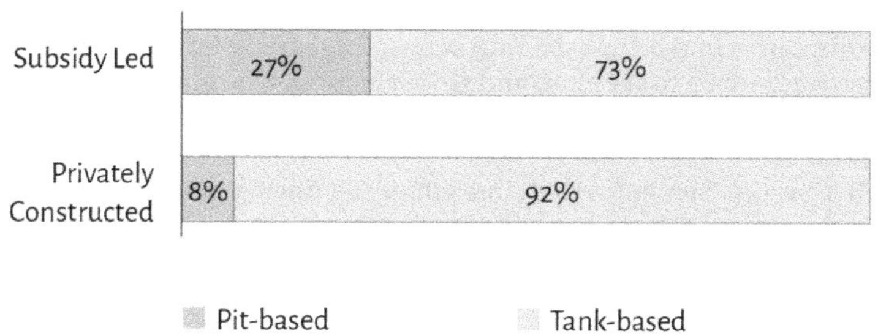

Figure 2.
Type of on-site system based on financing of toilet construction.

Parameter	Average Septic Tank Effluent Characteristics	Standard for Wastewater Treatment per Notification issued by Ministry of Forests, Environment, and Climate Change (MoEFCC), 2017		Proposed Standard for Wastewater Treatment as per National Green Tribunal, 2019 (for mega and metropolitan cities)
		Metro cities and state capitals	All other regions	
Biochemical Oxygen Demand (mg/l)	**203**	20	30	10
Chemical Oxygen Demand (mg/l)	**619**			50
Total Suspended Solids (mg/l)	**2377**	50	100	20
Total Kjeldahl Nitrogen (mg/l)	**318**			10
Dissolved Phosphorous (mg/l)				1
pH	**6.69**	6.5–9	6.5–9	
Faecal Coliform (Most Probable Number per 100 ml)	**1.63×10^7 Colony Forming Units per 100 ml**	1000	1000	230

***Authors' study based on a sample of 32 septic tanks in Udaipur, Rajasthan.*

Table 1.
Characteristics of septic tank effluent and standards for wastewater treatment.

the epidemiological impact of this phenomenon in peri-urban areas of Bolivia has related it to an increased incidence of diarrhoea in children under age five. It cautions against the poor quality and mismanagement of tank effluent attenuating the gains from increased access to toilets and improved on-site sanitation systems [11].

Just as significantly, greywater, or wastewater from activities such as washing, bathing, and other non-toilet related purposes, produced by the households too ends up in these drains, with 92% of all on-site systems being receiving only blackwater as input. Only 8% of the households reported treating the greywater in the same on-site system as the one for their blackwater or a separate one. Although greywater is minimally pathogenic compared to blackwater, it still contains pollutants and microcontaminants from residual pharmaceuticals, personal care products, aerosols, pigments, and other such products. Due to a lack of interception of the drains and treatment of waste flows, the disposal of tank effluent and greywater into drains holds the potential to not only cause adverse outcomes in health at source but also serve as a diffuse source of water pollution.

2.3 Household preference for septic tanks that are an order of magnitude larger than the recommended size

The issuing of the National Policy on Faecal Sludge and Septage Management, 2017, unlocked investments for the creation of city-level FSM infrastructure and assets. The Policy arrived two years into the Atal Mission for Rejuvenation and Urban Transformation (AMRUT), a massive urban infrastructure development programme with a total outlay of INR 77,640 crores (USD ~10.41 billion) covering 500 of the country's largest cities. The programme allocated 95% of its outlay towards water supply, wastewater management, and drainage. However, at its inception, AMRUT did not feature FSM as a component of wastewater management. Due to the National Policy and continuing advocacy on the importance of FSM to achieve citywide sanitation, AMRUT recognised and incorporated FSM as an investment area in its purview. Now, in 2021, the Covid-19 pandemic has emerged as the new foreground for reinvigorated investments in water supply and wastewater management. In India, MoHUA announced the second phase of SBM (2021–2026), which promotes FSM as a wastewater management solution for all cities with a population of less than 1,00,000.

The increased influx of national investments would bolster the smooth scaling up of FSM already underway in the country – going from standalone pilots 2015 onward to scale-up of FSM in AMRUT cities and further across all cities and towns in states like Maharashtra and Odisha that have been early champions of FSM. These investments usually mean setting up FSTPs in the city and acquiring vacuum trucks to desludge the on-site systems and convey faecal sludge to the FSTP(s). Though the capacity of local governments – big and small - to provide mechanised desludging services is on the rise, the engagement of informal and small-scale service providers, including manual labour, for desludging continues to be a reality of the non-networked sanitation ecosystem in India.

Owing to the pernicious entrenchment of sanitation-work within caste-based social hierarchies in India, the national government had notified 'The Prohibition of Employment as Manual Scavengers and their Rehabilitation Act' in 2013. The Act does not disallow per se the engagement of manual labour for desludging provided they adopt the prescribed safety equipment and protocols. However, largely, the engagement of manual labour takes the form of 'hazardous cleaning' or the manual cleaning of a septic tank without the prescribed protective gear, cleaning equipment, and safety precautions, which the Act deems a criminal offence [12]. More generally, the traditional norms of purity and pollution too have shaped the sanitation practices in India, with a significant body of research finding that these notions impact whether or not a household chooses to own and use a toilet facility [13, 14].

Within this context, the authors' survey finds that both households and masons consider an on-site system that does not require frequent maintenance, and thus engagement with the system, the gold standard in design. One of the masons interviewed as part of the primary data collection reported with confidence that the last septic tank he constructed would not require emptying for the next 40–50 years. Another mason acknowledged that with the large sizes of the tanks and a small number of users, the tanks would take 25–30 years to fill up. Overall, in the perception of both the households and the masons, on-site systems appear to be largely divorced from their role as a treatment system and are instead viewed as a mere containment structure that should be able to store faecal waste for as long as possible. Accordingly, while the Indian Code of Practice recommends a septic tank size of ~1,100 litres for five users, the average size of the septic tank for the same number of users is ~11,000 litres, as reported on the ground. The size shows a clear relationship with the economic status of the household, but not the size of the household as theory and the technical standard would dictate (**Figure 3**).

Along with the household's economic status, the lot size of the dwelling presents a physical constraint to the size of the septic tank and is positively associated with it. The third factor which strongly associates with the septic tank size, albeit

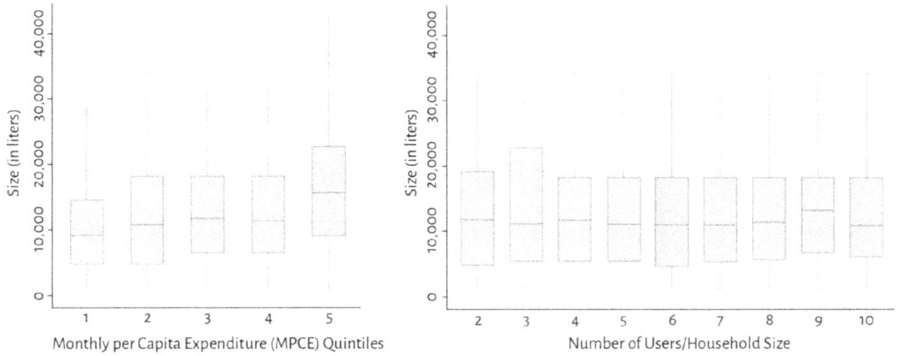

Figure 3.
Variation in septic tank sizes with respect to monthly per capita expenditure (MPCE) and number of users.

negatively, is whether the household constructed the toilet on their own or with support from the government programme. In the case of the latter, the average reported size of the septic tank dropped down by 50% to ~5,620 litres. Winneberger remarked, "Modern septic tank design has evolved mostly as a function of construction convenience, low cost, and repetitive practice" about the evolution of septic tank design in 1984 [15]. As it holds, his remark bears insight into the deviations constituting contemporary construction practices and the phenomenon of the household's preference for large septic tank sizes too.

2.4 Desludging frequencies running into decades due to large sizes

Like any wastewater management system, on-site systems require periodic maintenance too. Leaching pits are simple in their operation and perform the function of dispersing the incoming wastewater into the surrounding subsurface. Over time, the remnant solids occupy the full volume of the pit requiring its desludging. On the other hand, the accumulation of solids in the septic tank begins to constrain its settling performance long before they fully fill it up to the point of non-usability. As the volume of sludge builds up in the tank, the hydraulic retention time of the incoming wastewater reduces, in turn reducing the BOD removal rate and, resultingly, the quality of the exiting tank effluent. The Indian Code of Practice recommends desludging the tank when the scum layer at the top of the septic tank and the sludge layer together exceed half of the effective septic tank depth. Guidance on appropriate desludging rates from other countries like Australia and Ireland use the same yardstick, with limiting values for the volume of sludge ranging from 30% to 50% of the total working volume of the system.

Applying the principle to calculate the desludging rate for the average urban Indian septic tank with five users leads to a safe frequency of 8–10 years (**Table 2**). This means, that in theory, a septic tank under these conditions would continue to impart the acceptable level of performance until 8–10 years of operation. Nonetheless, in the absence of sludge level sensors, subsoil dispersion systems that begin to clog as septic tank performance deteriorates, and a periodic inspection programme for septic tanks, households cannot be expected to know when the sludge has crossed the halfway mark. Accordingly, as per the survey, 65% of the households reported issues like the clogging of their toilet and backflow from the tank to the toilet as the triggers for seeking desludging services. This means that households tend to desludge the tank when the sludge has accumulated as high as the water line, way beyond the recommended

Recommended Desludging Frequency (in years)							
Number of Users	Size of Septic Tank (in litres)						
	1,000	3,000	5,000	7,000	9,000	10,000	13,000
2	2	6	10	14	18	20	25
5	1	2	4	5	7	8	10
8	<1	1	2	3	4	5	6

Table 2.
Estimated desludging frequencies (in years) for different sizes of septic tank and number of users.

level. Then it is not a surprise that with their large sizes, the septic tanks that have been desludged have been in operation for 21 years on average. Overall, only 13% of all tanks had been emptied even once in their lifetime (13 years on average).

3. Improving on-site systems to achieve Sustainable Development Goal 6

Due to their unchecked and unregulated proliferation, on-site systems have mutated on the ground in response to the needs of the households (**Figure 4**). In urban India, households maximise the size of their on-site system subject to constraints of capital and space to reduce the incidence of maintenance or desludging events. The behaviour evinces the household's conception of on-site systems not as an active decentralised wastewater management system, but instead as a passive faecal waste containment structure (possibly rooted in the desire to 'flush and forget', if they can afford to, like sewered households). Overall, the phenomenon is not endemic to India, and similar issues in the quality and common perception of on-site systems prevail in countries like Bangladesh, Indonesia, Vietnam, and others in the Global South [16].

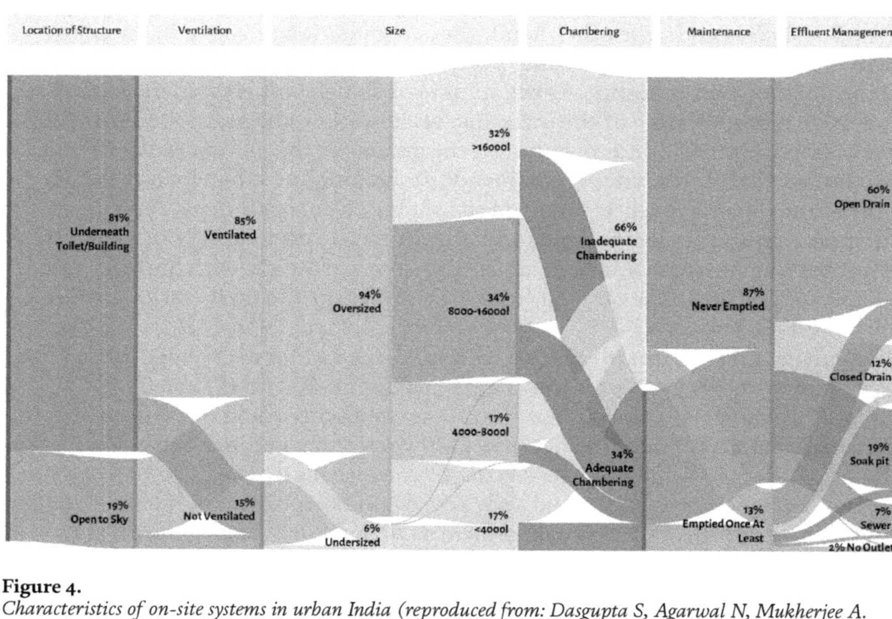

Figure 4.
Characteristics of on-site systems in urban India (reproduced from: Dasgupta S, Agarwal N, Mukherjee A. Unearthed - facts of on-site sanitation in urban India. Centre for Policy Research: New Delhi. https://doi.org/10.13140/RG.2.2.11717.06887).

As non-networked sanitation begins to find a place in mainstream planning and governance systems for citywide sanitation, it would be critical for city, state, and local governments to correct for the deficiencies in the household-level on-site systems for maximising the gains from sanitation investments. A three-point agenda, as discussed below, can guide the way for improving the entire ecosystem surrounding on-site systems towards achieving Sustainable Development Goal 6.

3.1 Shifting paradigm to on-site treatment without depending on soak pits and dispersion trenches

A septic tank, as a standalone unit, is not enough to manage wastewater on-site. A subsoil dispersion system together with the tank constitutes the conventional 'septic tank system' as a complete solution. Without a soak pit or dispersion trench, which release the tank effluent into the subsurface for further nature-based remediation, the effluent must either be treated more completely at the household level before being discharged into the environment or conveyed to an off-site treatment facility through closed channels for treatment. The applicability of each strategy changes based on context. For instance, soak pits and dispersion trenches are a low-cost and low-maintenance solution for effluent management in rural and low-density peri-urban areas. In areas with high density, conveyance and off-site treatment of tank effluent could work if retrofitting and interception of existing drainage channels is possible, or if the costs of creating such a system (like a small bore sewer system) anew are still lower than that of developing a full-sized sewerage system. Alternatively, higher in-situ treatment of the wastewater could help achieve a high level of sanitation without requiring significant investments in city-level infrastructure.

Each of the three strategies demands significant systemic changes to the broader ecosystem within which to implement them. For instance, both the construction of soak pits alongside existing septic tanks and the upgradation of septic tanks to newer, more advanced on-site systems require the willing participation of the household. The feasibility of the latter is additionally contingent on the availability of a flourishing prefabrication industry for on-site systems. Similarly, conveyance and treatment systems require sustained funding to build and operate.

Despite their conventionality, subsoil dispersion systems are unsuited to urban areas. Hydrogeological conditions form only one set of factors influencing the suitability of subsoil dispersion systems. Their spatial density also acts as a critical and limiting factor - with the recommended threshold of spatial density varying in the literature from as low as 16 to 495 units per square kilometres. In India, most cities lie at the higher end of the range and are denser still at the neighbourhood level, rendering the promotion of subsoil dispersion systems an unsuitable option [9]. Therefore, it is imperative that governments move on from viewing subsoil dispersion systems as a simple and appropriate fix to other strategies (**Figure 5**).

3.1.1 Learning from Japan

Up until the Second World War, Japan was primarily an agrarian society and relied on pit toilets, the faecal waste and sludge from which would be evacuated and used as a soil conditioner in farming. The government pursued the development of sewerage systems in the 1970s as the country started urbanising and densifying. With a rising level of affluence, even households in unsewered areas began transitioning to pour-flush toilets and created a need for a system that could serve as a complete on-site treatment system in the absence of a sewer connection.

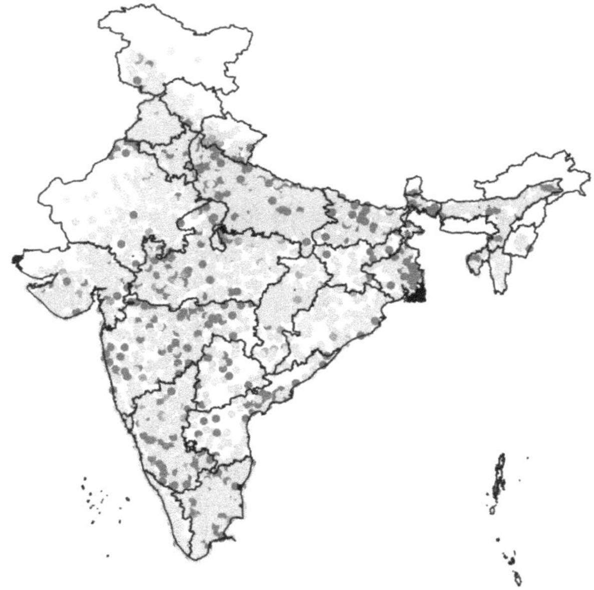

Figure 5.
Density of septic tanks at the city-level in India (reproduced from: Dasgupta S, Agarwal N, Mukherjee A. Moving up the on-site sanitation ladder in urban India through better systems and standards. J. Environ. Manage. 111656. https://doi.org/https://doi.org/10.1016/j.jenvman.2020.111656).

The Tandoku-shori Johkasou (translated as blackwater-only on-site treatment system) gained popularity among households during this period and witnessed proliferation alongside the sewerage system, albeit without governmental regulation. However, within a couple of decades, the persisting issues of water pollution, ascribed to dysfunctional Johkasou systems, emerged at the forefront. To plug the gaps in sanitation and environmental management, the government enacted the Johkasou Law, or the Packaged Aerated Wastewater Treatment Plant (PAWTP) Law, in 1983. The Law enabled the standardisation of the Johkasou for complete treatment of blackwater, its manufacturing, installation and maintenance. The national and local governments created a subsidy programme to enable the rapid diffusion of the improved Johkasou among non-sewered households. In 2000, recognising that treating only blackwater was not enough for environmental protection, the government further amended the PAWTP Law to phase out Tandoku-shori Johkasou in favour of the Gappei-shori Johkasou that treats both black and greywater in the same system [16, 17]. As per the latest data from JMP (2017), Johkasou and older on-site systems continue to serve 23% of the country's total population.

3.2 Encouraging adoption of prefabricated on-site systems to improve performance and standardisation

The speed of diffusion of improved on-site systems and technology, in general, is dependent on a mix of social, economic, and technical factors. Existing research has described the adoption of innovation as 'primarily the outcome of a learning or communications process' [18]. In a densely-populated and urbanising country like India with low levels of baseline technical expertise on safe on-site systems among masons and weak local governance capacities for their regulation, achieving diffusion of new systems at speed and scale would follow a tedious and long trajectory with in-situ construction.

A small set of, and often regional, prefabrication industries for on-site systems already exists in the country. The national and state governments should collaborate with the industrial players to create a portfolio of prefabricated on-site systems that perform advanced (secondary/tertiary) treatment of incoming blackwater and greywater. As part of such a strategy, the government should consider subsidising either the industry or the households directly to bring down the cost of prefabricated on-site systems, the latter like in the case of Japan, and make them competitive with the dominant practice of in-situ construction. Alternatively, or in complementing the subsidisation, the government could adopt a command-and-control approach where it mandates the adoption of certified prefabricated on-site systems among certain categories of users, such as commercial centres, institutional buildings, apartments, and others.

3.2.1 Learning from Malaysia

Malaysia has been one of the flag-bearers of non-networked sanitation and FSM among developing countries, with 20% of its population dependent on on-site sanitation as per JMP (2017). The country has experimented with different frameworks to streamline the co-existence of non-networked sanitation and sewerage systems, as well as, created specific models for the governance of the former, including scheduled desludging. Until the 1990s, septic tanks constructed in-situ were the predominant on-site systems in the country. As a small prefabricated industry for on-site systems began to flourish from then onwards, the Malaysian regulators took cognisance of the opportunity to effect a fundamental shift in the sanitation sector and issued the Malaysian Standard 2441–1 and 2441–2 for the quality-control of the prefabricated systems.

In its first part, the standard notified the design of an improved or enhanced septic tank combining a settling unit with an anaerobic filter for up to 30 population equivalent (PE). The second part covers those systems that perform higher treatment still through aeration and are appropriate for applications with 31 to 149 PE. The distinction between the two types – aeration-based for higher treatment and non-aeration-based for moderate treatment – realistically accounts for the need for incremental improvement. Within a couple of decades, in-situ construction of on-site systems is on its way out, with the prefabricated system being cost-competitive and more convenient for households.

3.3 Creating robust city-level planning and regulatory ecosystems for on-site systems

Rapid urbanisation and laggard service delivery systems have created new landscapes for the implementation of non-networked sanitation. Innovation in system design helps meets public health and environmental needs in these evolving contexts. However, the adoption of innovation and continuous process improvements are not possible without fundamental shifts in the encompassing ecosystem for planning and regulating urban infrastructure. Strong city-level planning systems are imperative to ensuring that households pick the correct option in on-site systems and construct or install it as per the prescribed guidelines. Secondly, a robust regulatory could help foster regular engagement with on-site systems and enable better performance through (a) monitoring of its overall compliance and quality and (b) identifying the need for desludging for improving operational performance. For example, in the case of urban India, the latter could look like local governments contracting desludging service providers to undertake scheduled inspections of on-site systems in addition to their primary responsibility.

3.3.1 Learning from Ireland

Ireland has one of the significant dependence on non-networked sanitation among countries of the Global North. As per JMP (2017), 32% of Ireland's total population depends on on-site systems – with the proportion being more than twice as high at 77% in rural areas. Since low-density rural areas are the major contributors to the dependence, the septic tank system continues to be a viable and the dominant type of system in use. Unlike India, where the Code of Practice recommends against treating 'wastes containing excessive detergents, grease, and disinfectants' in the septic tank, the Irish Environmental Protection Agency (EPA) clearly states that 'greywater in all circumstances be directed to the wastewater treatment system'.

The recently updated 2021 Code of Practice (CoP) for Domestic Waste Water Treatment Systems provides detailed guidance on on-site systems serving PE of 10 or less. The CoP behooves households to ensure that their on-site system complies with EN 12566, the standard for prefabricated assembled/packaged on-site systems, including septic tanks. The CoP requires households to select from the available on-site systems in consultation with the local authority following a site characterisation of their lot. It also discusses the appropriate desludging rates for septic tanks based on the different number of users and sizing. What is unique to Ireland is not its guidance and regulatory framework for on-site sanitation but its data-led inspection plan for monitoring and continuously improving the state of existing on-site systems.

Following the European Union Court of Justice ruling against Ireland under the 1975 EU Waste Framework Directive (Case C-188/08) in 2009, the country promulgated the Water Services (Amendment) Act 2012, which requires the EPA to prepare a national plan for inspection of at least 1,000 on-site systems annually [19]. The Act also requires households to maintain records of desludging. Since then, the EPA has carried out inspections in 2013 and 2015, with the third inspection plan for 2018–2021 underway. The latest inspection report from 2019 found that 51% of the inspected systems had failed, and 26% were a risk to human health or the environment. Under its new grant scheme, these failing systems are eligible for a grant worth €5,000 for improvements. The report noted that 73% of the systems that failed in previous inspections had been fixed.

4. Conclusion

Non-networked sanitation is a viable and necessary alternative to sewerage systems for public health and environmental management in the Global South. However, an erstwhile exclusive focus on developing sewerage infrastructure and viewing non-networked sanitation as a stopgap arrangement has led to poor institutional engagement with the state of the latter. On-site systems have proliferated under a laissez-faire regime, with households determining conventional design practices as a function of cost and convenience. These deviations from the scientific design have come at the expense of increased epidemiological risks and water pollution. In the run-up to the end of the SDG era, the agenda for citywide sanitation cannot exclude improving the quality of on-site systems and their performance. High-settlement densities necessitate a shift to advanced packaged-type systems for urban and peri-urban areas coupled with prefabrication to drive the change at scale and speed. Moreover, since operational performance is a function of both the design of the system and its maintenance, a regulatory programme and strengthening local governance capacities to deliver it are critical to long-term success.

Acknowledgements

The present work was supported by the Bill and Melinda Gates Foundation (BMGF), India (under the grant number OPP1136373).

Conflict of interest

The authors declare no conflict of interest.

Author details

Shubhagato Dasgupta* and Neha Agarwal
Scaling City Institutions for India, Centre for Policy Research, New Delhi, India

*Address all correspondence to: shubhagato@cprindia.org

References

[1] Schellenberg T, Subramanian V, Ganeshan G, Tompkins D, Pradeep R. Wastewater Discharge Standards in the Evolving Context of Urban Sustainability–The Case of India. Front Environ Sci [Internet]. 2020 Apr 17 [cited 2020 Apr 30];8:30. Available from: https://www.frontiersin.org/article/10.3389/fenvs.2020.00030/full

[2] World Health Organization (WHO). Guidelines on sanitation and health. 2019;

[3] Schrecongost A, Pedi D, Rosenboom JW, Shrestha R, Ban R. Citywide Inclusive Sanitation: A Public Service Approach for Reaching the Urban Sanitation SDGs. Front Environ Sci [Internet]. 2020 Feb 28 [cited 2020 Apr 30];8:19. Available from: https://www.frontiersin.org/article/10.3389/fenvs.2020.00019/full

[4] Supeck Septic Services L. The History of the Septic System – Supeck Septic Services [Internet]. [cited 2021 Apr 9]. Available from: https://supeckseptic.com/blog/the-history-of-the-septic-system/

[5] Schertenleib R, Lüthi C, Mintje AP, Depinder B, Abishek K, Narayan S, et al. A Sanitation Journey – Principles, Approaches & Tools for Urban Sanitation [Internet]. 2021 [cited 2021 Apr 9]. Available from: www.susana.org

[6] Dasgupta S, Agarwal N, Mukherjee A. Unearthed - Facts of On-Site Sanitation in Urban India [Internet]. New Delhi; 2019 [cited 2020 Feb 17]. Available from: https://doi.org/10.13140/RG.2.2.11717.06887. 2019.

[7] WaterAid. Quality and sustainability of toilets - A rapid assessment of technologies under Swachh Bharat Mission-Gramin [Internet]. 2017 [cited 2021 Apr 9]. Available from: https://www.wateraidindia.in/sites/g/files/jkxoof336/files/quality-and-sustainability-of-toilets.pdf

[8] Singh A. Building Regulations for Faecal Sludge Management : Review of Building Regulations. New Delhi; 2018.

[9] Dasgupta S, Agarwal N, Mukherjee A. Moving up the On-Site Sanitation ladder in urban India through better systems and standards. J Environ Manage [Internet]. 2020;111656. Available from: http://www.sciencedirect.com/science/article/pii/S0301479720315814

[10] Johnson S. The ghost map : the story of London's most terrifying epidemic--and how it changed science, cities, and the modern world [Internet]. Riverhead Books; 2006 [cited 2021 Apr 9]. 299 p. Available from: https://books.google.co.in/books/about/The_Ghost_Map.html?id=cWtglGzhPPEC&redir_esc=y

[11] Bancalari A, Martinez S. Exposure to sewage from on-site sanitation and child health: A spatial analysis of linkages and externalities in peri-urban Bolivia. J Water Sanit Hyg Dev. 2018;8(1):90-99.

[12] Manish, Singh T. Manual cleaning of sewers and septic tanks | Centre for Policy Research [Internet]. New Delhi; 2017 [cited 2021 Apr 9]. Available from: https://www.cprindia.org/research/reports/manual-cleaning-sewers-and-septic-tanks

[13] Gupta A, Coffey D, Spears D. Purity, pollution, and untouchability: challenges affecting the adoption, use, and sustainability of sanitation programmes in rural India. [cited 2021 Apr 9]; Available from: http://www.developmentbookshelf.com/doi/pdf/10.3362/9781780449272.017

[14] Mohanty R, Dwivedi A. Culture and Sanitation in Small Towns - An

Ethnographic Study of Angul and Dhenkanal in Odisha. Econ Polit Wkly [Internet]. 2015 Jun 5 [cited 2021 Apr 9];54(41):7-8. Available from: https://www.epw.in/journal/2019/41/special-articles/culture-and-sanitation-small-towns.html

[15] D'Amato VA. Factors Affecting the Performance of Primary Treatment in Onsite Systems | IWA Publishing [Internet]. IWA Publishing; 2008 [cited 2020 May 1]. 112 p. Available from: https://www.iwapublishing.com/books/9781843397816/factors-affecting-performance-primary-treatment-onsite-systems

[16] Hashimoto K. Institutional Mechanisms for Sustainable Sanitation: Lessons from Japan for Other Asian Countries [Internet]. 2019 Sep [cited 2020 May 5]. Available from: https://www.adb.org/publications/institutional-mechanisms-sustainable-sanitation-lessons-japan-other-asian-countries

[17] Gaulke LS. On-site wastewater treatment and reuses in Japan. In: Proceedings of the Institution of Civil Engineers [Internet]. Water Management; 2006 [cited 2021 Apr 10]. p. 103-9. Available from: http://courses.washington.edu/onsite/ICEPaperGaulkeJohkasou.pdf

[18] Brown LA. Diffusion: Geographical Aspects. Int Encycl Soc Behav Sci [Internet]. 2015 Jan 1 [cited 2021 Apr 10];406-10. Available from: https://www.sciencedirect.com/science/article/pii/B9780080970868720113

[19] Withers PJA, May L, Jarvie HP, Jordan P, Doody D, Foy RH, et al. Nutrient emissions to water from septic tank systems in rural catchments: Uncertainties and implications for policy. Environ Sci Policy [Internet]. 2012 Dec 1 [cited 2020 May 6];24:71-82. Available from: https://www.sciencedirect.com/science/article/abs/pii/S1462901112001293

Chapter 4

Reducing Pollution of Stabilized Landfill Leachate by Mixing of Coagulants and Flocculants: A Comparative Study

Mlika Kastali, Latifa Mouhir, Abdelaziz Madinzi, Abdeslam Taleb, Abdelkader Anouzla and Salah Souabi

Abstract

The physico-chemical process of coagulation-flocculation is very efficient and economical for the treatment of leachate. The latter can have considerable impacts on the environment. The leachate from the landfill of the city of Mohammedia is characterized by a high COD content which varies between 2200 and 2700 mg/l, a total Kjeldahl nitrogen concentration varying from 1080 to 1405 mg/l while the ammonium content has a concentration varying between 587 and 1410 mg/l. Organic matter is not readily biodegradable (BOD5/COD: 0.2 to 0.13). Metal concentrations ranged from 0.1 to 4.2 mg/l for Cr, 40 to 5 mg/l for Cd, and 0.3 to 0.8 mg/l for lead. For monitoring the leachate treatment, several coagulants and flocculants were used ($FeCl_3$, $Al_2(SO_4)_3$, Alginate, cationic flocculants, anionic flocculants). In parallel with the monitoring of the physicochemical parameters we followed the production of the volume of the settled sludge over time. Treatment with all coagulants and flocculants used is pH dependent. Ferric Chloride has been shown to be effective at a pH of 6.5 while for Aluminum Sulfate the optimum pH is 5.3. The results showed that coagulation-flocculation by Ferric Chloride and Aluminum Sulfate is very effective in reducing turbidity. This reduction reaches 95 and 98% respectively for $FeCl_3$ and $Al_2(SO_4)_3$, while the reduction in COD for the two coagulants is around 60%. Organic flocculants alone do not lead to a significant reduction in turbidity and COD, while their combination with coagulants marks a good reduction in pollution. Hydrated iron hydroxides precipitate more easily than flocs formed by aluminum, resulting in more efficient removal of pollutants than that obtained at lower pH values. The order of introduction strongly influences the coagulation flocculation. The optimal doses of the various coagulants and flocculants chosen for the study vary from one reagent to another. $FeCl_3$ remains the most suitable coagulant to further eliminate organic and metal pollution. The cost associated with the treatment using flocculants remains much higher when the flocculant is used in admixture with a coagulant.

Keywords: leachate, coagulation and flocculation, test jar, optimization

1. Introduction

Leachate is the juice produced during the fermentation of household waste stored in public landfills, which can pose many problems during the design and maintenance of a landfill. Leachate from landfills has been identified as potential sources of contamination of soil, groundwater and surface water, as it can percolate through soils, causing pollution of waterways and groundwater, s' they are not properly collected, processed and safely disposed of [1–4].

The climate and landfill are the main factors influencing the production and composition of the leachate. Where the climate is prone to higher levels of precipitation, there will be no more water penetration into the landfill, and therefore no more leachate generated. Another factor is the topography of the site, which influences the runoff regimes and the water balance of the site.

The treatment of landfill leachate is a complicated process due to the type of contaminants it contains and the variation in volume. The percolation of rainwater through municipal landfill waste from leachate produced by the biological and chemical processes that occur in the waste increases the volume of leachate juice.

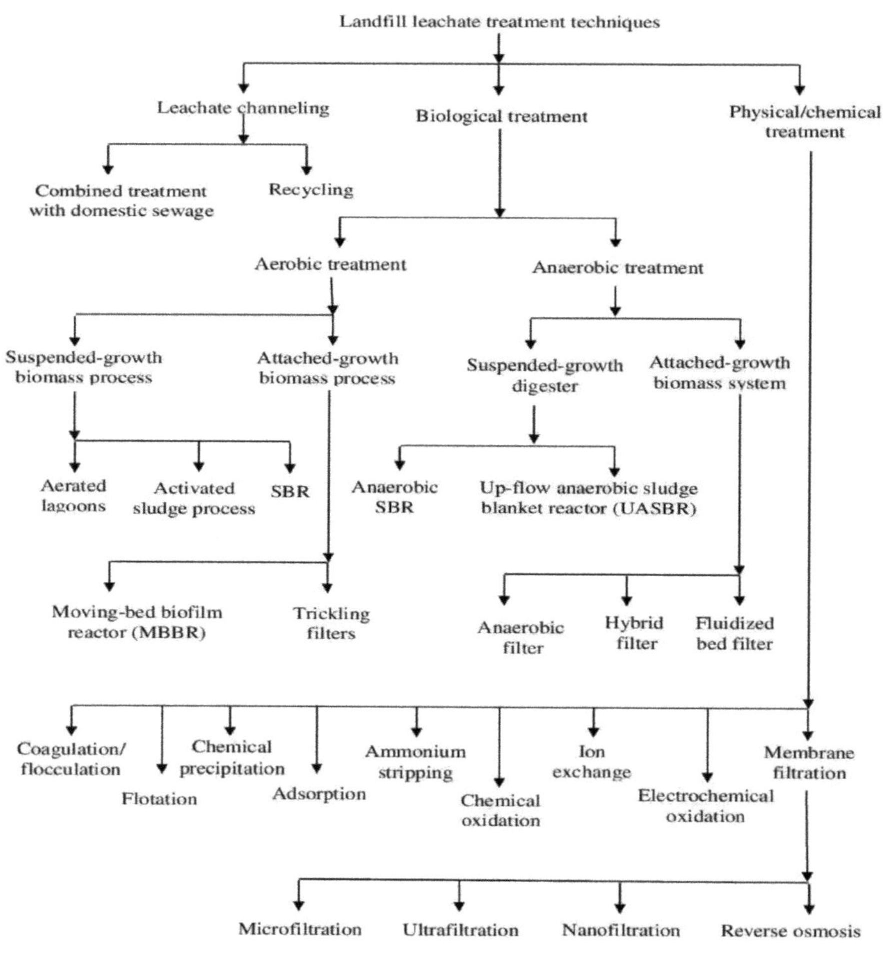

Figure 1.
Diagram of landfill leachate treatment techniques, based on Abbas et al. [6]; Renou et al. [7], Shuokr et al. [8].

The combination of the above factors could generate an effluent whose properties also largely depend on the age of the landfill [2–5].

Solid waste from municipal landfills is considered a very important source of pollution since it contains enormous amounts of organic and mineral matter, some types of organic matter of which are biodegradable, where humic and fluvic acids represent a significant amount in old leachate. Optimizing the factors controlling the treatment of this liquid effluent can greatly increase the efficiency of the process. The physico-chemical treatment process can be applied to landfill leachate without being affected by the toxicity of the leachate and could provide a simple, selective and economically acceptable alternative to traditional methods. The different treatment techniques often used to reduce pollution from leachate discharges are illustrated in **Figure 1** [6, 8].

The flocculation coagulation methods which are the most widely applied for the fight against pollution from leachate discharges [9–12]. State-of-the-art physico-chemical treatment processes have been developed [13, 14] and applied for the decontamination of leachate discharges. These different techniques depend on several parameters: leachate age, quality, cost and waste to be treated (household and industrial waste). Biological treatment processes such as activated sludge is problematic due to the low kinetics of degradation and foam production [15]. In the treatment of leachate many factors can influence the effectiveness of treatment by coagulation flocculation), such as the type and the optimal concentration of the coagulant/flocculant and the optimal pH [16–19]. The sanitary landfill method for final solid waste disposal continues to be widely accepted and used because of its economic benefits in developing countries [20].

The main objective of this study is the optimization of the conditions of the coagulation flocculation process in the treatment of landfill leachate, and the determination of the most appropriate dose for different coagulants and flocculants such as ferric chloride, sulphate aluminum, Alginate, ... at optimum pH which considerably reduces organic matter, suspended solids and metals present in leachate.

2. Materials and methods

2.1 Sampling techniques

The leachate samples were collected from the Mohammedia town landfill in 50 L plastic bins, transported to the laboratory and stored at 4° C. The leachate samples were placed for 2 hours at room temperature before performing the flocculation coagulation tests. Then, the samples were thoroughly shaken to resuspend the deposited solids before further tests were performed.

2.2 Coagulants/flocculant dosage

Several coagulants and flocculants have been tested for the treatment of leachate discharges such as ferric chloride ($FeCl_3.6H_2O$), aluminum sulphate ($Al_2(SO_4)_3.18H_2O$), alginate, ... for destabilize suspended solids and colloids and eliminate pollution afterwards.

In addition, two flocculants such as the Astral flocculant and the cationic polyelectrolyte Superfloc supplied by companies in Casablanca, the flocculants Chemic1, Chemic2, Chemic3 supplied by an Italian company.

The experimental process consists of three steps: a rapid mixture of leachate containing coagulation reagents of the flocculation reagents at 160 rpm for 10 min, followed by slow agitation for 20 minutes and 30 rpm, then a step of final settling for 1 hour. The coagulation-flocculation was carried out with the optimized and previously determined operating parameters.

Furthermore, the treatment tests were carried out by the Jar test technique using six polyethylene beakers of volume equal to 1 liter to examine the different doses of coagulant with a well-defined initial pH (optimal pH). The tested samples were mixed thoroughly to resuspend the deposited solids, and the appropriate volume of the sample was transferred to the corresponding beakers. First, the optimum pH for $FeCl_3$ activity was determined. A known volume of the solution of ferric chloride, aluminum sulfate or other coagulants and flocculants was added to 1 L of landfill leachate at various pH values adjusted with H_2SO_4 and NaOH. To study the optimum dose of coagulant, the pH of the leachate solution is maintained at the optimum value and variable doses of $FeCl_3$ or $Al_2(SO_4)_3$ were then added. After 60 minutes of decantation, the supernatant was taken for analysis. To evaluate the effectiveness of ferric chloride, aluminum sulphate or other coagulants and flocculants for the treatment of leachate, the following parameters were determined: turbidity, chemical oxygen demand (COD)... settled sludge and metallic elements not eliminated.

2.3 Analytical techniques

The turbidity was determined by a HI 93703 microprocessor turbidimeter. The Chemical Oxygen Demand (COD) and the other physicochemical parameters (NTK, total phosphate, etc.) for the characterization of the leachate were determined according to standard methods [21].

The pH of the solutions was measured using an "Accumet Basic AB15 pH-meter" from the Fisher Scientific brand with a combined Ag/AgCl glass electrode according to standard NF T 90-008 February 2001 (T90-008). The conductivity was measured using a conductivity meter brand "YK-2001PH intelligent conductivity pH-meter" according to standard NF EN 27888 January 1994 (T90-031). The COD was carried out according to the AFNOR standard in force [NF T90-101 February 2001 (T90-101)]. The measurement of the biological oxygen demand after five days (BOD5) was facilitated by the use of the gauge method [(EN 1899 May 1998) (T90-103)] using the BOD5 meter of the VELP brand. The absorbance measurements were carried out using a UV-visible spectrophotometer.

Spectrophotometer 9,200 RAYLEIGH 2-beam 1 nm bandwidth. Turbidity was measured using a turbidimeter according to NF EN ISO 7027 March 2000 (T 90-033). The determination of the materials in suspension was carried out by the centrifugation method of the standard [NF T 90-105 January 1997 (T 90-105)]. The phenolic compounds were determined by the colorimetric method using the Folin–Ciocalteu reagent [22]. The nitrate assay was carried out by the spectrometric method in the presence of sulfosalicylic acid according to standard EN ISO 78-90 January 1997 (T 90–045). The determination of the total phosphorus was carried out by spectrometric method according to NF T 90–023 January 1997. The determination of ammoniacal nitrogen NH4 was carried out by the spectrophotometric method with indophenol blue according to AFNOR NF T 90–015 January 1997. The method of heavy metal analysis is atomic absorption spectrophotometry with a graphite furnace (VARIAN AA 20 model).

3. Results and discussions

3.1 Leachate characteristics

To assess the impacts of a landfill on the environment, it is necessary to characterize the effluents it generates. Indeed, whatever the mode of operation of a landfill, the leachate constitutes, if it is not treated before its discharge, a source of

Parameters	Values	Average	Moroccan Standards
pH	7.7–8.92	8.3	6.5–8.5
Conductivitéms/cm	25.6–35.9	31.2	2.7
Turbidity NTU	63–140	102.2	—
HPO_4^{2-} mg/l	592.4–2128	1693.3	—
Sulphate mg/l	77.47–218.7	156.04	—
Tot phosphate mg/l	1226.6–2217	1879.5	10
TKN mg/l	1080–1405	1289.75	30
COD mg/l	2153–2707	2473.9	500
BOD5 mg/l	526–290	399	—
BOD5/COD	0.2–0.135	0.16	—
O_2 mg/l	0–0.2	0.03	
NO_3^- mg/l	36.3–453.9	173.2	—

Table 1.
Physico-chemical parameters of leachate (mg/l) from Mohammedia landfill.

nuisance which is added to the numerous problems of contamination of the surrounding environment. These liquids loaded with mineral and organic substances resulting from the decomposition of waste can be entrained by runoff and reach surface water, or infiltrate through the bedrock of the landfill and contaminate the water of the water table which is not deep.

The different physicochemical parameters analyzed in the landfill leachate are presented in **Table 1**. In addition, the results of the analysis of metals (Cu, Zn, Cr, Ni, Pb, Sb and Sn) in the three sampling companies were carried out (**Table 2**).

The characteristics of a leachate can generally be represented in terms of basic parameters such as COD, BOD, BOD5/COD ratio, color, pH, content of metallic elements [4]. These results showed that the leachate is characterized by high concentrations of organic matter and high concentrations of ammonium and nitrogen compound (**Table 1**). The organic matter, in terms of COD varies between 2153 and 2707 mg/l (stabilized leachate), while high concentrations of ammoniacal nitrogen (587 to 1410 mg/l) and NTK (1080 to 1405 mg/l) have been detected. The main concentrations of heavy metals are between 0.1 to 4.2 mg/l for Cr, 0.04–0.005 mg/l for cadmium and 0.8 to 0.3 mg/l for Pb. The characterization of the average leachate showed that the BOD5/COD ratio varies between 0.2 to 0.13, which shows that the leachate is rich in organic matter and not biodegradable (humic and fulvic substances).

In addition, turbidity and conductivity are very high values, far exceeding the standards for treated wastewater. This shows that decision-makers in Morocco must make an effort to save the current situation of public landfills in order to protect the

Sampling date	Cu	Zn	Cr	Cd	Ni	Pb	Sb	Sn
25/03/2000	0.7	0.2	0.1	0.035	0.3	0.5	1.3	—
10/8/2002	1.2	2.3	4.2	0.018	0.4	0.3	0.9	—
5/10/2007	1.2	1.9	3.2	0.005	0.2	0.8	0.5	0.6

Table 2.
Analysis of the metallic elements of leachate from the Mohammedia landfill.

health of the population. The low values of the BOD5/COD ratio (0.2–0.13) thus show that the leachate is rich in non-biodegradable organic matter, which can cause several impacts on surface water and groundwater [2]. Souabi et al. [1], showed that for leachate discharges from Mohammedia (main collector), the BOD5/COD ratio varies between 0.2 and 0.13, showing that the leachate is not easily biodegradable and can therefore cause several impacts on surface water. (Oued El Maleh). The same authors have shown that the COD values obtained vary between 2301 and 2750 mg/l and remain much lower than the content detected by [23] discharged into the sea. The variation in the characteristics of the leachate has been attributed to many factors, such as variations in the composition of the solid waste, the age of the landfill, the hydrogeology of the landfill, precipitation and specific weather conditions. and waste moisture [7, 24, 25]. From 5 to 10 years, the landfill is known as "middle age" and its leachate has a COD of between about 3000 to 15000 mg/l [20]. After 10 years, a landfill contains less biodegradable material and the leachate has a COD value of less than 2000 mg/l [4, 11].

For a given leachate, fluctuations in pH, flow, COD and BOD5 contents, etc. have been observed over time [4, 11]. This can influence the efficiency of the elimination by different treatment techniques and disturb the receiving environment if the leachate is rejected without treatment, which justifies the installation of a homogenization basin. The age of the landfill is one of the main factors that also influences the characteristics of the leachate.

Landfill leachate contains chemicals, including metal ions such as iron. Indeed, efficient and cost-effective leachate treatment techniques are difficult to implement [26]. Rivas and Gimento [27] pointed out that old landfills produce stabilized leachate with a relatively low COD content ranging from 500 to 5000 ppm, a slightly basic pH of 7.5 to 8.5, low biodegradability (BOD5/COD less than 0.1) and a significant amount of heavy metals and high molecular weight compounds (humic and fulvic substances). Leachate exhibits considerable variation in composition [11]. The concentration of contaminants are mainly influenced by the age of the landfill, as well as by the type of waste deposited at the landfill and other hydrogeological factors [11, 17].

The characterization of the average leachate has shown that the BOD5/COD ratio varies between 0.2 to 0.13, which shows that the leachate is rich in organic matter and not biodegradable (humic and fulvic substances) which can cause several impacts on the water surface and groundwater [28].

3.2 Leachate settling

The study of the elimination of leachate pollution by sedimentation is presented in **Table 3**. The settling time varies around 120 minutes. The supernatant was collected to analyze the COD after a stabilization time of 120 minutes.

Raw leachate (COD mg/l)	Decanted leachate (COD mg/l)	Abatement %
2707	1800	34.5
2301	1632	29
2153	1536	29.5
2688	2544	5
2240	1728	23
2540	1866	26.5

Table 3.
Study of leachate sedimentation for six sampling campaigns settling time 120 min.

The COD removal rate varies between 5 and 34.5%, which is essentially a function of the quality of the leachate collected. Indeed, sedimentation remains essential to reduce leachate pollution at the lowest cost.

Settling is a process to reduce turbidity by allowing the water to stand for 2–24 hours for the particles to settle to the bottom of the basin. The advantage of settling is that it does not require any equipment other than settling tanks. However, the drawbacks of this method require several settling tanks when the polluting load and the flow rate are high.

The removal of suspended particles by sedimentation depends on the size and density of these particles. Settleable solids are measured as the visible volume accumulated at the bottom of an Imhoff cone after settling for one hour.

Unhindered settling is a process that removes discrete particles at a very low concentration without interference from nearby particles. The re-stabilization of the system by adding excess coagulant is not effective, since increasing the settling time promotes clarification of the supernatant beyond the critical coagulation concentration and the charge reversal point.

3.2.1 Effects of Fe^{3+} and Al^{3+} on the removal of leachate pollution

The coagulation results for the $FeCl_3$ and $Al_2(SO_4)_3$ leachate are shown in **Figures 2** and **3**.

The comparative study of coagulation-flocculation by Fe^{3+} and Al^{3+} is given in the **Table 4**.

3.2.2 Effect of pH on $FeCl_3$ leachate coagulation

In the coagulation-flocculation process [29, 30]. It is very important to adjust the pH since coagulation occurs within a specific pH range for each coagulant and depending on the type and characteristic of the raw effluent to be treated.

The COD removal efficiency tests, using $FeCl_3$ were performed for pH values between 2 and 12 (**Figure 4**). The optimum pH of the raw leachate, before the addition of the coagulant is 6.5. At this pH, the COD and the turbidity dropped by 84% and 96% respectively. This conclusion is in agreement with that of [27].

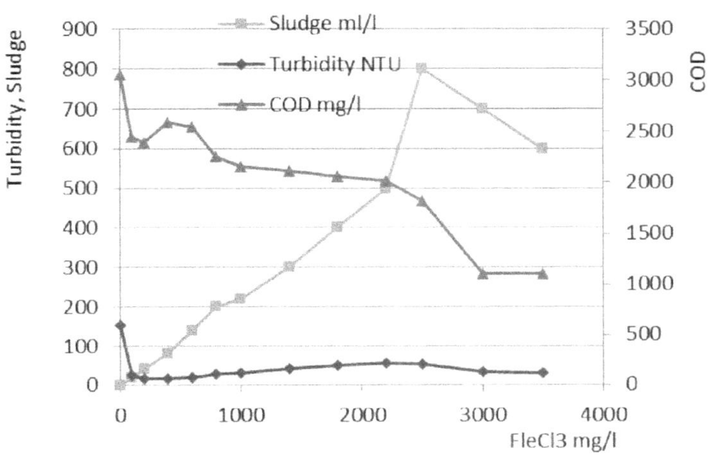

Figure 2.
Effect of $FeCl_3$ on the elimination of leachate pollution. Experimental conditions: initial COD of the leachate = 3175 mg/l and initial turbidity = 128 NTU, pH = 7.8.

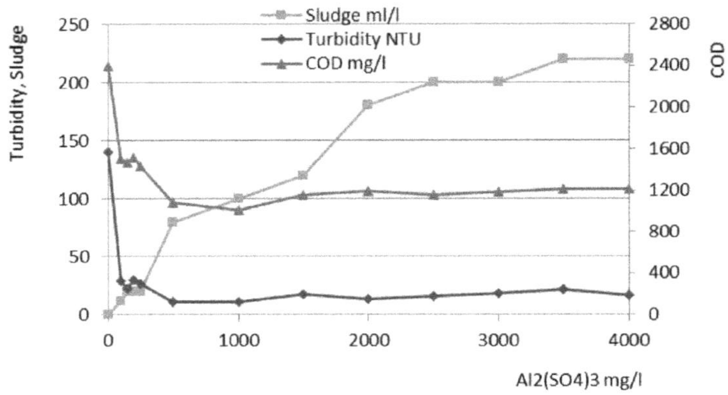

Figure 3.
Effect of $Al_2(SO_4)_3$ on COD removal, turbidity and settled sludge. Experimental conditions: initial COD of leachate = 2400 mg/l, initial turbidity = 140 NTU, pH = 7.8.

	Optimal concentration mmol/l	%Turbidity removal	%COD removal	Sludges ml/l	optimal pH
Fe^{3+}mmol/l	18.5	95	67	800	6.5
Al^{3+}mmol/l	5.82	98	60	230	5.3

Table 4.
Comparative study of coagulation-flocculation by Fe^{3+} and Al^{3+}.

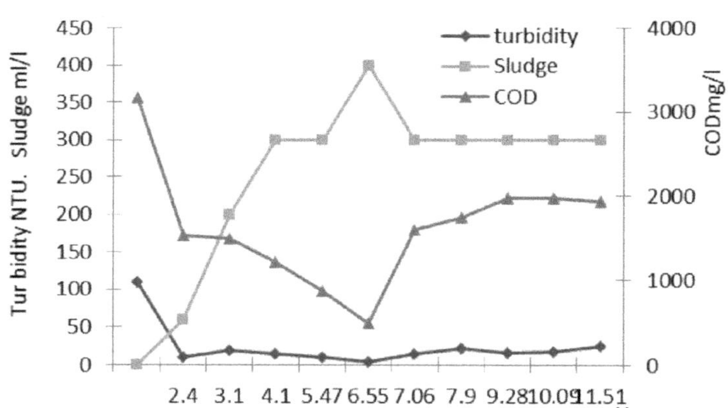

Figure 4.
Effect of pH on leachate coagulation using $FeCl_3$. Experimental conditions: (optimal $FeCl_3$ concentration: 3500 mg/l), initial leachate COD = 3168 mg/l, initial turbidity = 110 NTU and pH 7.8.

3.2.3 Effect of pH on leachate coagulation using $Al_2(SO_4)_3$

Figure 5 shows the effect of pH on leachate coagulation using aluminum sulfate. The results show a removal of turbidity which varies around 84% at pH 5.3. The maximum sludge volume, generated at optimum pH, is 240 ml/l. Partial dissolution of aluminum oxide and the appearance of a net positive charge on the surface should be considered.

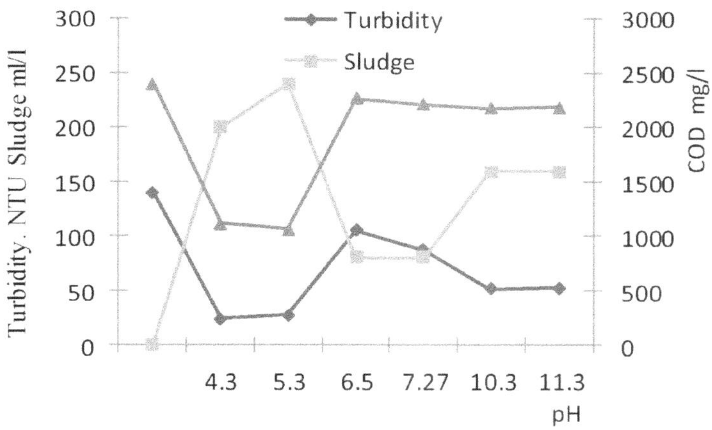

Figure 5.
Effect of pH on leachate coagulation using $Al_2(SO_4)_3$. Experimental conditions: (optimal concentration of $Al_2(SO_4)_3$: 1000 mg/l), initial leachate COD = 2.400 mg/l, initial turbidity = 140 NTU and pH 7.8.

Flocs generated under strongly acidic or basic conditions were significant, but in very small numbers, especially in an acidic environment. The reduction in pH is due to the acidic character of Al^{3+} from $Al_2(SO_4)_3$. For the other coagulant doses tested, the flocs were microscopic and similar in size.

4. The effect of coagulants and flocculants on the removal of COD and turbidity

4.1 Effect of the mixture: Astral Flocculant + $FeCl_3$

To improve the elimination of leachate pollution, we tested a flocculant supplied by the company. This flocculant is currently used at the wastewater treatment plant which treats the wastewater of company by coagulation flocculation. The effect of Astral flocculant on turbidity and COD removal is shown in **Figure 6**.

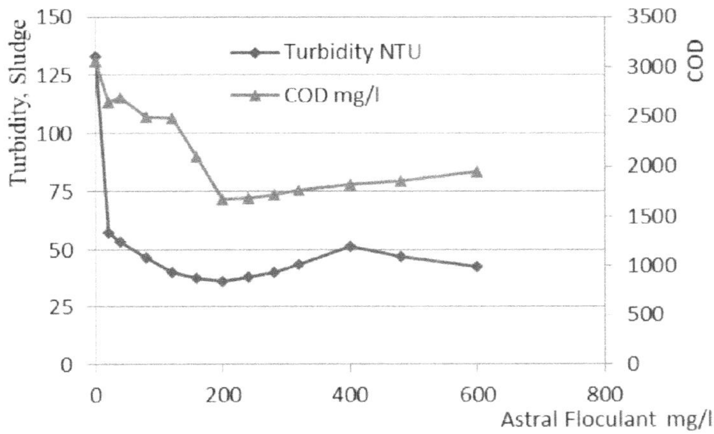

Figure 6.
Reduction of turbidity and COD by the Astral Flocculant alone.

The results show that the COD and turbidity parameters decrease with the increase in the concentration of Astral flocculant. The optimum concentration of the flocculant varies around 200 mg/l. From this value optimal, the concentration of COD and turbidity increases with the increase in the concentration of flocculant. The COD goes from 3300 mg/l to 1600 mg/l and the turbidity goes from 140 to 40 NTU with a removal efficiency of 53% and 71% respectively for the COD and the turbidity.

Indeed, the mode of action of polymers is however very different and depends mainly on their electrical charge properties and the concentration of flocculant. The stabilized leachate may contain too much organic matter (biodegradable, but also refractory to biodegradation) consisting mainly of humic substances [31, 32] as well as ammoniacal nitrogen, heavy metals, organochlorines and inorganic salts [33].

The pH is an essential parameter to be taken into account for the physicochemical treatment of liquid discharges by coagulation flculation. Indeed, we have studied the effect of pH on coagulation flocculation by the flocculant Astral. The results are shown in **Figure 7**. The effect of pH on the elimination of pollution from leachate discharges by coagulation flocculation has shown that there is no variation in turbidity and COD in the field. With a pH of between 2.5 and 12. The quantity of sludge formed during treatment remains lower. In addition, the results showed that the turbidity of raw leachate increases from 115 NTU to 40 NTU starting from acidic pH 2.5 while the COD goes from 3300 mg/l to 1550 mg/l with a yield of 65% and 53% respectively for turbidity and COD.

The study of coagulation flocculation by $FeCl_3$ (2500 mg/l) in the presence of variable concentrations of Astral flocculant is illustrated in **Figure 8** while monitoring the performance by measuring the parameters of COD, Turbidity and sludge production. These results showed that the increase in the concentration of Astral Flocculant made it possible to considerably reduce the COD and turbidity parameters while increasing the production of sludge. The turbidity value stabilizes around 15 NTU while it appears that the COD is around 1150 mg/l for a flocculant concentration of 600 mg/l with a yield of 62% and 89% respectively for the COD and the turbidity. The volume of sludge produced is around 800 ml/l with complete elimination of the coloring. at pH 6,5.

Furthermore, the study of the reduction in the pollution of leachate discharges by $FeCl_3$ in the presence of a constant concentration of Astral flocculant (200 mg/l) is given in **Figure 9**. The results have shown that the increase in

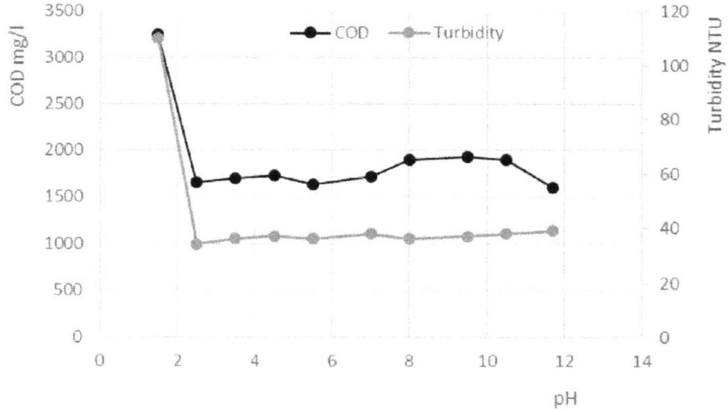

Figure 7.
Effect of pH on the reduction of turbidity and COD by the Astral Flocculant alone (200 mg/l).

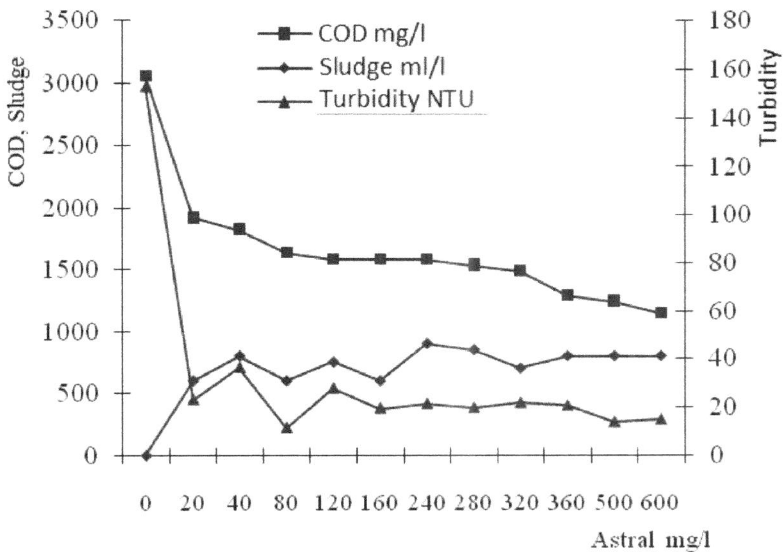

Figure 8.
Study of the mixture: $FeCl_3$ (2500 mg/l $FeCl_3$) + Astral flocculant variable flocculant COD = 3056 mg/l, pH = 6.5.

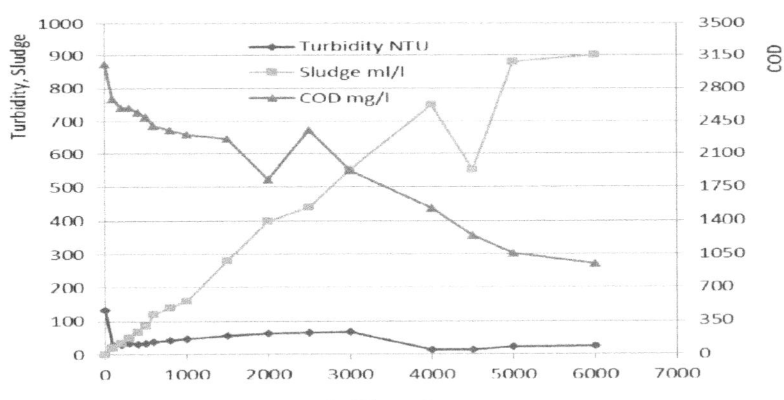

Figure 9.
Study of the mixture: $FeCl_3$ + ASTRAL flocculant (200 mg/l) variable $FeCl_3$. COD = 3100 mg/l, pH = 6.5.

addition of $FeCl_3$ increases the removal of COD and turbidity while increasing the production of sludge that requires treatment. It appears that the optimum concentration varies around 5000 mg/l of $FeCl_3$ for a pH of 6.5. Indeed, in our study, the elimination of leachate pollutants was improved by the addition of cationic polyelectrolytes (Astral and Lesieur Flocculant). It should be noted that at this stage hydrolysis, precipitation and adsorption reactions of leachate pollutants are greatly affected by the presence of humic and fulvic substances. Indeed, specific interactions can appear between humic substances, the surface of flocculates and dissolved ferric species, influencing the efficiency of the coagulation-flocculation process. The effect of a coagulant and flocculant mixture addition on the removal of COD and partially stabilized leachate turbidity could improve leachate remediation efficiency.

4.2 Effect of the mixture: Flocculant Lesieur + $FeCl_3$

To get an idea of the effectiveness of the leachate treatment by another flocculant used by the company Lesieur in Casablanca for the depollution of wastewater by SBR (sequential batch reactor), we carried out coagulantion flocculation tests by the flocculant alone or mixed with $FeCl_3$. The effect of the Lesieur flocculant on the removal of turbidity and COD is illustrated in **Figure 10**. The results showed that the COD and turbidity parameters decrease with increasing concentration of Lesieur flocculant. The optimum concentration of the flocculant varies around 200 mg/l (**Figure 10**). From this value the COD concentration increases with the increase in the flocculant concentration. The results showed that the COD goes from 3300 to 1300 mg/l and the turbidity goes from 140 to 35 NTU (optimal value) with a removal efficiency of 39% and 75% respectively for the COD and the turbidity.

To compare the effect of pH on Astral flocculant versus Lesieur flocculant, we studied the effect of pH on coagulation flocculation by Lesieur flocculant. The results are shown in **Figure 11.** The effect of pH on the elimination of pollution from leachate discharges by coagulation flocculation has shown that the optimum

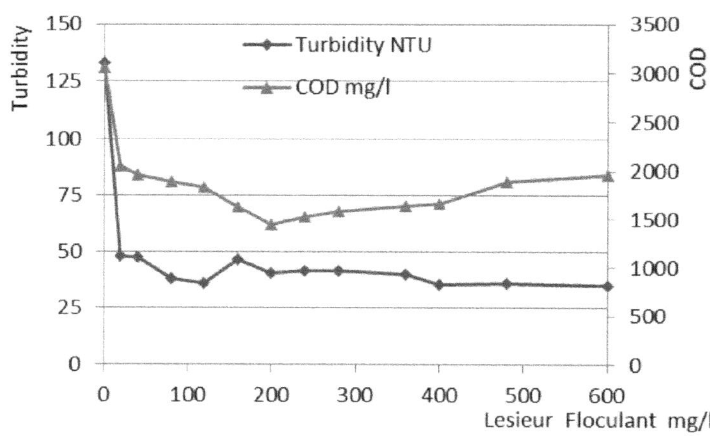

Figure 10.
Reduction of turbidity and COD by Lesieur Flocculant alone COD = 3300 mg/l, Turb = 130 NTU.

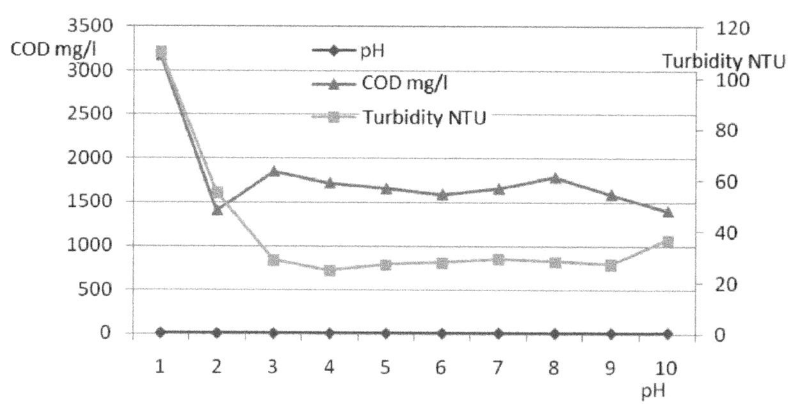

Figure 11.
Effect of pH on the reduction of turbidity and COD by Lesieur Flocculant (200 mg/l) COD = 3300 mg/l, Turb = 115 NTU.

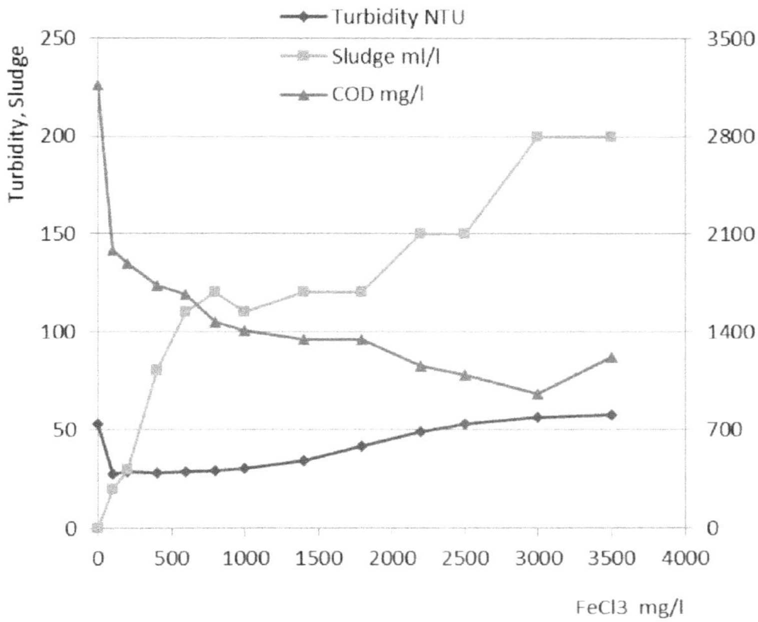

Figure 12.
Study of the mixture: $FeCl_3$ + Flocculant Lesieur (200 mg/l flocculant) variable $FeCl_3$. COD = 3200 mg/l, Turb = 130 NTU to be reviewed.

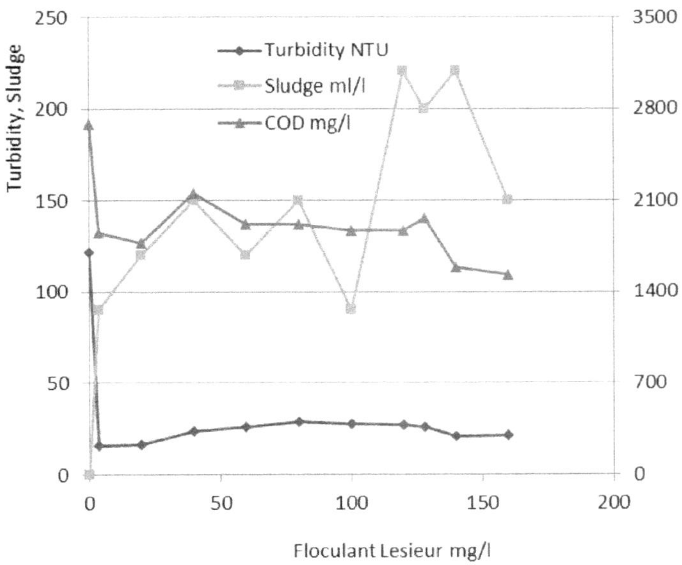

Figure 13.
Study of the mixture: $FeCl_3$ (2500 mg/l) + Lesieur Flocculant. Turb = 125 NTU.

pH varies around 6. In addition, the turbidity of raw leachate increases from 115 NTU to 30 NTU while the COD drops from 3300 mg/l to 1550 mg/l for the optimal concentration of 200 mg/l of the flocculant with a yield of 74% and 54% respectively for turbidity and COD.

$FeCl_3$ as a coagulant alone or as a mixture with other flocculants remains the most appreciated for better elimination of pollution from leachate discharges [34] in the form of COD and turbidity. We therefore studied the effect of $FeCl_3$ (200 mg/l of the flocculant, pH = 6) on the Lesieur flocculant.

Figure 12 shows that the mixture ($FeCl_3$ + Flocculant Lesieur) made it possible to reduce pollution, with a reduction in COD from 3200 mg/l (crude) to 800 mg/l for an optimal concentration of 200 mg/l of flocculant of Lesieur and 3000 mg/l of $FeCl_3$ while the turbidity has a minimum value for a concentration of 100 mg/l of FeC13. The volume of the settled sludge increases to reach a maximum of 200 ml/l for the concentration of 3000 mg/l of $FeCl_3$ as the optimum value (**Figure 12**).

To get an idea of the efficiency of the leachate treatment with the cationic flocculant used at the Lesieur company wastewater treatment plant in Casablanca, we studied the flocculation coagulation of leachate discharges by fixing the $FeCl_3$ concentration while at the same time varying that of the lesieur cationic flocculant. The results are illustrated in **Figure 13**. These results showed that the mixture made it possible to reduce the pollution, with a decrease in the COD from 3200 mg/l (crude) to 1500 mg/l (200 mg/l of Lesieur flocculant). The volume of the settled sludge increases to reach a maximum of 220 ml/l. Certainly, it can be concluded that the optimal dose of the cationic flocculant in the mixture ($FeCl_3$ + Lesieur flocculant) ($FeCl_3$ 2500 mg/pH 6) is 20 mg/l for the lesieur flocculant.

4.3 Effect of the mixture: Alginate + $FeCl_3$

4.3.1 Alginate alone

The study of the elimination of the pollution of leachate by coagulation flocculation by the alginate alone is given in **Figure 14**. The results obtained showed that the optimal dose of alginate for the elimination of COD and the turbidity are respectively 60 and 75% with an optimal dose of 120 mg/l of alginate, while producing a small quantity of sludge (20 ml/l).

The effect of pH on alginate flocculation coagulation (**Figure 15**), showed that the latter has little effect on the removal of COD and turbidity. For a pH between

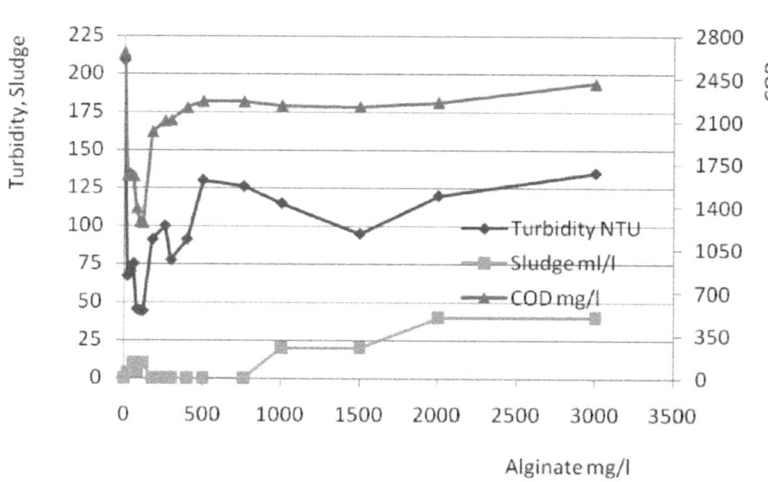

Figure 14.
Effect of alginate alone on COD removal and turbidity Turb = 125 NTU.

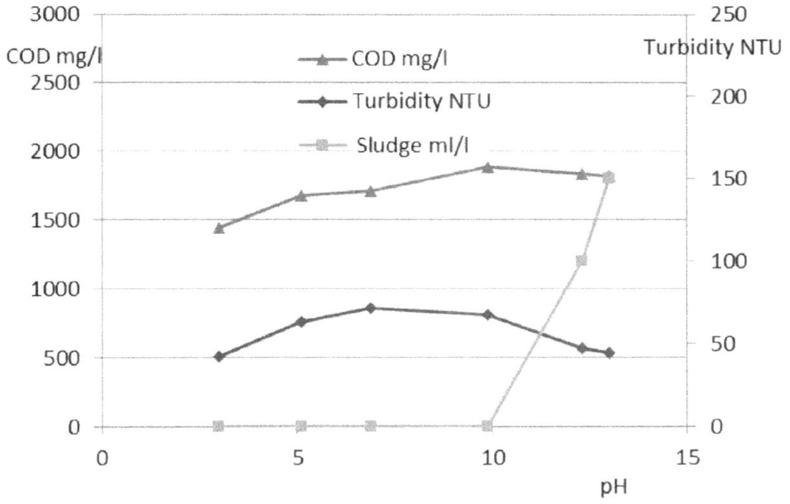

Figure 15.
Effect of pH on the reduction of turbidity and COD by alginate (120 mg/l).

1 and 10, no sludge production was observed for Alginate concentrations below 800 mg/l, while the volume of sludge increases from pH 10.

Furthermore, the study of the elimination of pollution from leachate discharges by the mixture of $FeCl_3$ and alginate is given in **Figure 16** (fixed alginate: 120 mg/l and variable $FeCl_3$).

The results obtained showed that the mixture of $FeCl_3$ and Alginate has an optimal concentration of around 120 mg/l of Alginate and a variable concentration of $FeCl_3$ increases the COD from 2900 to 1100 mg/l with a yield 60% COD 65% turbidity. The COD value decreases with the increase in the $FeCl_3$ concentration. As for the variation in turbidity, this remains negligible (30 NTU) from a concentration of 120 mg/l of alginate. The amount of sludge formed increases with an increase in alginate. The optimal concentrations for the removal of COD and turbidity by Alginate vary around 20 mg/l with a $FeCl_3$ concentration of 2500 mg/l at pH 6.5.

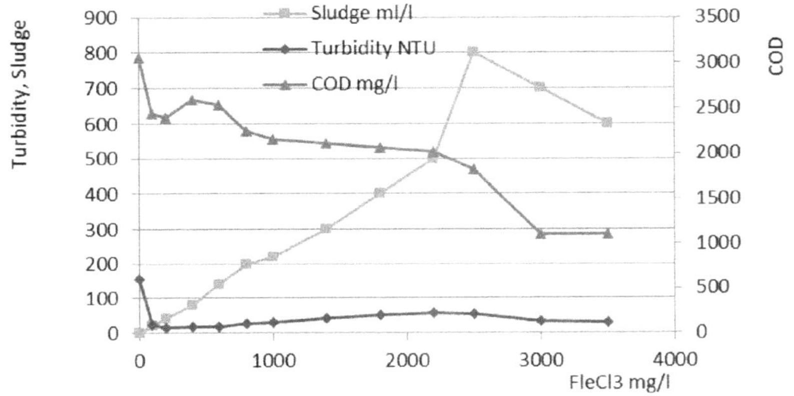

Figure 16.
Study of the mixture: Alginate (120 mg/l) + variable $FeCl_3$.

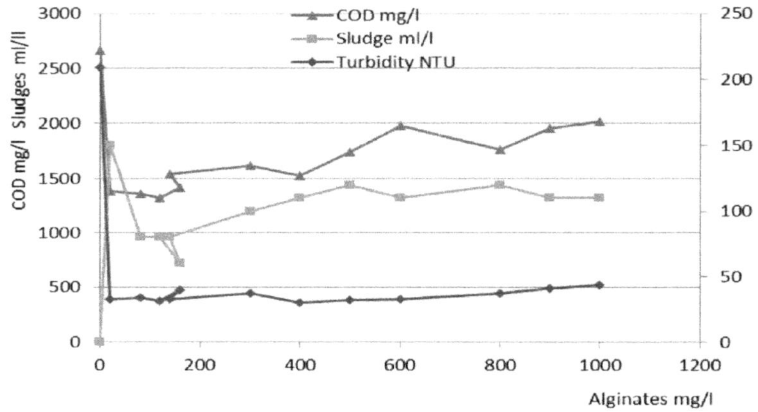

Figure 17.
Study of the mixture $FeCl_3$ (2500 mg/l) + alginate.

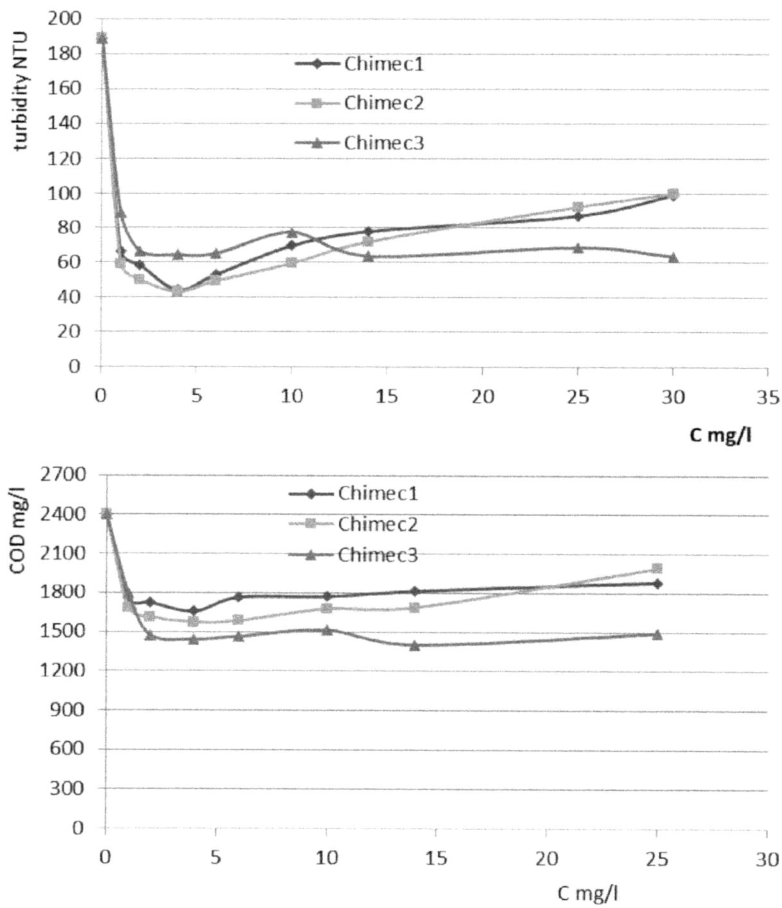

Figure 18.
Variation of turbidity (a) and COD (b) during coagulation flocculation by flocculants supplied by an Italian company.

Furthermore, **Figure 17** illustrates the effect of Alginate on flocculation coagulation while keeping a fixed concentration of $FeCl_3$ (2500 mg/l).

The results showed that the Alginate and $FeCl_3$ mixture has an optimal concentration of around 2500 mg/l, which resulted in very high COD removal with a 50% removal efficiency. The COD value increases with that of the Alginate The turbidity which varies around 30 NTU and remains constant from 50 mg/l of Alginate, while the volume of sludge produced increases with the increase of the Alginate stabilizes around 125 ml/l. The optimum concentration of Alginate is 120 mg/l. COD and turbidity values for optimum $FeCl_3$ and Alginate values show values of 1360 mg/l and 30 NTU, respectively.

4.4 Effect of flocculants chemec 1, 2 and 3 supplied by an Italian company

We carried out a comparative study on the elimination of pollution from leachate using three flocculant (Chimec 1, 2 and 3) supplied by an Italian company. The results (**Figure 18a**) showed that the turbidity decreases from 190 to 40 NTU for Chimec 1,2, for an optimal concentration of 4 mg/l then increases to 100 NTU for 30 mg/l of Chimec1 and 2. As regards the flocculant Chemic 3, the results showed a final elimination of the turbidity which is around 60 NTU for the same optimal concentration (4 mg/l) while the turbidity remains stable for Chimec 3 for a concentration of 10 mg/l.

As for the COD content (**Figure 18b**) during the treatment with the three flocculants, the results showed a decrease up to 1500 mg/l for 4 mg/l of flocculant, with an elimination efficiency of 40%, then increased for Chimec 1 and 2 arriving at around 2000 mg/l for 30 mg/l of flocculant. The COD remains almost stable for Chimec3 from 4 mg/l. In fact, no significant difference was observed as regards the elimination of COD by the three flocculants while producing a small amount of sludge in the case of the three flocculants.

5. Comparative study of the elimination of leachate pollution by different coagulants and flocculants

The comparative study on the elimination of turbidity and COD by different coagulants and flocculants is shown in **Figure 19**.

These results show that $FeCl_3$ gives a significant removal of COD and Turbidity with a high yield compared to other coagulants and flocculants. Aluminum sulphate allows elimination comparable to that obtained with $FeCl_3$. With regard to the flocculants, the results showed that the Astral flocculant alone allowed a very interesting elimination of 53% and 75% respectively for the COD and the turbidity. No significant difference was observed for the removal efficiency of COD and turbidity by the flocculants Chimec supplied by the Italian company.

The effect of optimal concentrations of coagulant FeC13 and flocculants (Astral, Supefloc, Alginate) alone or mixed on the production of sludge produced during the coagulation/flocculation process Coagulant type and dose volume of sludge is given in **Table 5**.

The addition of organic flocculants has been examined to improve the removal of organic matter.

$FeCl_3$ + Superfloc showed a removal efficiency of 30 and 66% respectively of COD and turbidity (**Figure 20**). These values are lower than the results obtained for the $FeCl_3$ + Astral or $FeCl_3$ + Alginate mixture.

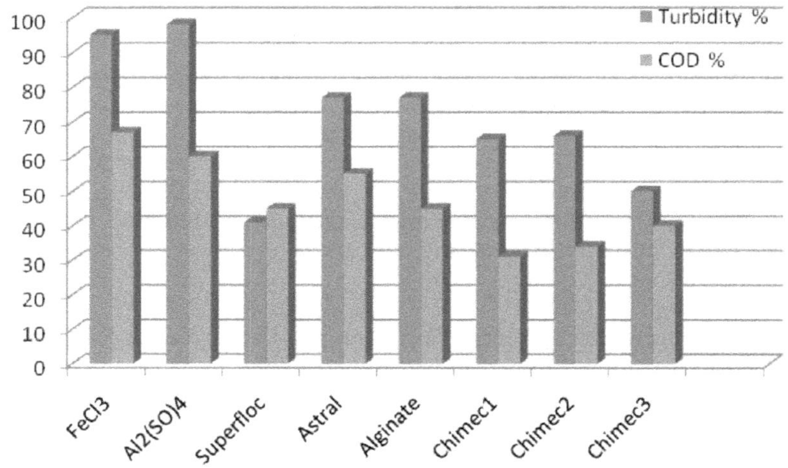

Figure 19.
Comparative study of the elimination of COD and turbidity by different coagulants and flocculants.

	Optimal concentrations alone mg/l	Optimal concentrations in mixture mg/l $FeCl_3$ + Flocculants	Sludge in mixture ml/l $FeCl_3$ + flocculants
$FeCl_3$	2500	—	—
Astral	192	500	800
Superfloc	200	140	230
Alginate	120	20	80

Table 5.
Effect of optimal concentrations of coagulant and flocculants alone or mixed on the production of sludge.

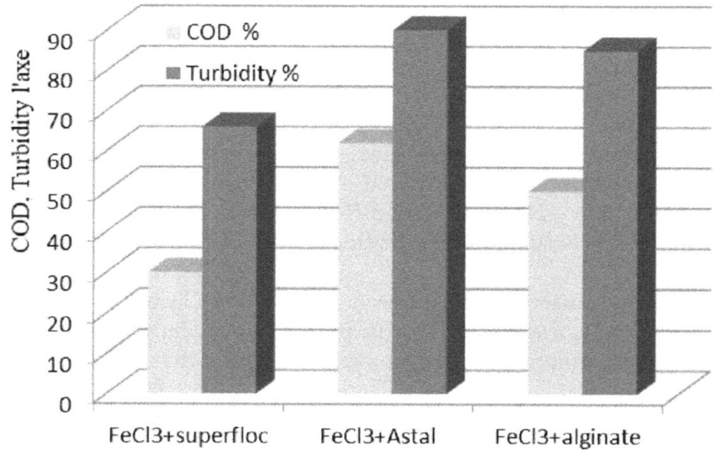

Figure 20.
Effect of $FeCl_3$ mixture, Superfloc flocculant, Astral flocculant using optimal doses on reduction of COD and turbidity.

The combined action of ferric chloride-polyelectrolyte mixtures was investigated. Addition of flocculant at a coagulant: flocculant ratio (Astral 2.5: 0.5, Superfloc 2.5: 0.14 Alginate 2.5: 0.02) (g), gave removal capacities of COD and variable turbidity (**Figure 6**).

Similar results were observed, during the addition of polyelectrolyte K1370 and A321 to stabilized leachate samples without pH correction [26]. Addition of polyelectrolyte superfloc did not substantially affect organic matter removal, which did not exceed 30%, as compared with the results $FeCl_3$ + Astral (62%), and $FeCl_3$ + Alginate (50%). However, the removal of pollutants was enhanced during the addition of polyelectrolytes in the samples. It should be mentioned at this point that hydrolysis, precipitation and adsorption reactions of ferric cation in leachate samples are greatly affected by the presence of humic substances. Specific interactions may appear between the humic substances, the surface of flocculates and the dissolved ferric species, influencing the efficiency of coagulation–flocculation process.

6. Removal of heavy metals

The removal of metallic elements by ferric chloride $FeCl_3$ is given in **Table 6**.

The concentration of heavy metals (Zn, Cu, Cd, Cr and Ni) in the leachate exceeds the maximum authorized values.

The flocculation coagulation made it possible to eliminate a yield varying between 80 and 99% (**Table 6**) for the various metallic elements studied (Cu, Zn, Cr, Cd, Ni, Pb and Sb). The results concerning the elimination of Chromium obtained during the present study are comparable with the results obtained for the treatment of leachate with FeCl3 [35] with a removal efficiency of 71% during the treatment with FeCl3 alone, whereas treatment with the latter in the presence of lime resulted in a yield of 90% of chromium [35, 36]. The same authors have shown that the aluminum sulphate allowed an elimination yield of 83% (**Table 7**).

Landfill leachate	Cu	Zn	Cr	Cd	Ni	Pb	Sb
Before Traetment	**1.20**	**2.30**	**4.20**	**0,02**	**0.35**	**0.30**	**0.90**
After treatment	0.10	0.01	0.21	—	0.12	0.01	0.03
Removal	91.70	99.6	95	—	80	97	97

Table 6.
Analysis of metals in stabilized leachate before and after coagulation flocculation-using $FeCl_3$ (concentration mg/l).

	As mg/l	Cd mg/l	Cr mg/l	Cu mg/l	Fe mg/l	Mn mg/l	Ni mg/l	Pb mg/l	Sb mg/l	Zn mg/l
Raw leachate	0.14	4.36	2.04	0 .4	33.72	2.58	3.74	0.18	0.63	4.68
$FeCl_3$	< 0.01	<0.01	0.6	0.03	232.4	—	0.33	0.07	0.44	0.53
$FeCl_3$+ lime	< 0.01	—	0.18	0.03	4.50	0.42	0.23	<0.01	—	0.14
$Al_2(SO_4)_3$	< 0.01	—	0.33	0.03	4.91	—	0.19	<0.01	—	0.32
$Al_2(SO_4)_3$ + lime	< 0.01	—	0.20	0.02	0.22	0.04	0.12	<0.01	—	0.15

Table 7.
Comparative study of the removal of metals by coagulation flocculation [35].

Lime has been used traditionally as a coagulant in the treatment of leachate for many years, requiring doses of around 1 to 15 g/l [35]. Amokrane et al. [37] have shown that the removal of heavy metals, such as Fe, Cd, Cr, reaches up to 90% efficiency during lime treatment. In fact, the removal of COD and heavy metals can be obtained at a pH of 10, which results in a yield of 28% and 86% respectively for COD and heavy metals, with the addition of 2,000 mg/l of ferric chloride [38–40]. In this study, the results indicate that iron (III) chloride [L5] coagulation-flocculation is very effective in reducing metallic elements; the reduction reaching 80 and 99.5% at optimal concentrations of 18.5 mmol/l Fe^{3+} achieved at a pH of 6.5. Similar results were obtained during the coagulation flocculation of leachate discharges from the city of Fez landfill by $FeCl_3$ [37].

Previously, the low removal of heavy metals in the leachate landfill was observed by Silva et al. [41] during the coagulation/flocculation process.

7. Effects of coagulation flocculation on sludge production

In general, the amount and characteristics of the sludge produced during the coagulation flocculation process are highly dependent on the specific coagulating and flocculating agent used and the operating conditions. The volume of wet sludge settled after the coagulation flocculation process is an interesting parameter to take into account when choosing the coagulant used for the treatment. The volume (ml/l) of the settled sludge can be is represented as a function of the dose of the coagulant.

The effect of the optimal concentrations of $FeCl_3$ coagulant and flocculants (Astral, Supefloc, Alginate) alone or in mixture in the production of sludge is given in **Table 6**.

The addition of organic flocculants has been investigated for improving the removal of organic material. The $FeCl_3$ + Superfloc mixture showed a removal efficiency of 30 and 66% respectively of COD and turbidity. These values are higher than those obtained in the case of the $FeCl_3$ + Astral or $FeCl_3$ + alginate mixture.

From **Table 8**, it is observed that the volume of sludge produced was considerably reduced with increasing dose of polyelectrolyte in the coagulation process. This may be due to the cationic nature of the polyelectrolyte used in this study. In fact, the high molecular weight of the polyelectrolyte allowed an improvement in the growth of the particles, which facilitates the settling. The cationic flocculant also has the ability to attract and retain colloidal particles at the polar sites of the molecule. In general, organic polymers generate less sludge than inorganic salts since it does not add weight or combine chemically with other ions in the water to form a precipitate. Thus, the sludge produced by the use of ferric chloride in combination with a polyelectrolyte is greatly reduced.

Reagents	Optimal concentrations mg/l	Optimal concentration in the $FeCl_3$ + flocculants mixture mg/l	Sludge in the mixture ml/l $FeCl_3$ + flocculants
$FeCl_3$	2500–2400	2500	—
Astral flocculant	192	500	800
Superfloc	200	140	230
Aliginate	120	20	80
Cactus ml/l	32	25	195

Table 8.
Effect of optimal concentrations of coagulants and flocculants alone or in mixture on sludge production.

The combination of Ferric Chloride, Alginate and Superfloc produces less sludge (ml/l) than when Ferric Chloride is used with Astral Flocculant.

8. Effect of the order of introduction of coagulants and flocculants

The effect of the order of introduction of the flocculant FeC13 and Astral on the removal of organic matter (COD), turbidity and sludge production are shown in (**Figure 21**).

Beyond the type of tests we performed in coagulation, we tested the influence of the method of adding the coagulant and flocculant on the properties of the leachate destabilized by coagulation/flocculation. In practice, in addition to the procedure described above where the reagents were added separately (coagulant + flocculant, flocculant + coagulant), we carried out a simultaneous addition of the coagulant and the flocculant. The protocol is then similar to that of coagulation on Jar test, but instead of the coagulant alone, the flocculant is added after the coagulant.

The results obtained show that when ferric chloride ($FeCl_3$) is introduced first, followed by the flocculant, the yield of COD and turbidity varies around 81% and 79% respectively. When $FeCl_3$ is introduced at the same time as the flocculant, the turbidity is considerably reduced (56%), while the COD is around 78% which does not show a significant difference between when $FeCl_3$ is introduced first, followed by by the flocculating agent. In addition, the results obtained when the flocculant is introduced before $FeCl_3$ showed a significant decrease in COD (59%) and turbidity (58%). However, the reduction in organic matter (COD) during the addition of coagulant-polyelectrolyte mixtures is greater than the results obtained by the addition of similar and single doses of $FeCl_3$. In addition to the removal of pollutants, sludge production was considered in this work, as it may affect the economic feasibility of the proposed treatment method. The sludge produced during the physico-chemical treatment of landfill leachate (**Table 9**) is composed by the amount of colloidal organic matter and suspended solids, as well as by the compounds formed due to the possible addition of chemical reagents.

The quantity of sludge produced by the introduction of $FeCl_3$ followed by the flocculant is 200 ml/l (compacted sludge) which remains low compared to the results obtained by introducing the Astral flocculant the first followed by $FeCl_3$

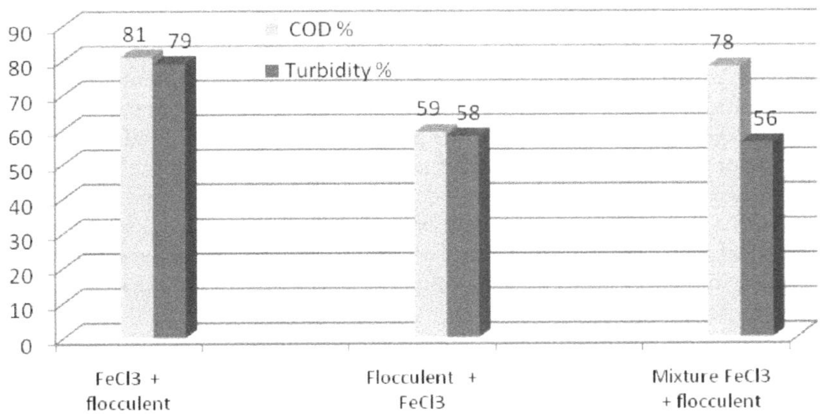

Figure 21.
Effect of the order of introduction of the dose dose of coagulant and flocculant $FeCl_3$ and Astral on the elimination of organic matter (COD) and turbidity.

Order of introduction	Sludges ml/l
$FeCl_3$ + Flocculant	200
9Flocculant + $FeCl_3$	300
Mixture ($FeCl_3$ + Flocculant)	750

Table 9.
Effects of the order of introduction of the dose of $FeCl_3$ and Astral flocculant on sludge production. Optimal concentrations: $FeCl_3$: 2500 mg/l, Flocculant: 500 mg/l and pH = 7.

(300 ml/l). In addition, the study of the coagulation of the mixture (flocculant + $FeCl_3$) showed a large quantity of uncompacted sludge (750 ml/l). In conclusion, the addition of $FeCl_3$ first, followed by the flocculant results in a small amount of compacted sludge volume.

9. Discussion

Knowing the composition of the waste (household waste + industrial waste) makes it possible to assess the risks of percolation through the soil (leaching). During the solubilization by rainwater, metal oxides and chemicals, often highly toxic contained in the waste, pass into the leachate water. Ecologically, the alarm bells have already been sounded, because in addition to the air pollution, the waters of the Oued Al Maleh which is close to the landfill (10 m) are heavily polluted due to the leachate produced by the old public dump of Mohammedia [1, 4].

To assess the impact of a landfill on the environment, it is necessary to characterize the effluents it generates. Indeed, whatever the mode of operation of a landfill, the leachate constitutes, if it is not treated before its discharge, a source of nuisance which is added to the numerous problems of contamination of the surrounding environment. These liquids loaded with mineral and organic substances resulting from the decomposition of waste can be carried away by runoff and reach surface water, or infiltrate through the substratum of the landfill and contaminate the water of the water table which is not deep (case of the city of Mohammedia). The results of **Tables 1** and **2** have shown that the leachate is characterized by high concentrations of organic matter, ammonium and nitrogen compounds..... The leachate from these separate stages contains different constituents and therefore different characteristics.

In the coagulation - flocculation process [4]. It is very important to adjust the pH since coagulation occurs within a specific pH range for each coagulant and flocculant and depending on the type and characteristic of the raw effluent to be treated.

Coagulation/flocculation is a commonly used process for wastewater treatment in which reagents such as ferric chloride and/or ferric polymer are added to landfill leachate in order to destabilize colloidal materials. This causes the agglomeration of the small particles into easily settling flocs. Several studies have reported the examination of this process for the treatment of landfill leachate, in particular in relation to the optimization of the performance of coagulant/flocculant, the determination of the experimental conditions, the evaluation of the pH, and the search for the addition of flocculant [4, 24].

To improve the coagulation/locculation process, the addition of some commercial polyelectrolytes has been investigated, including two cationics (Astral and Superfloc). The treatment of the leachate by coagulation flocculation using several coagulants has shown that the percentage of elimination of various pollution parameters such as COD, BOD5, turbidity and sludge formed during the treatment vary with the type of coagulant or flocculant chosen for study.

The optimal process variables for landfill leachate coagulation using Fe (III) and Al (III) were found at pH 6.5 for Fe (III) and 5.3 for Al (III) at coagulant doses of 18.5 mmol/l Fe (III) and 5.82 mmol/l Al (III). Although the doses required were identical (0.035 mol/l of Fe^{3+} or Al^{3+}), with an initial COD concentration of 4100 mg/l, $FeCl_3$ led to a higher elimination of organic compounds (55%) than 'aluminum (42%). Indeed, the results obtained during our study made it possible to show that $FeCl_3$ is more interesting in terms of reducing pollution, in particular the elimination of COD and turbidity with a yield of 95 and 67% respectively and the COD. In addition, the results showed that the pH considerably affects the coagulation and flocculation by the different coagulants and flocculants tested. The decrease in pH due to Fe + Al cations which present acidic characteristics; therefore, hydrolysis took place under acidic conditions caused by precipitation of metal hydroxides. Several studies have examined coagulation-flocculation for the treatment of landfill leachate, aimed at optimizing performance, namely selection of the most suitable coagulant, determination of experimental conditions, evaluation of the effect of pH, and the choice of flocculant [42]. In addition, during the precipitation process, coagulation, flocculation and adsorption appear to contribute to the removal of organic matter from the leachate [43, 44].

As for other coagulants and flocculants the results showed the yield of COD and turbidity varies from one reagent to another. The Astral and Lesieur flocculants in a mixture with FeCl3 were able to improve the reduction of leachate pollution. No significant difference was observed in the reduction of COD and turbidity by the flocculants supplied by the Italian company (Chimic 1, 2, 3) during flocculation coagulation. In addition, the order of introduction of $FeCl_3$ and Astral flocculant showed that the reduction of pollution (COD and Turbidity) is better when introducing FeCl3 first (elimination of 81% of COD and 79% of turbidity) while the introduction of the flocculant before the $FeCl_3$ resulted in a yield of 59%of the COD and 58% of the turbidity.

It was shown by Hamzeh et al. [45] that at an initial concentration of 5690 mg/L and at a pH of 4.8, a maximum COD removal of 56% was obtained with 0.8 g/l of $FeCl_3$, compared to 39% with 0.4 g/l of $Al_2(SO_4)_3$. In addition, Ez Zoubi et al. [46] showed during the treatment of leachate produced by the public landfill of the city of Fez with $FeCl_3$ that the COD content goes from 53199.6 mg/l to 41933 mg/l with a yield of 21% while Bakraouy et al. [25] showed that $FeCl_3$ could remove a yield of 65% of COD. This shows that the pollution removal efficiency varies with the coagulant used, the age and the quality of the leachate.

The treatment of leachate is a difficult and expensive process [25]. Although, the leachate can be treated biologically, the COD removal efficiency is generally low due to the high ammonium ion content and the presence of toxic compounds such as metal ions. The results suggest that $FeCl_3$ may be a viable coagulant in managing COD problems associated with landfill leachate. In addition, the treatment of the leachate by coagulation-flocculation has led to a reduction in the physicochemical (COD, BOD5, ...) and suitable microbiological parameters while the coagulation flocculation combined with a biological treatment of SBR type has allowed eliminate 99% of the COD from leachate produced by the public landfill in the city of Fez [47].

As regards the study of the elimination of metals by coagulation flocculation with $FeCl_3$, the results have shown that the efficiency of elimination of the metallic elements by the various coagulants and flocculants varies between 80 and 99.6. This proves that the flocs formed during coagulation flocculation allow most of the metal elements to be adsorbed in the leachate.

Khalill et al. [35] have shown that flocculation coagulation is a very effective technique for reducing metal pollution from leachate produced at the landfill in the city of Fez. However, the efficiency of removing the metallic elements varies from one coagulant to another and the combination of lime on the one hand with ferric chloride and on the other hand with Alumina Sulfate improves the efficiency of elimination of the elements Cr (90%), Fe (96%) and Mn (99%) [35].

It was shown by Hamzeh et al. [45] that at an initial concentration of 5690 mg/l and at a pH of 4.8, a maximum COD removal of 56% was obtained with 0.8 g/l of $FeCl_3$, compared to 39% with 0.4 g/l of $Al_2(SO_4)_3$. In addition, Ez Zoubi et al. [46] showed during the treatment of leachate produced by the public landfill of the city of Fez with $FeCl_3$ that the COD content goes from 53199.6 mg/l to 41933 mg/l with a yield of 21% while Bakraouy et al. [25] showed that $FeCl_3$ could remove a yield of 65% of COD. This shows that the pollution removal efficiency varies with the coagulant used, the age and the quality of the leachate.

Although, the leachate can be treated biologically, the COD removal efficiency is generally low due to the high ammonium ion content and the presence of toxic compounds such as metal ions. The results suggest that $FeCl_3$ may be a viable coagulant in managing COD problems associated with landfill leachate. In addition, the treatment of the leachate by coagulation-flocculation has led to a reduction in the physicochemical (COD, BOD5, ...) and suitable microbiological parameters while the coagulation flocculation combined with a biological treatment of SBR type has allowed eliminate 99% of the COD from leachate produced by the public landfill in the city of Fez [47].

However, it should be noted that the precipitation and adsorption of ions in leachate samples is strongly affected by the amount of humic compounds present, which impairs the efficiency of coagulation.

Tatsi et al. [26] in a study of coagulation flocculation for the removal of COD, showed that the addition of Aluminum to fresh leachate resulted in a 25–38% reduction in COD using a dose of 3 g/l d 'Aluminum. Amokrane et al. [37] have shown that ferric chloride is more effective than Aluminum Sulphate with a yield of 94 and 87%, respectively, in removing turbidity from landfill leachate. The removal rates of COD and color are 41% and 70% respectively by adding 2.5 g/l of ferric chloride as Fe^{3+} [45].

The addition of Superfloc polyelectrolytes did not significantly affect the elimination of organic matter, which does not exceed 30%, compared with the results obtained with the mixture $FeCl_3$ + Astral (62%), and $FeCl_3$ + alginate (50%) Similar results were observed during the addition of polyelectrolytes K1370 and A321 for the treatment of stabilized leachate without pH correction [25]. However, the removal of pollutants was improved by the addition of polyelectrolytes to the samples. It should be noted that at this stage the hydrolysis, ferric cation precipitation and adsorption reactions in the leachate are greatly affected by the presence of humic and fulvic substances. Indeed, specific interactions can appear between humic substances, the surface of flocculants and dissolved ferric species, influencing the efficiency of the coagulation-flocculation process. The effect of addition of coagulant and flocculant mixture on COD removal and partially stabilized leachate turbidity could improve leachate remediation performance.

10. Conclusion

The establishment of landfills in sites that are not suitable or not specifically designed for this purpose increases the risk of contamination of surface and groundwater, and consequently human health, knowing that water is the source of life. Following a bio-physico-chemical evolution of this piled up waste and the action of the rains, a juice called leachate is generated. This juice constitutes a source of pollution for the environment.

In this study, the treatment of leachate from the public landfill in the city of Mohammedia by a flocculation coagulation process was evaluated. Landfill leachate was characterized by a low pH value and a high concentration of pollutants. Organic matter varies between 2153 and 2707 mg/l of COD, and from 1080 to 1405 mg/l of total nitrogen. As for turbidity, however, the elimination of turbidity remains dependent on the efficiency of the coagulation, ie the coagulant used for the study.

In addition, the results obtained showed that ferric chloride is more effective than aluminum sulphate in removing COD, especially when the pH is above 9. Hydrated iron hydroxides precipitate more easily than flocs formed. by aluminum, which results in a more efficient removal of pollutants than that obtained at lower pH values. The optimal doses of the various coagulants and flocculants chosen for the study vary from one reagent to another. However, the reduction in pollution by the flocculants alone does not show an efficiency of elimination whereas the coagulant and flocculant mixture allows a good elimination of the pollution. $FeCl_3$ remains the most suitable coagulant to further eliminate organic and metal pollution. In addition, flocculation coagulation has significantly reduced metal pollution.

It can be concluded that the physicochemical treatment by coagulation flocculation proposed for the treatment of leachate is effective. The technique has several advantages:

- low cost,
- good pollution elimination efficiency, ease of implementation.

It can be concluded that $FeCl_3$ could have a considerable impact on reducing pollution compared to other results obtained with other coagulants and flocculants.

Author details

Mlika Kastali, Latifa Mouhir, Abdelaziz Madinzi, Abdeslam Taleb, Abdelkader Anouzla* and Salah Souabi
Department of Process Engineering and Environment, Faculty of Science and Technology Mohammedia, Hassan II University of Casablanca, Morocco

*Address all correspondence to: aanouzla@gmail.com

References

[1] Souabi S, Tawzar K, Chtioui H, Khalil E. Problématiques du chrome et du plomb dans lesdécharges publiques: cas de la ville de Mohammedia et de Fès Déchets Sciences et Techniques,Revue Francophone d'écologie industrielle. 2010; 58(2) : 37-43.

[2] Magda M, Abd Salam Gaber I, Abu-Zuid. Impact of landfill leachate on the groundwater quality: A case study in EgyptEl Journal of advanced research. 2015; 6: 579-586. https://doi.org/10.1016/j.jare.2014.02.003

[3] Bakraouy H, Souabi S, Digua K, Bahlaoui M, Dkhissi W, Jada A, Oubrayeme H, Dkhissi O, Chatoui M; Assessment of the Effectiveness of Ouled Berjal Landfill Leachate Treatment by Sequential Batch Reactor Technique: Elimination of Nitrogen Pollution, Phenolic Compounds and Phytotoxicity .2018. Chapter ID: 57856 Book 73-94, ID : 15201 Book Title: Sequencing Batch Reactors: An Overview

[4] Kastali M, Mouhir L, Assou M, Anouzla A, Abrouki Y. Diagnosis of leachate from a closed landfill, impact on the soil, and treatment by coagulation flocculation with alginate and ferric chloride Desalination and Water Treatment, Desalination and Water Treatment. 2020; 206: 307-314. DOI: 10.5004/dwt.2020.26303.

[5] Javier R, Fernando B, Fatima C, Benito A, Olga G. Stabilized leachates: sequential coagulation flocculation + chemical oxidation process. J Hazard Materials. 2008;150: 468-493. DOI: 10.1016/j.jhazmat.2004.07.022.

[6] Abbas AA, Jingsong G, Ping LZ, Ya PY, Al-Rekabi WS. Review on landfill leachate treatments. Journal of Applied Sciences Research, 2009; 5(5): 534-545.

[7] Renou S, Givaudan JG, Paulain S, Dirassouyan F, Moulin P. Landfill leachate treatment: review and opportunity. J Hazard Mater. 2008; 150: 468-493. https://doi.org/10.1016/j.jhazmat.2007.09.077.

[8] Shuokr Q.A, Hamidi A, Mohammed J.K. Bashir , Mojiri A. Landfill Leachate Treatment Techniques: An Overview Wastewater Engineering: Types, Characteristics and Treatment Technologies. 2014; 9(2): 1-18. DOI: 10.12983/1-2014-03-01.

[9] Anouzla A, Souabi S, Safi M, Rhbal H, Abrouki Y, Majouli A. Valorisation d'un rejet industriel riche en chlorure ferrique : application aux traitements des eaux résiduaires. Chimie şi Inginerie Chimică, Biotehnologii, Industrie Alimentară. 2010 ; 11 (2): 255 – 264. ID:CSCC6201011V02S01A0002.

[10] Nour A, Hamidi A, Mohd S. The use of Polyaluminum Chloride for the treatment of Landfill Leachate via Coagulation and Flocculation processes. Res J Chem Sci. 2011;1(3). 34-39.

[11] Abouri.M, Elmaguiri.A , Souabi.S, Aboulhassan.M.A. Valorisation of a wastewater in the treatment of leachate from municipal solid waste in Morocco. Int. J. Environment and Waste Management. 2019; 23(1): 27-39. DOI: 10.1504/IJEWM.2019.10016796.

[12] Bakraouy H, Souabi S, Digua K, Dkhissi O, Sabar M, Fadil M. Optimization of the treatment of an anaerobic pretreated landfill leachate by a coagulation-flocculation process using experimental design methodology H, Process Safety and Environmental Protection .2017; 1 0 9: 621-630. https://doi.org/10.1016/j.psep.2017.04.017.

[13] Aguilar MI, Saez J, Llorens M. Improvement of coagulation–flocculation process using anionic polyacrylamide as coagulant aid. Chemosphere. 2005; 58: 47-56. DOI: 10.1016/j.chemosphere.2004.09.008

[14] Tuba Y, Selami A, Ali B. Coagulation-Flocculation and Air Stripping as a Pretreatment of Young Landfill Leachate. The Open Environ Eng J. 2010; 3: 42-48.

[15] Dhouib A, Hamad N, Hassaïri I, Sayadi S. Degradation of anionic surfactants by Citrobacter braakii. Proc Biochem. 2003; 38: 1245-1250. https://doi.org/10.1016/S0032-9592(02)00322-9

[16] Mohd SMZ, Mahyun AW, Tamizi MS, Norsyazwani CM. Landfill Leachate treatment by a Coagulation flocculation process, International Conference on environment and Industrial Innovation IPCBEE, 2012; V12, Press Singpore.

[17] Bakraouy H, Souabi S, Digua K, Jada A. Effect of order of introduction of reagents on effectiveness of the treatment of landfill leachate by coagulation flocculation process 4th international congress on technology engineering and science August 5/6/2017 kuala lumpur Malaysia. 2017.

[18] Abouri.M, Taleb.A, Souabi.S, Pala.A. Removal of phenol and colour of leachate of municipal solid waste by physico-chemical treatment using a liquid waste as a coagulant, J. Mater. Environ. Sci. 2016;7:4290-4298.

[19] Kastali M, Mouhir L, Chatoui M, Souabi S, Anouzla A. Removal of Turbidity and Sludge Production from Industrial Process Wastewater Treatment by a Rejection of Steel Rich in FeCl3 (SIWW). Biointerface Research in Applied Chemistry. 2021; 11(5): 13359-13376. DOI: 10.33263/BRIAC115.1335913376.

[20] Javaheri H, Nasrabadi T, Jafarian MH, Rowshan GR, Khoshnam H. Site selection of municipal solid waste landfills using analytical hierarchy process method in a geographical information technology environment in Giroft. Iran J Environ Health Sci & Eng. 2006; 3(3): 177-184.

[21] AFNOR, Protocole d'evaluation d'une methode alternative d'analyse physico-chimique par rapport a une methode de reference [Protocol of evaluation of an alternative method of physico-chemical analysis relative to a method of reference], Norme NF XPT [Standard NF XPT], 1999;Vol. 58: 90-210.

[22] Macheix J.J., A. Fleuriet & J. Billot, Fruit phenolics. Boca Raton, 1990 :378p.

[23] Navarro A, Veron J. Treatment strategies, International Environment Day, Poitiers. 1992.

[24] Rassam A, Boukhriss B, Chaouch A, El Watik L, Chaouki H, Ghannami M. Caractérisation de lixiviats des décharges contrôlées au Maroc et solutions de traitement: Cas de lixiviats de la ville d'Al Hoceima, Sci Lib Environ. 2012; 4: 1-9.

[25] Bakraouy H, Souabi S, Digua K. and Levent Y. Treatment of leachate from the Ouled Berjal Landfill in Morocco by coagulation flocculation Flocculation : Process and applications, NOVA EditorEleonora Vollan.2019: 217- 245.

[26] Tatsi AA, Zouboulis AI, Matis KA, Samaras P. Coagulation–flocculation pretreatment of sanitary landfill leachates. Chemosphere. 2003; 53: 737-744. https://doi.org/10.1016/S0045-6535(03)00513-7.

[27] Rivas FJ, Gimento O. Stabilized leachates: sequential coagulation–flocculation + chemical oxidation process. J Hazard Mater. 2004; B116: 95-102. DOI: 10.1016/j.jhazmat.2004.07.022

[28] Laaouan M, Souabi S, Aboulhassan M. A, Tahiri M. Impact of stabilized leachate residues from the uncontrolled landfill of Mohammedia

city on the "Oued El Maleh" river and on the soil, J. Mater. Environ. Sci. 2017; 9(12) : 4487-4495. DOI: 10.26872/jmes.2017.8.12.474

[29] Duan, J., Gregory, J. Coagulation by hydrolysing metal salts, Advances in Colloid and Interface Science. 2003; 100: 475-502. https://doi.org/10.1016/S0001-8686(02)00067-2.

[30] Anouzla A, Souabi S, Safi S, Rhbal H, Abrouki Y, Majouli A. Valorization of an Industrial Waste rich in Ferric Chlorid: Application in the Treatment of Industrial Wastewater. Chemistry & Chemical Engineering, Biotechnology, Food Industry. 2010;11(2): 255-264. DOI: CSCC6201011V02S01A0002.

[31] Kang KH, Shin HS, Park H. Characterization of humic substances present in landfill leachates with different landfill ages and its implicationsWater Res.2002; 36(16): 4023-4032. https://doi.org/10.1016/S0043-1354(02)00114-8

[32] Wang ZP, Zhang Z, Lin YJ, Deng NS, Tao T, Zhuo K. Landfill leachate treatment by a coagulation–photooxidation process, J Hazard Mater. 2002; 95(1/2): 153-159. DOI: 10.1016/s0304-3894(02)00116-4

[33] Chemlal R., Azzouz L., Kernani R., Abdi N., Lounici H., Grib H., Mameri N., Drouiche N., Ecological Engineering.2014; 73: 281-289.

[34] Assou M., El Fels L., El Asli A., Fakidi H., Souabi S. Hafidi M. Landfill leachate treatment by a coagulation-flocculation process: effect of the introduction order of the reagents, Desal. Water Treat. 2016;57: 21817-21826. https://doi.org/10.1080/19443994.2015.1127779

[35] Khalil F,.Bouaouine H, Chtioui M, Souabi S, Aboulhassan M.A, Ouammou A. Treatment of Landfill Leachate by coagulation-flocculation. J. Mater. Environ. Sci. 6 (5) (2015) 1337-1342.

[36] Anouzla A, Souabi S. Treatment of industrial discharges loaded with dyes and surfactant. Scholars' Press.2020.

[37] Amokrane A, Comel C, Veron J. Landfill leachates pretreatment by coagulation-flocculation. Water Res. 1997; 31: 2775-2782. https://doi.org/10.1016/S0043-1354(97)00147-4.

[38] Afshin M, Mohammad A Z, Hassan I, Reza R. Composting Plant Leachate Treatment by Coagulation-Flocculation Process. Am Eurasian J Agric Environ Sci. 2009; 5 (5): 638-643.

[39] Anouzla A, SouabiS., Safi M, Abrouki Y, Loukili H, Rhbal H. Waste to Treat Waste of Landfill Leachates, Int. J. Environ. Prot. Policy. 2014; 2 : 50-53. doi: 10.11648/j.ijepp.20140202.12

[40] Anouzla Abdelkader. Valorisation des rejets liquides du secteur sidérurgique Application au traitement des eaux usées. Editions universitaires europeennes, 2019.

[41] Silva AC, Dezotti M, Sant'Anna GL. Treatment and detoxification of a sanitary landfill leachate. Chemosphere. 2004; 55: 207-214. https://doi.org/10.1016/j.chemosphere.2003.10.013

[42] Sletten RS, Benjamin MM, Horng JJ, Ferguson JF. Physical–chemical treatment of landfill leachate for metals removal. Water Res. 1995; 29(10): 2376-2386. https://doi.org/10.1016/0043-1354(95)00030-O

[43] Yimin S, Tichang S, Jiaqing C,. Cunzhen L. Flocculation Process Optimization of a Novel Coagulant for Landfill Leachate Pretreatment Bioinformatics and Biomedical Engineering, ICBBE. The 2nd International Conference Coll. of Civil & Environ. Eng., Univ. of Sci. Technol. Beijing, Beijing. 2008.

[44] Tatsi AA, Zouboulis AI. A field investigation of the quantity and quality of leachate from a municipal solid waste landfill in a Mediterranean climate (Thessaloniki, Greece), Advs in Environ Res. 2002; 6: 207-219. https://doi.org/10.1016/S1093-0191(01)00052-1.

[45] Hamzeh AJ, Amir HM, Ramin N, Foorogh V, Ghasem AO. Combination of Coagulation-Flocculation and Ozonation Processes for Treatment of Partially Stabilized Landfill Leachate of Tehran. World Appl Sci. 2009 ; 5: 9-15.

[46] Ez Zoubi Y, Merzouki M, Bennani L, El Ouali Lalami A, Benlemlih M. Procédé pour la réduction de la charge polluante du lixiviat de la décharge contrôlée de la ville de Fès, déchets, sciences et techniques - revue francophone d'écologie industrielle - n° 58 - 2eme trimestre 2010). 10.4267/dechets-sciences-techniques.3008.

[47] Merzouki M, Fadel H, Benlemlih M. traitement des effluents urbains et industriels : originalité et performance Revue Agrobiologia 2014; N°6, 36-41.

Chapter 5

Plastic Pollution in the Mediterranean and Public-Private Partnerships to Manage It - A Case Study in Lebanon

Michel Soto Chalhoub

Abstract

Hazards of plastic pollution in the oceans threaten human, animal, and vegetation life. Sources of plastic pollutants include marine transport activity, shore-to-shore movement by waves and currents, and waste transported from land to sea by rivers. Industries in several countries in the Mediterranean region, which generate waste dispose it in rivers or into municipal networks. The justify their activities as drivers of local economies, while a closer look shows the opposite. A case study is presented about Lebanon, a country on the Mediterranean easternmost boundary serving as a maritime transit gate to the rest of the Middle East. Private sector companies could play a major role in curbing plastic pollution through innovation to migrate toward green products and substitutes to plastics. Both remedial and preventive strategies in the private sector would be better realized through support from public sector entities. Therefore, public-private partnerships are recommended to alleviate current pressures exerted on local communities willing to fight plastic pollution and help them operate within known and supported norms. As such, we recommend incentive-based public policies.

Keywords: plastic pollution, ocean life, river load, public-private partnership, incentive-based policies

1. Introduction

Plastic litter transport in the oceans is a complex phenomenon. In particular, the accumulation of floating debris is a serious problem in the Mediterranean whose hydrodynamics comprise an inflow of surface water from the Atlantic. Several researchers argue that plastic litter is owed in large quantities to traveling vessels [1, 2]. It was argued that about 90% of consumer goods worldwide are moved through an international fleet of cargo ships and most of these goods are contained or wrapped in plastic. Hundreds of containers tip over in rough seas every year and eventually sink and break open, releasing their contents in the ocean. There are several cases of tipped containers that were abandoned on the seafloor. Off the coast of Monterrey Bay, California, over twenty-four containers were lost in a February 2004 storm, one of which is still resting on the seafloor at a depth of about 1500 meters [3].

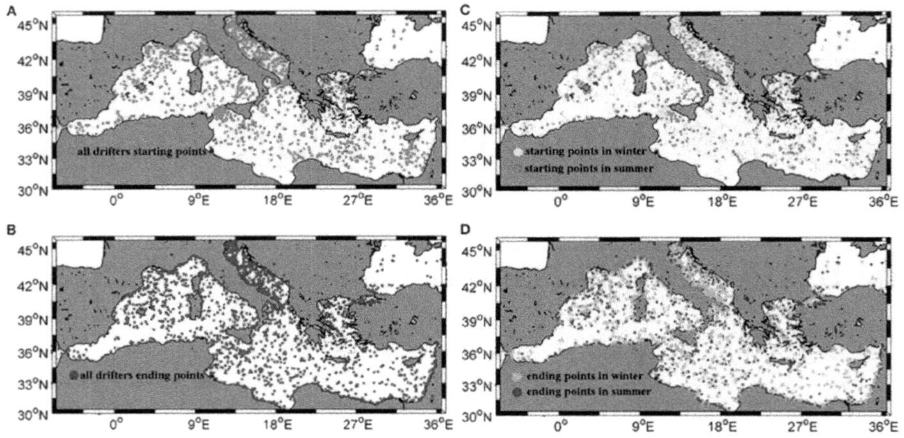

Figure 1.
Drifter starting and ending points in total; starting and ending points in summer and winter. Source: Zambianchi et al. [5].

Significant plastic loads originate from the shore from various sources such as solid waste dumps, trash conveyed from dry land to shore through rivers, and ocean currents carrying plastic debris from shore to shore. There have been several documentaries by environmental activists showing that rivers are a significant source of solid waste, in particular plastic, that make it into the marine environment [4]. There is no evidence yet that the Mediterranean contains a permanent trash island, but there are signs of litter accumulation. Possible retention areas can be identified by analyzing historical data to compute the probability of debris particles circulating into subbasins. The prediction of the location of floating trash islands becomes feasible once accumulation rates are quantified. Climatological reconstructions were performed using empirical data to study the evolution of litter concentration. Floating litter has a general tendency to concentrate in the southern portion of the Mediterranean [5]. A long-term accumulation of litter seems to be forming in the southern and southeastern Levantine basin.

Based on data collected and processed by Zambianchi et al., note how the near-surface drifters were used to track currents starting from a dispersed status (red dots) and ending along coasts on the East Mediterranean including Lebanon and North African countries [5]. Besides the Adriatic Sea portion, and focusing on the Mediterranean, a large percentage of the ending-points concentrate on the East Mediterranean coast, including Lebanon for both summer and winter seasons (**Figure 1**). As such, the author recommends that special attention be placed on the Levantine area to estimate existing, and forecast potential, plastic debris accumulation.

2. Rivers and challenges related to Land-To-Ocean data

Several sources of secondary data in the literature provide quantitative estimates about plastic pollution at large. In Europe and the United States, significant progress was made in data collection and availability in relation to weight, volume, and movement of plastics from their original points on dry land to the oceans. However, such data is not as available or reliable in Lebanon and several countries around the Mediterranean. In subsequent parts of this chapter, it is recommended that fieldwork, surveys, and quantification techniques be developed over the next few years to build a database in support of decision-making and policy design.

It is estimated from various studies that about 8 million metric tons of plastic waste per year travels to oceans worldwide and this figure is expected to increase. Studies in the U.S. and Australia present computational models that analyze data from 192 countries with coastlines. Starting from a total amount of solid waste generated as household refuse per capita, an assumption is made about its percentage of plastics. Another assumption is made about the proportion that will reach the oceans to estimate these amounts over the next decade on the basis of census data and population growth [6].

Results from different sources show corroboration that marine plastic debris, which originates inland and travel the most through rivers. A simplified infographic in **Figure 2** shows residential, commercial, and industrial conglomerates mismanaging plastic waste and discarding it in rivers, which in turn carry it to the oceans, terming the process as "plastic load." A study of 57 rivers investigated the concentration of plastic bags, bottles, fibers, and beads, and used the river flow to compute the total weight of plastic transported by the river to the ocean. Plastic litter per day per person was computed for each river and compared with littering onshore. Rivers were proven to be substantial conveyors of plastic debris into the marine environment. Schmidt et al., compiled global data on plastics in the water in rivers of a wide range of flows, including macroplastics (particles >5 mm) and microplastics (particles <5 mm). They identified mismanaged plastic waste (MMPW) discharged over river catchments basins, transported along the main river artery and into the sea [7]. They concluded that the mathematical relationship is not linear. Major rivers surrounded by densely populated areas generate a higher fraction of MMPW. Further, they concluded that 88–95% of the global plastic river load is conveyed through the ten top-ranked rivers, with an estimated range between 410 tons and 4 million tons per year [7]. This large disparity is owed to uncertainty in data. In fact, such a model requires additional parameters related to seasonality, climate change, hydrological factors, and local or regional precipitation [8]. There has been a misconception related to river loads in the articles attributed to ten rivers that these

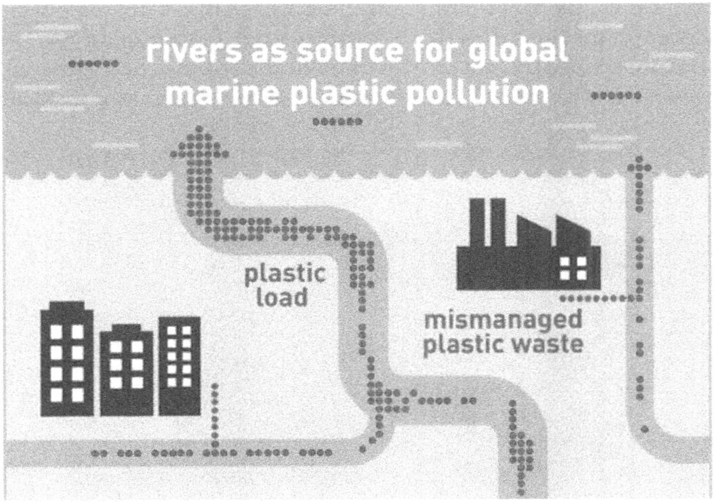

Figure 2.
Rivers exert "plastic loads" from common use and mismanaged plastic waste that make their way to the oceans Schmidt et al. [7].

ten rivers take 90% of total plastic pollution in the oceans. It should be clarified that the 90% estimate of the top ten river load is a percentage of total river load and not total ocean pollution.

3. River plastic load: a global problem and a Mediterranean concern

Most studies on river plastic loads address the largest ones across continents, while little attention was given to smaller rivers in countries around the Mediterranean. Nevertheless, it is useful to provide some context by comparing the Nile, which is the largest river with an estuary on the Mediterranean, with other major rivers worldwide. The top 10 rivers worldwide that were listed among polluters include the Nile and Niger, both of which are African rivers, and the others are Asian rivers. Note that the Yangtze alone was estimated to carry about 2.75 tons of plastic yearly into the sea [9]. Alarming documentaries have been shared on social media showing the Yangtze, among other rivers exhibiting the same problem, covered in opaque blotches of plastic waste (**Figure 3**).

The Nile River flows over 6600 kilometers and runs through (or along the border of) South Sudan, Sudan, Ethiopia, Uganda, Kenya, Congo, Rwanda, Tanzania, Burundi, and Egypt into the Mediterranean Sea making it the longest river in the world. The river has been critical in the development of ancient Egypt as it provided for irrigation, transportation, and fishing among other features. In recent years, over 90% of the Egyptian population lives only within a few kilometers of the Nile riverbanks using ferries, water taxis, and private boats for commute, leisure, or tourism. Today, the Nile is ranked among the top ten polluting rivers (**Figure 4**).

Research in the literature shows that the Mediterranean Sea suffers from high concentrations of floating plastic. This is an indicator that a trend is developing akin to the accumulation zones in the five subtropical ocean gyres. According to a study in the year 2015, an average density of plastic was found to be about 1 item per 4 m^2. It also showed that the frequency of occurrence is 100%, in the sense that all sampled sites showed an occurrence (presence) of plastic debris in the water. Plastic items found were in the range of millimeters. Large plastic items were also found to be in higher proportions than those documented in the oceanic gyres [10]. Most likely, this is due to the fact that sources of pollution around the Mediterranean are closer. Floating plastic in the Mediterranean Sea was estimated to be between

Figure 3.
The Yangtze River with workers collecting floating garbage (source: www.news.cn, 2019).

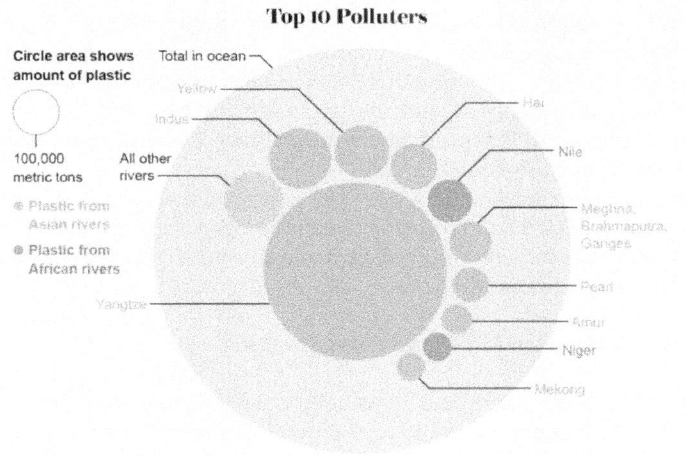

Figure 4.
Top 10 river polluters, among them the Nile flowing into the Mediterranean. Source: "Export of Plastic Debris by Rivers into the Sea," by Christian Schmidt et al. [7] (Artwork credit Amanda Montanez 2018).

1000 and 3000 tons. Schmidt et al. found the Nile to be the fifth river among the top ten polluting rivers worldwide [7]. **Figure 4** shows the contributions of the top ten polluting rivers with the estimated quantities of plastic transport in hundred thousands of metric tons. Ten countries sharing the benefits of the Nile bordering or running through them have a moral obligation toward each other to curb plastic waste at the source. They also have an obligation toward countries around the Mediterranean that are recipients, as well as contributors, of plastic waste on their shores. Therefore, the problem requires collaboration at a regional level.

4. Environmental and social challenges - case of Lebanon

4.1 Challenges pertaining to river loads

In terms of solid and plastic waste, the case of Lebanon carries even more uncertainty due to challenges in data availability, collection, analysis, and estimation. Lebanese rivers convey large amounts of solid waste and plastic debris into the Mediterranean, but disproportionately large amounts are due to direct dumps of solid waste and landfills on its coast. Landfills along the Lebanese shore are the source of sea pollution in the direct vicinity of the beaches. This makes the estimation of river plastic load even more complicated to relate to the river's water discharge rate. A previous estimate by the author used a model that combined population density around major Lebanese rivers, industrial activity, and average yearly discharge. The estimation model at the time focused on percentages rather than absolute numerical values with the objective of directing efforts for awareness and advocacy within the context of general solid waste inclusive of, but not limited to, plastics [8].

It would be necessary to pursue these estimates by collecting primary data from landfills, rivers, and direct dumps to update a geographic mapping focused on plastics transported through rivers into the sea. If we consider river flows exclusively, then we would find that Nahr el Kabir, Ostuene, Araqa, El Bared, Abou Ali, and

Al Jaouz would constitute about 24% of total Lebanese river discharge. Nahr Ibrahim would constitute about 13% and Nahr el Kalb 6% of total Lebanese river discharge. However, the presence of landfills and industrial activity yield different numerical values. For example, even though Nahr Beirut contributes about 3% of Lebanese river discharge, the presence of landfills, population density, and industrial activity tripled the percentage in that particular zone yielding 10% and 11% between Narh el Kalb and Nahr Beirut (**Figure 5**).

The question remains: Is solid waste at large a good indicator or proxy for plastic waste? By most standards, the proxy between the two indicators is close enough to proceed with a subsequent phase of primary data collection, documentation, analysis, and awareness building.

4.2 Challenges related to MSW and demographics

Several studies were performed about solid waste in Lebanon but there is a need to develop detailed observations and recommendations specific to plastics. According to a Country Report on Solid Waste Management in Lebanon, 1.57 million tons of municipal solid waste (MSW) was generated in Lebanon in 2009 [11]. Knowing the challenge of reaching an accurate census with the refugee situation in Lebanon, and using a simplified estimated population, the average waste generation per day per capita is estimated at 1.1 kg/day/capita in urban areas and 0.7 kg/day/capita in rural areas, with about 50% of the waste being organic. Nevertheless, plastics constitute 13% while paper, pulp products, and cardboard constitute 17%. It is expected that, in absence of focused public policies, waste generation will continue to rise annually by 1.65% [11]. The same study in 2010 reports that 30% of MSW is dumped in the

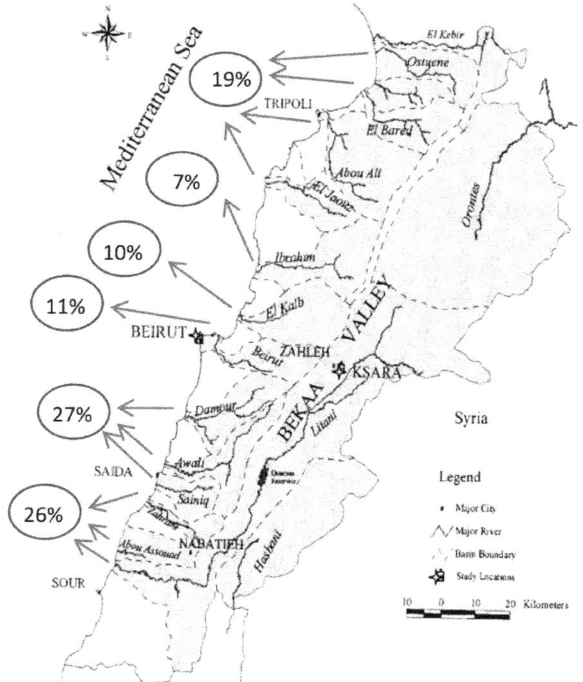

Figure 5.
Percentage estimates of solid waste distribution along the Lebanese coast. (Source: Chalhoub [8]).

open, 53% is land-filled, while only 9% is composted and 8% recycled. In Lebanon, the largest landfill is in Naameh, south of Beirut, which was closed following a public uproar [12]. Beirut generates the highest proportions of MSW in the country due to the fact that about 50% of the population lives in the capital and its direct suburbs, in addition to being a tourist attraction with a concentration of hotels and restaurants.

The Syrian refugee crisis affected demographics in Lebanon. By May 2014, Lebanon received over 35% of the region's Syrian refugees with an estimate of an additional 1000 tons/day of solid waste. Under such considerations, there are projections that by 2025, MSW would surpass 2.4 million tons [11, 13]. Studies showed that 37% of MSW in Lebanon could be recycled or reused, except for organic waste which can be composted into other products such as fertilizers [14]. Since there has not been a clear national strategy for solid waste management, MSW remains a critical problem with several environmental, economic, and public health impacts. Even though MSW in large Lebanese cities such as Tripoli, Beirut, Zahle, and Sidon is collected through private companies, the Lebanese end-user should adopt a preventive approach by reducing waste generation including plastics, and by looking for alternatives [8].

4.3 Challenges related to the private sector

Lebanese plastic companies serve local buyers but have well-established export markets. In 2014, Lebanon imported raw materials for the manufacturing of plastic semifinished and finished products in the value of $695 Mn, while it exported a total value of $131 Mn in raw materials and finished products [15]. Among the top seven Lebanese plastics manufacturers, there are those who produce food packaging, followed by containers, bottles, then piping products, furniture, agricultural materials, hospital consumables, bags, and other industrial materials. While only 10% of discarded plastics are recycled, the remaining quantities go to landfills and the sea. Three sectors, shipping, fishing, and tourism are briefly addressed to illustrate their socio-economic impact and highlight the role that they could fulfill in curbing marine plastic pollution.

4.3.1 Shipping

Historically, Lebanon is known for its shipping and transit activities. Despite the civil war in the 1970s and the current economic meltdown, maritime transport still plays an important role in the Lebanese economy. There are dozens of small ports all along Lebanon's coast used for limited activities and primarily fishing, in addition to twelve marine centers for leisure. But the main commercial ports in Lebanon where the bulk of maritime activities reside are located in Beirut, Tripoli, and Saida [16, 17].

Stretched on a 1.18 km^2 plot at the foothill of Ashrafieh, the Port of Beirut constitutes the main port of trade in Lebanon transiting products to Iraq, Jordan, the Gulf States, Syria, among other countries. The recent August 4, 2020 explosion crippled its activities but despite the extensive damage that it has endured, it started to limp back into a running operation in the following few months [18]. The port of Tripoli is ranked as the second commercial port in Lebanon. It covers a larger plot of about 2.9 km^2, but it is still less technically developed than the one in Beirut.

Secondary data indicates that, over the time span between 2014 and 2018, Tripoli docked between 500 and 870 ships per year while Beirut docked between 1600 and 2000 ships. Over the same time period, Beirut Port processed an average of 8 million tons of merchandise per year tonnage while Tripoli processed between

1.3 and 1.9 tons. As for Sidon Port (Saida), it is of a different character; more of a celebrated historic site, of lesser commercial stature, used mainly for small boats and about 190 ships per year [18]. Shipping is both a contributor to plastic pollution as well as a sector that suffers from plastics at docking facilities and potential hindrance at sea.

4.3.2 Fishing

Fishing in Lebanon has primarily three segments; sea fishing, fish farms, and imports. We focus on sea fishing as it is the one relevant to plastic pollution in Lebanese waters and on its shores. Lebanese fishing activities are considered as small businesses consisting of a single person each, with a crew of two or three helpers, hence closer to artisanal than industrial. With Mediterranean waters housing off the coast of Lebanon over 1700 marine fauna species, with over 82 fish species sold on the local market. Commonly used tools include small mesh nets used to fish near the seafloor. "Ghost fishing" is a term used to indicate lost nets. These nets are made of plastic wire mesh and cause various sorts of hindrance and death of untargeted marine organisms. Most fishing is performed at depths between 40 m and 65 m, and about 92% of fishermen operate at about a nine-kilometer radius from their base harbors. Ghost fishing is one of the concerns related to plastic pollution in marine waters.

The Ministry of Agriculture comprises a Fisheries and Wildlife Department that publishes data sporadically. There has been an increase in sea fishing activity between 1995 and 2005. In 1994, small-operation fishermen totaled about 4100 with a fleet of approximately 2050, while in 2005, the number was between 4500 and 9600 commensurate with the active seasons most of whom were Lebanese (89%).

Fishermen are considered among the poor population segment because their annual income is less than the minimum wage annual income population. Secondary data indicates that the annual average range between \$800 and \$2100 while the minimum wage corresponded (in 1999) to \$5400 per year [18, 19]. Research by Kanbar shows a distinctive difference in income between those who own their boats, averaging \$7400 per year, and those who lease or are loosely employed by boat owners, averaging \$ 3000 [17]. Fishing contributes to plastic pollution and simultaneously suffers from plastic litter, which reduces productivity, fish reproduction (quantity), and fish quality. Further, fishing boats are also hindered at sea.

4.3.3 Tourism

Lebanon has always depended on tourism in its economy. There are various dimensions through which tourism contributes to economic growth. Earnings from tourism provide foreign currencies, which in turn support imports. Further, destination marketing enhances healthy competition among local service providers and hospitality establishments [20–22]. Another indirect effect of tourism is that it creates demand for skilled human resources and new infrastructure, which requires investment. Tourism increases demand for products and services in construction, manufacturing, transportation and rental vehicles, and financial services such as insurance and banking [23, 24].

Tourism in Lebanon showed an overall upward trend between 1961 and 2011. Between 1996 and 2010, arrivals of tourists in Lebanon increased by a factor of 2.5. The tourism sector is sensitive to security and political developments, which explains fluctuations including a drop down from 7.8 million arrivals in 2004 to 5.9 million in 2005. In 2011, when the civil war broke out in Syria, Lebanon saw another drop in total arrivals from 9 million in early 2011 to 5.8 in 2016 [25].

In 2018, the total contribution of tourism and travel to Lebanon's GDP was 19%, down from 27% in 2010 and 18% in 2017 [26]. That was the result of several events including travel bans, the refugee situation, regional and internal political tensions, and most of all local mismanagement in the public sector. Most of the inbound tourists are Lebanese living overseas or Arabs, with the percentage of Arab tourists decreasing from 59% in 2013 to around 41% in 2018. The tourism sector is affected by solid waste crises, among others, as was seen in the last two decades [18, 26, 27].

Tourism contributes directly and indirectly to job creation. Despite the drop in arrivals, there were about 395 thousand jobs in 2018, up from 365 thousand in 2017, while overall, the percentage of total employment decreased to 18% in 2017, down from 24% in 2010 [26]. Besides hotel services, travel agents, leisure, and such jobs are directly related to tourism, there are indirect jobs such as cleaning, food and beverage, suppliers to companies providing hospitality services, local tours activities, and the like. Therefore, the percentage affected by the tourism sector would be in the range of 33%, which is significant.

Plastic pollution in rivers, on the beaches, and in the streets have a drastic effect on touristic, hence economic activity. For instance, in 2017, hotels officially registered in the Syndicate of Hotel Owners reached 408 with a total of 21,804 rooms most of which are located on the coast. Secondary data from 2008 indicate that 68 beach resorts occupy 7.5% of the coastal square footage. By 2017, their number increased to 200, of which 65% are located between Byblos and Beirut, over a 38-kilometer distance along the Mediterranean coast [28]. Therefore, the way solid and plastic waste are managed by those resorts has a large impact on marine pollution.

The rush in the mushrooming of beach resorts caused an overdevelopment on the shore including several environmental breaches bypassing environmental impact assessments and permitting processes. This phenomenon has a double effect; excessive waste generation as well an effect on environmental quality. While plastic pollution has an obviously negative visual effect for tourists, microplastics have a health effect as it is transmitted to humans from fish and seafood. A study by the author on tourism entities operating on the coast between Adonis City and Tabarja shows that those establishments generate six-fold the waste in summer compared to winter. Tourism contributes to plastic waste but it is also negatively impacted by plastic pollution which spoils the beauty of the shores, the attractiveness of leisure sea trips, and increases risks of digestive diseases in hospitality establishments due to microplastics in fish and seafood.

The above sections show that the economic impacts of marine plastic pollution on shipping, fishing, and tourism are disconcerting. Cleanup costs, losses in fishing, ghost fishing, boat damage, economic losses in tourism, and ship hindrance are all effects that require prevention of plastic litter rather than remediation. There should be a joint effort between the private and public sectors to collect reliable data, on a continuous basis, and categorize plastic waste by description (type) and quantities. Such data would help develop a more accurate evaluation of how marine litter impacts these three areas in the private sector. Additionally, the more challenging quantification pertains to marine ecosystems and the reduction in marine life reproduction and mobility.

5. Public-private partnership - a roadmap and recommendations

We continue our illustration with the case of Lebanon as it represents a less developed country, located on the Mediterranean, subject to plastic pollution, and faced with public policies and management challenges. Local authorities such as municipalities at a town or city level have been traditionally entrusted with solid waste collection and disposal. In recent decades, nongovernmental organizations intervened and started to provide services, some funded by international agencies and some based on volunteerism. Either way, a significant social cost is incurred to remove marine litter. For beach cleanup projects, which became in vogue in the last ten years, there is a cost of mobilization, time away from the job (for volunteers), and cost of labor when done as paid professional services. Cleanup cost includes collection, loading, transportation, disposal, and when applicable, recycling. Therefore, the economic opportunity cost of cleaning depends on the line of business that is being forfeited within the local economy.

There have been attempts to quantify such activities in highly developed countries, whereby such studies were performed by the public sector. In the United Kingdom, port authorities spent Euros 2.3 million on debris removal from harbors, while the cost of removing plastic bags on beaches was estimated Euros 340,000/year. Other examples from Belgium and the Netherlands show that about Euros 10 million/year were spent to remove solid waste off beaches [29, 30].

Various studies showed that beach cleanliness ranks as a top priority for tourists and visitors [31]. An analysis of litter impact on beach visitors in the Cape Peninsula in South Africa found that 97% of visitors would not be allowed to a beach with 10/m^2 or more of large litter items. This indicates that marine litter threatens the image of a country like Lebanon and ultimately leads to a decline in its tourism, which corresponds to 20% of its GDP as seen in previous sections. Another area of public-private cooperation is that, according to UNEP, tourism not only drops from the marine litter but also contributes to it [32].

5.1 Public-private partnerships for remedial actions

Several activities led by NGOs and advocacy groups, while noteworthy in terms of community service in fighting plastic pollution, are considered by the author as merely reactive. Granted that beach cleaning campaigns, distribution of trash containers for plastic collection, and offering trucking services from trash collection points to recycling plants are all necessary remedial activities, they fall short of offering a long-term solution to plastic pollution. The circle of manufacturing, consuming, dumping, collecting, and recycling plastics has its own carbon footprint problems that should be thoroughly evaluated and gradually replaced by preventive strategies.

Private sector establishments in Lebanon, namely the ones that are active in plastics trading and manufacturing have an opportunity to play a critical role in partnering with the public sector in a national and regional effort. New process innovations, manufacturing techniques, and new product development must be implemented in the Lebanese manufacturing sector. To reach such operational achievements, concepts of corporate social responsibility must become an integral part of the companies' vision and strategy.

There has been a flawed argument that there is tension between industrial activity and job creation on one side, and environmental preservation on the other side. Numerous examples confirm the opposite in that sustainability in strategic planning and environmental consciousness are aligned with long-term results in business development. Private sector entities, plastic traders, producers, and corporate users are increasingly subjected to changes in consumer awareness about plastics as hazardous waste. Therefore, they need to embrace corporate social responsibility to align and anticipate market needs.

Figure 6 summarizes the relationships among various stakeholders and how actions among private sector establishments, public sector entities, and the citizen

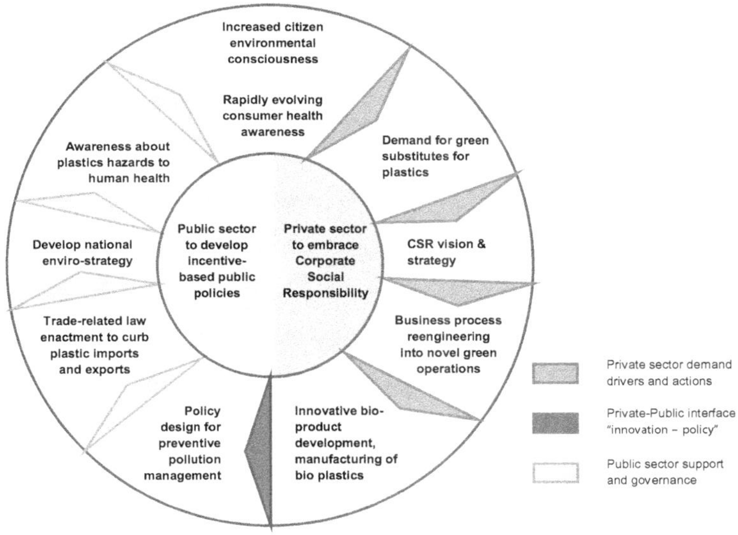

Figure 6.
A citizen- and consumer-centered view to a proposed interaction and public-private partnership in fighting plastic pollution.

are interrelated. The local population must be engaged in awareness campaigns, and the manufacturing sector is to be part of advocacy campaigns. Radical changes are required through preventive strategies. Since the Lebanese coast is not only a source of plastic litter but is also a destination, a collaboration at a regional level would serve best the common interest to protect this shared sea [33].

6. Conclusions

Among multiple sources of plastic pollution, rivers carry solid waste from inland to the ocean from residential, industrial, and agricultural areas. There has been an increased awareness about the hazards of plastic pollution and threat to human, animal, and vegetation life. While the maritime transport industry was blamed for many decades as the main source of marine plastic pollution, it is found that river load and dumps on the shores are major contributors. The problem is exacerbated by movements from shore to shore by waves and currents. Our overview about river solid waste loads calls for urgent actions to be taken by the private sector by embracing corporate social responsibility. The Mediterranean, which is particularly fragile because of its enclosed geography, suffers from industries in several countries around the basin that generate toxic or solid waste disposed of in rivers and municipal sewage networks. A practical application was presented using data from Lebanon, located on the easternmost shore of the Mediterranean, and whose economy depends by and large on service sectors including transit from its harbors to inland countries in the region. The private sector is expected and recommended to play a leading role in curbing plastic pollution by partnering with the public sector. Companies are encouraged to be proactive in the process and product innovation, and the public sector is recommended to stimulate such preventive corporate strategies through the enactment of thoughtful and forward-looking public policies. While remedial actions such as cleanup and recycling are necessary, the solution resides in migration toward green products and the development of bio-substitutes to plastics. A concerted effort to fight plastic pollution onshore and in the marine environment is required through partnerships between companies and local governments.

Author details

Michel Soto Chalhoub
Notre Dame University, Louaize, Lebanon

*Address all correspondence to: mchalhoub@live.com

References

[1] Culin J, Bielic T. Plastic pollution from ships. Journal of Maritime and Transportation Science. 2016;**51**(1): 57-66

[2] Cirino E. Plastic Pollution: From Ship to Shore. Tucson, Arizona: The Revelator, Center for Biological Diversity. Tucson, Arizona; 2017. Available from: https://therevelator.org/plastic-pollution-ship-shore/

[3] Monterey Bay National Marine Sanctuary. Scientists to Give a Lots Shipping Container a Second Look. Available from: https://montereybay.noaa.gov/resourcepro/mt/2013cruise.html

[4] Bellini A. 10 Rivers 1 Ocean. California, USA: Video Documentary; 2019

[5] Zambianchi E, Trani M, Falco P. Lagrangian transport of marine litter in the Mediterranean Sea. Journal of Frontiers in Environmental Science. 2017. DOI: 10.3389/fenvs.2017.00005

[6] Jambeck JR, Geyer R, Wilcox C, Siegler TR, Perryman M, Andrady A, et al. Plastic waste inputs from land into the ocean. Science. 2015;**347**(6223):68-771. DOI: 10.1126/science.1260352

[7] Schmidt C, Krauth T, Wagner S. Export of plastic debris by Rivers into the sea. Environmental Science & Technology. 2017, 2017;**51**(21): 12246-12253

[8] Chalhoub MS. Modeling Solid Waste Conveyance into the East Mediterranean: Uncertainties and Challenges in Engineering and Public Policy. Working paper. Vol. 2016. Lebanon, Louaize; 2016

[9] Christou L. The Yangtze Deposits 55% of all River Marine Plastic Pollution – But China Is Finally Taking Action. London, UK: The Verdict Newsletter; 2018. Available from: https:// www.verdict.co.uk/yangtze-river-plastic-pollution/

[10] Cózar A, Sanz-Martín M, Martí E, González-Gordillo JI, Ubeda B, Gálvez JA, et al. Plastic accumulation in the Mediterranean Sea. PLoS One. 2015;**2015**. DOI: 10.1371/journal.pone.0121762

[11] SWEEP-net country report. Country Report on Solids Waste Management. Sweep-Net, GIZ and German Cooperation; April 2014

[12] Chalhoub MS. Public policy and technology choices for municipal solid waste management: A recent case in the East Mediterranean. Journal of Environmental Science, Taylor & Francis. 2018;**4**(1):1-18

[13] UNDP. Lebanon Environmental Assessment of the Syrian Conflict and Priority Intervention. 2014

[14] Ismail IA, Chaaban JK, Al-Rabaa AR, Shaar AA. Solid waste Management in Lebanon: Challenges and recommendations. Journal of Environment and Waste Management. 2017;**4**(2):53-63

[15] BLOM. The Lebanese Plastic Industry: Leveraging its Strengths Locally and Abroad. 2015

[16] Chalhoub MS. A Comparative Study of Coastal Ports in Lebanon towards a National Maritime Transport Strategy. Working paper. Vol. 2010. Louaize; 2010

[17] Kanbar N. Mediterranean regional activity – Lebanon. In: GEF: Governance and Knowledge Generation Socio-Economic Evaluation of Maritime Activities. Lebanon: GEF Plan Bleu; 2015

[18] Chalhoub MS. The port of Beirut explosion: Disaster, response and observations. In: Online Conference by Region 9 of the American Society of Civil Engineers, and the State of

California Governor's Office of Emergency Services; March 31, 2021, California, USA; 2021

[19] MoA. Census of Lebanese Fishing Vessels and Fishing Facilities. Vol. 2005. Ministry of Agriculture, Directorate of Rural Development & Natural Resources Department of Fisheries & Wildlife; 2005

[20] Krueger AO. Trade policy as an input to development. American Economic Review. 1980;**70**(2):188-292

[21] Ashley C, Mitchell J. Can Tourism Help Reduce Poverty in Africa? London: Overseas Development Institute (ODI), Briefing Paper, ODI; 2006

[22] Troy L, Shane L, Brian F. Tourism receipts contribute to the sustainability of current account deficits: A case study of Barbados. International Journal of Tourism Research. 2013;**15**(6):620-624

[23] Spurr R. Tourism satellite accounts. In: Dwyer L, Forsyth P, editors. International Handbook on the Economics of Tourism, Cheltenham. U.K.: Edward Elgar Publishing; 2009

[24] Lee CC, Chang CP. Tourism development and economic growth: A closer look at panels. Tourism Management. 2008;**29**:180-192. Scientific Research Publishers. DOI: 10.1016/j.tourman.2007.02.013

[25] Central Administration of Statistics. Census Report. 2018. Available from: www.cas.gov.lb. 2016-2018

[26] WTTC. Travel and Tourism Lebanon Economic Impact 2018. World Travel and Tourism Council; 2018

[27] MoET. Quarterly Economic Bulletin". Issue 8, March. Ministry of Economy and Trade, Lebanon; 2013

[28] Lebanon opportunity databank. Available from: http://www.databank.com.lb/doc.asp?ID=1811 and http://www.databank.com.lb/doc.asp?ID=1809

[29] Mouat T, Lopez-Lozano R, Bateson H. Economic Impacts of Marine Litter. KIMO (Kommunenes Internasjonale Miljoorganisasjon); 2010. p. 117

[30] Marine Conservation Society. Submission from the Marine Conservation Society: Environmental Levy on Plastic Bags (Scotland) Bill. Ross-on-Wye: Marine Conservation Society; 2005

[31] Ballance A, Ryan PG, Turpie JK. How much is a clean beach worth? The impact of litter on beach users in the Cape Peninsula, South Africa. South Africa Journal of Science. 2000;**96**:5210-5213

[32] UNEP. "Results of the Assessment of the Status of Marine Litter in the Mediterranean", United Nations Environment Programme. Athens: UNEP/MAP; 2009

[33] Chalhoub MS. Need for a collaborative natural resourxce management strategy for the marine environment – The case of plastics in the Mediterranean. In: Natural Resource Management and Biological Sciences. InTech Open-Sage Publishers; 2021

Section 2

Habitat

Chapter 6

The Impacts of Air Pressure Differences on Microclimatic Wind Comfort among Low-Rise Buildings in the Historical Urban Landscape of the Bay of Kotor Region, Montenegro

Enes Yasa and Kadir Özdemir

Abstract

Urban design and urban form can affect ventilation potential by causing flow turbulences around and at the top of buildings, which result in higher wind velocity. The air velocity is either increased or decreased by building blocks, and the solar energy is trapped in the urban canyons formed by buildings on both sides of the streets. The aim of this study was to investigate the effect of building orientation and forms, and street orientations in terms of pedestrian- level microclimatic within the dense structure of the city of the case study area, which is considered the historical texture of the Montenegro region. The another aim was to answer the questions on the relation of the prevailing wind with the wind behavior in the built-up area. This is a multidisciplinary study between urban architecture, and urban physics. The data collection analysis and its interpretation are the numerical part of the study. When the results of the analyses on all prevailing wind directions and flows are examined in detail, building layouts can be revised and optimized to allow sufficient pressure on the facades of buildings with the lowest pressure values around each group of buildings. Otherwise, buildings with insufficient wind flow and therefore buildings with low-pressure values will exposed the insufficient natural ventilation performance.

Keywords: historical texture in urban context, urban design, air exchange rate, pedestrian level wind microclimatic condition, the effect of building orientation

1. Introduction

Due to the rapid increase in urbanization in recent years, urban microclimate studies are gaining popularity. In the meetings held by the United Nations in recent years, "making cities and human settlements climate-resistant and sustainable" has started to be promoted as one of the sustainable development goals [1]. Especially after the Covid-19 pandemic, which emerged all over the world in 2019 and caused the death of thousands of people by affecting their health, researches on sustainable healthy cities-habitats with the issue of natural ventilation of the city and buildings gain importance and will continue to gain importance in the coming years.

Approaches that emphasize microclimatic comfort sensitivity as part of the urban planning processes implemented to date are rarely included in the design process because there is a general lack of knowledge on how to do this among urban planning practitioners. Many studies conducted so far have documented that urban microclimate can affect building energy performance and occupant thermal comfort balance, especially its effects on human health [2–6]. Urban comfort, which is the most important topic in the field of urban physics, deals with the relationship between wind/thermal comfort of pedestrians and pollutants and wind, which examines the urban air quality to ensure a healthy and happy life for the residences living in the city. Should the importance of urban form in urban design is developed in accordance with the context of urban microclimatic comfort, it can improve the quality of life of millions of people living in cities. The importance of climatically sensitive urban design is very important on the concept of sustainability, which has been a popular decision of recent years. Appropriate urban design enables the use of renewable energy sources for passive natural ventilation at city scale and passive heating and cooling at building scale while increasing pedestrian comfort and efficiency.

2. The characteristics of wind in a built environment

The average wind speed profile near the ground (interface layer) is governed by pressure differences due to the presence of buildings, vegetation, and topography. The nature of the obstacles regulates the turbulence level. When the wind velocity is greater than 10 m/s, the influence of surface friction is predominant in distorting and generating a turbulent flow. Flow disruption depends on the shape and height of the obstacles. The wind does not reach a full speed up to a certain height above the ground (called gradient wind); this height depends on local obstacles and is called surface roughness. Surface roughness and obstacles usually reduce wind speed, but can also have an acceleration effect on the wind. It occurs when airflow passes through a smaller cross-section (for example, passing through a building). It can also happen near tall buildings. Many features of the built environment and atmosphere affect wind speed. Wind speed in the built environment, therefore, exhibits a very complex behavior that is difficult to model.

3. Pedestrian level comfort in urban texture

In recent years, the number of studies on pedestrian comfort levels around buildings has increased in urban textures where building densities have increased. Due to the necessity of analyzing the negative comfort conditions that may occur at the pedestrian level, pedestrian health, and safety conditions very well, the urban texture and buildings have started to be analyzed in detail. The wind is the most important microclimatic parameter that affects pedestrian level comfort around the building. Wind movement manifests itself in basically two ways at the pedestrian level: it can either be felt like a wind speed that affects the heat exchange between people and the environment, or it can be felt as a force from the sum of the pressure field on the human body [7]. Urban wind flow has many effects on pedestrian level comfort, including heat transfer via convection, penetration of rain, dilution of pollutants, noise, or dust removal. In this study, only the mechanical effects of wind on pedestrian comfort are discussed. Pedestrian thermal comfort threshold at pedestrian level corresponds to wind speeds of about 4.50 m/s [8]. Pedestrian comfort conditions between buildings depend on several parameters. Among these parameters, biological factors such as wind speed, local climate, ambient temperature, precipitation amount, humidity, the activity level in public spaces, clothing, age, and psychological states of people come to the fore. A preliminary assessment of wind behavior at ground level and around buildings can prevent excessive wind speeds [9]. Pedestrian level outdoor microclimatic comfort between buildings can be achieved by applying the right design strategies of building groups together with open/semi-open and closed spaces within the urban texture. For this reason, in advance, meteorological analysis, evaluating the data according to the microclimate of the settlements, and planning the building form and settlement will increase the quality of life.

4. Urban physics and microclimatic comfort analysis with CFD

When both the applications and the literature are examined, it is seen that the number of research studies and applications that take into account the wind, which is the most important parameter of the microclimatic comfort parameter in urban design, is inadequate. Although most of the literature studies generally focus on the details and technical aspects of wind simulation used in the analysis, there are not many studies for urban planning practitioners on how they can apply wind simulation to improve their designs. This naturally means that wind simulation is not used enough in city planning at the moment, which reduces the quality of the outdoor urban area, and unqualified designs are produced.

The application of wind simulation in urban planning in conceptual design, schematic design, and detail design processes in the urban planning process can be preferred especially in schematic and detail design processes since the conceptual design phase is not very detailed by nature. During the schematic design phase, wind behavior between buildings can be considered on a rather macro scale. In the detail stage, wind analyzes may not be very effective in the wind-design relationship, since it is a scale that can be handled at the scale of the building envelope, and at this stage the settlement, shape-form decisions are determined.

There are four methods for analyzing wind speeds and directions. The first is on-site measurements. These provide detailed information, but extensive field measurements are time-consuming and expensive. They only work when analyzing current situations, so their use in predicting the impact of changes on the built environment is limited.

The second is the testing of scale models in wind tunnels. The modeling process itself is fairly simple and sensors can be used to get precise data on wind speeds, but it has two drawbacks. First, measurements are only made where the sensors are located, so their placement becomes critical to the results. Second, a wind tunnel is a specialized piece of equipment and not everyone has physical and financial access to it, which may be seen by urban planners as a barrier to its adoption.

The third method consists of simplified calculation methods. Rather than simulating the actual physical processes that together determine wind behavior, they use simplified, empirical mathematical models to predict wind speed based on surrounding urban geometry. These techniques have a relatively low computational cost but are also less accurate. There is also a lack of user-friendly software for the implementation of these techniques, making them less suitable for practitioners [10].

The fourth method of analyzing wind is computational fluid dynamics (CFD). This is using a computer-based model to simulate real physical processes that together determine the behavior of the wind. CFD provides a complete picture of wind behavior across the entire model and is well established in a variety of fields, making it more accessible than field measurements, wind tunnel experiments, or simplified mathematical models in general. CFD is also becoming more applicable due to advances in computer technology [11].

Considering all the advantages and disadvantages, wind analyzes, whether alone or comprehensively as a part of microclimate analysis, cannot be used sufficiently in urban planning processes at present [3]. The barriers for CFD are lower than for other techniques, so CFD is the focus of this chapter. When we look at the historical background of urban microclimate studies, they have mostly been done with observational methods such as field measurements. In recent years, with advances in computational resources, numerical simulation approaches have become increasingly popular. Nowadays, especially CFD is frequently used to evaluate the urban microclimate. Computational simulations in urban physics and urban design studies can be used to study urban microclimate at different scales, from meteorological macro–micro scale to building scale [12–14]. Most of the CFD urban physics for microclimate studies have focused on parameters related to temperature, wind flow, thermal comfort, and heat transfer. CFD has repeatedly demonstrated its predictive ability in validation studies focusing on different parameters. CFD provides the possibilities of detailed indoor and outdoor comfort modeling of each building by evaluating inter-building microclimatic parameters at an urban scale. In the past, articles have been published that provide extensive reviews of meteorological micro-scale CFD studies [15, 16].

Advances in the application of computational simulations in recent years have allowed them to develop best practice guidelines in urban microscale studies, so the popularity of the use of CFDs has continued to grow steadily [13, 17, 18]. Micro-scale CFD studies in urban design, pedestrian level comfort between buildings, wind flow around buildings [19–23] pedestrian wind comfort [24, 25] pedestrian thermal comfort [26] the effect of wind-induced rain on buildings [27, 28]. It includes the distribution of urban air quality [29–32] etc. In the literature, there are studies on natural ventilation studies and convective heat transfer coefficients CFD studies for the analysis of the microclimate at the pedestrian level around the buildings at the building scale [12, 13, 15, 16, 21, 26, 33–36]. The smallest-scale studies using CFD on microclimatic analyzes at urban scale are the ones dealing with the indoor microclimatic comfort conditions of the building, where the horizontal distances between buildings are approximately 10 m and the focus is on the indoor climate. CFD has been used primarily for indoor ventilation studies and HVAC design issues in studies on this scale [22, 37–42]. In the last decade, the popularity of topics such as urban settlement/location, urban street canyons, building blocks, courtyards, and urban microclimate has been increasing year by year in studies with CFD on the microclimatic scale of urban physics [43–53]. Most of the studies on real urban areas appear to have been conducted in mid-latitude climates [54].

In the literature, CFD studies on urban physics and microclimatic comfort studies appear as validated and unvalidated studies. CFD studies on the unvalidated real urban area are mostly comparative studies comparing current real comfort conditions of different urban configurations, design parameters, neighborhoods, and districts within the same urban area. Most of these studies target to achieve best-case scenarios based on optimization of a target parameter (e.g. outdoor thermal comfort) [55–58] Most of the CFD urban microclimate studies are conducted without verification. The percentage share of unvalidated studies seems to have remained fairly stable in recent years. However, it is imperative that CFD urban microclimate studies include much more frequent validation to provide the desired reliability and predictive capability. The most common reason for the lack of validation in CFD microclimate studies may be the lack of relevant and well-documented measurement data [54].

When the field measurements method is used in microclimate studies in real urban areas, meteorological measurements such as field measurements of wind and air temperature around the street and building are made, this method is relatively simple. However, this methodology may not be possible to use in all urban studies. However, there may be certain limitations in the use of these data for scientific purposes and, in particular, their suitability for validation purposes. This is because the meteorological conditions in the measured urban area are complex and constantly changing, and not only requires careful measurement of a large number of parameters (to be used as boundary conditions in simulations), but also a fairly complete reporting of the urban area, measurement systematics, at the same time, a detailed and comprehensive validation study of the urban area, measurement scheme, measurement accuracy, etc., would not be possible without them [55–58].

When the related articles studies in the literature are examined, in addition to experimental wind tunnel tests and field measurements studies, numerical analysis studies with CFD have been increasing in recent years to examine pedestrian level comfort wind conditions in urban areas. Compared to both wind tunnel tests and field measurements, CFD has some advantages. One of the major advantages of CFD over wind tunnel testing is that it gives detailed flow area data of associated parameters across the entire calculation area.

Another advantage of CFD over wind tunnel measurements is that, in general, wind tunnel measurements are performed at only a few selected points in the model, while CFD provides a more detailed analysis of wind flow around the building(s) by providing data on relevant parameters at all points of the calculation areas [59–61].

This study aims to investigate the effect of building orientation and forms, and street orientations in terms of pedestrian level microclimatic comfort and natural ventilation of pedestrian level comfort conditions in the urban area within the dense structure of the city of the case study area, which is located in the historical texture of Montenegro region. The aim is to answer the questions on the relation of the prevailing wind and the wind behavior in the built-up area. For this purpose, in the case study area of Montenegro, which is a historical settlement area, wind analyzes were carried out in 10 different directions (North, South, East, West, North-East, North-West, South-East, South-West, North- North-East, East- North-East) using the highest wind speed of 30.5 m/s, considering the worst scenarios in the light of meteorological data, as well as cardinal and intercardinal directions as boundary conditions.

This study focuses on the role of wind, which is the most important parameter affecting urban microclimatic comfort, which should be considered in the urban design process. Wind affects primarily urban air pollution and air pressure, as well as the energy exchange of buildings and users with the effect of convective heat transfer. Thus, it becomes one of the main driving forces of urban physics and urban microclimate. To evaluate the natural ventilation potential in the hot-humid climate of the Bay of Kotor region of Montenegro, the air exchange coefficients of the buildings in the case study region were examined. In the study of Moreau and Gandermer [62], on the evaluation of natural ventilation and pedestrian level comfort conditions in the urban area, a table is given about the air exchange rates

Level of natural ventilation efficiency	ΔCp range
ACH too low	$\Delta Cp < 0.17$
ACH enough	$0.17 \leq \Delta Cp < 0.39$
ACH good	$0.39 \leq \Delta Cp < 0.53$
ACH very good	$0.53 \leq \Delta Cp$

Table 1.
Guidelines for natural ventilation potential [62].

of the buildings in the urban texture and the relationship between natural ventilation (**Table 1**). Guidelines are based on the pressure coefficient differential ΔCp between upwind and downwind sidewalls of a building.

5. Characteristics of case study area

This study was carried out in the region of the Bay of Kotor Region, Montenegro, located in the historical texture of Montenegro with traditional stone buildings and painted shuttered windows on the edge of the Bay of Kotor. This residential area of this coastal city of Montenegro is located on the Bay of Kotor (**Figure 1**). It is one of the youngest cities on the Adriatic, formerly part of the Ottoman Empire and the Republic of Venice; it characterizes architecture that reflects a mix of Venetian and picturesque architectural styles (**Figure 2**).

Montenegro the Bay of Kotor region has a hot-humid climate with much more precipitation in winter than in summer. Its distinctive topography and high mountains make it one of the wettest places in Europe. This residential area is sunny about 200 days a year. Local meteorological data for this region as relative air humidity is the highest 80% indicator in autumn. It is seen in the summer period with the lowest level of 63%. The average temperature throughout the year is 15°C. The lowest recorded temperature (monthly average) of the studied region was measured at −1°C in January 2017, and the highest temperature (monthly average) was measured in July 2015 at 29°C (**Figure 3**).

Annual average local atmospheric wind conditions for the Bay of Kotor Region, Montenegro are shown in the wind rose plotted in **Figure 3**. It is clear that northerly

Figure 1.
The bay of Kotor region, architectural and urban characteristic and settlement pattern of the region where the study was conducted (https://elevation.maplogs.com/poi/bijela_montenegro.436217.html).

Figure 2.
The façade architecture and street façade texture characteristic of the region where the study was conducted (https://tr.depositphotos.com/275544506/stock-photo-narrow-streets-in-the-old.html).

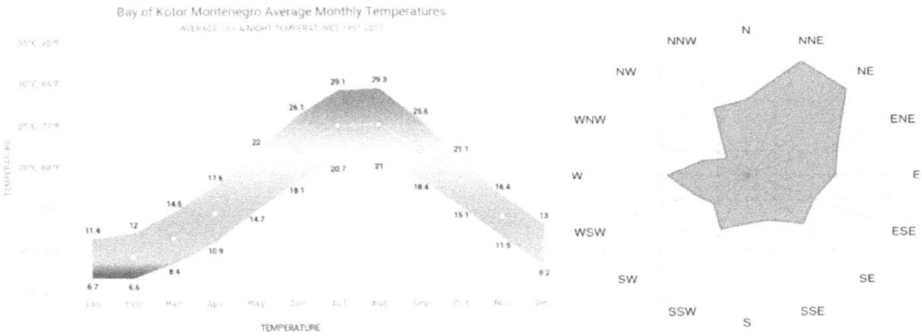

Figure 3.
Meteorological measurement data of 1951–2017, average temperature values, and wind rose for the bay of Kotor region, Montenegro.

winds prevail throughout the year. Also, in **Table 2**, maximum wind speeds are given for all directions.

The Bay of Kotor Region, Montenegro, the case study area located in the heart of Boka Bay, is close to the two historic medieval towns of Perast and Kotor and the Adriatic Coast. The area of Kotor has been classified as a UNESCO World Heritage Site since 1979 due to its historical and cultural significance (**Figure 4**).

6. Methodology and numerical modeling

CFD software is the most popular tools used to calculate the wind flow to balance the microclimate within the built environment in the urban texture. These allow easy understanding and interpretation of the flow characteristics of the wind around buildings in any urban area. For urban designers and architects, the wind flow velocity and pressure values obtained as a result of CFD analysis during the design process are used to optimize the urban texture draft project in terms of layout approaches, location, and orientation of buildings to provide the correct microclimate. It also facilitates the detailed evaluation of the comfort conditions in the texture and the wind comfort condition for pedestrians.

Direction	N	NNE	NE	ENE	E	ESE	SE	SSE	S	SSW	SW	WSW	W	WNW	NW	NNW
Maximum wind velocity (m/s)	18.7	30.5	30	21	18.9	15.5	17	12	12	14.4	10	12.3	17	10	6	18

Table 2.
Wind direction & velocities for Montenegro.

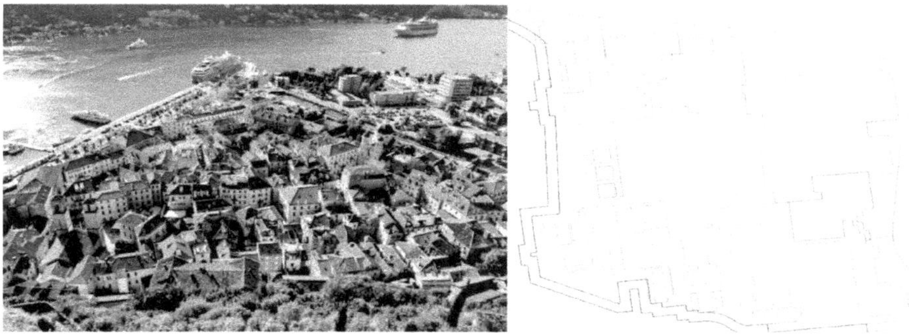

Figure 4.
Plan and landscape view of the case study area.

In this study, CFD Fluent was preferred to simulate pedestrian level comfort conditions and wind condition environments due to both the bureaucratic and economic constraints encountered for field measurements and the more comprehensive analysis parameters provided by numerical simulation. The CFD simulations were performed using CFD code Fluent and the 3D steady RANS equations. The closure was provided by the realizable (k-ε) turbulence model. The choice of this turbulence model was based on recommendations by Franke et al. [63] and earlier validation studies for pedestrian-level wind conditions [64]. Sensible modeling of the atmospheric boundary layer in CFD is one of the most important criteria in external aerodynamic analyzes around the building. Many of the analysis software conduct flow analysis for materials with a low roughness coefficient, and therefore the roughness coefficient is defined as 0 in the CFD. Depending on the region where the structure is located, the roughness coefficient should also be defined. Since it is an open zone surface, the surface roughness is defined as 0.2 m [9].

Pressure differences occur on the surfaces of buildings exposed to wind. Due to the pressure difference in the building envelope caused by the wind and the density difference between the indoor and outdoor air, it causes air exchange around the building and in the buildings. Pressure coefficients largely depend on the shape of the buildings and the influence of neighboring buildings. The pressure field in a complex urban area can be analyzed to reveal the potential for natural ventilation in the urban texture. Modeling of wind flow and velocity around buildings in urban texture has traditionally been applied with full-scale measurements and wind tunnel tests when studies in the literature are examined. However, the creation and adaptation of atmospheric flow conditions in wind tunnel tests is a serious problem. Numerical simulations based on CFD are quite common as a tool to support the assessment of airflow around buildings in urban texture. CFD solves the problem of establishing and adapting atmospheric flow conditions encountered in a wind tunnel by providing both the actual wind flow velocity of the study area and the distribution of turbulence over the entire study area. The case study area of wind modeling, which takes into account regional terrain conditions and meteorological period average data of the region, includes surface roughness modeling in an atmospheric boundary layer [60, 65, 66].

Although RANS remains very popular in research projects, especially in the areas of wind flow and comfort between buildings, urban air pollutants and pollution dispersion, urban thermal performance, urban natural ventilation, and indoor airflow, the application of the large eddy simulation (LES) technique allows taking into account the characteristics of the wind at the atmospheric scale. The LES provides a deeper insight into the unstable flow properties. Many situations that are interesting for urban planning applications still seem to be beyond the reach of such simulations today [60].

Pressure fluctuations occurring on building surfaces depending on the average wind speed lead to both laminar and turbulent flow through leaks from the surface and between buildings [67]. High-frequency fluctuations around buildings create a turbulent distribution of air across inter-building openings containing eddies of similar or smaller size. The frequency-domain analysis of wind speed and wind pressure on the building facades is effective on the rate and amount of air exchange.

Wind-induced air change rate ACH (1/h) is given by the following equation.

$$\mathrm{ACH}d(\mathrm{t}) = \left(\frac{3600}{\mathrm{V}}\right)\sum_{J=1}^{n}\left(Kd{,}j(Vq)\right)Aj \tag{1}$$

$$\left[0.5\rho\left(Cp_{d,j}^{ext} - Cp_{d,j}^{\mathrm{int}}\right)V_d^2(\mathrm{t}) + 0.04\mathrm{z}_j\Delta\,\mathrm{T}(\mathrm{t})\right]^{0.5} \tag{2}$$

This equation describes the calculated air exchange rate for different building components that are exposed to a positive pressure difference or a negative pressure difference caused by the wind blowing from d at time t.

Kd,j in the formula; a leakage function presented as a linear function of Vq regarding the flow rate from the building openings to the area of the building component j and the corresponding pressure drop across the openings for the wind blowing from there, d($\sqrt{m^3 / kg}$); vq—“frictionless flow rate” (m/s) through openings; n—the number of elements of the building envelope facing only positive or only negative pressure difference; V—volume (m^3); Aj—area of jth element (m^2); ρ air density (kg/m^3); $Cp_{d,j}^{ext}$; assumed external pressure coefficient (−) for facade j exposed to wind from direction d; $Cp_{d,j}^{\mathrm{int}}$; assumed internal pressure coefficient for facade j exposed to wind from direction d (−); vd (t)—wind blowing from direction d (m/s); zj—the vertical distance from the neutral pressure layer to the center of the jth building element (m); ΔT(t)—10-min mean temperature difference between outside and inside (K) treated later on as slowly changing 1-hour mean.

Pressure differences and fluctuations in wind flow caused by turbulence around buildings affect airflow through openings and cracks in the building envelope and between buildings. The character of the wind flow depends on the scale of the wind flow length and the geometrical properties of buildings and their cracks in relation to the Reynolds number for airflow [68, 69].

7. Computational domain settings-parameters and meshing system

A solid model of the case study area was created with the information obtained from the 2-D architectural project and site plans of the buildings. Three-dimensional model of the project is illustrated in **Figure 5**. The definition of wind direction is illustrated in **Figure 3**. The CFD model represents buildings set along with the real topography of their location. The 1000 m × 1000 m topography, where the case study buildings are situated has been obtained from the Google Earth software. For the atmospheric boundary layer to be formed correctly, a denser grid was used in regions with rapid changes in geometry and near the surface. As a result, the quality of the grid affects the precision when the results are compared with the experimental values. Using the grid tuning twice during the analysis caused the grid

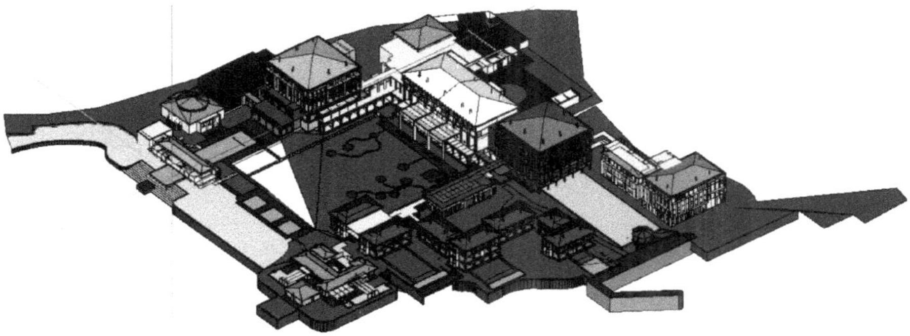

Figure 5.
3D model view of the case study.

to become denser where necessary and the flow solution to converge in the continuous flow regime. It was applied automatically in every 300 iterations depending on the average pressure changes on the predetermined surfaces in the buildings. The design of buildings must account for wind loads, and these are affected by wind gradients. The respective gradient levels, usually assumed in the Building Codes, are 500 m for cities, 400 m for suburbs, and 300 m for flat open terrain [70].

The approaching wind was created from a power-law model to approximate the mean velocity profile:

$$U = U_r + \left(\frac{Z - d}{Z_r} \right)^{\alpha} \tag{3}$$

where; U = mean wind speed, Zr = reference height, Ur = wind speed at reference height Zr, d = zero plane displacement, and α = power-law exponent. The exponent α varies according to the type of terrain; α = 0.14, 0.25, and 0.33 for open country, suburban, and urban exposures, respectively. At the inlet condition, the power-law equation is used to simulate a mean wind velocity of 30.5 m/s at the building height according to an exponent α, which depends upon the surface roughness of the terrain surrounding the building model. The input parameters for wind density, ρ, and wind dynamic viscosity, η are based on the real wind characteristic.

Mean wind velocity 30.5 m/s was used as inlet boundary conditions at ten directions. A total of 30.5 m/s maximum wind velocity was used as inlet boundary conditions at ten directions as shown in **Table 1**, so that the worst scenarios could be considered.

The accuracy of simulation results is highly dependent on the appropriate computational modeling, such as domain size, grid size, and grid discrepancy. Therefore, the CFD simulation modeling for the validation approach discussed in this study complies with the AIJ (Architectural Institute of Japan) guidelines, which is one of the standards in the literature for the urban pedestrian wind environment. AIJ guidelines are based on a series of cross-comparisons between CFD, wind tunnel experiments, and field measurements. In contrast, another popular guideline, cost recommendations, is based on a literature review [71]. The calculation area size for the validation experiment is 500 m × 500 m × 50 m (W×L×H). The domain is divided into 125,170 grid points. Pressure velocity coupling was taken care of by the simple algorithm. Second-order discretization schemes were used for viscous terms of the governing equations. Simulations were performed for ten wind directions as seen in **Table 3**. The iterations were terminated when the scaled residuals showed a very little further reduction with an increasing number of iterations. The following minimum values were reached:

Description of the terrain	Power law exponent, α	Gradient height, z_g
For open country, flat coastal belts, small islands situated in large bodies of water, prairie grasslands, tundra, etc.	(0.14)	900 ft. (274 m)
For wooded countryside, parkland, towns, outskirts of large cities, rough coastal belts	(0.29)	1300 ft. (396 m)
For centers of large cities	(0.40)	1700 ft. (518 m)

Table 3.
Power law exponents for various descriptions of terrain.

Figure 6.
Computational domain mesh numerical grid system.

For x, y, z-velocity components: 10^{-8}. For (k –ε): 10^{-7}. For continuity: 10^{-6}

Four layers (layer height: 0.5 m) are arranged below the assessment height (2.25 m above ground) to comply with AIJ guidelines. In the first step, a flow volume is created around the buildings. This area is called the computational area. This area is knitted with the network structure while creating the mathematical model. Then, boundary conditions are defined. After these definitions are made, the equations are solved and the result is reached. In all simulations, a denser network structure has been created in areas where velocity and pressure gradients are predicted to be high.

The first step is to discretize a part of the continuous space around the considered building. This part of space is named the computational domain. The domain was divided into a finite volume. For each volume of the computational domain, the basic equations were set up. Subsequently, the equations are solved given a set of initial and boundary conditions. For all performed simulations a mesh is used which is denser in regions where velocity gradients or pressure gradients will be high. An example of the mesh used is illustrated in **Figure 6**. The computational domain mesh consisted of about 12 million polyhedral and hexahedral cells.

8. Results and discussion

Pressure differences occur on the surfaces of buildings exposed to wind. Due to the pressure difference in the building envelope caused by the wind and the density difference between the indoor and outdoor air, it causes air exchange in/around the buildings. Evaluation of the effect of wind on the air exchange rate is generally limited to analysis of hourly average wind speed. The wind pressure and the pressure coefficient in the leeward area mostly depend on the form characteristics of the building according to the wind direction. The frequency-domain analysis of wind speed and wind pressure on the building facades is effective on the rate and amount of air exchange. Thus, due to the changing rate and amount of air exchange around the building, the amount of air exchange around the building will vary in the urban texture, and both the urban air quality and the pedestrian level will be effective on microclimatic comfort values. Air exchange in buildings and around the buildings is caused by the pressure difference in the building envelope caused by the wind and the density difference between the outside and indoor air. So, the minimum and maximum wind pressure difference on buildings causes air exchange around and inside the building [69]. For this reason, in this study, the minimum and maximum pressure values that affect the amount of air exchange around the buildings in the urban texture were examined. Evaluation of the effect of wind on the air exchange rate is generally limited to analysis of hourly average wind speed.

It was observed that the region with the highest pressure difference occurred in the region where the C01-C05-SPA buildings and TOWER buildings are located (**Figures 7** and **8**). In the case of northerly wind flow, the highest air exchange rate between buildings was observed in the region where the C01-C05-SPA-TOWER buildings are located. When the ACH around the buildings is evaluated according to the ΔCp values in **Table 1**, it is seen that it is an enough and good level in the regions where there are other building groups other than the building groups where the lowest and highest pressure differences are seen.

It was observed that the region with the highest pressure difference occurred in the region where the C01-C05-SPA buildings are located (**Figures 9** and **10**). In the case of southerly wind flow, the highest air exchange rate between buildings was observed in the region where the C01-C05-SPA is located. When the ACH around the buildings is evaluated according to the ΔCp values in **Table 1**, it is seen that it is an enough and good level in the regions where there are other building groups other than the building groups where the lowest and highest pressure differences are seen.

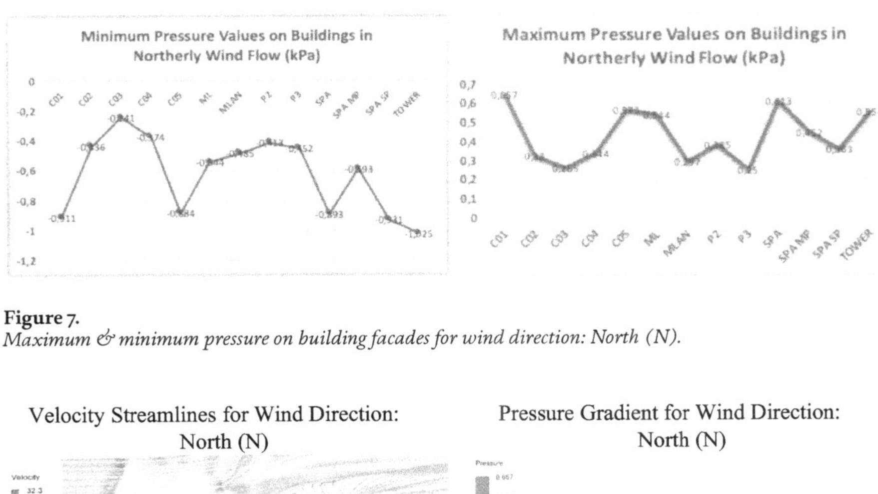

Figure 7.
Maximum & minimum pressure on building facades for wind direction: North (N).

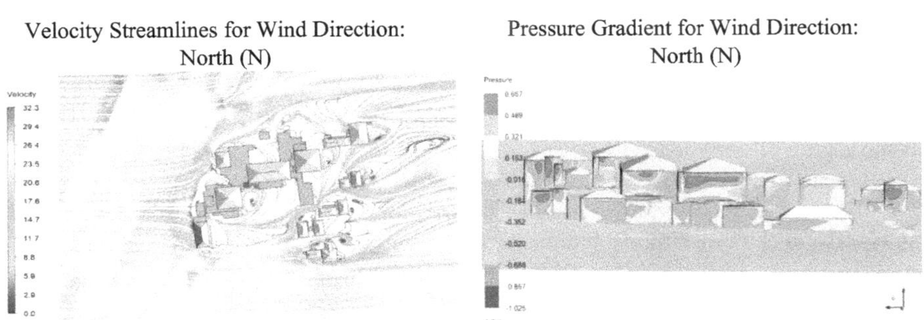

Figure 8.
Velocity streamlines and pressure gradient for wind direction: North (N).

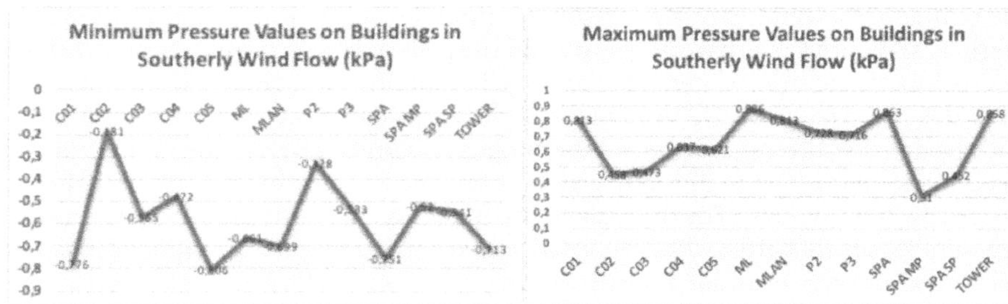

Figure 9.
Maximum & minimum pressure on building facades for wind direction: South (S).

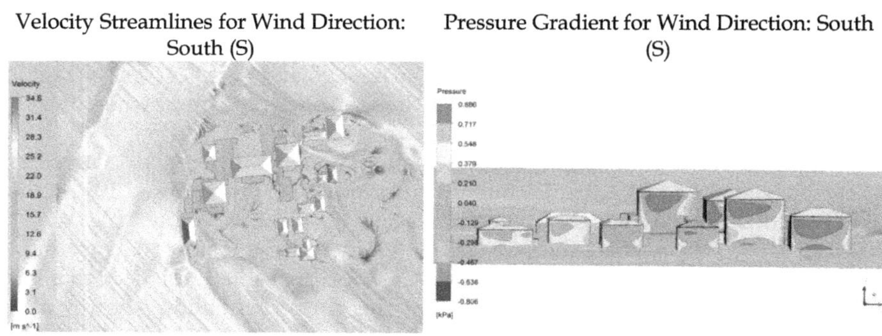

Figure 10.
Velocity streamlines and pressure gradient for wind direction: South (S).

It was observed that the region with the highest pressure difference occurred in the region where the C01-ML-SPA-MP buildings are located (**Figures 11** and **12**). In the case of East wind flow, the highest air exchange rate between buildings was observed in the region where the C01-ML-SPA-MP are located. When the ACH around the buildings is evaluated according to the ΔCp values in **Table 1**, it is seen that it is an enough and good level in the regions where there are other building groups other than the building groups where the lowest and highest pressure differences are seen.

It was observed that the region with the highest pressure difference occurred in the region where the C01-C04-ML-P2-SPA buildings are located (**Figures 13** and **14**). In the case of west wind flow, the highest air exchange rate between buildings was observed in the region where the C01-C04-ML-P2-SPA buildings are located. When the ACH around the buildings is evaluated according to the ΔCp values in **Table 1**, it is seen that it is an enough and good level in the regions where there are other building groups other than the building groups where the lowest and highest pressure differences are seen.

It was observed that the region with the highest pressure difference occurred in the region where the C01-ML-SPA buildings are located (**Figures 15** and **16**). In the case of North–East wind flow, the highest air exchange rate between buildings was observed in the region where the C01-ML-SPA buildings are located. When the ACH around the buildings is evaluated according to the ΔCp values in **Table 1**, it is seen that it is an enough and good level in the regions where there are other building groups other than the building groups where the lowest and highest pressure differences are seen.

It was observed that the region with the highest pressure difference occurred in the region where the C02-P2-P3-SP buildings are located (**Figures 17** and **18**).

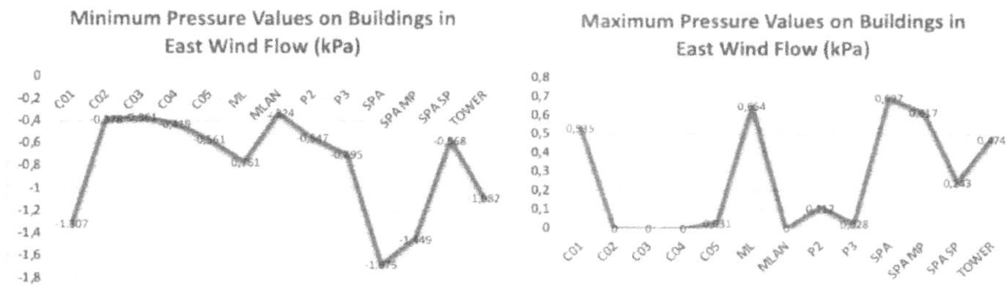

Figure 11.
Maximum & minimum pressure on building facades for wind direction: East (E).

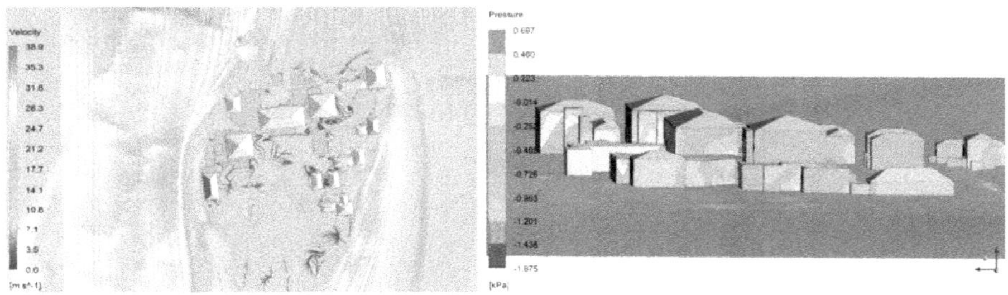

Figure 12.
Velocity streamlines and pressure gradient for wind direction: East (E).

In the case of North-West wind flow, the highest air exchange rate between buildings was observed in the region where the C02-P2-P3-SP buildings are located. When the ACH around the buildings is evaluated according to the ΔCp values in **Table 1**, it is seen that it is an enough and good level in the regions where there are other building groups other than the building groups where the lowest and highest pressure differences are seen.

It was observed that the region with the highest pressure difference occurred in the region where the C01-C05-P2-TOWER buildings are located (**Figures 19** and **20**). In the case of South–East wind flow, the highest air exchange rate between buildings was observed in the region where the C01-C05-P2-TOWER buildings are located. When the ACH around the buildings is evaluated according to the ΔCp values in **Table 1**, it is seen that it is an enough and good level in the regions where there are

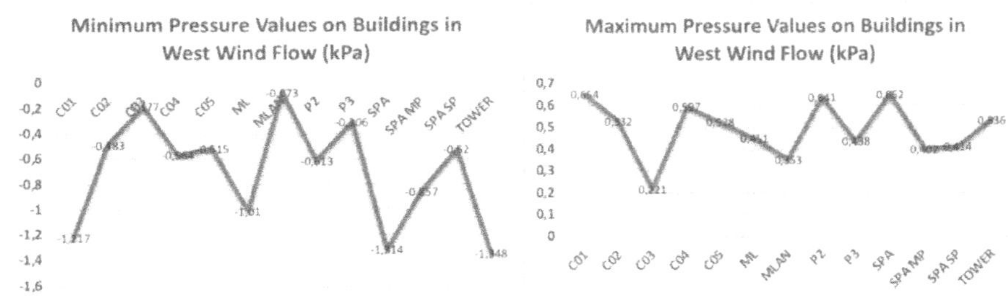

Figure 13.
Maximum & minimum pressure on building facades for wind direction: West (W).

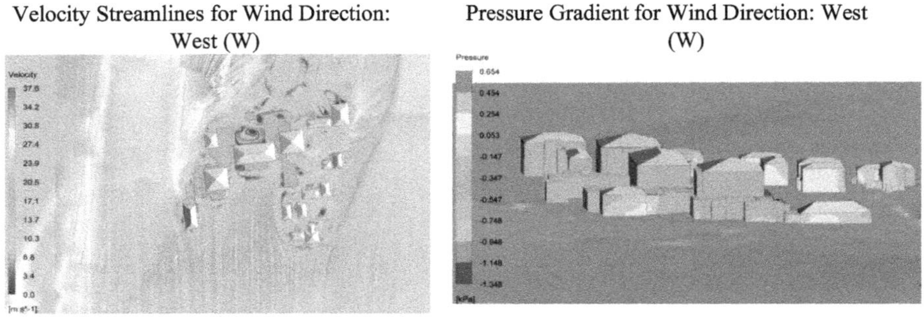

Figure 14.
Velocity streamlines and pressure gradient for wind direction: West (W).

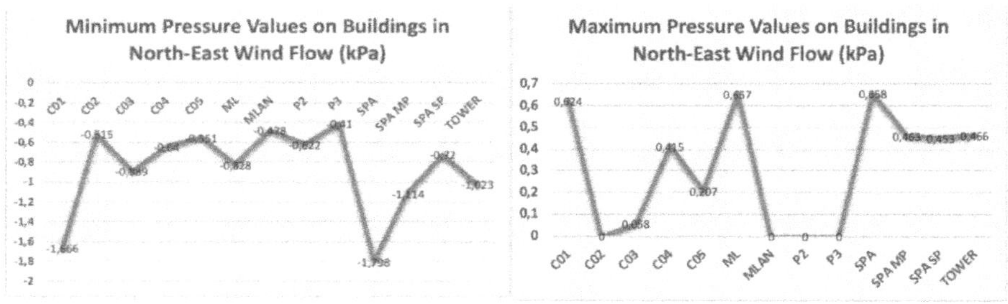

Figure 15.
Maximum & minimum pressure on building facades for wind direction: North-East (NE).

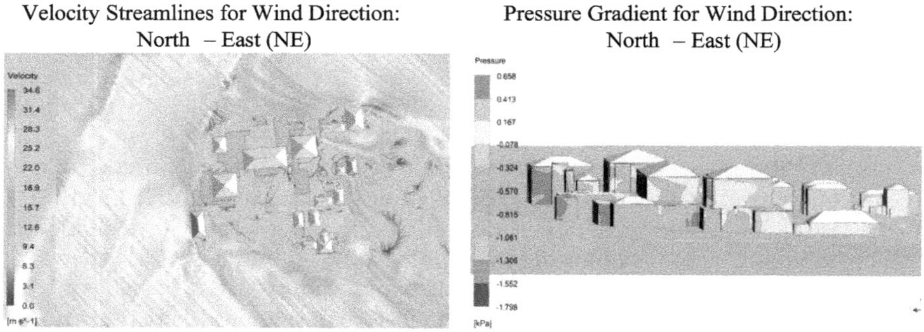

Figure 16.
Velocity streamlines and pressure gradient for wind direction: North-East (NE).

other building groups other than the building groups where the lowest and highest pressure differences are seen.

It was observed that the region with the highest pressure difference occurred in the region where the C01-ML-SPA-SP buildings are located (**Figures 21** and **22**). In the case of South–West wind flow, the highest air exchange rate between buildings was observed in the region where the C01-ML-SPA-SP buildings are located. When the ACH around the buildings is evaluated according to the ΔCp values in **Table 1**, it is seen that it is an enough and good level in the regions where there are other building groups other than the building groups where the lowest and highest pressure differences are seen.

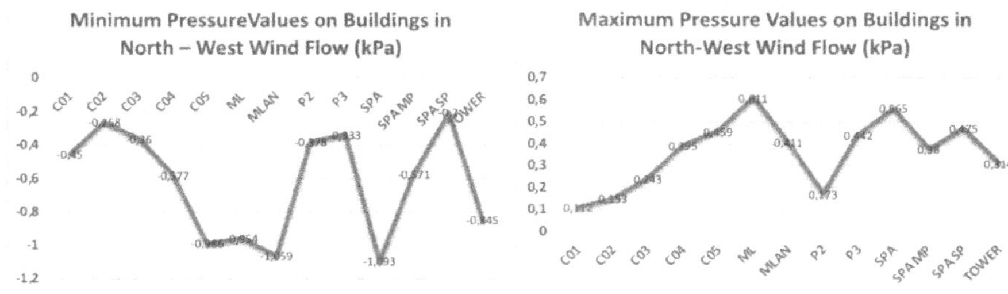

Figure 17.
Maximum & minimum pressure on building facades for wind direction: North–West (NW).

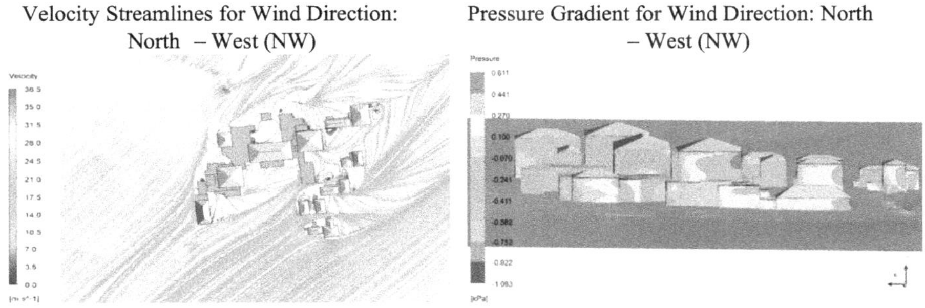

Figure 18.
Velocity streamlines and pressure gradient for wind direction: North-West (NW).

When the maximum and minimum wind pressure values resulting from the wind flows coming from different directions on the roof surfaces of the buildings in the study area were observed, the lowest pressure values were caused by the wind flows coming from the NE and NNE directions (**Figure 23**).

In this study, a total of ten wind directions, four cardinal directions, and six intercardinal directions were discussed on the settlement pattern in the historical Montenegro region, which was considered as a case study. In this chapter, the results of four main directions and four intermediate directions are evaluated in detail. Air exchange in and around buildings is caused by the pressure difference of the wind on the building envelope and the density difference between the outside and indoor air. Therefore, in this study, pressure differences on buildings, which are one of the sources of air changes occurring around the building, are discussed in detail. In this context, the wind directions that cause the most air change on the buildings in the

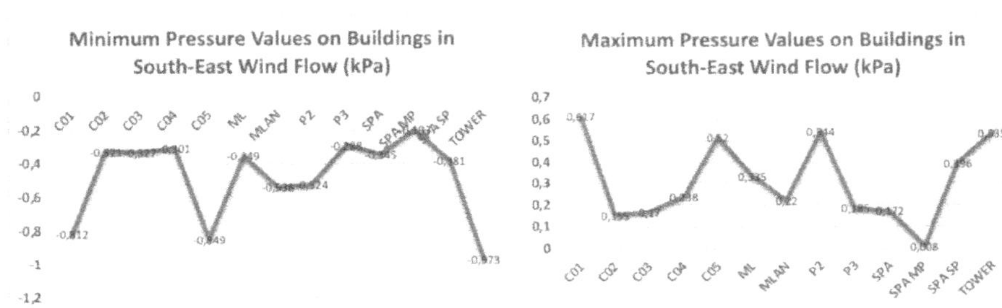

Figure 19.
Maximum & minimum pressure on building facades for wind direction: South-East (SE).

Velocity Streamlines for Wind Direction: South – East (SE)

Pressure Gradient for Wind Direction: South – East (SE)

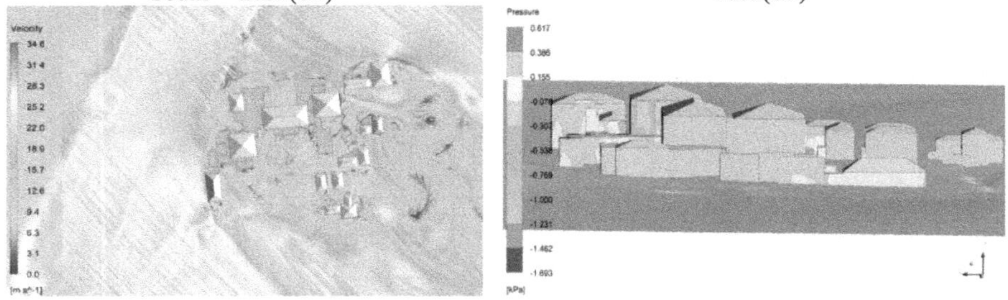

Figure 20.
Velocity streamlines and pressure gradient for wind direction: South-East (NW).

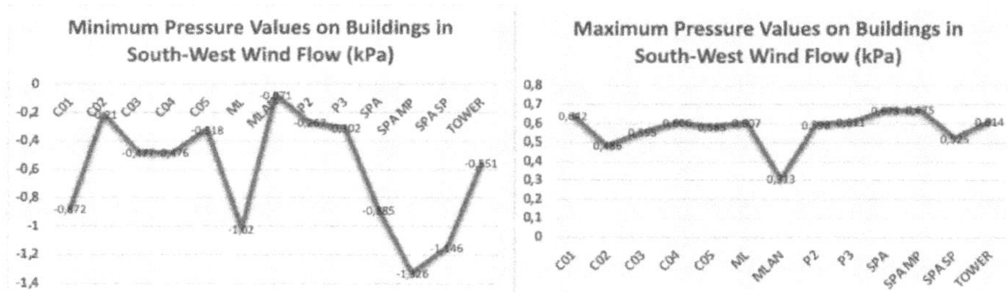

Figure 21.
Maximum & minimum pressure on building facades for wind direction: South-West (SW).

Velocity Streamlines for Wind Direction: South – West (SW)

Pressure Gradient for Wind Direction: South – West (SW)

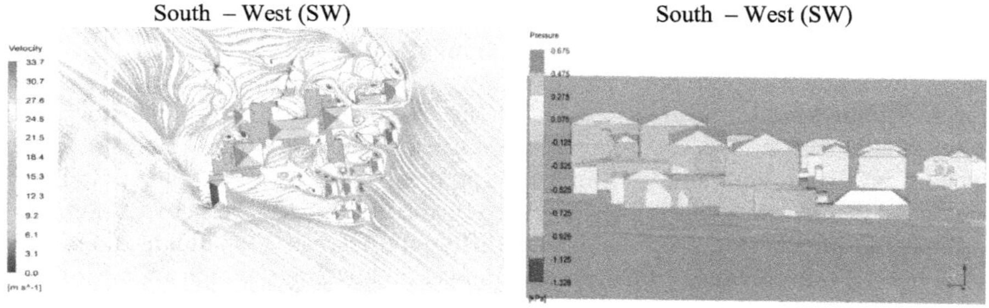

Figure 22.
Velocity streamlines and pressure gradient for wind direction: South-West (SW).

urban texture, which is considered first, are the wind flows coming from the NE and NNE directions.

According to the relationship between the rates of change in the surface pressure differences of the buildings and the air variability between the buildings, the data obtained as a result of the analyzes were examined in detail, it was observed that the C01-C05-ML buildings were the building group with the highest pressure difference and showing similar characteristics in all wind directions. The positive wind pressure is the pressure acting toward the wall, whereas the negative pressure/suction is the pressure acting away from the wall of models. From the pressure contours, it can be observed that on the windward face a positive pressure distribution is observed. The maximum positive pressure is 0.75 kPa at the C01 building on the NNE–ENE

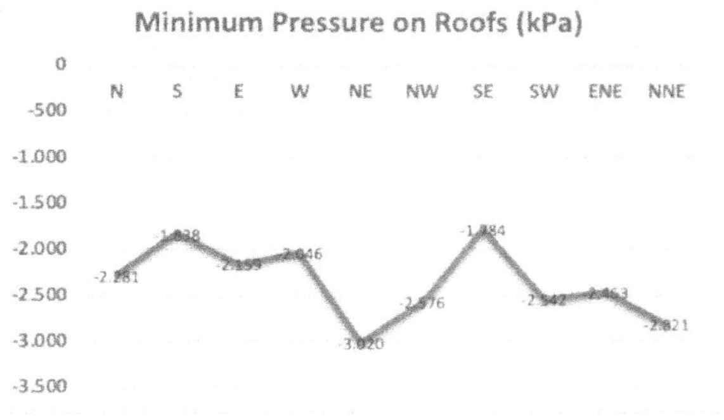

Figure 23.
Maximum & minimum pressure on roofs.

wind direction. Maximum negative pressures (suction pressures) occurred mostly at the ridges and edges of buildings as shown from pressure gradient results.

The wind load also varies between points on the building envelope, with ridges, corners, and edges most susceptible to high wind pressures. These locations are likely to require careful detailing.

When the ACH around the buildings is evaluated according to the ΔCp values in **Table 1**, it is seen that it is an enough and good level in the regions where there are other building groups other than the building groups where the lowest and highest pressure differences are seen.

When the results of the analyzes on all prevailing wind directions and flows are examined in detail, building layouts can be revised and optimized to allow sufficient pressure on the facades of buildings with the lowest pressure values around each group of buildings. Otherwise, buildings with insufficient wind flow and therefore buildings with low-pressure values will be exposed the insufficient natural ventilation performance.

9. Conclusion

The chapter focused on a numerical methodology to assess the effect of building orientation and forms, and street orientations in terms of pedestrian level micro-climatic comfort and natural ventilation of pedestrian level comfort conditions in historical urban texture within the dense structure of the city of the case study area, which is located in the historical texture of Montenegro region. The microclimatic conditions around the buildings in the urban texture depend on the layout design decisions of the buildings forming the texture and accordingly the actual wind condition conditions between the buildings. The actual wind condition is the result of the interaction of all kinds of ground obstacles around the buildings with the wind as well as the coming together of the buildings. It depends on the wind speed and direction at different levels from the ground and the shape of the obstacles (architectural form, physical plan), building airtightness (or permeability), and the position of adjacent buildings relative to each other (urban plan).

Making the design suitable for the microclimate in the urban texture; can be achieved by analyzing the wind speed and pressure differences between the buildings, choosing the appropriate place according to the natural morphology of the land, consciously designing the form of the building, placing the adjacent buildings, and arranging the distances between them correctly. The results obtained in the case study in question showed that; it has been observed that the desired air flows are obtained even at very high wind speed in the areas between buildings, with the effect of the correct settlement in the urban texture and the correct spaces left between the buildings.

Consequently, architects and urban planners need to use wind and comfort analysis software effectively in the design process in-line with microclimatic comfort and sustainable urban planning sensitivity, both when making settlement decisions in historical texture and when making urban design and building architectural project design decisions in open land.

Author details

Enes Yasa[1*] and Kadir Özdemir[2]

1 Faculty of Architecture, Department of Architecture, Istanbul University, Istanbul, Turkey

2 Faculty of Engineering, Department of Mechanical Engineering, Uludag University, Bursa, Turkey

*Address all correspondence to: enesyasa@istanbul.edu.tr

References

[1] United Nations. Transforming Our World: The 2030 Agenda for Sustainable Development. Vol. 2015. New York: Sustainable development.un.org-United Nations Publications; 2015

[2] de Schiller S, Evans JM. Bridging the gap between climate and design at the urban and building scale: Research and application. Energy and Buildings. 1990;**15**(1-2):51-55. Available from: http://linkinghub.elsevier.com/retrieve/pii/037877889090115Y

[3] Ebrahimabadi S. Outdoor Comfort in Cold Climates Integrating Microclimate Factors in Urban Design. Luleå, Sweden: Luleå University of Technology; 2015. Available from: https://www.diva-portal.org/smash/get/diva2:999481/FULLTEXT02.pdf

[4] Erell E. The application of urban climate research in the design of cities. Advances in Building Energy Research. 2008;**2**(1):95-121. Available from: http://www.tandfonline.com/doi/abs/10.3763/aber.2008.0204

[5] Mills G et al. Climate information for improved planning and management of mega cities (needs perspective). Procedia Environmental Sciences. 2010;**1**(1):228-246

[6] Oke TR. Towards a prescription for the greater use of climatic principles in settlement planning. Energy and Buildings. 1984;**7**(1):1-10

[7] Bênia M, Dolz C. Criteria Evaluation for Determining People's Comfort and Safety Conditions Facing Wind Action. Porto Alegre, Brazil: Dissertaxcã o (Grau de Mestre), Departamento de Escola de Engenharia, Universidade Federal do Rio Grande do Sul; 2010. 139 f

[8] Lopes A, Oliveira S, Marques da Silva F. Thresholds of comfort from tests in the wind tunnel: First results. Lisbon: Cities and climate changes. What future? In: Portuguese; Design Guide for Wind, District Plan. Design Guides, Non-statutory: For Guidance Only. 15-16 Maio 2000. Vol. 2. Lisboa: Universidade de Lisboa; 2008

[9] Yasa E. Microclimatic comfort measurements evaluation of building physics: The effect of building form and building settled area, on pedestrian level comfort around buildings. Journal of Building Physics. 2016;**40**(5):472-500. DOI: 10.1177/1744259115621979

[10] Broekhuizen I. Integrating outdoor wind simulation in urban design [master thesis]. Luleå, Sweden: Luleå University of Technology Department of Civil, Environmental and Natural Resources Engineering; 2016. Available from: https://www.diva-portal.org/smash/get/diva2:1028220/FULLTEXT02.pdf

[11] Jun Chung D, Choo M-L. Computational fluid dynamics for urban design: The prospects for greater integration. International Journal of Architectural Computing. 2011;**9**(1):33-54. DOI: 10.1260/14780771.9.1.33

[12] Blocken B. 50 years of computational wind engineering: Past, present and future. Journal of Wind Engineering and Industrial Aerodynamics. 2014;**129**:69-102. DOI: 10.1016/j.jweia.2014.03.008

[13] Blocken B. Computational fluid dynamics for urban physics: Importance, scales, possibilities, limitations and ten tips and tricks towards accurate and reliable simulations. Building and Environment. 2015;**91**:219-245. DOI: 10.1016/j.buil-denv.2015.02.015

[14] Moonen P, Defraeye T, Dorer V, Blocken B, Carmeliet J. Urban physics: Effect of the microclimate on comfort, health and energy demand. Frontiers

of Architectural Research. 2012;**1**:197-228. DOI: 10.1016/j.foar.2012.05.002

[15] Blocken B, Stathopoulos T, Carmeliet J, Hensen JLM. Application of CFD in building performance simulation for the outdoor environment: An overview. Journal of Building Performance Simulation. 2011;**4**:157-184. DOI: 10.1080/19401493.2010.513740

[16] Murakami S. Current status and future trends in computational wind engineering. Journal of Wind Engineering and Industrial Aerodynamics. 1997;**67-68**:3-34. DOI: 10.1016/S0167-6105(97)00230-4

[17] Franke J, Hellsten A, Schlünzen H, Carissimo B. Best Practice Guideline for the CFD Simulation of Flows in the Urban Environment. Hamburg: COST Office; 2007

[18] Roache PJ. Perspective: A method for uniform reporting of grid refinement studies. Journal of Fluids Engineering. 1994;**116**:405-413. DOI: 10.1115/1.2910291

[19] Ai ZT, Mak CM. Modeling of coupled urban wind flow and indoor airflow on a high-density near-wall mesh: Sensitivity analyses and case study for single-sided ventilation. Environmental Modelling & Software. 2014;**60**:57-68. DOI: 10.1016/j.envsoft.2014.06.010

[20] Meroney RN. Ten questions concerning hybrid computational/physical model simulation of wind flow in the built environment. Building and Environment. 2016;**96**:12-21. DOI: 10.1016/j.buildenv.2015.11.005

[21] Murakami S, Ooka R, Mochida A, Yoshida S. CFD analysis of wind climate from human scale to urban scale. Journal of Wind Engineering and Industrial Aerodynamics. 1999;**81**:57-81. DOI: 10.1016/S0167-6105(99)00009-4

[22] van Hooff T, Blocken B. Coupled urban wind flow and indoor natural ventilation modelling on a high-resolution grid: A case study for the Amsterdam ArenA stadium. Environmental Modelling & Software. 2010;**25**:51-65. DOI: 10.1016/j.en-vsoft.2009.07.008

[23] Xie X, Liu C-H, Leung DYC. Impact of building facades and ground heating on wind flow and pollutant transport in street canyons. Atmospheric Environment. 2007;**41**:9030-9049. DOI: 10.1016/j.atmosenv.2007.08.027

[24] Blocken B, Janssen WD, van Hooff T. CFD simulation for pedestrian wind comfort and wind safety in urban areas: General decision framework and case study for the Eindhoven University campus. Environmental Modelling & Software. 2012;**30**:15-34. DOI: 10.1016/j.envsoft.2011.11.009

[25] Stathopoulos T. Computational wind engineering: Past achievements and future challenges. Journal of Wind Engineering and Industrial Aerodynamics. 1997;**67-68**:509-532. DOI: 10.1016/S0167-6105(97)00097-4

[26] Mochida A, Lun IYF. Prediction of wind environment and thermal comfort at pedestrian level in urban area. Journal of Wind Engineering and Industrial Aerodynamics. 2008;**96**:1498-1527. DOI: 10.1016/j.jweia.2008.02.033]

[27] Blocken B, Carmeliet J. A review of wind-driven rain research in building science. Journal of Wind Engineering and Industrial Aerodynamics. 2004;**92**:1079-1130. DOI: 10.1016/j.jweia.2004.06.003

[28] Choi EC. Simulation of wind-driven rain around a building. Journal of Wind Engineering and Industrial Aerodynamics. 1993;**46**:721-729. DOI: 10.1016/0167-6105(93)90342-L

[29] Gousseau P, Blocken B, Stathopoulos T, van Heijst GJF.

CFD simulation of near-field pollutant dispersion on a high-resolution grid: A case study by LES and RANS for a building group in downtown Montreal. Atmospheric Environment. 2011;**45**: 428-438. DOI: 10.1016/j.atmosenv. 2010.09.065

[30] Lateb M, Meroney RN, Yataghene M, Fellouah H, Saleh F, Boufadel MC. On the use of numerical modelling for near-field pollutant dispersion in urban environments—A review. Environmental Pollution. 2015;**208**:271-283. DOI: 10.1016 j.envpol.2015.07.039

[31] Okaze T, Takano Y, Mochida A, Tominaga Y. Development of a new k–ε model to reproduce the aerodynamic effects of snow particles on a flow field. Journal of Wind Engineering and Industrial Aerodynamics. 2015;**144**:118-124. DOI: 10.1016/j.jweia.2015.04.016

[32] Tominaga Y, Mochida A, Okaze T, Sato T, Nemoto M, Motoyoshi H, et al. Development of a system for predicting snow distribution in built-up environments: Combining a mesoscale meteorological model and a CFD model. Journal of Wind Engineering and Industrial Aerodynamics. 2011;**99**:460-468. DOI: 10.1016/j. jweia.2010.12.004

[33] Defraeye T, Blocken B, Carmeliet J. Convective heat transfer coefficients for exterior building surfaces: Existing correlations and CFD modeling. Energy Conversion and Management. 2011;**52**: 512-522. DOI: 10.1016/j.encon-man. 2010.07.026

[34] Kato S, Murakami S, Mochida A, Akabayashi S, Tominaga Y. Velocity-pressure field of cross ventilation with open windows analyzed by wind tunnel and numerical simulation. Journal of Wind Engineering and Industrial Aerodynamics. 1992;**44**:2575-2586. DOI: 10.1016/0167-6105(92)90049-G

[35] Montazeri H, Blocken B, Derome D, Carmeliet J, Hensen JLM. CFD analysis of forced convective heat transfer coefficients at windward building facades: Influence of building geometry. Journal of Wind Engineering and Industrial Aerodynamics. 2015;**146**:102-116. DOI: 10.1016/j.jweia.2015.07.007]

[36] Ramponi R, Blocken B. CFD simulation of cross-ventilation for a generic isolated building: Impact of computational parameters. Building and Environment. 2012;**53**:34-48. DOI: 10.1016/j.buildenv.2012.01.004

[37] Ai ZT, Mak CM. Comparison of single-sided ventilation characteristics between single-story and multi-story buildings due to wind effect. International Journal of Ventilation. 2015;**14**:181-190. DOI: 10.1080/ 14733315.2015.11684079

[38] Chow WK, Hong T. Application of computational fluid dynamics in building services engineering. Building and Environment. 1996;**31**:425-436. DOI: 10.1016 0360-1323(96)00012-1

[39] Launder BE, Kato M. Modelling flow induced oscillations in turbulent flow around a square cylinder. In: Proc Forum on Unsteady Flows. Vol. 157. ASME FED; 1993. pp. 189-199. Available from: https://ci.nii.ac.jp/naid/80007747037/

[40] Li Y, Nielsen PV. CFD and ventilation research. Indoor Air. December 2011;**21**(6):442-453. DOI: 10.1111/j.1600-0668.2011.00723.x

[41] Meroney RN. CFD prediction of airflow in buildings for natural ventilation. In: 11th Am. Conference Wind Eng; San Juan, Puerto Rico; 2009. pp. 1-11

[42] van Hooff T, Blocken B, van Heijst GJF. On the suitability of steady RANS CFD for forced mixing ventilation at transitional slot Reynolds numbers. Indoor Air. 2013;**23**:236-249.

DOI: 10.1111/ina.12010. Available from: https://www.engr.colostate.edu/~meroney/PapersPDF/CEP09-10-1.pdf

[43] Bottillo S, Vollaro A, de L, Galli G, Vallati A. CFD modeling of the impact of solar radiation in a tridimensional urban canyon at different wind conditions. Solar Energy. 2014;**102**:212-222. DOI: 10.1016/j.solener.2014.01.029

[44] Hong B, Lin B. Numerical study of the influences of different patterns of the building and green space on micro-scale outdoor thermal comfort and indoor natural ventilation. Building Simulation. 2014;**7**:525-536. DOI: 10.1007/s12273-014-0167-6

[45] Johansson E, Spangenberg J, Gouvêa ML, Freitas ED. Scale-integrated atmospheric simulations to assess thermal comfort in different urban tissues in the warm humid summer of São Paulo, Brazil. Urban Climate. 2013;**6**:24-43. DOI: 10.1016/j.uclim.2013.08.003

[46] Kim J-J, Pardyjak E, Kim D-Y, Han K-S, Kwon B-H. Effects of building-roof cooling on flow and air temperature in urban street canyons. Asia-Pacific Journal of Atmospheric Sciences. 2014;**50**:365-375. DOI: 10.1007/s13143-014-0023-8

[47] Lee RX, Kardinal Jusuf S, Wong NH. The study of height variation on outdoor ventilation for Singapore's high-rise residential housing estates. International Journal of Low-Carbon Technologies. 2013:1-19. DOI: 10.1093/ijlct/ctt013

[48] Ma J, Li X, Zhu Y. An hourly simulation method for outdoor thermal environment evaluation. Building Simulation. March 2015;**10**(1):15-33. DOI: 10.1007/s12273-014-0206-3

[49] Perini K, Magliocco A. Effects of vegetation, urban density, building height, and atmospheric conditions on local temperatures and thermal comfort. Urban Urban Green. 2014;**13**:495-506. DOI: 10.1016/j.ufug.2014.03.003

[50] Vollaro AL, de Simone G, Romagnoli R, Vallati A, Bottillo S. Numerical study of urban canyon microclimate related to geometrical parameters. Sustainability. 2014;**6**: 7894-7905. DOI: 10.3390/su6117894

[51] Wang Y, Zhong K, Zhang N, Kang Y. Numerical analysis of solar radiation effects on flow patterns in street canyons. Engineering Applications of Computational Fluid Mechanics. 2014;**8**:252-262. DOI: 10.1080/19942060.2014.11015511

[52] Yahia MW, Johansson E. Influence of urban planning regulations on the microclimate in a hot dry climate: The example of Damascus, Syria. Journal of Housing and the Built Environment. 2013;**28**:51-65. DOI: 10.1007/s10901-012-9280-y

[53] Yahia MW, Johansson E. Landscape interventions in improving thermal comfort in the hot dry city of Damascus, Syria—The example of residential spaces with detached buildings. Landscape and Urban Planning. 2014;**125**:1-16. DOI: 10.1016/j.landurbplan.2014.01.014

[54] Toparlar Y et al. A review on the CFD analysis of urban microclimate. Renewable and Sustainable Energy Reviews. 2017;**80**(2017):1613-1640

[55] Blocken B, Carmeliet J. High-resolution wind-driven rain measurements on a low-rise building—Experimental data for model development and model validation. Journal of Wind Engineering and Industrial Aerodynamics. 2005;**93**:905-928. DOI: 10.1016/j.jweia.2005.09.004

[56] Schatzmann M, Rafailidis S, Pavageau M. Some remarks on the

validation of small-scale dispersion models with field and laboratory data. Journal of Wind Engineering and Industrial Aerodynamics. 1997; **67-68**:885-893. DOI: 10.1016/S0167-6105(97) 00126-8

[57] Schatzmann M, Leitl B. Issues with validation of urban flow and dispersion CFD models. Journal of Wind Engineering and Industrial Aerodynamics. 2011;**99**:169-186. DOI: 10.1016/j.jweia.2011.01.005

[58] van Hooff T, Blocken B. Full-scale measurements of indoor environmental conditions and natural ventilation in a large semi-enclosed stadium: Possibilities and limitations for CFD validation. Journal of Wind Engineering and Industrial Aerodynamics. 2012; **104-106**:330-341. DOI: 10.1016/j.jweia.2012.02.009

[59] Blocken B, Stathopoulos T, van Beeck JPAJ. Pedestrian-level wind conditions around buildings: A review of wind-tunnel and CFD techniques and their accuracy for wind comfort assessment. Building and Environment. 2016;**100**(2016):50-81

[60] Blocken B. LES over RANS in building simulation for outdoor and indoor applications: A foregone conclusion? Building Simulation. 2018;**11**:821-870

[61] Yoshie R, Mochida A, Tominaga Y, Kataoka H, Harimoto K, Nozu T, et al. Cooperative project for CFD prediction of pedestrian wind environment in the Architectural Institute of Japan. Journal of Wind Engineering and Industrial Aerodynamics. 2007;**95**(2007):1551-1578

[62] Moreau S, Gandemer J. Guide sur la climatisation naturelle de l'habitat en climat tropical humide. Tome III Principes aérodynamiques de la ventilation naturelle dans l'habitat tropical collectif—CSTB. 2002. ISBN 2-86891-302-4

[63] Franke JC, Hirsch AG, Jensen HW, Krüs M, Schatzmann PS, Westbury SD. et al. Recommendations on the use of CFD in wind engineering. In van Beeck JPAJ, editor. Proceedings of the International Conference on Urban Wind Engineering and Building Aerodynamics: COST Action C14—Impact of Wind and Storm on City Life and Built Environment, May 5 - 7, C.1.1 - C.1.11. Belgium: Rhode-Saint-Genèse; 2004. ISBN: 2-930389-11-7

[64] Blocken B, Persoon J. Pedestrian wind comfort around a large football stadium in an urban environment: CFD simulation, validation and application of the new Dutch wind nuisance standard. Journal of Wind Engineering and Industrial Aerodynamics. 2009;**97**(5-6):255-270

[65] Pietrzyk K. Probabilistic modelling of air infiltration and heat loss in low-rise buildings. In: Building technology/building physics, school of architecture [Ph.D. thesis]. Sweden: Chalmers University of Technology; 2000

[66] Pietrzyk K, Czmoch I. On Risk and Reliability Studies of Climate-Related Building Performance, Risk Assessment. Valentina Svalova: IntechOpen; 2018

[67] Handa K, Kärrholm G, Lindquist T. BFR, Report T3, Stockholm. 1979

[68] Ginger JD, Mehta KC, Yeatts BB. Journal of Wind Engineering & Industrial Aerodynamicss. 1997;**72**: 163-174

[69] Pietrzyk K. Analysis of wind speed and wind pressure on the facades in frequency domain for the modelling of air change rate. In: E3S Web of Conferences 172, 9005 0 (2020). 2020. DOI: 10.1051/e3sconf/20201720 005

[70] Foss RN. Ground Plane Wind Shear Interaction on Acoustic Transmission. WA-RD 033.1. Washington State

Department of Transportation. Available from: http://www.wsdot.wa.gov/Research/Reports/000/033.1.htm; 1978 [Accessed: May 30, 2007]

[71] Tominaga Y, Mochida A, Yoshie R, Kataoka H, Nozu T, Yoshikawa M. et al. AIJ guidelines for practical applications of CFD to pedestrian wind environment around buildings. Journal of Wind Engineering and Industrial Aerodynamics. 2008;**96**(10-11):1749-1761

Chapter 7

Trajectories of RNA Virus Mutation Hidden by Evolutionary Alternate Reality Thermodynamic Endpoints in Transformations in Response to Abiotic Habitat Stresses

Farida Hanna Campbell

Abstract

Viruses ensure the vital redistribution of nutrients to maintain sustainability in an ecosystem. This includes repair and survival, growth and evolution thanks to the efficient nutrient recycling and infectious rates of viruses throughout a stressed-ecosystem. If evolution in space–time can be defined by multiple planes which change position according to the evolution rate of the habitat, then the locations and volumes of returning chronic infectious viruses will appear in a logical predictable fashion based on the lissajous trajectory based on thermodynamic modeling.

Keywords: SARS-CoV-2, Mutation, Habitat, Sustainability, livestock, ecology

1. Introduction

Virus outbreaks are largely RNA viruses whose rapid spread triggers overwhelming reduction in population and disease, following abiotic habitat stress extremes. The ability to predict a future outbreak has been significant to much research in epidemiology, many of which target statistical socioeconomics and victim genetic parameters, rather than the brutal biophysics of virus outbreak timing in its source environment. To do so requires an introduction to thermodynamics.

Virus life cycle thermodynamics are well documented [1–5] including models for the statistical mechanics and thermodynamics of virus evolution, mutations and host-infection [5, 6]. A virus always would have a stronger negative Gibbs free energy than its host in order to drive the synthesis of viral components through the hijacking of host life machinery to develop its growth products - namely virion nucleic acid, virion protein capsid and occasionally a virion lipid envelope [7]. Cross-species infection by virus are intrinsic to immunity gene instruction sharing which teaches the host how to survive abiotic stresses such as drought and frost. In this way, evolution from gene transfer and resulting changes in biodiversity are mutually interdependent. Later in this chapter we refer to this as alternate reality

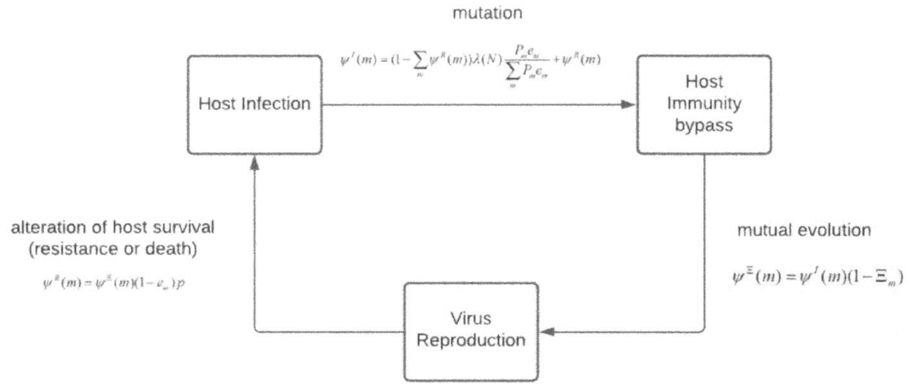

Figure 1.
Virus life cycle, adapted from Jones et al. The changing states of all viruses must be computed self-consistently over the entire virus life cycle. The figure shows three important stages of the model virus life cycle: 1. infection (entering the host cell), (I); 2. virus mutation-based positive host-immune by-pass (Ξ); and, the successful reproduction and progeny release from the infected host cell (R). Also shown are the equations for cell occupancy at each stage [5], ψ.

formation, representing the conjoined species and habitat changes, following the stress-impetus. If so, then micro-environments may be defined as a microbial system of eco-thermodynamic symbionts which exchange nutrients mutually between them and their shared habitat [8]. The habitat might represent the microbiome of a gut system of a human. The thermodynamic balance throughout the habitat includes a maximally-sustained growth between the habitat's microbial biodiversity [6, 9]. It follows therefore, that changes to the eco-thermodynamics from abiotic and biotic stressors to the environment [9–11] results in key genetic signaling responses. These include the non-coding RNA polymerases that help species respond to disruptions to the ecothermodynamic stability. The genetic signals enable the microorganism to escape the stresses [12–16]. Species motility allows them to arrive where nutrient and moisture resources are more readily available. Virus infection and reinfection triggers resistance signaling and repair to any cellular and genetic damage [17, 18]. In so doing, the stress response can also trigger conversion of nonpathogenic bacteria and viruses into pathogenic versions. The coronavirus is also a good example of this, with mutations correlated to the stressed habitat conditions [19–21] resulting in infectious outbreaks [22]. The outbreaks help biodiversity readiness to survive. In this chapter we refer to this survival process as via thermodynamically-driven rates of virus infection and species evolution (**Figure 1**).

2. Abiotic stresses and relationship to virus outbreaks

Earlier we introduced the definition of general stress response (GSR) which is an advanced subject describing multiple gene expression, mutation, protein transcription, mRNA translation, intracellular endoplasmic reticulum repair, DNA recombination and repair, epigenetic imprinting and motility [23]. It also includes specific RNA polymerases, such as in alphaproteobacteria, where the GSR is under the transcriptional control of the alternative sigma factor EcfG. EcfG regulates genes for proteins that are associated with the regulation of motility (escape) and biofilm formation (adhesion), by binding to the RNA polymerase to redirect general protein transcription towards stress response genes [12]. The stress response can include conversion from non pathogenic to pathogenic mechanisms to acquire nutrients under harsher, more competitive conditions. Infections prepare the now-pathogenic bacteria to withstand diverse host environments [24] defined by any range of abiotic stresses, whether in acidity, alkalinity, radioactivity, temperature extremes, nutrient and resource scarcity, drought or any mixed combinations of stresses and durations. Viruses may exploit the presence of these stress responses, including the RNA-dependent RNA polymerases for replication of their genomes or, in retroviruses, the reverse transcriptase to produce new viral DNA which can be integrated into the host DNA under its integrase function [25]. Interestingly, the arrival of virulence and infection of genes at specific, appropriate times, frequencies and sites also stimulates patterns that resemble wide-sweeping oscillations of outbreaks (**Figure 2**) [24, 26].

Formalisms in statistical mechanics and thermodynamics have been used previously in order to describe the lifecycle of pathogenic viruses, from mutation to evolution and infection [5].

Viral mutation rates are caused by a number of processes including:

- Polymerase errors
- Ability of a virus to correct DNA mismatches by proofreading and/or post replicative repair
- Host's enzymes
- Spontaneous nucleic acid damage
- Special genetic mutator elements.

Retroviruses are viruses with RNA-containing virions and a cellular DNA stage [27]. Para-retroviruses are viruses with DNA-containing virions and a cellular RNA stage [20]. Both mutate and evolve at rates similar to riboviruses. Riboviruses are non-reverse transcribing RNA viruses [28].

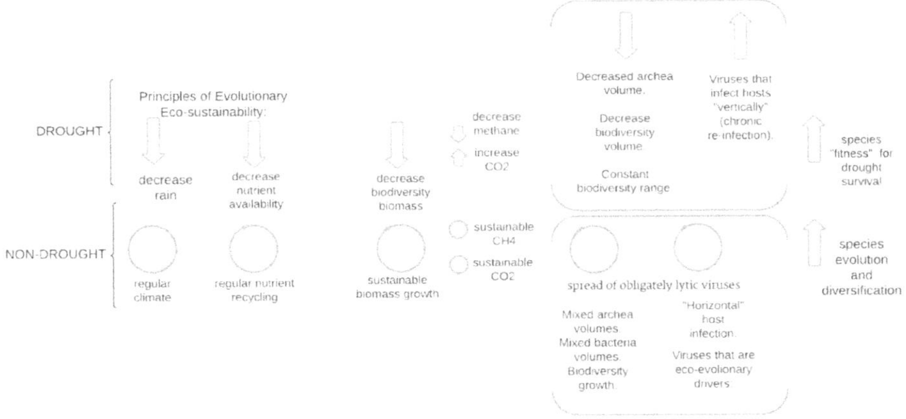

Figure 2.
Comparison of drought and non-drought virus infection patterns, where drought represents an example of abiotic stress impact on infectiousness-patterns: Circles represent cycles of growth, and cycles of nutrient (gas) exchange between symbiont species in a given habitat; Drought triggers vertical (chronic re-infection of a host), likely due to the limited host-population growth in times of drought-related resource limitations. Horizontal infection results in chronic virus re-infection, and can include host DNA to virus transfer. Source: the author, F.H. Campbell.

In general, the list of habitat stresses on bacterial mutation rates can result in:

a. Hyper-mutations based on mutator mutations over very short periods of time; this may be momentary for physiological or growth benefits, as well as for more established evolution [29, 30], referred to later in this chapter as vertical evolution;

b. Microbial mutation rates such as via transient mutators from what seems to resemble *errors* of transcription, translation, and molecular segregation (later in this chapter, we dispute the definition of errors based on changing the planar dimensions of evolution); microbial mutation rates can contribute to slight and single mutations or to vibrant multiple mutations per genome per replication [31, 32].

c. Bacterial hypermutation for rapid survival, such as immediate stress-response related DNA synthesis [32–34]; Hyper-mutability changes are driven by only a few cells in any population at any time and include translesion bypass, which leaves lesions un-repaired during starvation situations. Drake and Ripley cite examples among microbes that include fully constitutive, as in phage T4 [32, 35] to strongly inducible hypermutations described in Walker (1984) for *E. coli* SOS responses. The latter dramatically increase mutation rates in one full cell generation, even in undamaged parts of the genome [30].

d. Stress-related chemical reaction-type mutations, such as sudden transfer of microbial organisms into alien environments; this represents immediate and complex adaptation; later in this chapter, this can describe lateral evolution mutations. At least 10 genes can generate mutator mutations such as for *E. coli* populations which generate roughly 10^{-6}–10^{-5} mutator mutants per replication [32].

e. DNA damage-related hypermutations, such as in resting genomes and in a replication-independent fashion; when non-rest state DNA replication resumes, this may even alter transcription to produce a mutant phenotype before replication [32, 35, 36].

In Drake et al., mutation-rate calculations for DNA-type viruses are based on the effective genome size G_e for transforming a mutant frequency f into a mutation rate, where f is measured for large populations that had accumulated mutants in the putative absence of selection. In Zhao et al., the mutation rate in the SARS-CoV genome was estimated to be 0.80–2.38 × 10–3 nucleotide substitution per site per year, well within the magnitude of RNA viruses. The most recent common ancestor of the 16 sequences was inferred to be present as early as the spring of 2002, the outbreak of SARS [37]. Khailany et al. describe the current SARS-CoV-2 with genome size between 29.8 kb to 29.9 kb and 116 mutations implicated in the severity of infection and spread - including the three most common mutations: 8782C > T in ORF1ab gene, 28144 T > C in ORF8 gene and 29095C > T in the N gene [38]. For comparison, examples of mutation rates for non-SARS viruses in general are shown in the table below (**Table 1**).

Pathogenic RNA viruses that encode complex RNA-dependent RNA polymerase bearing a 3′ exonuclease domain will mutate slowly [40, 41] and indeed, the SARS-CoV-2 viruses mutate in four months in order to accumulate knowledge about the infective host [19] and successfully bypass the host immunity, including those who were early-vaccinated such as with mRNA, mod-mRNA vaccines and possibly

Class	Virus	Genome size (kb)	Mean mutation rate (s/n/c)
ss(+)RNA	Bacteriophage Qβ	4.22	1.10E-03
	Tobacco mosaic virus	6.4	8.70E-06
	Human rhinovirus 14	7.13	6.90E-05
	Poliovirus 1 (PV-1)	7.44	9.00E-05
	Tobacco etch virus (TEV)	9.49	1.20E-05
	Hepatitis C virus (HCV)	9.65	1.20E-04
	Murine hepatitis virus (MHV)	31.4	3.50E-06
ss(−)RNA	Vesicular stomatitis virus (VSV)	11.2	3.50E-05
	Influenza A virus (FLUVA)	13.6	2.30E-05
	Influenza B virus (FLUVB)	14.5	1.70E-06
dsRNA	Bacteriophage ϕ6	13.4	1.60E-06
Reverse transcribing	Duck hepatitis B virus (DHBV)	3.03	2.00E-05
	Spleen necrosis virus (SNV)	7.8	3.70E-05
	Murine leukemia virus (MLV)	8.33	3.00E-05
	Bovine leukemia virus (BLV)	8.42	1.70E-05
	Human T-cell leukemia virus (HTLV-1)	8.5	1.60E-05
	Human immunodeficiency virus type 1 (HIV-1)	9.18	2.40E-05
	HIV-1 (free virions)		
	HIV-1 (cellular DNA)		
	Foamy virus		
	Rous sarcoma virus (RSV)	9.4	1.40E-04
ssDNA	Bacteriophage ϕX174	5.39	1.10E-06
	Bacteriophage M13	6.41	7.90E-07
dsDNA	Bacteriophage ƛ	48.5	5.40E-07
	Herpes simplex virus type 1	152	5.90E-08
	Bacteriophage T2	169	9.80E-08

Table 1.
Mutation rates of non-SARS pathogenic viruses and genome size. Adapted from Sanjuán et al. [39].

others will inevitably show success by activation of cellular anti-viral proteins known as zinc antiviral proteins (ZAP) and APOBEC-3. ZAP and APOBEC-3 diminish a virus by detecting its foreign CG-dinucleotide before it infects, simply by comparing it to its own native RNA as part of natural innate immunity response. However, the slow-rate (four months) SARS mutations allow the virus to successfully bypass this antiviral protein in mass-vaccinated humans.

Thermodynamic models in the research all consistently recognize that a cell is infected with one or more virus particles, and that each infecting genome is copied iteratively such that complementary strands accumulate in the host, eventually producing final strands of the same polarity as the infecting strand, so that these final strands are then packaged and released throughout the host [30]. It is assumed that "final" strands rarely (or never) re-enter the beginning of the cycle within a single infection. In this way, the mutation frequency f is the same as the mutation rate μ per replication. And so, if n number of complementary strands are copied from a template and if μ is the mutation rate per copying event, then the number of mutations will be $n\mu$, and $f = n\mu/n = \mu$.

But, thermodynamic research of habitats does not establish relationships between mutations and spreadrate /infectiousness locations in a habitat and what drives the location: Is it just the population dysbiosis? Is it just the habitat stress?

For example, J might represent a infectious spread rate and N_j the infected population, the number of mutations occurring in a pathogenic outbreak could be described an effective infection rate μ_{ij} per habitat.

$J_i = \sum_{j=1}^{n} \mu_{ij} N_j$ for pathogenic virus infection spread rate requiredwhere, μ_{ij} is the infection matrix which in the limit as $\lim_{N_j \to 0} \left(\frac{\partial J_i}{\partial N_i} \right)$ and is symmetric when $\mu_{ij} = \mu_{ji}$ and which could be crudely integrated over an entire habitat per host-species non-homogeneously over time. However, this sort of model evaluation is largely unable to describe the wavelike nature of outbreaks in the infections caused by virus mutation following an ecological threat. In addition, no part of it satisfactorily allows sensitivity to the interaction between the host and virus, as a thermodynamic instability which would result in the oscillatory periodic moment of spread. We need a method to include entropy production $\frac{\partial s}{\partial t} + \nabla J_s = \sigma; \sigma \geq 0$ and the flux of pathogenic virus throughout a habitat in response to a habitat stress, resulting in a non-uniform infectiousness.

But how can we forecast thermodynamic stability of a habitat in this equation? What are the specific thermodynamic limits and how is this represented or accommodated in mutation responsive virus nature?

We might try to show that, when an ecosystem's resources are severely constrained, a higher re-infection rate occurs. This requires investigation of models from the research to do with the replication conditions in RNA viruses that predominate post-stress outbreaks. If so, we find from Drake et al. and Pathak and Temin [32, 42]:

1. Linear replication RNA virus conditions: mutation rate $\mu_{lin} = f$ regardless of the extent of growth

2. Binary replication RNA virus conditions: $\mu_{bin} = (f - f_0)/\ln(N/N_0)$ where N_0 is the initial and N is the final population size, including for $N_0 > 1/\mu_{bin}$, for $N_0 < 1/\mu_{bin}$, and $\mu_{bin} = f/\ln(N\mu_{bin})$

3. The average of μ_{bin} and μ_{lin} is μ_m. μ_{lin} is at a maximum always at least an order of magnitude greater than μ_{bin}

4. Lytic virus mutation rates from repeated replication of the virus in each infective cycle. One infected cell yields viruses carrying several new mutations per particle, the majority of which are deleterious. That is, a relatively high mutation rate is correlated with characteristic low specific infectivities (infectious particles per physical particle) in pathogenic RNA.

5. Mutation rates in retrovirus or retrotransposon chromosome elements replicate exactly three times per infective cycle.

   a. Transcription by the host RNA polymerase produces one RNA genome.

   b. Reverse transcriptase then catalyzes two replications in order to generate a DNA-based chromosome that integrates into the host chromosome, including of a different cell for packaged retroviruses, or of the same cell in the case of a retrotransposon.

c. Thereafter it assumes a far lower mutation rate so that the resulting mutant frequency is the sum of the mutation rates of all three steps. Drake [43] notes that retro-element rates are roughly an order of magnitude lower than the RNA-virus rates and that retroviral mutation rates do not appreciably reduce specific infectivity and render more resistance to increased mutation rates (e.g., Spleen necrosis virus, which is obliterated only after a roughly 13-fold increase.)

After obtaining the entropy production and mutation rates for given species of infectious viruses, we need an understanding of the host immunity resistance proteins and their interactivity with virus mutability [41, 44]. Mutability of the viruses is correlated inversely with genome size [30, 41]. Unfortunately the solution for modeling becomes much more complex because each host immunity resistance proteins are transient in very short intervals of expression and mutating virus variants are population-wide processes rather than merely intracellular-driven [41].

It is worthwhile to insert a comment here: For example, SARS-CoV-2 viruses colonize specifically anaerobic proteobacteria commonly found in the gut of livestock. These bacteria likewise have a range of mutations according to abiotic environmental stress related gene-signaling. They include *Prevotella* (found in the gut of bovine, ovine, swine, avian livestock); Streptococcus (bovine, ovine and camel), *Bacterioides* (gut of swine, and hind-gut of avians) and *Mycoplasma pneumoniae*, *Haemophilus influenzae and Pseudomonas aeruginos,* which can be hosted by all the previously listed livestock. It is interesting to observe that livestock experience the most significant of stresses in rapid successive seasonal intervals (every six and nine months) when livestock are brought in large herds to be slaughtered. The slaughter process supports full resistance mutation processes resulting in the pathogenic conversion of these bacteria: animal confinement stress, heat-stress, food-stress (particularly before slaughter), dehydration stress, anxiety-panic stress, and trauma to the tissue from slaughter (and related death practices, such as live-animal steaming) and, of course, maternal stress towards offspring also butchered en measles. Vascular swelling from butchering [45–47] is part of the explosive discharge of gut-related bacterial organisms from slaughterhouse events into the ambient environment: This explains the relatively constant high per-genome mutation rate observed (0.003 per round of copy) [41] and at levels of 1,000,000 animals per week per slaughterhouse neighborhoods and livestock post-butchering products are all visibly the same location where COVID19, dementia, gastrointestinal diseases outbreaks are their absolutely highest [45, 48, 49]. In the period of 2019 through the year of this chapter's writing, COVID19 disease outbreaks were consistently describable as oscillatory or wavelike with dense centers and radiating lines of trajectory between the centers [50–52]. The locations did not repeat but also showed a pattern of shifting so that new outbreak locations or "hotspots" were observed. In mapping these outbreaks, the author noticed a clever relationship to mathematical lissajous-like oscillations. Would it be possible to describe the relationship between infectious spread so-called waves of outbreaks as a lissajous parametric trajectory?

3. Lissajous parametric equations: the requirements for describing virus-mutation evolution relative to infection and evolution, thermodynamically

The Lissajous figures graphically represent the relationship between two quantities that have an oscillatory behavior as a function of a certain variable, usually but

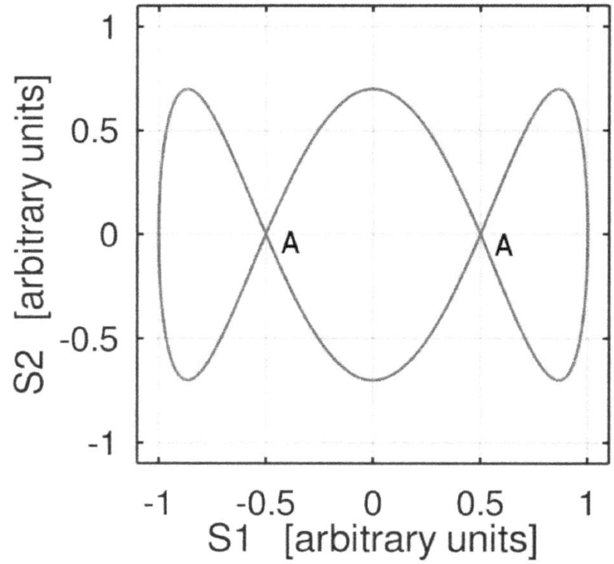

Figure 3.
Example of a Lissajous figure for variables that oscillate with different periods.

not necessarily, time. In general, suppose that the two quantities have amplitudes S_1^0 and S_2^0 and repeat themselves with periods T_1 and T_2. Their behavior as a function of time can be represented by the two relations:

$$S_1(t) = S_1^0 \bullet sin\left(2\pi \frac{t}{T_1}\right) \tag{1}$$

$$S_2(t) = S_2^0 \bullet sin\left(2\pi \frac{t}{T_2} + \varphi\right) \tag{2}$$

The quantities in brackets are called phases, and the term ϕ is the delay with which the variable S_2 follows the variable S_1. The Lissajous figures are completely determined by the amplitudes S_1^0 and S_2^0, by the periods T_1 and T_2 and by the delay ϕ; these parameters can be reconstructed from their shape.

In particular, the Lissajous figures have nodes (see A in **Figure 3**) when the periods of oscillation T_1 and T_2 are not equal. In the case of the interaction between host and virus it is very unlikely that this will happen, since the mutations of one are strictly a consequence of the other and it is improbable that the mutations of the virus (for example, represented by the thermodynamics that describes specific genes involved in mutator mutations), oscillate many times within a single oscillation of mutations of the host. This requires evaluation of evidence from experimental data. For now, we will limit ourselves to the case where $T_1 = T_2$ and call T_R their common period of oscillation, which in this case is the repetition time for repeated infectious outbreaks. In general it will depend on the mutation rate μ (representing linear, binary, lytic or other type of RNA mutation), so we can generically indicate the phasic term $2\pi/T_R$ as $\delta(\mu)$.

We therefore obtain:

$$S_1(t) = S_1^0 \bullet sin\,(\delta(\mu)) \tag{3}$$

$$S_2(t) = S_2^0 \bullet sin\,(\delta(\mu) + \varphi) \tag{4}$$

When the two curves have the same period, the shape of the Lissajous figure can be a straight line (such as direct infection of an immediate host as seen in person-to-person pathogenesis), or an ellipse or a circle, depending on the amplitudes S_1^0 and S_2^0 and on the delay ϕ over increasing time. This takes on an important meaning: it is the speed with which the viral mutation responds to that of the host. For ecothermodynamic stability to be preserved, the range of mutations and spread in virus outbreaks would be isenthalpic, such that the sum of each mutation (infection) redistributes the energy equivalent to the volume of excess, so that the enthalpy remains unchanged.

Human dysbiosis is known to be created by the presence of anaerobic proteobacteria species [53–55] that are found in the hindgut and gut of livestock, mentioned earlier. Specifically, we noted that they include the same species upon which SARS-CoV-2 virus infect leading to disease in their human hosts: we observe virus-infection represents symbiont-driven breakdown within the human oro-tracheal and gastrointestinal tracts [56], and not only for COVID19 disease [57–59] repeatedly in locations of high-resource consumption (slaughterhouse districts) that continue to operate during and following a severe drought.

We can therefore summarily describe three limiting cases that have in fact been matched with infectious spread in the SARS-CoV-2 outbreaks and which make the Lissajous model ideal:

1. Immediate response. The viral-host infectious adaptation is immediate and $\phi = 0$. In this case the Lissajous figure is reduced to a straight line, whose angle is given by the ratio S_2^0/S_1^0 (**Figure 4**).

2. Quadrature response: In this case, the Lissajous figure becomes an ellipse describing the rate of infection from the SARS-CoV-2 mutations, with width

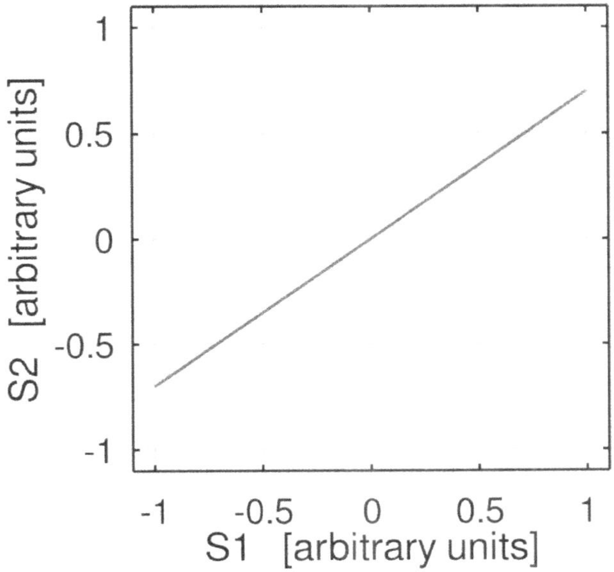

Figure 4.
Example of a Lissajous figure with zero delay, degenerating into a line.

S_1^0 and height S_2^0 within repeated intervals. These can be correlated to mutation frequency per 400th infected patient [60] or relative to the habitat as described earlier [19, 60]. Formally we have $\phi = \frac{\pi}{2}$; from the mathematical point of view it corresponds to the fact that the maximum amplitude of the pathogenic mutations and the **maximum rate of change** of the virus mutations coincide (and vice versa) with the eco-thermodynamics of the habitat as it gravitates towards a new evolved thermodynamic equilibrium. This period theoretically is an estimate of the transition time for mutation-related events (infecting survivors, reduction of population) on behalf of thermodynamic sustainability of the habitat after abiotic stress. This case therefore appears significant from an evolutionary point of view because it indicates that the maximum adaptive effort of the host/virus occurs in response to the peak of virus/host mutations.

In this case, if the phase shift is $\phi = \frac{\pi}{2}$ the second function is transformed into the cosine of the phase and the term ϕ disappears (**Figure 5**).

3. Response in antiphase. It corresponds to the case in which $\phi = \pi$ and the Lissajous figure again becomes a line, with a negative angle this time. It corresponds to the case in which the maximum of host-virus infectious-mutations, and their rates of change are of the opposite sign: the mutations of the virus increase while those of the host decrease (and vice versa). In fact, the most important part of a public health anti-outbreak effectiveness strategy of a technology would be based on measured reduction of the delay component for a given pathogen outbreak, thermodynamically. This alone, according to the author, means that that the relationship between delay $\phi = \pi$ and a strategy to prevent outbreaks can be evaluated based on a valid virus-specific spread-moment relationship to the habitat (**Figure 6**).

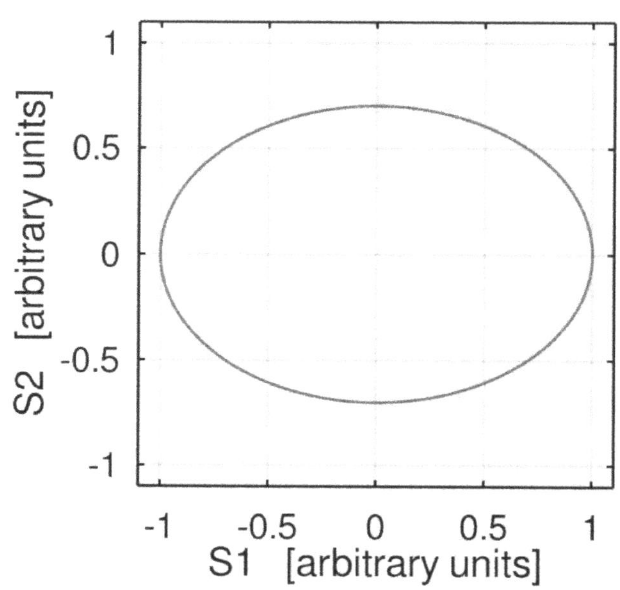

Figure 5.
Example of a Lissajous figure with $\frac{\pi}{2}$-delay.

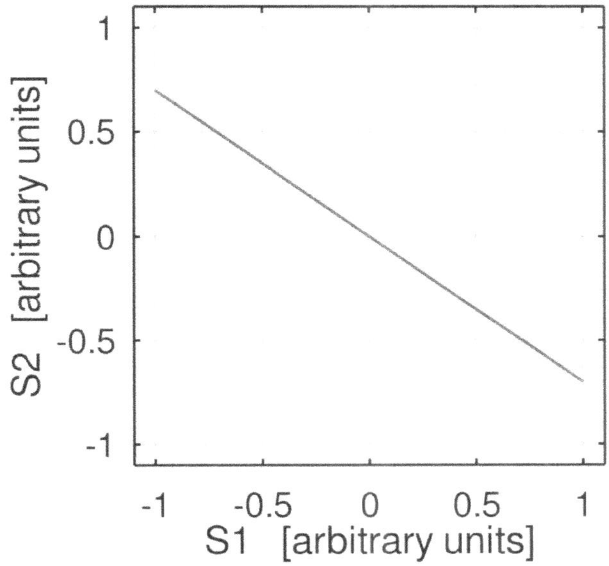

Figure 6.
Example of a Lissajous figure with π delay, again degenerating into a line.

The real case will be intermediate between the three listed above and the figure of Lissajous will be an inclined ellipse; the most important parameters, namely the delay ϕ and the amplitudes S_1^0 and S_2^0 are derived from the figure without need to know the period T_R. This is significant because the period can be difficult or impossible to determine if the exact time point in the cycle at which the mutations were detected is unknown. If the period is known from the experimental data, it is obviously of great importance too.

Letting T_R be the repetition time, then using the Lissajous trajectory equation, we know the duration of the outbreak to be based on the virus-bacteria mutation frequency under stressed-habitat response conditions:

$T_R = \frac{N}{\mu_{bacteria}} = \frac{N-1}{\mu_{virus}} = \frac{N(N-1)}{\mu_R}$ where the duration can be estimated as $\frac{1}{\mu_R}$ and N represents the susceptible host-population size.

And so, the Lissajous curve obtained by plotting the characteristic phase associated for expected infectivity might be drawn for mutation rate per virus species, and the corresponding phase angle δ and S extracted from the solution describing, for example, $S(\mu_{host})$ and $S(\mu_{virus})$ based on these equations.

Using the lissajous trajectory model in three dimensions, however, reveals a new opportunity to include evolution as both lateral and vertical. We can also define the amplitude $S^0(x, y, z)$ as the volume of the stress response for an ecothermoydnamic habitat as that which is vulnerable to evolution. If so, we can consider the phase of intersecting signals within the lissajous model as genomic natural mutation frequency, w_x, affected by the intensity of stress. The intensity of thermodynamic stress frequency includes an interesting ratio, $n_x : n_y : n_z$ which would describe the periodicity of infections in order to achieve the maximum number of points of intersection (infection), for specific evolutionary-spacetime stages (planes). This ratio is a new property that is very powerful in understanding the habitat stress relationship to resulting infections, and not found in any prior reference in the research by the author, to-date. Evolution is described by the position of the set of planes defining the thermodynamic stable balance between the habitat

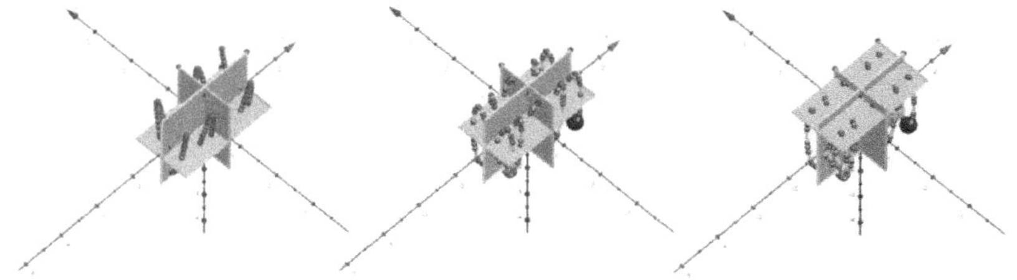

Zero phase to increased phase representing increased infection for the same range of mutation, *left and middle image*, in present state of evolution (i.e., the current reality) and resulting in reduced observed infectiousness in the final alternate reality of evolution. Vertical evolution within the x-y plane can represent arrival of new species, in this model.

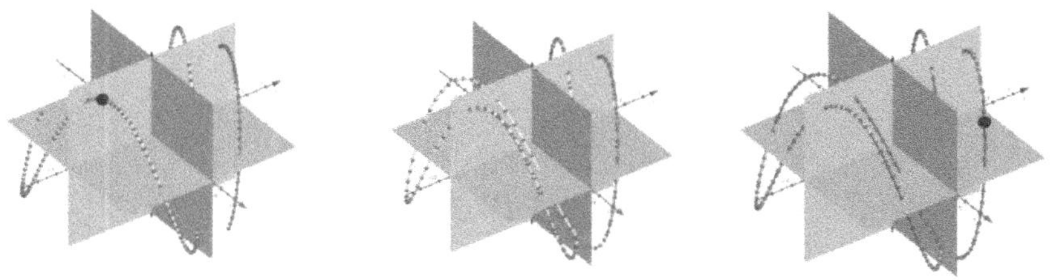

Increased mutation resulting in the observation of increased intensity and wavelike return($left\ to\ right$: $w_x = 1, w_x = 2, w_x = 20$) of infections.

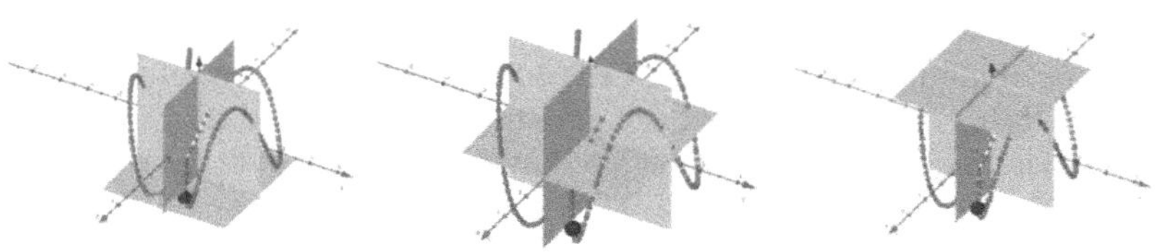

For the same characteristic virus species, the locations and frequency of infectious outbreaks will appear to be less at the start (left) and end (right) stages of evolution described in this chapter as *Alternate Realities* of a habitat and its incumbent species to the stage in present time (middle image), based on the role of virus outbreak. Evolution is shown vertically here in the xy-plane.

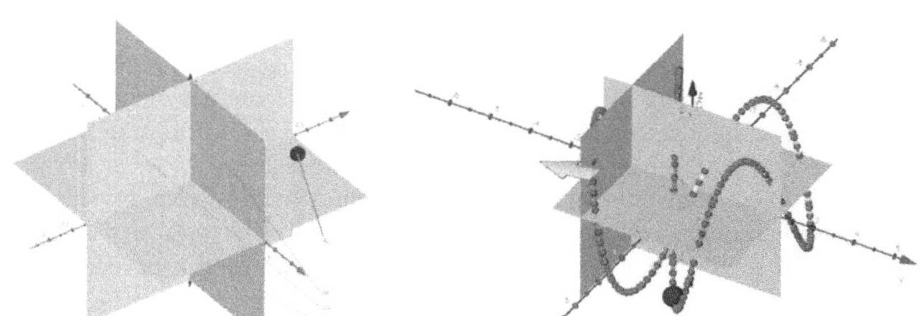

Left image: (A) virion particle in the xz-plane (B), yz-plane (C), xy-plane (D); Right image: direction of lateral evolution such as what might represent horizontal virus and DNA infection.

Figure 7.
Schematic demonstration of evolution planes modeled with comparative mutation rates and expected infectiousness (changes in phase). Adapted with Geogebra software [61] and R. Chijner [62].

environment and its incumbent microecology. If so, the lissajous model for the system also could include the phase delay in at least two of those dimensions, such as a_{yx} and a_{yz}, which represents the expected rate of infectious particle multiplication and the rate of infectious spread, as a function of the varying $V_{vulnerable}$ respectively, throughout the course of evolution from one Alternate Reality to the next stage of evolutionary ecothermodynamic stability.

At any given stage of evolution, the species and the conditions of that habitat may be considered a particular Alternate Reality for which all biodiverse species are sustained and survive. When the conditions requiring new evolution are visible in new stresses, then a new alternate reality evolves and it may be one of many (**Figure** 7).

For exactness, one would expect to find the suitable species mutation and infectiousness rate, for the virus species and host volume. Like livestock at slaughter, this could include the infection of their gut microbiome bacterial organisms dispersed in the habitat shared with human gut deleteriously. Considering that none of these species migrate or evacuate as they would for natural herd immunity, there is no alternative except to endure virus attack in significant pandemics. This means, for a volume of evolution-vulnerable hosts in a given habitat defined by

$$V_{vulnerable} = A_x A_y A_z \tag{5}$$

We represent

$$S_x(x) = A_x \cos(w_x x) \tag{6}$$

$$S_y(x) = A_y \cos(w_y x + a_{yx}) \tag{7}$$

$$S_z(x) = A_z \cos(w_z x + a_{yz}) \tag{8}$$

The dimensions for lateral evolution represented by $xz-$ and $yz-$ planes while vertical evolution in the xy-plane. Thus, for each evolution transition, based on stress response that includes arrival of foreign species (vertically) and/or the transition of species within the same habitat (laterally) we observe a snapshot of the same virus spread trajectory involved in the same mutation rate but with different points of intersection and different numbers of intersection. Each represents a characteristic frequency of a specific virus genome: the mutations are consistently carried by the thermodynamic moment of the habitat response to a stress, as the habitat system transitions from one alternate reality to the next. Where researchers traditionally describe mutations as mistakes [63], the lissajous thermodynamic model can disprove the assumption and demonstrate precisions in these genomic departures thorough transitions in alternate reality formation. Otherwise, in two-dimension models, the enthalpic energy is represented by amplitudes S_1^0 and S_2^0, generated by the periods T_1 and T_2 representing the process of transition from one evolutionary isenthalpic state to another future evolutionary state where energy of the habitat system is fully conserved; and that the delay ϕ facilitates the spread width and height for efficient distribution of the mutations necessary. Mutation-spread can be described in space time as edges of the trajectory whilst centres of the Lissajous can be correlated to dense locations of chronic mutation-infections. The pathogen's natural moment is self-sustained during the period of an outbreak, until there is no location in the habitat that still needs to evolve towards a stable state. When eco-thermodynamic equilibrium is reached, it returns to zero and represents the point at which mutations cease, theoretically, and the arrival when a new reality following the outbreak is complete. At this point, the evolution process is satisfied by nutrient distribution for the sustainable growth of each species.

4. Conclusion

The goal of virus outbreaks pertains to ensuring habitat sustainability when resources for habitat biodiversity survival are threatened. The Lissajous parametric equation affords the incorporation of wavelike oscillatory phenomena of outbreaks that is both observable in pandemic outbreaks and that is much needed to describe virus-host coevolution stability thermodynamically. The method of using Lissajous equations offers the opportunity to incorporate multiple types of mutation rates relative to the thermodynamic stress of the environment and stages of lateral or vertical evolution in a habitat, referred to in this chapter as Alternate Realities. Application of the lissajous-model may provide a more accurate description of viruses behavior relative to infectious spread, duration and volume per Alternate Reality.

Glossary

Thermodynamic enthalpy	In this chapter, thermodynamic enthalpy is part of a compensation phenomena with entropy that may be observed in the transfer process of energy in order to achieve stability of a system; this can include, any and all sub-processes of cellular exchange, host rates of infection, nutrient exchange and so on.
Lissajous	Lissajous refers to a pattern of elliptic oscillation in mutual frequency and phase resonance; in this chapter Lissajous refer to distribution of energy transformation including in terms of Cartesian variables, and that can also be defined implicitly in polar variables from the oscillations' partial differential equations.
Gibbs-free energy	Gibbs free energy refers to a mathematical function that describes mass action of any ingredients in a multi-phase system. When the Gibbs free energy is at a minimum, the mass action laws are satisfied and the system is stable. This has been proven in the analysis of complex chemical systems. In this chapter, the concepts are presented with regards to the synthesis of viral components.
RNA polymerases	RNA polymerases are enzymes in cellular organisms; in this chapter, they refer to enzymes which help generate stress proteins for rapid changes in cellular behavior.
mRNA translation	Cellular genes are regulated by the arrival of messenger ribonucleic acids (mRNAs); this controls the genes that are individually responsible for activating or deactivating the cell's biological processes throughout a 24 hour period; in this chapter, mRNA translation is described as a vital part to virus

	multiplication and so, infection is the process by which viruses use the host cell's mRNA translation to transfer genetic information that teaches the host how to survive abiotic threats directly. Viruses use this process to help their hosts strengthen their immune resistance; traditional beliefs assume the fittest of a species is genetically independent of this process and that the fittest also becomes dominant. However, dominance is disruptive to thermodynamic equilibrium, leading to pathogenic reduction.
intracellular endoplasmic reticulum repair	The domains of the cellular endoplasmic reticulum (ER) are responsible for vital stress response handling, include delivery and assembly of necessary proteins, phospholipids and steroids on the cytosolic side of the ER membrane, the management and storage of specific ions and various protein-related activities that protect cells from stress and/or clear dead cells; the ER stress pathway is involved in vascular diseases
Microbial dysbiosis	Dysbiosis represents pathological disruption to normal bacterial and other syntrophic species which represent sub-components of habitat ecosystem; it usually refers to the imbalance of function occurring within the gut, in skin, brain and other parts of the individual host; dysbiosis is directly linked to pathologies that emerge in the habitat to the host, eg., human or livestock
Lytic viruses	Viruses which rupture the cellular membrane as part of infectious multiplication cycles.

Author details

Farida Hanna Campbell
De 7 Provinciën, Leiden, The Netherlands

*Address all correspondence to: fhcampbell@7provincien.com

References

[1] Katen S, Zlotnick A. The thermodynamics of virus capsid assembly. *Methods Enzymol*. 2009;455: 395-417. doi:10.1016/S0076-6879(08) 04214-6

[2] Jover LF, Effler TC, Buchan A, Wilhelm SW, Weitz JS. The elemental composition of virus particles: implications for marine biogeochemical cycles. *Nat Rev Microbiol*. 2014;12(7): 519-528. doi:10.1038/nrmicro3289

[3] Demirel Y. Thermodynamics and Biological Systems. *Nonequilibrium Thermodynamics*. Published online 2014: 485-562. doi:10.1016/b978-0-444-59557-7.00011-4

[4] von Stockar U. Optimal energy dissipation in growing microorganisms and rectification columns. *J Non-Equilib Thermodyn*. 2014;39(1). doi:10.1515/ jnetdy-2013-0027

[5] Jones BA, Lessler J, Bianco S, Kaufman JH. Statistical Mechanics and Thermodynamics of Viral Evolution. *PLoS One*. 2015;10(9):e0137482. doi: 10.1371/journal.pone.0137482

[6] Rhodes CJ, Demetrius L. Evolutionary entropy determines invasion success in emergent epidemics. *PLoS One*. 2010;5(9):e12951. doi: 10.1371/journal.pone.0012951

[7] Popovic M, Minceva M. A thermodynamic insight into viral infections: do viruses in a lytic cycle hijack cell metabolism due to their low Gibbs energy? *Heliyon*. 2020;6(5): e03933. doi:10.1016/j.heliyon.2020. e03933

[8] Nobu MK, Narihiro T, Mei R, et al. Catabolism and interactions of uncultured organisms shaped by eco-thermodynamics in methanogenic bioprocesses. *Microbiome*. 2020;8(1): 1-16. doi:10.1186/s40168-020-00885-y

[9] Fuhrman JA. Marine viruses and their biogeochemical and ecological effects. *Nature*. 1999;399(6736):541-548. doi:10.1038/21119

[10] Yang Y, Cai L, Zhang R. [Effects of global climate change on the ecological characteristics and biogeochemical significance of marine viruses–A review]. *Wei Sheng Wu Xue Bao*. 2015;55 (9):1097-1104. https://www.ncbi.nlm.nih.gov/pubmed/26762022

[11] Lovisolo O, Hull R, Rösler O. Coevolution of viruses with hosts and vectors and possible paleontology. *Adv Virus Res*. 2003;62:325-379. doi:10.1016/ s0065-3527(03)62006-3

[12] Gottschlich L, Geiser P, Bortfeld-Miller M, Field CM, Vorholt JA. Complex general stress response regulation in *Sphingomonas melonis* Fr1 revealed by transcriptional analyses. *Sci Rep*. 2019;9(1):9404. doi:10.1038/ s41598-019-45788-7

[13] Alternative Sigma Factor RpoX Is a Part of the RpoE Regulon and Plays Distinct Roles in Stress Responses, Motility, Biofilm Formation, and Hemolytic Activities in the Marine Pathogen *Vibrio alginolyticus*. Accessed July 10, 2021. https://journals.asm.org/ doi/abs/10.1128/AEM.00234-19

[14] Enck P, Holtmann G. Stress and gastrointestinal motility in animals: a review of the literature. *Neurogastroenterology & Motility*. 2008;4 (2):83-90. doi:10.1111/j.1365-2982.1992. tb00084.x

[15] Holtmann G, Enck P. Stress and gastrointestinal motility in humans: A review of the literature. *Neurogastroenterol Motil*. 2008;3(4):245-254. doi:10.1111/ j.1365-2982.1991.tb00068.x

[16] Mitchell JG, Kogure K. Bacterial motility: links to the environment and a

driving force for microbial physics. *FEMS Microbiol Ecol*. 2006;55(1):3-16. doi:10.1111/j.1574-6941.2005.00003.x

[17] Xu P, Chen F, Mannas JP, Feldman T, Sumner LW, Roossinck MJ. Virus infection improves drought tolerance. *New Phytol*. 2008;180(4): 911-921. doi:10.1111/j.1469-8137.2008.02627.x

[18] Baron S, Fons M, Albrecht T. Viral Pathogenesis. In: Baron S, ed. *Medical Microbiology*. University of Texas Medical Branch at Galveston; 2011. https://www.ncbi.nlm.nih.gov/pubmed/21413306

[19] Wei Y, Silke JR, Aris P, Xia X. Coronavirus genomes carry the signatures of their habitats. *PLoS One*. 2020;15(12):e0244025. doi:10.1371/journal.pone.0244025

[20] Eid S. Biological and molecular studies on plant para-retroviruses associated with Dahlia spp. in natural and managed ecosystems. Pappu H, ed. Published online 2010. https://www.proquest.com/dissertations-theses/biological-molecular-studies-on-plant-para/docview/821341070/se-2

[21] Nasrollahi V, Mirzaie-Asl A, Piri K, Nazeri S, Mehrabi R. The effect of drought stress on the expression of key genes involved in the biosynthesis of triterpenoid saponins in liquorice (*Glycyrrhiza glabra*). *Phytochemistry*. 2014;103:32-37. doi:10.1016/j.phytochem.2014.03.004

[22] Sun Z, Thilakavathy K, Kumar SS, He G, Liu SV. Potential Factors Influencing Repeated SARS Outbreaks in China. *Int J Environ Res Public Health*. 2020;17(5). doi:10.3390/ijerph17051633

[23] Foster PL. Stress responses and genetic variation in bacteria. *Mutat Res*. 2005;569(1-2):3-11. doi:10.1016/j.mrfmmm.2004.07.017

[24] Fang FC, Frawley ER, Tapscott T, Vázquez-Torres A. Bacterial Stress Responses during Host Infection. *Cell Host Microbe*. 2016;20(2):133-143. doi:10.1016/j.chom.2016.07.009

[25] Poltronieri P, Sun B, Mallardo M. RNA Viruses: RNA Roles in Pathogenesis, Coreplication and Viral Load. *Curr Genomics*. 2015;16(5): 327-335. https://www.ingentaconnect.com/content/ben/cg/2015/00000016/00000005/art00008

[26] Gahan C, Hill C. Relationship between Stress Adaptation and Virulence in Foodborne Pathogenic Bacteria. *Microbial Stress Adaptation and Food Safety*. Published online 2002. doi:10.1201/9781420012828.ch7

[27] Menéndez-Arias L. Mutation rates and intrinsic fidelity of retroviral reverse transcriptases. *Viruses*. 2009;1(3):1137-1165. doi:10.3390/v1031137

[28] Torrence PF. *Antiviral Drug Discovery for Emerging Diseases and Bioterrorism Threats*. John Wiley & Sons; 2005. https://play.google.com/store/books/details?id=QZl7GzhTsb8C

[29] Bradwell K, Combe M, Domingo-Calap P, Sanjuán R. Correlation between mutation rate and genome size in riboviruses: mutation rate of bacteriophage Qβ. *Genetics*. 2013;195(1): 243-251. doi:10.1534/genetics.113.154963

[30] Drake JW, Holland JJ. Mutation rates among RNA viruses. *Proc Natl Acad Sci U S A*. 1999;96(24): 13910-13913. doi:10.1073/pnas.96.24.13910

[31] Ninio J. Transient mutators: a semiquantitative analysis of the influence of translation and transcription errors on mutation rates. *Genetics*. 1991;129(3):957-962. https://www.ncbi.nlm.nih.gov/pubmed/1752431

[32] Drake JW, Charlesworth B, Charlesworth D, Crow JF. Rates of spontaneous mutation. *Genetics*. 1998; 148(4):1667-1686. https://www.ncbi.nlm.nih.gov/pubmed/9560386

[33] Foster PL. Nonadaptive mutations occur on the F' episome during adaptive mutation conditions in *Escherichia coli*. *J Bacteriol*. 1997;179(5):1550-1554. doi: 10.1128/jb.179.5.1550-1554.1997

[34] Torkelson J. Genome-wide hypermutation in a subpopulation of stationary-phase cells underlies recombination-dependent adaptive mutation. *The EMBO Journal*. 1997;16 (11):3303-3311. doi:10.1093/emboj/16.11.3303

[35] Drake JW, Ripley LS, Karam JD. Induced mutagenesis and isolation of T4 mutants. *Molecular biology of bacteriophage*. 1994;4:447-451.

[36] Auerbach C. Spontaneous mutations in dry spores of Neurospora crassa. *Z Vererbungsl*. 1959;90:335-346. doi: 10.1007/BF00888808

[37] Zhao Z, Li H, Wu X, et al. Moderate mutation rate in the SARS coronavirus genome and its implications. *BMC Evol Biol*. 2004;4:21. doi:10.1186/1471-2148-4-21

[38] Khailany RA, Safdar M, Ozaslan M. Genomic characterization of a novel SARS-CoV-2. *Gene Rep*. 2020;19: 100682. doi:10.1016/j.genrep.2020.100682

[39] Sanjuán R, Nebot MR, Chirico N, Mansky LM, Belshaw R. Viral mutation rates. *J Virol*. 2010;84(19):9733-9748. doi:10.1128/JVI.00694-10

[40] Smith EC, Sexton NR, Denison MR. Thinking Outside the Triangle: Replication Fidelity of the Largest RNA Viruses. *Annu Rev Virol*. 2014;1(1): 111-132. doi:10.1146/annurev-virology-031413-085507

[41] Sanjuán R, Domingo-Calap P. Mechanisms of viral mutation. *Cell Mol Life Sci*. 2016;73(23):4433-4448. doi: 10.1007/s00018-016-2299-6

[42] Pathak VK, Temin HM. 5-Azacytidine and RNA secondary structure increase the retrovirus mutation rate. *J Virol*. 1992;66(5):3093-3100. doi:10.1128/JVI.66.5.3093-3100.1992

[43] Ripley, Lynn S., and John W. Drake. "Bacteriophage T4 particles are refractory to bisulfite mutagenesis." *Mutation Research/Fundamental and Molecular Mechanisms of Mutagenesis* 129.2 (1984): 149-152.

[44] Fu M, Blackshear PJ. RNA-binding proteins in immune regulation: a focus on CCCH zinc finger proteins. *Nat Rev Immunol*. 2017;17(2):130-143. doi: 10.1038/nri.2016.129

[45] Urrea VM, Bridi AM, Ceballos MC, Paranhos da Costa MJR, Faucitano L. Behavior, blood stress indicators, skin lesions, and meat quality in pigs transported to slaughter at different loading densities. *J Anim Sci*. 2021;99 (6). doi:10.1093/jas/skab119

[46] Li Y, Guo Y, Wen Z, Jiang X, Ma X, Han X. Weaning Stress Perturbs Gut Microbiome and Its Metabolic Profile in Piglets. *Sci Rep*. 2018;8(1):18068. doi: 10.1038/s41598-018-33649-8

[47] Stalder KJ. Effects of porcine stress syndrome genotype on maternal traits in swine. doi:10.31274/rtd-180813-10131

[48] Beneke B, Klees S, Stührenberg B, Fetsch A, Kraushaar B, Tenhagen B-A. Prevalence of methicillin-resistant *Staphylococcus aureus* in a fresh meat pork production chain. *J Food Prot*. 2011; 74(1):126-129. https://meridian.allenpress.com/jfp/article-abstract/74/1/126/173068

[49] Serra HRH, Oliveira VDS. Covid-19 spatial circulation through the

slaughterhouses in the south and southeast parÁ: Spatial impacts of an "essential activity" in the midst of a pandemic. *Revista Brasileira de Gestao e Desenvolvimento Regional*. Published online 2020:191-205. https://www.rbgdr.com.br/revista/index.php/rbgdr/article/download/5983/1025

[50] Chua GT, Wong JSC, Lam I, et al. Clinical Characteristics and Transmission of COVID-19 in Children and Youths During 3 Waves of Outbreaks in Hong Kong. *JAMA Netw Open*. 2021;4(5):e218824. doi:10.1001/jamanetworkopen.2021.8824

[51] Costa GS, Cota W, Ferreira SC. Outbreak diversity in epidemic waves propagating through distinct geographical scales. *Phys Rev Research*. 2020;2(4):043306. doi:10.1103/PhysRevResearch.2.043306

[52] Solis J, Franco-Paredes C, Henao-Martínez AF, Krsak M, Zimmer SM. Structural Vulnerability in the U.S. Revealed in Three Waves of COVID-19. *Am J Trop Med Hyg*. 2020;103(1):25-27. doi:10.4269/ajtmh.20-0391

[53] Iljazovic A, Roy U, Gálvez EJC, et al. Perturbation of the gut microbiome by Prevotella spp. enhances host susceptibility to mucosal inflammation. *Mucosal Immunol*. 2021;14(1):113-124. doi:10.1038/s41385-020-0296-4

[54] Spadoni I, Pietrelli A, Pesole G, Rescigno M. Gene expression profile of endothelial cells during perturbation of the gut vascular barrier. *Gut Microbes*. 2016;7(6):540-548. doi:10.1080/19490976.2016.1239681

[55] Dethlefsen L, Relman DA. Incomplete recovery and individualized responses of the human distal gut microbiota to repeated antibiotic perturbation. *Proc Natl Acad Sci U S A*. 2011;108 Suppl 1:4554-4561. doi:10.1073/pnas.1000087107

[56] Chakraborty S. Prevotella/Streptococcus and other anaerobes colonize the metagenome (nasopharyngeal swab) submitted by Emory University School of Medicine, Georgia in Covid19 patient, corroborating the hypothesis that SARS-Cov2 is enabling anaerobes. doi:10.31219/osf.io/qn32v

[57] Cohen D, Ferne M, Rouach T, Bergner-Rabinowitz S. Food-borne outbreak of group G streptococcal sore throat in an Israeli military base. *Epidemiol Infect*. 1987;99(2):249-255. doi:10.1017/s0950268800067716

[58] Miliotis MD, Bier JW. *International Handbook of Foodborne Pathogens*. CRC Press; 2003. https://play.google.com/store/books/details?id=sbwCpA-r9EQC

[59] Blanchard CK, Others. A Milk Borne Outbreak of Septic Sore Throat. *Public Health News*. 1934;18:131-139. https://www.cabdirect.org/cabdirect/abstract/19342701604

[60] Pathan RK, Biswas M, Khandaker MU. Time series prediction of COVID-19 by mutation rate analysis using recurrent neural network-based LSTM model. *Chaos Solitons Fractals*. 2020;138:110018. doi:10.1016/j.chaos.2020.110018

[61] Hohenwarter M, Hohenwarter M. GeoGebra. *Available on-line at http://www geogebra org/cms/en*. Published online 2002. https://sodilinux.itd.cnr.it/sdl6x2/documentazione/geogebra/intro-it.pdf

[62] Materials of Roman Chijner.2011. https://www.geogebra.org/u/roman

[63] Mihailovic MK, Chen A, Gonzalez-Rivera JC, Contreras LM. Defective Ribonucleoproteins, Mistakes in RNA Processing, and Diseases. *Biochemistry*. 2017;56(10):1367-1382. doi:10.1021/acs.biochem.6b01134

Chapter 8

Hunting and Deforestation: A Threat to the Existence of the Niger Delta Red Colobus Monkey (*Procolobus epieni*)

Lameed Gbolagade Akeem and Lateef Funmilayo Lewiska

Abstract

The Niger Delta in Nigeria is the largest wetland in Africa and the third largest mangrove forest in the world. The region is known for its richness in biodiversity as well as its oil and gas resources. Due to the high level of oil exploration, deforestation, hunting and insecurities in these areas, the wildlife especially endemic species like the Niger Delta red colobus becomes vulnerable to extinction. Most researches on their range have noted a significant reduction in their population and range distribution. Hence, up-to-date information on their current status is paramount to ensure proper and urgent conservation measures. Data was obtained through the use of field survey and secondary data. The species was recently discovered endemic to Niger delta region in Nigeria for about 23 years ago and recent studies observed that there has been a drastic reduction in their population and a shift in the range they formally occupied faulting this to anthropogenic activities. This study revealed that the location is under intense timber extraction and hunting and as a result, one of the location in the Apoi creek where it was reported to be present, record no species of Red colobus monkey. Only the red capped mangabey monkey (3) were sighted at the location with some evidence of alligator (10). Result also revealed that most of the communities (age ≤ 30) do not know or have seen the species. The situation at the location is exacerbated because of the level of poverty and insecurity in the areas. Going by the evidence of intense timber extraction and hunting at the location, the number of this species may have drastically reduced compared to what it was formally projected (±200 individuals). It is therefore strongly recommended that a follow up of the research is done in other location where it was reported to be present.

Keywords: Deforestation, Hunting, Niger Delta Red Colobus Monkey, Threat

1. Introduction

The Niger Delta red colobus monkey, *Piliocolobus epieni* [1] was listed one of the 25 most threatened species in the world. It was made known to science as a result of a wide range of survey conducted in the South–South region of Nigeria [2]. Formally, it classified geographically as a close relative to the red colobus populations; Preuss's red colobus (*Procolobus preussi*), located in over 240 kilometers away along the Nigerian-Cameroon border and also the Bioko red colobus (*Procolobus pennantii pennantii*) was also classified as a close relative prior to the survey. As a result, it was categorized as a subspecies of *Procolobus badius* in the *pennantii* group [3]. After some years, Groves [4, 5] and Ting [6] studied the species with focus on vocalizations and mitochondrial DNA and arrived at the conclusion that the species is distinct (*Procolobus epieni*). However, before the study of the aforementioned author, the species was only studied by Werre between 1994 and 1997 Werre [7], where he established the location of the rare species, which he stated to occur only in the Niger Delta's freshwater swamp forest, with a year-round, high water table but with no deep flooding or tidal effects [8]. Studies on their habitat revealed that [8] the more clustered distribution of plant species peculiar the forests was a key factor restricting the monkey to its limited range of about 1,500 km^2, demarcated by the Forcados River and Bomadi Creek in the northwest, the Sagbama, Osiama and Apoi creeks in the East, and the mangrove belt to the South [8] in the Central Niger Delta, Bayelsa State, Nigeria. Unfortunately for the species, they exist outside protected areas of the southern region except for the Apoi creek which is protected. This wetlands region on the other hand, play a vital role in the hydrological cycle, acting as sinks into which surface water and/or groundwater flows from the surrounding catchment. Some replenish groundwater and some regulate river flows. Some also clean water, removing pollutants and sediment. But smaller, less well-known wetlands are also enormously important, acting as a source of food and water for people living nearby. Cumulatively these small wetlands play a significant role in reducing poverty and supporting both livelihoods and biodiversity. However, human activities, either within the wetland, or in the catchment in which they are situated, can alter these natural processes or accelerate the rate of change, threatening the wetland's continued existence especially endemic species which depends on it. These threats are likely to grow in the next few decades, as populations rise and demand more food and greater economic development. The Niger Delta Coastal settlements, which are already under stress of demographic pressure and unsustainable oil exploitation, are equally under the threat of sea level rise.

As the world's populations grow and competitions for scarcely available resources increase, pressure is mounting on the available natural resources. According to Makenzi (2011) and Nordas and Gleditsch [9], the effects are characterized by deforestation; depletion of biodiversity; air and water pollution; global warming; increased poverty and food insecurity. Awotodunbo and Adewumi [10] also maintain that resources upon which the "rural poor" in developing economies depend are being progressively threatened. This paper seeks to ask the way forward to ensure sustainable conservation amidst increasing poverty, population increase and conflict in regions with endemic species. The study highlights some field experiences and pressing issues threatening the existence of the Niger Delta Red Colobus monkey in Apoi creek forest reserve.

2. Materials and methods

The Apoi Creek forest reserve is located in the central part of the Niger Delta in Bayelsa State (carved out of the former River State), in the central Niger Delta. It is located in the old Koluama Divison (latter Southern Ijaw Local Government Area) and bounded by Gbaraun and Paratubo to the North, Okubie and Lobia to the East, Apoi Creek to the South and Ekinigbene/Kokologbene village to the West. The land area is 29 213 ha with an elevation of 2–4.5 m. a.s.l. It is mainly of marsh and mangrove forests as well as fresh water swamps. It is very significant due to the presence of populations of fauna life, most particularly the endemic Niger Delta Red Colobus monkey [11].

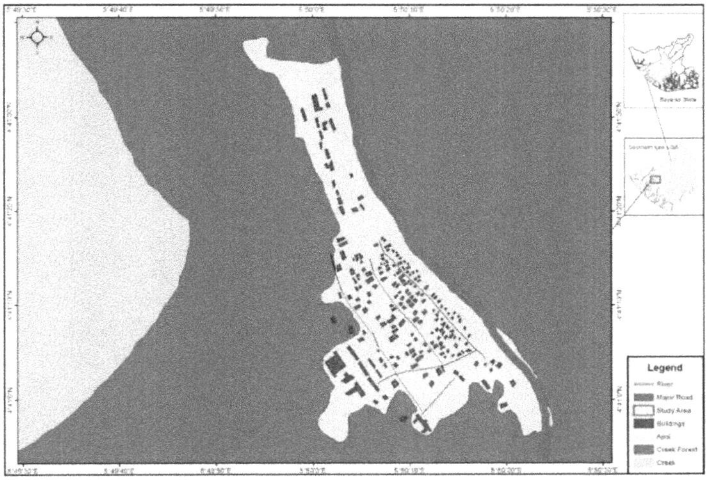

Figure 1.
Apoi creek forest with major road/river.

The study adopted an observational and socio-economic procedure in data collection. Mixed methods of data collection as recommended by Malgosia et al. (2013) was used in data collection, and these include combining data from surveys, document reviews, and information from key informants (**Figure 1**).

3. Results and discussion

The survey discovered that as a result of intense hunting and deforestation at the creek, there was no species of the Niger Delta red colobus monkey present after a three days survey of the Gbaraun axis of the reserve. Although in the 1990s, visitors to the forests near the town of Gbanraun observed *P. epieni* relatively easily [7]. It was also reported that the Werre [12] estimated the entire population of *P. epieni* may have fallen below 10,000 individuals. However, a more recent study by Ikemeh (2015) estimated the population of Epieni to be more or less than 200 individuals. Ikemeh (2015), findings also revealed that there was presence of the species in the Gbaraun axis of the forest, although they were unable to site any individuals directly only report from communities. This study however, did not observe any species even though report gathered from the community confirmed their presence. It was also observed that people who claimed to see and are knowledgeable of the species were folks of age between the range of 40–50 years and above, those below this age range have not seen or heard about the species. Other species like Aliigator, birds and Mangabey monkey (*Cercocebus torquatus*) were sited. There were more than five logging points at the location, leaving the forest with little or no trees and as a result rendering wildlife species especially the Niger Delta red colobus money homeless. An unfortunate situation during the survey happened when the supposedly individual that the community chiefs suggested to go with me during the survey (from the Gbaraun village), left me at the center of the forest to kill a mother of Mangabey monkey with its infant who narrowly escaped death as the bullet happened to hit the infants' eye (see **Figures 2–4**). His reason was income to take care of his family! With what he did, it was concluded that the forest is in serious threat and in no time, there would not be a single wildlife species let alone the endemic

Figure 2.
Apoi forest.

Figure 3.
Logging activities at different locations within the Apoi creek.

Figure 4.
Mother and infants of a Mangabey monkey shot by the guard that was supposed to guide the researcher.

species in the reserve. The implication is, there is no fear of state government or fear that I could report him to a body that would not even implement the law.

This experience is just a measure of many of Africa's problems. The growing population, conflicts between different ethnic groups, national political instability, and unsustainable exploitation of natural resources are all the problems affecting conservation in the area. Roger (2007), highlighted some basic problems frustrating research effort in the area which he listed to be lack of development, electricity only in a few of the Delta's towns and absent of fresh water and health care facilities as well as the kidnappings.

The human population of the Niger Delta is growing rapidly, with the result that most of the natural resources (for example, fish and timber) there have either been reduced to a level where they are insufficient to meet the local needs, or have been depleted altogether. As a result, the only local large scale economic activity that provides cash comes from the exploitation of the Delta's other natural resource; trees. From experience and observation during the course of this study, the following was observed to be the major problem militating against conservation:

- Access route to the location: The route to the creek is basically by water with several check point owing to the frequent occurrence of sea pirate. Furthermore, the location of the forest cannot be surveyed successfully during the peak of wet season due to the terrain which is highly water-logged. It is practically inaccessible on foot only by speed boat and this could limit thorough survey during wet season because of a lot of thickets and climbers' species that could prevent easy see through within the forest.

- Security: The location as record of several kidnapping occurrences, there were numerous check points on water along the route to the forest which implies that the location is not safe for researchers especially non indigene. Apart from this, communities have conflicting issues regarding the boundary of the forest.

- Lack of awareness: most of the youth are not aware of the importance of the forest when it comes to the rare wildlife being housed by the forest. The forest is important to them because of the oil and timber. To them, wildlife is bush meat! Report from this survey is evident that if nothing is done urgently to protect the forest, the endemic species will be history as it is already happening where no single species can be found where they were once many.

4. Conclusion

The study was conducted as a follow-up on the current status of the critically endangered species, Niger Delta red colobus monkey in one of its location where it was reported to be sighted in the Gbaraun axis of Apoi creek. The survey discovered that they are not present in the said location owing to intense timber extraction and hunting. This is presumed to be worse because of the insecurities in the area that has prevented researchers and possibly the state government to implement any form of enforcement. Further research is strongly encouraged because of the ever increasing threat on the forest.

Author details

Lameed Gbolagade Akeem* and Lateef Funmilayo Lewiska
Department of Wildlife and Ecotourism Management, Faculty of Renewable Natural Resources, University of Ibadan, Ibadan, Nigeria

*Address all correspondence to: lamgbola2008@gmail.com

References

[1] Grubb, P. and Powell C. B. (1999). Discovery of red colobus monkeys (*Procolobus badius*) in the Niger Delta with the description of a new and geographically isolated subspecies. *J. Zool.,* Lond. 248: 67-73.

[2] Powell, C. B. (1993). Sites and Species of Conservation Interest in the Central Axis of the Niger Delta (Yenegoa, Sagbama, Ekeremor and Southern Ijo Local Government Areas). Report, recommendations to the Natural Resources Conservation Council (NARESCON), Abuja, Nigeria.

[3] Werre, J. L. R. and Powell C. B. (1997). The Niger Delta colobus discovered in 1993 and now in danger of extinction. Oryx 31: 7-9.

[4] Groves, C. P. (2001). *Primate Taxonomy*. Smithsonian Institution Press, Washington, DC.

[5] Groves, C. P. (2007). The taxonomic diversity of the Colobinae in Africa. J. Anthropol. Sci. 85: 7-34.

[6] Ting, N. (2008). Molecular Systematics of Red Colobus Monkeys (*Procolobus* [*Piliocolobus*]): Understanding the Evolution of an Endangered Primate. PhD thesis, City University of New York, New York.

[7] Werre, J. L. R. (2000). Ecology and Behavior of the Niger Delta Red Colobus Monkey (*Procolobus badius epieni*). PhD thesis, City University of New York, New York.

[8] Oates J. F. and Were J. L. R. (2009). Primate in peril. The world's 25 most Endangered Primates 2008-2010. Distribution of the Olive Colobus Monkey.

[9] Nordas, R. and Gleditsch, N. P. (2007). Climate change and conflict. PoliticalGeography, 26, 627-638.

[10] Awotodunbo and Adewumi (2012): Agricultural Extension Strategies for Effective Mitigation against the Effects of Climate Change Proceedings, 17th Annual National Conference. AESON [11 – 14 March, 2012] ISSN: 1595 – 1421

[11] Werre L., (1997). Ecology and conservation of the Niger Delta Red Colobus. A report for general reference preliminary to completion of detailed technical information. Unpublished Ph.D. thesis.

[12] Oates, J. F. (1994). The Niger Delta's red colobus monkey: a new subspecies? *Research Notes, African Wildlife Update*, March–April 1994, 3(2): 4.

Section 3

Ecology

Chapter 9

Implications of Ethnoecological and Phytoecological Studies for the Sustainable Management of the Mozogo-Gokoro National Park (Cameroon)

Rodrigue Constant Sandjong Sani, Mama Ntoupka, Toua Vroumsia and Adamou Ibrahima

Abstract

Sustainable management planning of protected areas depends on data from their biophysical and human environment. Based on such a premise, and using established international and national standards, this chapter proposes to outline a range of measures that can be considered in this process, drawing on the results of ecological studies carried out in the Mozogo-Gokoro National Park, located in the Sudano-Sahelian dry zone in the Far North of Cameroon. Initially, determining attributes for conservation were identified, notably those relating to the richness of the flora and the structure of the vegetation, which are close to a reference ecosystem. Subsequently, recommendations for sustainable management were formulated and analyzed in turn, taking into account especially the destructive anthropization identified as a major threat to the stability of the park. These management orientations could also be applied to safeguard other ecosystems in the Sudano-Sahelian zone.

Keywords: Conservation, Ecological studies, Far North Cameroon, Management guidelines, Park, Valorization

1. Introduction

The extension of research results to the range of actors involved with natural resources is an essential operation for the sustainable management of plant formations. The concept of forest extension is described as a systematic process of exchanging ideas, knowledge and techniques that can change attitudes, practices, knowledge, values and behaviors for better forest and tree management [1, 2]. With the multiplicity of partnerships involved in sustainable forest management (local people, non-governmental organizations, private sector and government, scientists), there is a need for wider dissemination of forestry-related information and for flexible communication based on dialog, feedback and flexibility [3, 4]. Indeed, Kandzior and Rivas [4] consider forestry extension to be a minimum requirement for any forestry program targeting rural people. Decision-makers are aware of the importance of research results in the day-to-day management of forest sites. However, they cite obstacles such as accessibility and insufficient skills for their exploitation [5, 6]. There is therefore a great interest in synthesizing and making accessible to different stakeholders, the diversity of data from research considering the complexity of sustainable forest management processes.

The sustainability-oriented forest management process involves six key concepts [7]: better management practices/reduction of the impact of logging, biodiversity conservation, forest protection, multi-scale planning, participatory forestry and maintaining forest production. This conception is in line with the paradigm of "systemic forestry" of Nocentini *et al.* [8], who further specify that the sustainable management of vegetation must integrate multisectoriality, an implementation oriented towards a dynamic resilience-seeking process, the multifunctionality of ecosystems including ecological, social and economic components, and the plurality of actors. With this divergence of approaches, goals and specific realities, forest management has recently evolved towards the concept of sustainable forest management [9, 10]. The sustainable management of protected areas has its own particularities and is even more essential because of the major interest in *in situ* biodiversity conservation [10, 11], or the importance of the ecosystem goods and services it promotes, especially for the benefit of riparian communities [12, 13]. This observation justifies the multiple strategies put in place by organizations working in the fields of biodiversity conservation for greater efficiency in the management of these natural sites. They are working to permanently reduce, generally through guidelines, the lack of ownership of research results in forest governance.

Many steps in sustainable management planning for protected areas are supposed to be based on the results of prior studies [11, 14]. In reality, however, this governance is sometimes based on empirical considerations [5, 15], as has long been the case in Mozogo-Gokoro National Park, located in a semi-arid sudano-sahelian region in the Far North of Cameroon. In a context marked by strong edapho-climatic and anthropogenic constraints, this management is sometimes considered effective in the MGNP, due to its resilience [16]. With multiple publications describing this protected area [17–25], this chapter aims to be part of a process of sustainable management that respects international and national standards. Considering the complexity and uncertainty recognized in the study of natural environments [8, 26, 27], it is not intended to recommend rigorous actions on a scientific basis. Instead, with the identification of governance deficiencies, threats, pressures and valuation assets, sustainable management guidelines can be formulated based on reference documents [7, 8, 11, 14, 28–33].

In this chapter, the specific objectives set are, among others, to state the characteristics for the valorization of the MGNP, to determine the managerial insufficiencies, the pressures and the threats to its conservation, to identify and comment on the major axes of intervention in relation to the management objectives, all of this in confrontation with the principles or experiences known in the literature.

2. General information on the MGNP

The MGNP is located in a dry zone in the far north of Cameroon (10°56′ and 10°57′ North latitude and 13°54′ and 13°58′ East longitude.), Mayo-Tsanaga Department, Mayo Moskota Arrondissement (**Figure 1**). This site was created as a forest and fauna reserve by decree No. 165 of 12 June 1932 of the High Commissioner of the French Republic in Cameroon, and then set up as a national park by decree No. 120 of 5 December 1968 of the Secretariat for Development of

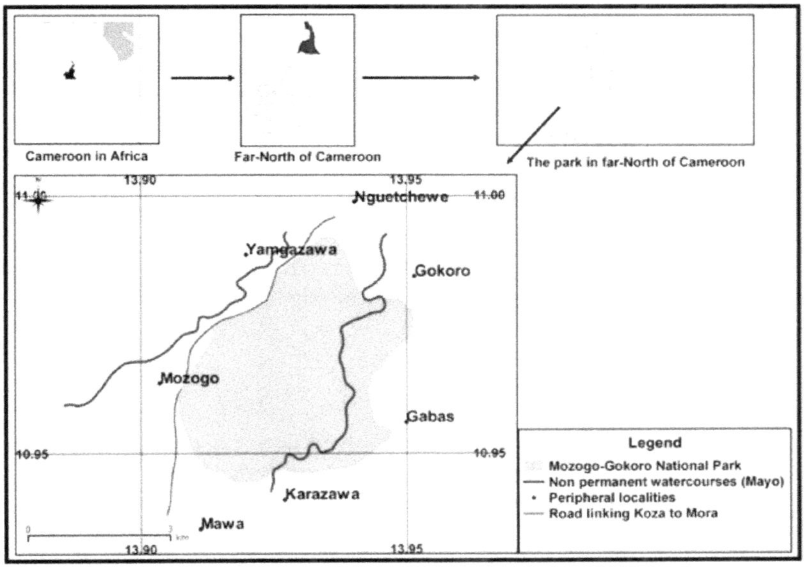

Figure 1.
Location of Mozogo-Gokoro National Park.

the State of Cameroon. Its governance is essentially state-owned, notably with the Cameroonian government's Order No. 911/MINEF of 12 April 1994, which guides its management through its designation as a 3rd category Technical Operational Unit, based on its surface area of 1400 ha (50,000 ha being the lower limit of the 2nd category). In Olson *et al.*'s [34] classification, it corresponds marginally to the Mandara Plateau mosaic ecoregion. However, in reality, its biodiversity is closer to the savannah ecosystems of eastern Sudan or the Sahelian savannahs with *Acacia* spp. The MGNP also belongs to the Ramsar site of the Waza-Logone floodplains, representing the 10% of wetlands in the West African sahel [35]. Its designation as a park is theoretically assimilated to category II of the IUCN classification, but it does not have a management plan in line with this status.

This protected area has been demarcated without cadastral reference [25]. Its boundaries can therefore be moved by the population according to their interests. In addition, the park lacks a buffer zone as provided for by the regulations. Difficulties in water supply constitute a factor degrading the habitat of the medium-sized fauna it contains, corresponding to mammals (patas monkeys, olive baboons, gray duikers, mongooses, burrowing squirrels, porcupines, Thomson's Gazelles, ...), birds (114 species), reptiles (monitor lizards, canine pythons and other snakes), and several batrachians and invertebrates [20]. As a solution to this problem, the forestry administration built two artificial ponds in 2009 (one of which is mostly dry) and a solar-powered pumping trough (currently non-functional). The administration has also worked to build twenty kilometers of tracks within the park, but these are often not maintained.

Three vegetation zones have been distinguished as Field Data Collection Units or (CU) in some of the work done in this protected area [16, 23]. These are CU1: Mosaic of gallery forests, dense dry forests and shrub thickets (392.73 ha), CU2: Mosaic of dense dry to clear forests and shrub thickets (836.33 ha), and CU3: Mosaic of clear dry forest to wooded savannahs and shrub thickets, (95.91 ha). The climate is megathermal with mean annual temperatures ranging from 26–28°C [16].

Rainfall variability (with the observation of intense episodes of drought with sometimes less than 800 mm of annual rainfall), or even climate change, and anthropisation supported by a population density of more than 300 inhabitants/km^2 [25], have not significantly impacted the vegetation of the park [22]. These are nevertheless real pressure factors, which although they have affected the vegetation (with several signs of degradation noted especially in CU3); have certainly not led to a loss of resilience [16]. Illegal resource harvesting [20], has led to the creation of several trails into the park. It is an ecoregion whose soils are mainly classified as Oxisols, Vertisols and Fluvisols [36]. Their fertility certainly justifies the strong land pressure in the riparian zone of the park, with the existence of multiple crop fields [25]. Evidence of grazing and human constructions are also observed at the edge of the park.

3. Methodological approach

The methodological approach initially involved assessing a range of available information on the MGNP, mainly publications describing the biophysical and human environments [16–25], and secondarily recent administrative reports. At the same time, it was necessary to draw on international guidance documents, national texts, and scientific literature on the sustainable management of natural ecosystems, in order to draw from this initial assessment, highlights and proposals for measures applicable in such a process to the MGNP.

The salient points arising from the analysis of the work carried out in the MGNP were defined in accordance with Cameroonian regulations and the guidelines presented by several authors [11, 28, 29, 31, 37–41]. The aim was to distinguish the elements of value for conservation, and then to identify the shortcomings in the management of the park, as well as the pressures and threats to its stability. In the end, management objectives were formulated based mainly on the same reference documents, and measures to conserve values and limit pressures and threats were proposed. **Figure 2** outlines the organization the methodological approach.

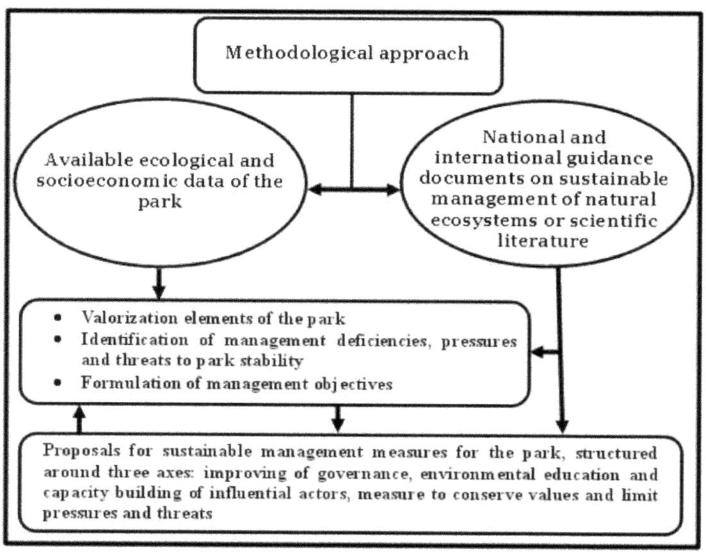

Figure 2.
Structuring of the methodological approach.

4. Valorization elements for a sustainable conservation of the park

4.1 Attributes of a reference ecosystem in the Sudano-Sahelian zone

A set of characteristics gathered from the present study of the MGNP constitute particular assets for this protected area. This analysis could lead to greater appreciation and a positive impact on the conservation of the park if an effective management approach were applied by the local communities and decision-makers.

The work carried out in the MGNP shows a structural vegetation dynamic with increasing density and size of individuals, and major socio-economic and ecosystem roles, as perceived by various stakeholders in the management process [25]. Phases of reforestation are observable from the analysis of its diachronic evolution by remote sensing [19, 25]. The other major indicators identified for the development of the MGNP are mainly related to the diversity of its flora and its structure, which is considered sufficiently stable [16–19, 23, 24]. This predominantly exuberant vegetation is illustrated by the two images in **Figure 3**. The anthropisation indices noted are certainly inherent to its functioning, and justify the characterization of its resilience. Its compositional diversity is particularly high, with a very rich flora constituting a gene bank (110 species of woody plants, Shannon-Weaver index evaluated at 4.54 bits and Simpson's index at 0.90). Several species that are rare in the natural environments surrounding the park and even vulnerable or threatened at the global level are found there (*Afzelia africana*, *Khaya senegalensis*, *Dalbergia melanoxylon*...). The importance value index (IVI) of families and species shows its great heterogeneity (floristic groups of ligneous plants with more than 25 species with a high IVI and 30 families). The density and basal area of individuals are also high (2694.16 stems/ha and 43.88 m^2/ha), indicating a low impact of the various environmental constraints. Its high woody phytomass indicates high production (331.73 tMS/ha on average for each CU). There is also a strong presence of specific Sudanian or Guinean elements, indicating adaptability to the quality of the soil and favorable climatic conditions. The specificities of the Oxisols, which are widespread in the region, are generally preserved. The high proportion of sarmentous and lianascious individuals sometimes makes the undergrowth impenetrable, and mechanisms of self-destruction or natural mortality indicate that this ecosystem has followed a trajectory towards quasi-typical Sudano-Sahelian vegetation without major disturbances. Remote sensing data show that savannization is certainly underway, especially in CU3, but to a limited extent.

With the implementation of an effective management system, these ecosystemic and scientifically beneficial values of the MGNP could make it eligible as

Figure 3.
Characteristics of exceptional vegetation in the Sudano-Sahelian zone: (a) Regreening of the mosaic of dense dry forest and shrub thickets in the rainy season; (b) image of a dense to open dry forest in the same season.

a UNESCO World Heritage Site. The MGNP presents itself as close to a natural habitat model for *in situ* conservation of biological diversity, representative of the ecological and biological processes involved in the evolution and development of ecosystems in this geographical area of Cameroon. Leaving aside the smallness of its area, this is also a feature in line with criterion C of the IUCN definition of key biodiversity areas [42]. Other plant formations in the Sudano-Sahelian zone can benefit from the sustainable conservation of the values identified in the MGNP.

4.2 Implications for the sustainable management of Sudano-Sahelian ecosystems

The assessment of the explanatory mechanisms of vegetation evolution in MGNP via remote sensing [22], did not reveal highly significant correlations between the characteristics of the park's flora on the one hand and rainfall and demographic factors on the other. Circumstances related to the inaccessibility of the flora, as well as the dangers of entering the park due to popular belief, would have sufficiently reduced anthropic pressures. This low anthropisation, combined with the irrefutable climatic variability in this region, has nevertheless resulted to increasing of savannization noticeable in CU3 [16].

In view of the floristic assets of the MGNP, there would therefore be a great benefit in respecting conservation measures, or even in implementing management plans for ecosystems in the Sudano-Sahelian zone, which give an important place to the safeguarding of the flora, with the hope of obtaining a regeneration of the vegetation similar to that of the MGNP. To confirm this hypothesis, the work carried out by Donfack [43] showed phytoecological characteristics of 30-year-old fallows that were quite similar to the vegetation of the MGNP. Ecological restoration and rehabilitation projects for Sudano-Sahelian ecosystems in the area could thus be based on the compositional and structural foundations of the MGNP.

5. Managerial shortcomings, pressures and threats to the conservation of values

The identification of multiple threats and pressures to the stability of the park, and the numerous arguments demonstrating inadequacies in management, represent risks of regression in values. **Table 1** presents these obstacles to the process of sustainable management of the park, ranked according to importance in terms of their recurrence in the analysis of various works on the park.

In the event of their persistence or accentuation, a rapid depreciation to the level of UNESCO's natural heritage in danger is conceivable, or even a reclassification in the permanent forest domain of the Cameroonian state. Also, it is necessary to point out a limitation of the valuing consideration of the MGNP, which is not based on the effectiveness of its management system and its governance system, particularly according to the principles of the IUCN green list [44, 45]. Despite the managerial shortcomings noted, the reference ecosystem values of the MGNP can be used for its sustainable management, given the official non-existence at the time of writing of a park management plan that complies with the texts in force in Cameroon.

6. Proposed management objectives

The use of information on the MGNP and the analysis of the management experiences of protected areas in Africa and in Cameroon in particular [35, 46–48],

Main elements of managerial shortcomings, pressures and threats to the stability of the park	Evaluation of importance*
• Lack of formal participatory and integrated sustainable management planning	Very important
• Poor governance of state actors, corruption and degradation of public morals	Important
• Lack of a framework for the conjunction of actions of the different actors	Less important
• Lack of a buffer zone, smallness and lack of ecological connectivity	Less important
• Perception of a regressive trend in animal and plant biodiversity	Important
• Land pressure from agro-pastoral practices, risk of encroachment and intrusion	Important
• Droughts, rapid population growth and large influx of refugees and displaced persons	Very important
• Illegal harvesting of resources (fuelwood, service wood, non-timber forest products), grazing and bush fires on the periphery of the park	Very important
• Removal techniques for woody plants often do not favor easy regeneration	Important
• Degradation of wildlife habitat, especially due to lack of water	Very important
• Indications of sahelisation, savannization, proliferation of thickets and regression of gallery forests	Important
• Presence of an exotic species such as *Azadirachta indica* within the vegetation	Less important
• Indices of soil fragility and degradation	Less important
• Ecological imbalance and significant rarity indices for several woody species	Less important
• Insufficient knowledge of wildlife resources	Important
• Insecurity and lack of ecotourism activities	Important

**Importance of elements of managerial inadequacy, threats and pressures assessed according to their recurrence in the analysis of available data on the park.*

Table 1.
Managerial shortcomings, pressures and threats to the stability of the park.

revealed shortcomings that led to the recommendation of the three main management objectives below:

- improve the governance of the protected area;
- educate and build the capacity of influential actors in park management;
- design strategies and actions to conserve values and limit pressures and threats.

The management measures and strategies attached to each of these objectives are applicable at different scales in this process, from the central state to local populations. The aim is to comply with the requirements of donors and international institutions in charge of biodiversity conservation programs, which support natural resource management based on participatory approaches [49, 50].

7. Areas of intervention for sustainable management of the MGNP

7.1 Improving governance

In the MGNP, in order to promote the effectiveness of integrated and participatory management that respects the norms, the State, which holds the property rights, must set up a consultation framework involving the various stakeholders. Forest administration actors are also invited to promote it, for its true recognition as a reference for plant conservation in the Sudano-Sahelian zone, and to work for the provision of financial resources, within the framework of the carbon market. In this process, they should establish the necessary partnerships, ensure the involvement of scientific and technical expertise, exploit the available data on the park, and gather all the necessary means for appropriate management. Wicander [46] believes that state governance in sub-Saharan Africa has indeed the potential to achieve effective biodiversity conservation. He adds that with the requirement for greater transparency and accountability, it can be more effective, increasing social inclusion for greater societal legitimacy, to reduce conflicts and inequities, maximize resources, capacities and skills for the benefit of stakeholders.

However, in a context of state governance of protected areas, distrustful attitudes and bureaucratic red tape often hinder the involvement of some stakeholders in the management process [51]. Evaluations of management effectiveness should therefore be regular exercises, integrated into the management and planning cycles of protected area administrations [40].

Considering the many constraints to compliance in protected area management, some authors do not exclude the use of alternative and palliative measures, essentially contributing to the maintenance of resilience [8]. Other studies recognize the importance of non-scientific sources of knowledge in forest management practices [52, 53]. Thus, the authorities involved in forest management should invest as much as possible in maintaining a rigorous protection of the park, minimizing the negative impact of humans on its entire extent, especially with the activities of the terrorist sect "Boko Haram", which have led to a massive influx of displaced people and refugees in the area. The aim here is simply to apply the law, which prohibits encroachment or access to the park for the purpose of collecting any products whatsoever. The use of Geographic Information Systems and other innovative technological tools, could improve governance, even in the face of insufficient staff. Ecotourism promotion is also essential in this management. However, in practice, it must be recognized that it is very difficult to apply strict restriction measures on intrusions into the park, with the multiple existing paths or tracks. It would therefore seem more appropriate to manage the park sustainably, based on less restrictive or dissuasive initiatives, including above all a good awareness-raising of all influential actors.

Furthermore, for a long-term improvement of governance, it is not unrealistic to recommend the design and implementation of legal texts that would focus attention on the particularities of dryland ecosystem management and give more value to the conservation of natural resources in this area. Gautier *et al.* [51] have argued for a reform of forest governance applied in semi-arid zones. In order to address the lack of joint action in favor of the park, the creation of an agency dedicated specifically to the management of protected areas could be envisaged at the national level, with regional branches.

The lack of a buffer zone is a legal loophole, constituting one of the major threats to the sustainable conservation of the biodiversity of the MGNP. The currently known limits, which correspond to the edge of the vegetation, cannot constitute a brake on the poaching and destructive intentions of the population in the vicinity. This contiguity with the riparian population is very pronounced in some places, with the establishment of social infrastructures (schools, health centers, and roads), dwellings and crop fields in almost its entire border (**Figure 4**), with the exception of a degraded zone separating the villages of Karazawa and Gabas.

As information from farmers indicates that animals may move between the park and the surrounding mountains, an extension of the park into such a corridor

Figure 4.
School (a) and cultivated area (b) at the periphery of the park.

may be suggested. In this area and other peripheral spaces, degraded land will be restored and agro-sylvo-pastoral practices will be implemented, favoring the resources desired by the farmers. Such actions must be carried out according to an agro-ecological approach. It aims to reconcile, in the long term, the productivity of agricultural systems and the preservation of natural resources [54]. According to Lausche [33], the emergence of climate change requires the extension of existing protected areas, the creation of new ones and the strengthening of environmental connectivity. Regarding the planting of woody species in the buffer zone, minimum interspecific spacing of 4.5 m, or intraspecific spacing of 3 m, have been suggested in the Sudanian zone [55]. In his book on the reconfiguration of protected areas in Africa, Chardonnet [48] advocated the establishment of an alternative to buffer zones called peripheral areas or conservancies, contributing more effectively as a transition zone to both the maintenance of values and the development of local communities.

There is therefore a possibility to create this transition zone, in accordance with the principle of ecological connectivity in such a space [56, 57], with real adhesion of the population, while respecting prior consultations and compensation measures concerning all expropriated persons. However, this is a solution that, although favorable to the MGNP, is limited by the high land pressure, already very visible in this densely populated area. The establishment of a dense natural protection barrier, such as a hedgerow, is another option to be considered in places where such an extension is not feasible.

7.2 Organization of environmental education of the stakeholders of influence of the park

Awareness raising, education and capacity building are important principles in sustainable forest management in sub-Saharan Africa [31]. Environmental education, having a major contribution in the extension process, is an essential activity for the effectiveness of protected area management. It will be necessary to integrate in its organization, the diversity of actors without discrimination (activities, gender, ethnicity, religion). Chalabi and Mahamadou [58] make this an important issue for the conservation of protected areas in the Sudano-Sahelian zones.

To make people understand the ideal of conservation, the approach to be recommended in raising awareness among the population results from their perception of species that are disappearing, decreasing or increasing. It should emphasize on the responsibility of man in the evolution of vegetation, as well as non-destructive use rights in relation to forestry legislation. The organization of meetings and discussions in influential groups are ways of spreading awareness messages.

Also, with formal education, young people can be influenced by ways of thinking, a new understanding of nature, and a more concrete perception of environmental preservation [25]. Education also involves the media and new technologies, which, through the play of permanent messages, can lead people to adhere to the ideal of biodiversity conservation. In the end, a good compromise is needed between the development of the local population and the preservation of the environment.

Significant knowledge of regeneration patterns is essential. For example, managers need to be aware of interventions that can enhance the potential for regeneration by sexual (viable seed stocks) or vegetative means. The importance of vegetative regeneration (adventitious or proventive stump sprouts, suckers) is noted in the area compared to Guinean regions [28, 59]. Bellefontaine *et al.* [60] thus advocate the inseparability of sexual reproduction and vegetative propagation (asexual reproduction) for a true enrichment in woody plants. He encourages the practice of regeneration techniques that are more accessible to populations, at lower cost, notably suckering and terrestrial layering. Such techniques must

Figure 5.
Base cutting of a Balanites aegyptiaca stem (left) and extensive debarking of Ziziphus spina-christi (right).

Figure 6.
Tadpole cutting of one individual of Dalbergia melanoxylon.

be popularized for the successful establishment of an agro-sylvo-pastoral zone, integrating agro-ecological practices, in the park's surroundings.

With the observation that totally destructive logging is sometimes practised, in the removal of ligneous and NTFPs (**Figures 5** and **6**), it would be essential to teach logging or cutting techniques that facilitate easy regeneration [60], in particular the so-called improved cuts that preserve rare species and individuals with small diameters. In the area, cutting and protection regimes (**Table 2**), including minimum exploitable diameter, duration of cutting rotation have been proposed by Catinot [59], Nouvellet [61], Peltier *et al.* [62], Ntoupka [63], Sokpon *et al.* [65], Faye *et al.* [64] and clearly, more species-specific cutting rotations are recommended for better stand recovery.

Managers must also become familiar with assisted natural regeneration techniques. Fire and grazing practices in a less degrading form, maintaining the fragile balance of the ecosystems, must also be known by the populations. These pressure factors have been reported to the MGNP [25]. **Figures 7** and **8**, show that these practices are present in the park. Several authors [66, 67] propose early annual fires as a possible solution, rather than late fires, as well as moderate grazing outside the rainy season.

Minimum diameters (Ø) or heights of cuts and species concerned found in the MGNP	Indication of the duration of the cutting rotation or protective measures	Authors
Between 8 and 15 cm Ø (simple coppicing) No species details	• Short rotation (7 years ±2 years) fuel-wood, fodder and miscellaneous uses • Average rotation (14 years ±2 years) timber and service wood	Nouvellet [61]
Coppice (cut to a sufficient diameter) No species details	• –7-8 years old without selection • 14 to 16 years old selection in clumps and service wood stems	Catinot [54]
• 6 cm Ø at the base for *Guiera senegalensis, Combretum micranthum* • 8 cm Ø at the base for *Combretum nigricans and C. glutinosum*	Can be cut to an ankle size (approximately 8 cm) or wrist size (approximately 6 cm)	Peltier *et al* [62], Ntoupka [63]
• 20 cm in height for *Combretum glutinosum and Guiera senegalensis*	//	Faye *et al.* [64]
• No operation recommended • *Anogeissus leiocarpa* and many other timber and service species	At least 6 years	Ntoupka [63]
• No operation recommended • NTFPs (fruit trees): *Tamarindus indica, Sclerocarya birrea, Senegalia senagal*	Protection until standing dead	Ntoupka [63]
• More than 2 m high • *B.aegyptiaca*, *Senegalia. nilotica*, *Stereospermum kunthianum*, *Ficus* sp., *Khaya senegalensis*	No flush cutting until standing dead, pruning or trimming tolerated	Ntoupka [63]
• 45 cm Ø for *A. leiocarpa*, 35 cm Ø for *D. mespiliformis* and *Pterocarous erinaceus*, 55 cm Ø for *P. kotschyi*	Between 15 and 30 years for the main exploitable species (Sudanese open forests in the north of Benin)	Sokpon *et al.* [65]

Table 2.
Examples of cutting regimes in the Sudanian or Sahelian zone.

Figure 7.
Evidence of grazing in the park.

Figure 8.
Area attacked by a late fire caused by carelessness one year earlier.

In addition, people need to be informed about the decline in quantity of several gallery forest species (Mayo-specific vegetation), so that they can take a greater interest in their conservation.

7.3 Measures to conserve values and limit pressures and threats

7.3.1 Special protection measures for some rare and coveted species

A number of species recorded are rare in the park (50.91% of the woody species recorded), and others are known from the IUCN red list. It would be important to draw up a national or even regional directory of these species, with images to facilitate their identification. This measure will help raise awareness among the various stakeholders of the need to preserve them. It is also a recommendation of the IUCN [68] to evaluate the risk of extinction of species and publish it in the red list for defined geographical areas.

On the other hand, the expression of the needs accorded to certain plant resources may favor the implementation of special measures for their valorization in the sense of the urgency of their conservation or more important restrictive measures if, in addition, they are rare or threatened. Among the species cited for their usefulness, some have been quantified with a certain rarity or even considered more or less endangered by the IUCN (*Dalbergia melanoxylon*, *Prosopis africana*, *Afzelia africana*, *Khaya senegalensis* ...). It would therefore be important to apply measures aimed at multiplying them, within the vegetation or in a buffer zone that can be delimited from the eastern periphery (selective thinning, enrichment with protection of seedlings, assisted natural regeneration). It will also be necessary to raise the awareness of the local population and even of all the actors involved in the management of these trees about their fragility, the risk of seeing them disappear, and to train them for their planting.

7.3.2 Special measures concerning invasive species

In exceptional cases, selective cutting, stump removal or girdling should be authorized to destroy invasive exotic species, which are known to induce an imbalance in phytocenoses. This is the case of *Azadirachta indica* (**Figure 9**), which could impoverish the native dry forest flora through its propensity to invade [69]. Triplet and Howard [70] argue that any exotic species should be managed as if it were potentially invasive until there is convincing evidence that it poses no threat. Invasive non-native species displace local fauna and flora, and in many cases affect ecosystem function [71].

7.3.3 Enrichment of gaps or windfalls

Beyond assisted natural regeneration, enrichment of gaps of vegetation can only be planned if there is evidence of significant extension. If the soil quality and nature of the bedrock allow it, it is preferable to opt for rare species in the park, or those whose regeneration has been analyzed as weak, slowed or disturbed [22]. This would be an exception to the legally prescribed restrictions on trespassing in this type of protected area. It is not out of the question to consider soil restoration in these areas, if real difficulties arise.

7.3.4 Improving the quality of wildlife habitat

Limitations in water supply, with a man-made pond drying up completely for 6–7 months a year (**Figure 10**), limited ecological connectivity and reduced surface area all act as barriers to animal flourishing in the MGNP. A drastic

Figure 9.
Proliferation of several stems of Azachdirata indica in the undergrowth.

Figure 10.
Pond without water in dry season in CU2.

decrease in the vertebrate community is a consequence of habitat degradation and habitat fragmentation [72]. Ponds constructed in the recent past have not achieved the desired objectives of permanent water conservation for wildlife, due to poorly conducted works. It is imperative to correct these shortcomings in the long term, at the risk of seeing a large part of the park's animal population perish in the near future. Also, the reduction of excessive overgrowth caused by the extension of thickets must be considered, notably by selective cutting of the species most concerned, which hinders the movement of certain animal species: *Senegalia ataxacantha*.

7.3.5 Proposed ecological monitoring indicators and parameters to be monitored

The essential values of the MGNP are linked to the exceptional vegetation cover in the Sudano-Sahelian zone, constituting a forest relic or an exemplary *in-situ* conservation area for the flora. In addition, it is a suitable habitat for several fauna species (avifauna, reptiles, and mammals) of varying degrees of rarity. According to the IUCN guidelines [32], ecological monitoring strategies should be oriented towards safeguarding these values for the well-being of present and future generations, but also towards limiting pressures and threats. A partnership with scientists is very often necessary for their implementation.

Therefore, for ecological monitoring of vegetation, it is more appropriate to proceed by permanent monitoring of its evolution based on remote sensing work. Information on the rate of progression of degraded forest or savannah and vegetation indices can be obtained to reflect the effectiveness of management actions. During the various patrols, it would also be important to identify and quantify the species taken in order to ensure the protection of rare and vulnerable species. With regard to fauna, beyond the need for more in-depth knowledge, regular inventories can help to control the park's animal populations in order to maintain them in balance with their habitat.

7.3.6 Ecological restoration of areas of advanced degradation in the park and its periphery

Ecological restoration makes it possible to recover ecological integrity, including the conservation of biodiversity with ecosystem goods and services [73].

Figure 11.
Areas of advanced degradation: (a) in MGNP, (b) in the periphery.

In MGNP, particularly in CU3 and its periphery, where there is evidence of degradation linked to savannization, and sometimes soil denudation (**Figure 11**), ecological restoration can take the various forms proposed by Keenleyside *et al.* [74], including the re-establishment of locally extinct or rare species, the deliberate removal of invasive non-native species, the reduction of certain pressures, enrichment interventions such as plantations, and the improvement of the physico-chemical properties of the soil. The periphery should also be addressed. Biodiversity conservation in protected areas located within human-dominated landscapes and ecological connectivity should be improved, through the restoration of these forest landscapes or small areas around these protected areas [75, 76]. Restoration actions should also respect the principles of effectiveness, efficiency and commitment [74].

With regard to CU3 in particular, anti-erosion management is recommended. Several approaches exist, but as a priority it will be necessary to find techniques adapted to tropical conditions and involving the population in their implementation. Roose [77] has mentioned the duration of these types of management (5 to 10 years), their dependence on the farmers' will and socio-economic contingencies. It may simply be proposed, as Ntoupka [63] did, to lay down branches in order to limit runoff, trap organic matter, increase water storage, and attract termites and earthworms. This technique increases microporosity, and in the medium term favors vegetation recovery. Roose *et al.* [78] conclude that in a favorable socio-economic context, with an improvement in the level of income of the populations and a limitation of land tenure problems, six rules should be respected to restore degraded soils and improve their biodiversity: adequate management of surface water (stone barriers, hedges, basins, etc.); reopening and reuse of land (e.g. by means of an irrigation system); and a reduction in the number of trees and shrubs. These include: adequate management of surface water (stone barriers, hedges, basins, etc.); reopening and stabilization of macroporosity (tillage and burial of organic matter); revitalisation of the surface horizon by adding humified organic matter; improvement of soil pH; plant nutrition; and a choice of locally adapted but non-invasive plants.

The re-greening process of certain degraded areas could be based on local plant species with favorable effects on soil fertility, mainly belonging to the Fabaceae family [79], or playing a role in soil protection and regeneration, such as *Leptadenia hastata* [80]. In the same vein, previous soil rehabilitation experiments in the North and Far North of Cameroon, which have proved to be conclusive, can be put into practice, notably surface development by reforestation [79] or by improving the water regime [81, 82]; planting techniques [83], or water saving and tillage techniques [84]. Some farming techniques that are sometimes considered beneficial (earth dams, tillage with plow or hoe, application of organic matter, integration of farming techniques such as fallow, crop association and rotation) cannot be overlooked, but could be improved with expert input [85].

7.3.7 Measures to improve monitoring and limit illegal resource extraction

The organization of surveillance patrols, not systematic and above all improvised, and sometimes at night in the dry season, is strongly recommended. No peripheral or internal area of the park should be excluded within the limits of accessibility. The use of civilian aerial drones, which are of great interest in forest management [86], would make a significant contribution to this surveillance, especially at the edges (entrances, fire pockets). In the absence of legal reform, this measure takes into account the legal prohibition in parks on flying aircraft below 200 m altitude [38]. In the event of infringements, the sanctions provided for by the regulations in force must be applied. However, these repressive actions are generally a last resort.

Indeed, other so-called palliative strategies favor the use of alternative sources of animal protein [87]. Development involving farmers would make it possible to reconcile the production of firewood, a scarce resource, with the sustainability of tree parks [88]. Bergonzini [89] proposes ways of reducing pressure on wood and fodder resources, such as improving the energy efficiency of stoves, using alternative energy sources, reducing the number of herds and controlling grazing and fire management techniques.

The collection of firewood is a constant concern of the farmers. The law does not allow this practice in the protected area, as the entire ecosystem balance must be preserved. Such a measure, as well as selective cutting of invasive bush species, could only be tolerated around tracks set up to facilitate travel during recreational visits. It is known that the fallen stems and branches of living or dead woody plants represent micro-habitats for micro-organisms in the more or less long term, which contribute to the enrichment of soil organic matter. In the Oti-Ke'ran National Park in North Togo, the sale of collected deadwood and the allocation of income to local people are proposed to managers to facilitate participatory management [90].

Most accounts did not mention the major destructive action of fires in the core of the vegetation. Culverwell [91] stated that the MGNP had not burned for at least 40 years. Nevertheless, a recent observation at the edge of an area of about 2000 m^2 consumed by a farmer's accidental fire confirmed the effectiveness of this threat. The protected area is not particularly fireproof and as its degradation intensifies, the hygrometry that limits the spread of bushfires will be reduced. This could lead to a total burning of the vegetation. It is therefore imperative to control and prevent early dry season fires and to enrich the edge of the forest with fire-breaking hedgerow species, also constituting a protective barrier. This natural protective barrier, using a few natural non-invasive plant species, can be put in place by involving the riparian population, especially in easily accessible areas, with human constructions or crop fields at the edge. It will also be necessary to monitor their proliferation on a permanent basis.

7.3.8 Guidelines for the implementation of a geographic information system (GIS)

With the obtaining of important spatial data of the park and its periphery, the implementation of a GIS could be done by exploiting the identification of land occupation units over the years. This multiple mapping will allow multi-date cross-referencing, with a view to detecting changes in land cover and carrying out simulations. The geo-referencing of spatial information, in the large vegetation units concerning climate, plant composition and structure, pedological data, anthropisation parameters, and remote sensing indices could favor ecological monitoring. These data should be renewed periodically, taking into account the resources available, in order to gauge the effectiveness of management measures, and thus guide new decision-making. The data collection points are integrated into the GIS. Thus conceived, this GIS would be part of a sustainable management dynamic for the MGNP.

8. Conclusion

In conclusion, this chapter has essentially allowed measures to be proposed in order to promote sustainable management of the MGNP. On the basis of information gathered from its physical and human environment, a number of values were identified, as well as management shortcomings, threats and pressures, with a view to formulating a number of management guidelines favorable to its sustainable conservation. The aim was to contribute to the popularization of the results of the research work on this park, presented in the form of guidelines applicable to the diversity of actors likely to interact with the resources or to be involved in its management. Other specialists in the field of natural resource management are therefore called upon, particularly in support of the design of better awareness-raising strategies, for the full appropriation and effective application of the proposed management measures. It is obvious that adherence to the results of this work will have to face certain reprehensible resistances. Indeed, these behaviors are in contradiction with the United Nations' vision of sustainable development, in favor of sharing benefits, goods and ecosystem services between present and future generations. These obstacles call for a real consideration of socioeconomic, sociocultural, psycho-affective (sensitivity to environmental issues), political and economic factors in the realization and operationalization of management plans for protected areas in general, and for the MGNP in particular.

Acknowledgements

The authors thank the International Foundation for Science (IFS) for its material and financial support, which made it possible to carry out preliminary research on the study site.

Author details

Rodrigue Constant Sandjong Sani[1*], Mama Ntoupka[2], Toua Vroumsia[3] and Adamou Ibrahima[3]

1 Faculty of Science, University of Maroua, Maroua, Cameroon

2 Institute of Agricultural Research for Development (IRAD Forest), Foumban, Cameroon

3 Faculty of Science, Department of Biological Sciences, University of Ngaoundéré, Ngaoundéré, Cameroon

*Address all correspondence to: sanirocos@yahoo.fr

References

[1] Anderson J, Farrington J. La vulgarisation forestière face aux défis d'aujourd'hui et de demain. Unasylva. 1996; 184(47):3-12.

[2] Samari D, Azadi H, Zarafshani K, hosseininia G, Witlox F. Determining appropriate forestry extension model: Application of AHP in the Zagros Area, Iran. *Forest Policy and* Economics, 2012;15(1):91-97.

[3] Dembner SA, Anderson J. Towards forestry information dissemination and communication strategies: new partners, priorities and technologies. Unasylva. 1996; *184*(47)

[4] Kandzior A, Rivas E. Forestry Extension as a Work Approach for Forestry Programs and Projects. In: Pancel L, Köhl M, editors. Tropical Forestry Handbook. Berlin: Springer Heidelberg; 2015. p. 1-20 p. https://doi.org/10.1007/978-3-642-41554-8_90-1

[5] Giehl ELH, Moretti M, Walsh JC, Batalha MA, Cook CN Scientific Evidence and Potential Barriers in the Management of Brazilian Protected Areas. PLoS ONE; 2017. 12(1): e0169917. https://doi.org/10.1371/journal.pone.0169917

[6] Rafidimanantsoa HP, Poudyal M, Ramamonjisoa BS, Patricia J, Gordon J. Mind the gap: the use of research in protected area management in Madagascar, Madagascar Conservation & Development 2018; 13(01):15- 24. http://dx.doi.org/1 0.431 4/mcd.v1 3i1 .3

[7] Foster BC, Wang D, Keeton WS, Ashton MS. Implementing sustainable forest management using six concepts in an adaptive management framework, journal of sustainable forestry. 2010; 2979-108. https://doi.org/10.1080/10549810903463494

[8] Nocentini S, Buttoud G, Ciancio O, Corona P. Managing forests in a changing world: the need for a systemic approach, a review. Forest Systems. 2017; 26(1):1-15. DOI:10.5424/fs/2017261-09443

[9] Douglas J, Simula M. The future of the world's forests: ideas vs ideologies. Dordrecht, the Netherlands: Springer; 2010. 214 p.

[10] Leroy M, Derroire G, Vendé J, Leménager T. La gestion durable des forêts tropicales. De l'analyse critique du concept à l'évaluation environnementale des dispositifs de gestion. France: Agence Française De Développement, Collection "À Savoir"; 2013. 236 p.

[11] Lee T, Middleton J. Lignes directrices pour la planification de la gestion des aires protégées. Gland. Suisse: UICN; 2011. 67 p.

[12] Watson JEM, Dudley N, Segan DB, Hockings M. The performance and potential of protected areas. Nature. 2014; 515:67-73. https://doi.org/10.1038/nature13947

[13] He M, Cliquet A. Challenges for Protected Areas Management in China, Sustainability 2020; 12, 5879 1-29 http://dx.doi.org/10.3390/su12155879

[14] UICN/PACO. Formations en gestion des aires protégées en Afrique de l'Ouest et centrale: Effets et recommandations. Ouagadougou. Burkina Faso: UICN; 2015. 52 p.

[15] Cook CN, Hockings M, Carter RW. Conservation in the dark? The information used to support management decisions. Frontiers in Ecology and the Environment. 2010; 8(4): 181-186, doi: 10.1890/090020

[16] Sandjong Sani RC, Ntoupka M, Vroumsia T, Ibrahima A. Phytoecological valorization attributes of Mozogo-Gokoro National Park

(Cameroon). Environmental Monitoring and Assessment. 2019; 191 (79): 1-21. DOI: 10.1007/s10661-019-7186-9

[17] Boutrais J, Boulet J, Beauvilain A, Gubry P, Barreteau D, Die'j M, et al., editors. Le Nord du Cameroun des Hommes, une région. Paris. Collection Mémoires No 102: Éditions de l'Office de la Recherche Scientifique et Technique Outre-mer; 1984. p. 539

[18] Yengué JL. L'évolution du couvert ligneux dans l'Extrême-Nord du Cameroun. Utilisation de la photographie aérienne et de l'imagerie satellitaire. Thèse de Doctorat en Géographie, Université Paris I—Panthéon-Sorbonne, version numérique; 2000

[19] Wafo T. Les aires protégées de l'Extrême-Nord Cameroun, Entre politiques de conservation et pratiques locales. Thèse de Doctorat. France: Université d'Orléans, Pôle Universités Centre Val de Loire; 2008. p. 325

[20] Sandjong Sani RC, Ntoupka M, Ibrahima A, Vroumsia T. Essai d'analyses de la conception paysanne de l'évolution, de la gestion et de l'utilité du Parc National de Mozogo-Gokoro (Cameroun) en vue de son aménagement. International Journal Biological and Chemical Sciences. 2013; 7(6):2434-2449. DOI: 10.4314/ijbcs.v7i6.24

[21] Sandjong Sani RC, Ntoupka M, Ibrahima A, Vroumsia T. Etude écologique du Parc National de Mozogo-Gokoro (Cameroun): prospections préliminaires de la flore ligneuse et du sol pour sa conservation et son aménagement. International Journal of Biological and Chemical Sciences. 2013; 7(6):2434-2449. https://doi.org/10.4314/ijbcs.v7i6.21.

[22] Sandjong Sani RC, Ntoupka M, Ibrahima A, Toua V, Etouna J. Inducement of sustainable management planning of Mozogo-Gokoro National Park (Cameroon) by images processing. Journal of Biodiversity and Environmental Sciences. 2017;11(5):74-91

[23] Sandjong Sani RC, Ntoupka M, Vroumsia T, Ibrahima A. Caractérisation structurale de la végétation ligneuse du Parc National de Mozogo-Gokoro (Cameroun). Flora et Vegetatio Sudano-Sambesica. 2018;21:7-24. DOI: 10.21248/fvss.21.56

[24] Sandjong Sani RC. Etude phytoécologique du Parc National de Mozogo-Gokoro dans l'Extrême-Nord Cameroun: implications pour une gestion durable. Thèse de Doctorat/Ph.D, Université de Maroua (Cameroun). Faculté des sciences. Spécialité: Biologie des Organismes Végétaux (Phytoécologie); 2019. 198 p.

[25] Sandjong Sani RC, Ntoupka M, Vroumsia T, Ibrahima A. Sustainable Management of Tropical Dry Forests: An Overview from Cameroonian Context and the Special Case of Mozogo-Gokoro National Park, Rhodes ER and Humood N, editors. Natural Resources Management and Biological Sciences. IntechOpen; 2020. DOI: 10.5772/intechopen.91982.

[26] Gallopín G, Funtowicz S, O'Connor M, Ravetz J. La science pour le XXIe siècle: du contrat social aux fondements scientifiques, Revue internationale des sciences sociales. 2001; 168:239-250.

[27] Vimal R., Des aires protégées aux réseaux écologiques: science, technique et participation pour penser collectivement la durabilité des territoires. Thèse de Doctorat de l'Université Montpellier II. Sciences et Techniques du Languedoc; 2010. 297 p.

[28] Bellefontaine R, Gaston A, Petrucci Y. Aménagement des forêts

tropicales sèches. Rome: FAO, Cahiers FAO Conservation 32; 1997. 321 p.

[29] Dupuy B, Maître HF, Amsallem I. Techniques de gestion des écosystèmes forestiers tropicaux: état de l'art. Working paper FAO/FPIRS; 1999. 146 p.

[30] Secretariat of the Convention on Biological Diversity. The Ecosystem Approach (CBD Guidelines). Montreal: Secretariat of the Convention on Biological Diversity; 2004. 50 p.

[31] FAO, Lignes directrices pour la gestion durable des forêts en zones arides d'Afrique subsaharienne. Document de travail sur les Forêts et la Foresterie en zones arides n°1; 2010. 56 p.

[32] UICN-PAPACO. La planification des aires protégées: études de cas portant sur l'élaboration et la mise en œuvre des plans de gestion d'aires protégées en Afrique du Centre et de l'Ouest. Nouvelles des Aires Protégées en Afrique N°50: UICN-PAPACO; 2012. 9 p.

[33] Lausche B. Lignes directrices pour la législation des aires protégées. Gland. Suisse: UICN; 2012. 406 p.

[34] Olson DM, Dinerstein E, Wikramanayake ED, Burgess ND, Powell GVN, Underwood EC, D'amico J, Itoua I, Strand HE., Morrison JC, Loucks CJ, Allnutt TF, Ricketts TH, Kura Y., Lamoreux JF, Wettengel WW, Hedao P, Kassem KR. Terrestrial Ecoregions of the World: A New Map of Life on Earth. BioScience. 2001; 51(11):933-938.

[35] Doumenge C, Palla F, Scholte P, Hiol Hiol F, Larzillière A. Aires protégées d'Afrique centrale, État 2015. OFAC. Kinshasa, République Démocratique du Congo et COMIFAC. Yaoundé, Cameroun; 2015. 256 p.

[36] Brabant P, Gavaud M, Les sols et les ressources en terres du Nord Cameroun (Provinces du nord et de l'Extrême-Nord): Cartes et notice explicative (Feuille 19), Chapitre III, 2e partie, Paris: ORSTOM; 1985. p. 121-182.

[37] Republic of Cameroon. Loi N°94/01 du 20 Janvier 1994 portant régime des forêts, de la faune et de la pêche au Cameroun. République du Cameroun; 1994. p. 24

[38] Republic of Cameroon. Décret N°95/531/PM du 23 aout 1995 fixant les modalités d'application du régime des forêts. République du Cameroun; 1995. p. 39

[39] Republic of Cameroon. Décret N°95/466/PM du 20 juillet 1995 fixant les modalités d'application du régime de la faune. République du Cameroun; 1995. p. 22

[40] Hockings, M., Stolton, S., Leverington, F., Dudley, N. et Courrau, J. (2008). Évaluation de l'efficacité : Un cadre pour l'évaluation de l'efficacité de la gestion des aires protégées 2ème édition. Gland, Suisse : UICN. 105pp.

[41] UNESCO. Trousse à outils, Amélioration de notre patrimoine, Evaluer l'efficacité de la gestion des sites naturels du patrimoine mondial. Centre du patrimoine mondial de l'UNESCO; 2008. 104 p.

[42] UICN. Standard mondial pour l'identification des Zones Clés pour la Biodiversité. Version 1.0. Première édition. Gland, Suisse: UICN; 2016. 43p.

[43] Donfack P. Végétation des jachères du Nord-Cameroun : typologie, diversité, dynamique, production. Thèse de doctorat d'Etat, Université de Yaoundé 1 (Cameroun). Faculté des sciences. Biologie et Physiologie végétale; 1998. 225 p.

[44] IUCN/WCPA. IUCN Green List of Protected and Conserved Areas: Standard. Version 1.1. Gland,

Switzerland: IUCN, World Commission on Protected Areas; 2017. 43 p.

[45] IUCN/WCPA/ASI. IUCN Green List of Protected and Conserved Areas. User Manual, Version 1.2. Gland, Switzerland: IUCN, World Commission on Protected Areas (WCPA), Assurance Services International (ASI); 2019. 110 p.

[46] Wicander S. State governance of protected areas in Africa. Case studies, lessons learned and conditions of success. UNEP-WCMC. UK: Cambridge; 2015. 71 p.

[47] Fouth D, Nkolo M, Scholte P. Analyse des modèles de Gouvernance des Aires Protégées et autres aires de conservation, Expériences pratiques des projets/programmes de la de la GIZ en Afrique. Deutsche Gesellschaft für Internationale Zusammenarbeit (GIZ) GmbH; 2017. 54 p.

[48] Chardonnet B. L'Afrique change: ses Aires Protégées doivent-elles évoluer ? Reconfigurer les Aires Protégées en Afrique. France: UICN; 2019. 45 p.

[49] Adams MA, Aveling R, Brockington D, Dickson B, Elliott J, Hutton J, Roe D, Vira B, Wolmer W. Biodiversity conservation and the eradication of poverty. Science. 2004; 306(5699):1146-1149. DOI: 10.1126/science.1097920

[50] Binot A, Joiris DV, Règles d'accès et gestion des ressources pour les acteurs des périphéries d'aires protégées. VertigO, la Revue Electronique en Sciences de l'Environnement. 2007; Hors-série 4. Consulté le 08 avril 2021. DOI : https://doi.org/10.4000/vertigo.759

[51] Gautier D, Garcia C, Negi S, Wardell DA. The limits and failures of existing forest governance standards in semi–arid contexts. International Forestry Review. 2015; 17(2) DOI:10.1505/146554815815834831

[52] Burnette B, DeHose J. The land has wisdom. In: Fortmann L, editor. Participatory research in conservation and rural livelihoods: doing science together. Oxford: Blackwell. 2008. p. 84-97.

[53] Fortmann L, Ballard H. Sciences, knowledges, and the practice of forestry. European Journal of Forestry Research. 2011; 130:467-477. https://doi.org/10.1007/s10342-009-0334-y

[54] Agrisud International. Guide l'agro-écologie en pratiques, Édition 2020. Agrisud; 2020. 246 p.

[55] Fonton HN, Atindogbe G, Fandohan B, Lejeune P, Ligot G. Structure spatiale des arbres des savanes boisées et forêts claires soudaniennes: implication pour les enrichissements forestiers. Biotechnologie, Agronomie, Société et Environnement. 2012; 16 (4): 429-440.

[56] Bennett AF. Linkages in the Landscape: The Role of Corridors and Connectivity in Wildlife Conservation. Gland, Switzerland and Cambridge, UK: IUCN; 2003. 254 p.

[57] Correa AC, Mendoza M, Etter A, Pérez-Salicrup D, Habitat connectivity in biodiversity conservation: A review of recent studies and applications. Progress in Physical Geography. 2016; 40:7-37.

[58] Chalabi B., Mahamadou S. Les aires protégées en milieu désertique, In: Manuel de gestion des aires protégées d'Afrique Francophone. Paris: Awely; 2009. p. 25-34.

[59] Catinot R. Aménager les savanes boisées africaines - un tel objectif semble désormais à notre portée. Bois et Forêts des Tropiques. 1994; 241: 53-69.

[60] Bellefontaine R, Meunier Q, Ichaou A, Morin A, Mapongmetsem PM, Belem B, Azihou F, Houngnon A, Abdourhamane H. La

régénération par graines et par multiplication végétative à faible coût (drageons et boutures de segments de racine). Cirad; 2018. 460 p.

[61] Nouvellet Y. Evolution d'un taillis de formation naturelle en zone soudanienne du Burkina Faso. Thèse Université Pierre et Marie Curie: Paris VI; 1992. 356 p.

[62] Peltier R, Lawali EM, Montagne P, Aménagement villageois des brousses tachetées au Niger. 1ère partie le milieu: potentiel et contraintes. Bois et Forêts des Tropiques. 1994; 242: 59-76. DOI: https://doi.org/10.19182/bft1994.242.a19804

[63] Ntoupka M. Impact des perturbations anthropiques (pâturage, feu, et coupe de bois) sur la dynamique de la savane arborée en zone soudano-sahélienne du Nord du Cameroun. Thèse de Doctorat de l'Université Paul Valery-Montpellier III; 1999. 260 p.

[64] Faye E, Diallo H, Samba SAN, Touré MA, Dramé A, Fall B, Lejoly J, Diatta M, Kaïré M, De Cannière C, Mahy G, Bogaert J. Importance de la méthode de coupe sur la régénération de Combretaceae du Bassin arachidier sénégalais. Tropicultura. 2013; 31(1): 44-52.

[65] Sokpon N, Biaou SH, Ouinsavi C, Hunhyet O.Bases techniques pour une gestion durable des forêts claires du Nord-Bénin rotation, diamètre minimal d'exploitabilité et régénération, Bois et Forêts des Tropiques. 2006; 287(1): 45-57.

[66] Schmitz A, Fall AO, Rouchiche S. Contrôle et utilisation du feu en zones arides et subhumides africaines. Cahiers FAO: Conservation N° 29; 1996. 211 p.

[67] Rakotoarimanana V., Feu, pâturage et dynamique des savanes à *Heteropogon contortus* (L.) P. Beauv. ex Roem. et Shut dans le Sud-ouest de Madagascar (Région de Sakaraha). Thèse de Doctorat troisième cycle: Université d'Antananarivo-Madagascar; 2002. 177 p.

[68] UICN. Lignes Directrices pour l'Application, au Niveau Régional, des Critères de l'UICN pour la Liste Rouge. Commission de la sauvegarde des espèces de l'UICN. Gland, Suisse: et Cambridge, Royaume-Uni: UICN; 2003. 44 p.

[69] Sanou L, Devineau J-L, Fournier A. Groupements floristiques et capacité de régénération des espèces ligneuses des sanctuaires boisés dans l'aire culturelle Bwaba (département de Bondoukuy, Ouest Burkinabé). Acta Botanica Gallica. 2013; 160(1):77-102. doi=10.1080/12538078.2013.797366

[70] Triplet P, Howard G., Gérer les espèces végétales et animales invasives. In: Manuel de gestion des aires protégées d'Afrique Francophone. Paris: Awely; 2009. p. 551-560.

[71] Davies J, Poulsen L, Schulte-Herbrüggen B, Mackinnon K, Crawhall N, Henwood, W.D., Dudley N, Smith J. Gudka M. Conservation de la biodiversité des zones arides. UICN, PNUE-WCMC et CNULCD; 2017. 84 p.

[72] Banks-Leite C, Pardini R, Tambosi LR, Pearse WD, Bueno AA, Bruscagin RT, Condez TH, Dixo M, Igari AT, Martensen AC, Metzger JP. Using ecological thresholds to evaluate the costs and benefits of set-asides in a biodiversity hotspot. Science. 2014; 345(6200): 1041-1045. doi: 10.1126/science.1255768.

[73] Woodley S. Ecological integrity: a framework for ecosystem-based management In: Cole D, Yung L, editors. Beyond Naturalness: Rethinking Park and Wilderness Stewardship in an Era of Rapid Change: Washington DC: Island Press; 2010. p. 106-124.

[74] Keenleyside KA, Dudley N, Cairns S, Hall CM, Stolton S. Restauration écologique pour les aires protégées: Principes, lignes directrices et bonnes pratiques. Gland, Suisse: UICN; 2013. 120 p.

[75] Brancalion PHS, Viani RAG, Strassburg BBN, Rodrigues RR. Financer la restauration des forêts tropicales. Unasylva. 2012; 63(239): 25-34.

[76] Janishevski L, Santamaria C, Gidda SB, Cooper HD, Brancalion PHS, Restauration des écosystèmes, zones protégées et conservation de la biodiversité. Unasylva. 2015; 66(245):19-28.

[77] Roose E. Gestion conservatoire des eaux et de la fertilité des sols dans les paysages soudano-sahéliens de l'Afrique Occidentale in Soil, Crop, and Water Management Systems for Rainfed Agriculture in the Sudano-Sahelian Zone In: proceedings of an International Workshop ICRISAT (International Crops Research Institute for the Semi-Arid Tropics); 7- 11 January 1987; Sahelian Center Niamey: Niger; Patancheru AP. 502324: India; 1989. p. 55-72

[78] Roose E, Bellefontaine R, Visser M. Six rules for the rapid restoration of degraded lands: synthesis of 16 case studies in tropical and Mediterranean climates. Sécheresse. 2011; 22(2): 86-96. DOI: 10.1684/sec.2011.0300

[79] Harmand JM. Rôle des espèces ligneuses à croissance rapide dans le fonctionnement biogéochimique de la jachère, effet sur la restauration de la fertilité des sols ferrugineux tropicaux (Bassin de la Bénoué au Nord-Cameroun). Thèse de Doctorat de l'Université de Paris VI en Biologie et Ecologie végétales tropicales. Volume 1. IRAD; CIRAD; 1997. 213 p.

[80] Kimba A, Delmas P. *Leptadenia hastata* (hanam ou yadiya), De superbes potentialités mais une plante oubliée. Réseau National des Chambres d'Agriculture du Niger, Note d'information. 2017; GDT 1: 1-5.

[81] Eyog Matig O. Modification du régime hydrique d'un sol par les aménagements de surface, in Les terres hardé, Caractérisation et réhabilitation dans le bassin du lac Tchad. In: Peltier R, Editeur Scientifique. Cahiers scientifiques N°11. Mémoires et travaux de L'IRA N°6. CIRAD-Forêt; ORSTOM; IRA; 1993. p. 99-111.

[82] Masse D, Donfack P, Floret C, Pontanier R, Seiny-Boukar L. Réhabilitation de vertisols dégradés (sols hardés) au Nord-Cameroun, In: Pontanier A, M'Hiri N, Akrimi J, Aronson E, Le Floc'h, Editeurs. L'homme peut-il refaire ce qu'il a défait? Paris: John Libbey Eurotext; 1995. p. 127-137

[83] Eyog Matig O. L'enracinement de quatre espèces ligneuses sur sol hardé. In: Peltier R, Editeur Scientifique. Les terres hardé, Caractérisation et réhabilitation dans le bassin du lac Tchad. Cahiers scientifiques N°11. Mémoires et travaux de L'IRA N°6. CIRAD-Forêt; ORSTOM; IRA; 1993. 111-119.

[84] Donfack P. Régénération de la végétation spontanée d'un sol hardé, In: Peltier R, Editeur Scientifique. Les terres hardé, Caractérisation et réhabilitation dans le bassin du lac Tchad. Cahiers scientifiques N°11. Mémoires et travaux de L'IRA N°6. CIRAD-Forêt; ORSTOM; IRA; 1993, P. 71-81.

[85] Tsozué D, Haiwe BR, Louleo J, Nghonda JP. Local Initiatives of Land Rehabilitation in the Sudano-Sahelian Region: Case of Hardé Soils in the Far North Region of Cameroon. Open Journal of Soil Science. 2014; 4: 6-15. http://dx.doi.org/10.4236/ojss.2014.41002

[86] Tang L, Shao G. Drone remote sensing for forestry research and practices. Journal of Forestry Research. 2015; 26(4): 791-797. DOI 10.1007/s11676-015-0088-y.

[87] Smektala G, Peltier R, Sibelet N, Leroy M, Manlay R, Njiti CF, Ntoupka M, Njiemoun A, Palou O, Tapsou. Parcs agroforestiers sahéliens: de la conservation à l'aménagement. VertigO. La Revue Electronique en Sciences de l'Environnement. 2005; 6(2). Consulté le 09 avril 2021; DOI : https://doi.org/10.4000/vertigo.4410

[88] ATIBT. Etude sur le Plan Pratique d'Aménagement des Forêts Naturelles de Production Tropicales Africaines. Application au cas de l'Afrique Centrale (Volet 3). Aspects Faunistiques. Paris: ATIBT; 2005. 99 p.

[89] Bergonzini J., Changements climatiques, désertification, diversité biologique et forêts. SILVA; RIAT; 2004. 146 p.

[90] Adjonou K, Bellefontaine R, Kokou K. Les forêts claires à *Anogeissus leiocarpus* du Parc National Oti-Ke'ran au Nord-Togo: structure, dynamique et impacts des modifications climatiques. Sécheresse. 2009; 20(4): 394-396.

[91] Culverwell J. Long term recurrent costs of protected area management in Cameroon, Monitoring of protected area, donor assistance and external financing, ecological and management priorities of current and potential protected area system. Yaoundé, Cameroon: WWF Cameroon and MINEF Report; 1997. 80 p.

Chapter 10

Ecological Restoration of Degraded Habitats of Jajang Iron and Manganese Ore Mines, Keonjhar, Odisha, India

Rabindra Kumar Mishra, Barun Kumar Behera, Anita Dash and Bidyut Kumar Patra

Abstract

Mining activities in Jajang iron and manganese ore mines located in Keonjhar district of Odisha, India starting from mineral explorations to production and transport are causing environmental damage in many ways, which includes deforestation, loss of topsoil, accelerated soil erosion, migration of wildlife and avifauna, and addition of air pollutants and dust to the atmosphere. In connection to this, the current study was an attempt to regain the original ecological status of the degraded areas of Jajang iron and manganese ore mines caused due to mining by Rungta Mines Limited. To achieve this indigenous plant species for restoration were selected from mining forests and plantations. Species selection from mining forests was made through systematic phytosociological analysis that involved measurement of Importance Value Index (IVI), regeneration values of tree species and their economic uses. On the other hand, species selection from plantations was made based on their growth, productivity, economic uses and adaptation to terrain and soil types. Shrubs and grasses were selected based on their relative index and abundance, respectively. The top 15 tree and 16 grass species as well as all six shrub species were selected from mining forests and plantations were considered for restoration. The findings of the study may also aids in the faster restoration of degraded habitats with initial human facilitation as the soils of degraded areas were similar to that of the mining forest. To speed up the recovery process after-care and monitoring have also been suggested or advised.

Keywords: Growth, Importance Value Index (IVI), Mining, productivity, Restoration, Vegetation

1. Introduction

Ecological restoration often known as eco-restoration is the process of recreating, initiating or accelerating the recovery of degraded habitats [1]. The adverse effect of disturbances include the full removal of vegetation cover and topsoil, which completely changes the topography of the area, deterioration of esthetics, impacts on surrounding ecosystems, and cause the major environmental changes that alter both ecosystem structure and function [2]. These disturbances are the negative outcome of opencast mining. In pacifying the adverse impacts caused due to mining activity on the local environment, mining-degraded areas are either reclaimed, by restoring a neglected area to some use or rehabilitated, by providing circumstances for a new and considerably different use [3] in order to mitigate the negative effects of mining activities on the surrounding ecosystem. To achieve this, two restoration techniques are to be used namely physical, technical, or engineering restoration, which is high cost and accounts for 60 to 90% of the total restoration cost and biological restoration, which is low cost and requires multi-disciplinary inputs [4].

The normal recovery of mining-degraded sites takes time for plant and animal species to colonize [5–7]. However, in many degraded areas, conventional recovery practices combined with biological restoration through human involvement can speed up the restoration process [8, 9]. Until now, there has not been much focus on restoring these degraded lands. Recent awareness followed by stringent enforcement of rules and regulations has generated consciousness about the environment. In some places of India restoration has been tried on an experimental basis [10–13]; [8] through the introduction of plantation programs. Plantation of indigenous plant species has attempted restoration through such approaches and as a consequence, the degraded areas have been restored [14].

Restoration is the recreation of entire communities of organisms that are closely modeled on those occurring naturally, whereas reclamation is any purposeful effort to return a damaged ecosystem to some type of beneficial usage [15–17]. In several situations, it would appear that it is reclamation rather than restoration which is attempted. Restoration needs knowledge of indigenous biological resources for understanding the species response to micro-environmental features and edaphic conditions [18–20]. Information on these aspects aids not only in the selection of species that are adapted to local conditions [13] but also in the rapid recovery of the ecosystem once such species have been planted [21, 22]. In these conditions, this piece of research is the outcome of a study that encompassed all of the factors needed to aid in ecological restoration of disturbed areas at Jajang iron and manganese ore mine in Keonjhar district, Odisha.

The Jajang iron and manganese ore mine area in Keonjhar district, Odisha has been disturbed due to mining since 1957. The area with dry deciduous forests contains good quality minable iron and manganese ore deposits. To undertake the mining activities some parts of the forest covers were cleared. Presently dumping is being done in well-vegetated valleys that adversely affected the vegetation. Thus the present study aimed to fix a set of phytosociological and growth related parameters of plant species that are linked to species success, as well as an ecological framework for selecting suitable species from the nearby mining forest and plantation to restore the degraded areas of Jajang iron and manganese ore mine, Odisha.

2. Study area

The Jajang Iron and Manganese Ore Mine (JIMOM) $21^0\ 55'\ 00''$ to $21^0\ 56'\ 35''$N latitude and $85^0\ 25'\ 00''$ to $85^0\ 27'\ 10''$ E longitude having a lease area of about 666.15 ha include 247 ha of forest area and 41.97 ha of dump area (**Figures 1** and **2**).

In this area, mining has been done in 377.18 ha and 41.97 ha or nearly about 42 ha have been used as a dump. The rate of extraction of ore is around 16.5 million tons per annum (MTPA) and the ore to waste ratio is 1:0.043. The mines lease area includes the following:

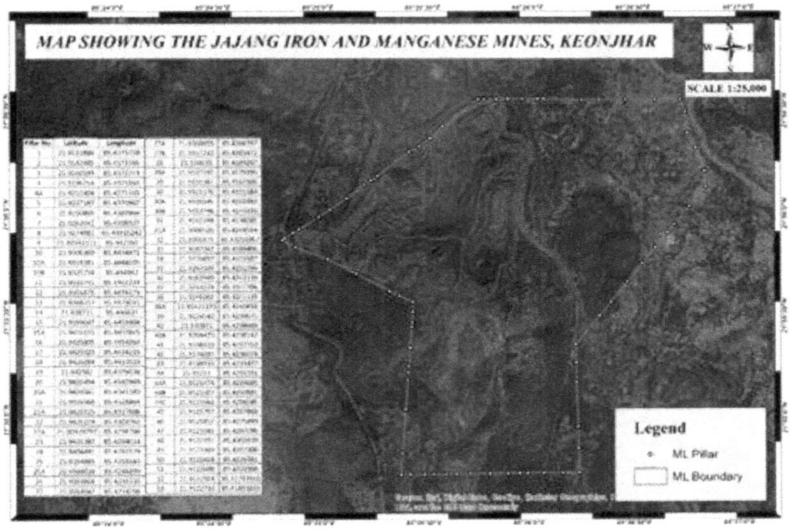

Figure 1.
Google earth view of Jajang iron and manganese ore mine at Keonjhar. ML: Mining lease.

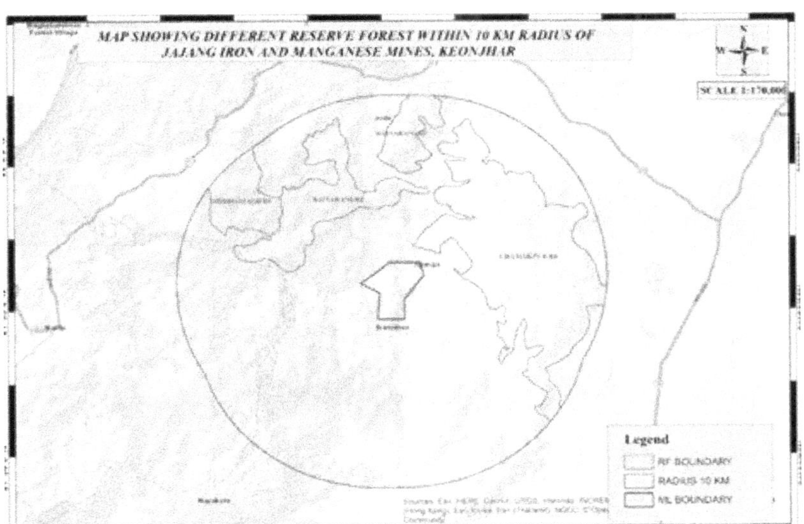

Figure 2.
Outline map within 10 km radius of Jajanga iron and manganese ore mine at Keonjhar. RF: Reserve Forest, ML: Mining lease.

i. Forest area (FA): 247 ha, where mining activities have not yet been taken up and have natural vegetation in some parts (**Figure 3**).

ii. Dump Area (DA): 41.967 ha i.e. equal to 42 ha, where the waste and topsoil were dumped in the past (**Figure 4**).

iii. Mining Area (MA): 377.18 ha, where mining has been done (**Figure 5**).

Figure 3.
Forest area (FA) of JIMOM.

Figure 4.
Dump area (DA) of JIMOM.

Soil analytic report comprises of some physical and chemical parameters are used to validate the fertility and health status of soil in this area is presented in **Table 1**. Physical parameters (sand, silt and clay percentage) related to the development of soil structure indicated that the soil of the area is loamy with some proportions of silt and clay. The depth varies from shallow (0-30 cm) and medium (31–50 cm) to moderately deep (51-80 cm). Most areas have medium-depth soil. More than half of the area has moderate to good water holding capacity. Chemical parameters encompass pH, nitrogen, phosphorus, potassium and organic carbon mostly related to soil fertility inferred that the soil is slightly acidic and adequate in the required nutrient parameters (potassium, phosphorus and nitrogen) to afford plant growth [23].

Figure 5.
Mining activity at JIMOM.

Parameters	Values (Mean ± SD)
Sand (%)	68.5 ± 3.18
Silt (%)	15.3 ± 0.76
Clay (%)	16.2 ± 1.32
Bulk density (g/cm^3)	1.18 ± 0.065
Soil Moisture (%)	16.73 ± 1.17
WHC (%)	48.3 ± 3.6
pH	6.42 ± 0.46
Nitrogen (kg/ha)	163.07 ± 18.62
Phosphorus (kg/ha)	4.25 ± 0.66
Potassium (kg/ha)	279.92 ± 24.3
Organic Carbon (%)	3.8 ± 0.12

Source: Soil analysis report of Jajang iron and manganese ore mine (JIMOM); WHC: Water Holding Capacity.

Table 1.
Soil physico -chemical characters (mean ± SD) of the study site.

3. Methods

A field survey was carried out from June, 2015 to May, 2017 in FA, DA and plantation (P). One hundred and fifty quadrats of 20 m × 20 m in sizes were laid down randomly at FA to obtain data on the composition and phytosociological attributes of tree species. In each quadrat, trees (≥ 30 cm GBH) such as girth at breast height (137 cm above ground), height, canopy height, canopy width and regeneration (plants <10 cm GBH) were recorded [24]. Tree height and canopy height were measured from the ground to the tree tip and up to the height from where the branching of canopy starts, respectively using a height-measuring rod.

To measure the canopy width each tree was viewed below from all sides to identify the longest axis. The diameter 'd_1' or length of the longest axis passing through the center of the canopy/crown was measured followed by the length of the shortest axis or diameter 'd_2' perpendicular to the longest (first) axis. The two diameters were then averaged to determine the canopy width (in meter) as:

$$CW = d_1 + d_2/2 \tag{1}$$

Where, d_1 = length of the longest axis of each tree canopy and d_2 = Length of the shortest axis of each tree canopy perpendicular to the longest axis.

Shrub species from the FA were analyzed by placing two quadrats of 5 m × 5 m sizes nested within each quadrat laid down for tree species. The density and frequency of each shrub species enumerated from the FA were calculated as:

$$\text{Density} = \text{Total number of individuals of a species/Total number of quadrats studied} \tag{2}$$

$$\text{Frequency} = \text{Number of quadrats in which species occur/Total number of quadrats studied} \tag{3}$$

The selection of shrub species from FA for restoration practice was recognized using relative index (RI) calculated as a sum of relative density (RD) and relative frequency (RF) [14]. Relative density (RD) is the study of the numerical strength of a species to the total number of individuals of all species and calculated as:

$$\text{Relative Density (RD)} = (\text{Number of individuals of a species/Number of individuals of all species}) \times 100 \tag{4}$$

Formulae to calculate the relative frequency (RF) as:

$$\text{Relative Frequency (RF)} = (\text{Frequency of a species/Frequency of all species}) \times 100 \tag{5}$$

Unlike shrub and tree species, herbaceous species were analyzed by placing 300 numbers of 1 m × 1 m size quadrats each at FA and DA. Only abundance (A) was calculated for herbaceous species. The abundance which is an appreciation of the number of individuals of different species in a community is calculated as [25]:

$$\text{Abundance (A)} = \text{Total number of individuals of a species/Total number of quadrats in which the species occurred} \tag{6}$$

In both FA and DA abundance of herbaceous species was estimated at regular intervals and categorized as rare, common and abundant. Further abundance rating (AR) was given to each herbaceous species. The rare species were rated as 1, while the common and abundant species were given a score of 2 and 3, respectively [26].

3.1 Species selection from forest

Tree species for restoration were selected in two phases. In the first phase, the top 15 species were selected based on the Importance Value Index (IVI). Remarking was given to each species based on the IVI. IVI was calculated as a sum of relative density (RD), relative frequency (RF), and relative dominance (RDo) [27, 28]. Formulae for measurement of RD and RF of tree species is similar to that of RD and RF of shrub species, but the relative dominance (RDo) of tree species was calculated as:

$$\text{Relative Dominance (RDo)} = (\text{Basal area of a species}/\text{Basal area of all the species}) \times 100 \tag{7}$$

The basal area which is regarded as an index of dominance of a species was calculated as:

$$\text{Basal area (BA)} = \pi r^2 \left(m^2\right) \tag{8}$$

$$\text{Importance Value Index (IVI)} = \text{RD} + \text{RF} + \text{RDo} \tag{9}$$

During the second phase of selection, regeneration potential was included. Tree species represented by more than 15 individuals per m^2 in the regeneration (seedling) stage (GBH $\leq$ 10 cm) were ranked 1, species having less than five number of individuals in the regeneration stage were ranked 3 and species having individuals in between 5 and 15 in the regeneration stage were ranked 2 [29]. Adding IVI and regeneration ranks, the top twelve tree species were selected for restoration. Shrub species were selected using relative index (RI) and herbaceous species on abundance ranking (AR).

3.2 Species selection from plantation

Tree species in "P" were selected based on their growth, productivity and adaptation. The growth was estimated using the size index [14] as:

$$\text{Size Index (SI)} = \text{Tree height (cm)} \times \text{gbh (cm)}. \tag{10}$$

Productivity potential of tree species was estimated using canopy index [14] as:

$$\text{Canopy Index (CI)} = (\text{Average canopy height} + \text{Average canopy width}) \times \text{no.of sample trees}. \tag{11}$$

Adaptation potential of species was evaluated as; species grown on the slopes were ranked 1, species grown on flat terrain were ranked 2, while those species are grown in valleys, stream bed or river bed were ranked 3 and 4, respectively. The species growing on shallow soils were ranked 1, while those on medium and deep soil were ranked 2 and 3, respectively. Adding the ranks for growth, productivity, terrain and soil, the top ten species were selected. Some species were included based on their properties to enrich the soil.

3.3 Economic rank (ER) of tree species selected for plantation

The economic rank of tree species was considered as an additional criterion to strengthen the process of tree species selection from mining forest areas and plantation for plantation in the mining waste site of JIMOM. To analyze the economic rank of tree species selected from FA and P for plantation the local people and forest officials were consulted and interviewed during the field visit days. Based on local use types (food, animal feed, timber, gum, edible fruit, ethnomedicine, edible oil, etc.) of such plant species for livelihood subsistence of the local community and industrial purposes their economic rank was calculated. As ER was an ordinal variable, it took values >0 and varied from 1 to 3. Species having a maximum number of economic uses were ranked as 1 and those having a minimum number of economic uses were ranked as 3. The other ones of economic uses intermediate between maximum and minimum were ranked as 2.

4. Results and discussion

4.1 Species richness and abundance

The study explored the presence of 67 plant species of 26 angiospermic families and 51 genera belonging to different strata i.e. tree, shrub and herb from FA, P and DA of Jajang Iron and Manganese Ore Mine (JIMOM) (**Tables 2–4**). From FA 62 plant species were recorded which includes 34 trees, 6 shrubs and 22 herbaceous species (**Tables 2–4**). However, in plantation only12 tree species were recorded. The number of tree species enumerated in FA was more or less 3 times of P. Tree species found similar to both FA and P are *Acacia nilotica*, *Samanea saman*, *Albizia lebbeck*, *Dalbergia sissoo*, *Madhuca indica*, *Gmelina arborea* and *Xylia xylocarpa*. Of these, *Samanea saman*, *Dalbergia sissoo*, *Albizia lebbeck* and *Gmelina arborea* performed better in "P" only. On the other hand, *Xylia xylocarpa* performed well in both. Compared to tree and herb layers, the diversity of the shrub layer in terms of the number of species was too low. Only six species of shrubs from families Lythraceae, Sterculiaceae, Oleaceae, Rubiaceae, Flacourtiaceae and Fabaceae were recorded from FA (**Table 3**). In the herb layer, all the 22 species were enumerated both from FA and DA and included under 3 families namely Caryophyllaceae, Cyperaceae and Poaceae. Based on species dominancy family Poaceae was species rich followed by Cyperaceae and Caryophyllaceae (**Table 4**). High species richness of trees in FA as compared to plantation may likely due to the high level of structural complexity and stratification of vegetation to attract wild animals which acts as the seed dispersers required for seed germination. Dispersal of seeds spatially by the dispersers to a greater extent and germination of seeds in newly arrived areas may one of the ways to maintain high species richness in FA. Inversely low species richness of trees in plantations may be due to lack of seed source and litter deposition and decomposition on the soil surface of plantation [30]. Further Plantations are mostly monocultures or include few species of interest leads to low species richness [4, 29].

4.2 Tree species selection from FA and "P"

Species selection from different vegetation layers of FA for plantation at mine waste sites (DA) through the use of some phytosociological parameters (abundance, frequency, IVI, etc.) is vital as a first step and was amplified by studying the economic use and regeneration status of trees, RI of shrubs and AR for herbs, respectively to reveal the suitability of species to survive in the existing edaphic and environmental conditions of mine waste sites. In the tree layer *Holarrhena antidysentrica* had maximum IVI followed by *Mitragyna parviflora, Anogeissus latifolia, Adina cordifolia, Buchnania lanzan, Lannea coromandelica, Miliusa velutina, Xylia xylocarpa* and *Bridelia retusa*. These tree species had IVI greater than 7. The rest of the species had IVI ranged from 0.31 to 5.78. The top 15 species with higher

Name of species	Family	IVI	Rank
Holarrhena antidysentrica (L.) Wall. Ex A. DC.	Apocynaceae	15.75	1*
Mitragyna parviflora (Roxb.) Koth.	Rubiaceae	15.40	2*
Anogeissus latifolia (Roxb. ex DC.) Wall. ex Bedome	Combretaceae	12.12	3*
Adina cordifolia (Roxb.) Brandis	Rubiaceae	10.96	4*
Buchnania lanzan Spreng.	Anacardiaceae	10.46	5*
Lannea coromandelica (Houtt.)Merr.	Anacardiaceae	10.44	6*
Miliusa velutina (Dunal) Hook. f. &Thomas	Annonaceae	9.91	7*
Xylia xylocarpa (Roxb.)Taub.	Mimosaceae	9.36	8*
Bridelia retusa (L.) Spreng.	Euphorbiaceae	7.19	9*
Schleichera oleosa (Lour.) Oken	Sapindaceae	5.78	10*
Syzygium cumini (L.) Skeels	Myrtaceae	4.89	11*
Garuga pinnata (Roxb.)	Burseraceae	4.65	12*
Wendlandia tinctoria (Roxb.) DC.	Rubiaceae	4.34	13*
Shorea robusta Gaertn. f.	Dipterocarpaceae	4.23	14*
Terminalia bellirica (Gaertn) Roxb.	Combretaceae	2.73	15*
Terminalia alata Heyne ex Roth.	Combretaceae	2.50	16
Dalbergia sissoo Roxb.	Mimosaceae	2.41	17
Elaeodendron glauca (Rottb) Pers.	Celastraceae	2.21	18
Morinda pubescens Sm.	Rubiaceae	2.13	19
Cassia fistula L.	Caesalpiniaceae	1.86	20
Madhuca indica Gmel.	Sapotaceae	1.55	21
Samanea saman (Jacq.) Merr.	Mimosaceae	1.43	22
Lagerstroemia parviflora Roxb.	Lythraceae	1.37	23
Butea monosperma (Lam.) Taub.	Fabaceae	1.22	24
Terminalia arjuna (Roxb. Ex DC.) Wight &Arn.	Combretaceae	1.2	25
Trema orientalis Linn. Blume	Ulmaceae	1.18	26
Albizia lebbeck (L.) Benth.	Mimosaceae	1.15	27
Acacia nilotica (Linn.) Willd. Ex Del.	Leguminosae	1.11	28
Pongamia pinnata (L.) Pierre	Leguminosae	1.08	29
Phyllanthus emblica L.	Euphorbiaceae	1.05	30
Hymenodictyon excelsum (Roxb.) Wall	Rubiaceae	0.58	31
Bauhinia racemosa Lam.	Caesalpiniaceae	0.46	32
Terminalia chebula Retz.	Combretaceae	0.41	33
Gmelina arborea Roxb.	Simaroubaceae	0.31	34

**Species selected for restoration.*

Table 2.
Importance value index (IVI) of tree species recorded in forest area (FA) of Jajang iron and manganese ore mine.

IVI values were selected from FA for economic use and regeneration studies. Considering all the criteria (IVI, economic rank (ER) and regeneration rank) of species selection, tree species selected from FA for plantation are presented in **Table 5**. To

Name of the species	Family	RI	Rank
Woodfordia fruticosa (L.) Kutz.	Lythraceae	23.71	1
Helicteres isora L.	Malvaceae	20.81	2
Nyctanthes arbortristis L.	Oleaceae	17.31	3
Wendlandia exerta (Roxb.) DC.	Rubiaceae	15.29	4
Flacourtia indica (Burm. f.) Merr.	Flacourtiaceae	13.17	5
Cassia auriculata L. (Roxb.)	Fabaceae	11.87	6

Table 3.
Relative index (R.I.) of shrub species at Jajang iron and manganese ore mine.

Name of the species	Family	Abundance	Rank
Apluda mutica L.	Poaceae	4	6*
Aristida setacea Retz.	Poaceae	6	4*
Cynodon dactylon (L.) Pers.	Poaceae	3	7*
Chloris barbata Sw.	Poaceae	6	4*
Chloris virgata Sw.	Poaceae	8	2*
Cryperus compressus L.	Cyperaceae	9	1*
Cyperus difformis L.	Cyperaceae	4	6*
Cyperus eleusiniodes (Lunth.) Haines	Cyperaceae	3	7*
Cyperus iria L.	Cyperaceae	3	7*
Cyperus sp.	Cyperaceae	2	8
Dactyloctenium aegyptium (L.) Beauv.	Poaceae	7	3*
Digitaria marginata Linn.	Poaceae	7	3*
Oplismenus burmannii (Retz.) Beauv.	Poaceae	2	8
Isellema laxum Hack.	Poaceae	5	5*
Dianthus sp.	Caryophyllaceae	2	8
Dichanthium annulatum Forsk.	Poaceae	4	6*
Paspalidium punctatum (Burm.) *A. Camus*	Poaceae	3	7*
Pennisetum sp.	Poaceae	1	9
Setaria verticillata (L.) Beauv.	Poaceae	5	5*
Sporobolus indicus (Linn.) Chase	Poaceae	2	8
Sporobolus sp.	Poaceae	2	8
Themeda arundinaceae (Roxb.) A. Camus	Poaceae	3	7*

**Species selected for restoration.*

Table 4.
Abundance rating (AR) of herbaceous species at Jajang iron and manganese ore mine.

rehabilitate the mine waste sites tree species selected as the planting material may not only act as one of the successful methods of ecorestoration but also establish an ecological condition for nutrient cycling in soil nutrient amelioration as well as create an ecological avenue for attracting avifauna and other wildlife to congregate in this area. Further, in the future, this ecologically restored area should be used

Name of the species	IVI		Regeneration rank	Multiple economic uses	Economic Rank (ER)	Total rank
	Value	Rank				
Holarrhena antidysentrica	15.75	1*	1	WS, AI,D, CM, P,M	1	3
Mitragyna parviflora	15.40	2*	1	HC, F, AI, M	2	5
Anogeissus latifolia	12.12	3*	1	HC, BF, FW, AI, M	2	6
Adina cordifolia	10.96	4*	2	FW,AF, M, AI	2	8
Buchnania lanzan	10.46	5*	2	BF, EF, M, FW	2	9
Lannea coromandelica	10.44	6*	2	AF, FW,G,M	2	10
Miliusa velutina	9.91	7*	1	FW, M	3	11
Xylia xylocarpa	9.36	8*	2	HC, BF, AF, EF, M	2	12
Bridelia retusa	7.19	9*	1	F, FW, HC, AI, M	2	12
Schleichera oleosa	5.75	10*	1	F, MO, EO, EF, FW, M	1	12
Syzygium cumini	4.89	11*	3	FO, CL,F, AI, EF, M	1	15
Garuga pinnata	4.65	12*	2	EF, F, G, FW	2	16
Wendlandia tinctoria	4.34	13*	1	M, AT	3	17
Shorea robusta	4.23	14*	3	W, AI, T, EO, M	2	19
Terminalia bellirica	2.73	15*	2	G, M	3	20

HC, House Construction; F, Furniture; AI, Agricultural Impliments; BF, Bio Fencing; P, Paper; AT, Arrack & Toddy; WS, Walking Stick;FW, Fuel Wood; M, Medicine; G, Gum; CL, Country Liquor; EF, Edible Fruit; CM, Carved Material;D, Dye; AF, Animal Feed; MO, Message Oil;EO, Edible Oil; W, Wood; T, Toothbrush.

Table 5.
Multiple economic uses, importance value index, regeneration and economic ranks of tree species in mine forest at Jajang iron and manganese ore mine.

to maintain socioeconomic goals (productivity) and to fulfill the biodiversity objectives.

Unlike FA, instead of IVI and regeneration rank important growth related parameters like growth rate and productivity of tree species at "P" was considered along with ER, terrain and soil depth to select species for plantation at mine waste sites. The age of tree species years after the plantation was ranged from 3 to 6 years. *Gmelina arborea* was the fast-growing species with a maximum growth rate (3867 cm^2/year) with minimum ER while *Xylia xylocarpa* gained maximum productivity (48 cm^2/year) and ER (**Table 6**). When adaptation to terrain and soil depth was included in the selection parameter, *Samanea saman* shared the top rank followed by *Flindersia australis, Dalbergia sissoo, Xylia xylocarpa*, *Albizia lebbeck* = *Peltophorum pterocarpum*, *Gmelina arborea*, etc.

Parameters used for the choice of species were to assess their ability to adapt and thrive in challenging environmental conditions. The inclusion of more than one parameter ensures that even if two species scored the same on one parameter, the difference in scores on other parameters assisted in deciding which species was the best. Aside from parameter selection, selecting species for plantation from several sampling locations (FA and P) aided in the development of a comprehensive list of species based on their performance in a variety of habitats. Only 12 tree species were grown in plantations, out of which 7 species did occur in FA and most of the species were native to the area. On the other hand, the FAs' comparatively large number of species contributed to more options for the selection of species. The top-performing native species in the neighborhood from a cumulative list of 21 tree

Tree species	Age	Growth rate GR/Y	Growth rate Rank	Productivity rate P/Y	Productivity rate Rank	T Rank	S Rank	Multiple economic uses	Economic Rank (ER)	Total Rank
Acacia auriculiformis	5	1862	11	28	11	2	1	D, FW, M	2	27
Acacia nilotica	4	1973	10	26	12	2	1	D, AF, FW, M	2	27
Samanea saman	6	3567	2	36	4	2	1	AF,FW,G	2	11
Albizia lebbeck	4	2963	5	32	7	2	1	HC, F, AI, M	2	17
Casia siamea	4	1435	12	31	8	1	1	D, FW	3	25
Dalbergia sissoo	4	2595	7	44	2	1	2	F, HC, M	2	14
Delonix regia	6	2147	9	35	5	2	3	D, FW	3	23
Flindersia australis	3	3279	3	42	3	2	1	F, HC	3	12
Madhuca indica	4	2888	6	29	10	1	1	CL, EO, M	2	20
Gmelina arborea	6	3867	1	30	9	2	3	F, AI, M	2	17
Peltophorum pterocarpum	4	3215	4	33	6	2	3	D, FW, M	2	17
Xylia xylocarpa	4	2583	8	48	1	2	3	HC, BF, AF, EF, M	1	15

GR/Y, growth rate/year; P/Y, Productivity/year; T, Terrain; S, Soil.
HC, House Construction; F, Furniture; AI, Agricultural Impliments; BF, Bio Fencing; FW, Fuel Wood; M, Medicine; G, Gum; CL, Country Liquor; EF, Edible Fruit; D, Dye; AF, Animal Feed; EO, Edible Oil.

Table 6.
Growth (cm^2/year), productivity (cm^2/year), terrain, soil and economic ranks of tree species at Jajang iron and manganese ore plantation area.

species, 11 from FA, 9 from plantations and one species common to both i.e. *Xylia xylocarpa* to encourage natural colonization (**Table** 7).

Furthermore, the study suggests that growing leguminous plants, which give nitrogen to the root zone in mine spoil, would be more beneficial in increasing mining wasteland fertility [19]; [33]. *Albizia lebbeck, Acacia auriculiformis* and *Acacia nilotica* are the species with strong nitrogenous activity in root nodules [6]; [34]. As a result, these tree species are recommended for planting on dumps and in degraded environments. In addition to these *Pongamia pinnata* is regarded as one of the most promising plants for mining overburden [35, 36] and should be planted on the mining waste site to enrich the soil. Critical analysis of the study envisages that tree species like *Samanea saman*, *Flindersia australis, Gmelina arborea* and *Peltophorum pterocarpum* are the topmost selected ones from "P" may do well when planted on dumps, as suggested. The list of tree species that have been suggested for plantation or revegetation both from mining forest and plantation based on the results of the present investigation and their unique ecological features to ameliorate the degraded conditions is presented in **Table** 7.

4.3 Shrub and herbaceous species selection

The relative index (RI) of shrub species in the FA ranged from 11.87 to 23.71. *Woodfordia fruticosa* had the highest RI followed by *Helicteres isora*, *Nyctanthes*

Species	Characteristics*	From mining forest area	From plantations
Holarrhena antidysentrica	Drought tolerant, light demander, fire tolerant and pioneer species	√	
Mitragyna parviflora	Esthetic, easy to grow, industrial woodware and wind breaker	√	
Anogeissus latifolia	Drought resistant, grow in well drained and low fertility soil and acts as soil stabilizer	√	
Adina cordifolia	Prefers moist and well drained soil,soil binder and drought resistant	√	
Buchnania lanzan	Light demander, prefers dry soil and grow in hill slopes	√	
Lannea coromandelica	Grow in poor soil condition and fire resistant	√	
Miliusa velutina	Grow in dry soil and drought resistant	√	
Xylia xylocarpa	Grow in adverse environmental conditions and nitrogen fixer	√	√
Bridelia retusa	Fast growing and fire resistant	√	
Schleichera oleosa	Slow growing, fire resistant grow in well drained and acidic soil, and light demander	√	
Syzygium cumini	Fast growing, drought tolerant and grow in shallow and rocky soils	√	
Garuga pinnata	Grow in well drained soil having moderate fertility and prefers acidic to neutral soil pH	√	
Samanea saman	Fast growing, prefers moderately to acidic soil, drought tolerant and nitrogen fixer		√
Flindersia australis	Fast growing, light demanding and grow in wide range of soil		√
Dalbergia sissoo	Leguminous, dust resistant and nitrogen fixer		√
Albizia lebbeck	Leguminous, Nitrogen fixer and soil binder		√
Peltophorum pterocarpum	Fast growing, nitrogen fixer and used as shelter belts		√
Madhuca latifolia	Grow in loamy and sandy loam soil and drought resistant		√
Gmelina arborea	Nitrogen fixer		√
Delonix regia	Fast growing, drought resistant and nitrogen fixer		√
Cassia siamea	Easy to grow, fast growing and nitrogen fixer		√

**Source: [31, 32].*

Table 7.
Tree species suggested for plantation on dumps.

arbor-tristis, *Wendlandia exerta* and *Flacourtia indica* while *Cassia auriculata* had the lowest RI (**Table 3**). All six species enumerated were suggested for use in rehabilitation efforts. In the understorey in addition to shrubs the floristic inventory of herbaceous species of the study area revealed that Poaceae had the maximum number of species indicating that members of this family had the greatest potential to colonize adverse iron and manganese mine spoil habitat. The ability of herbaceous species, particularly grass species to withstand drought, poor soil nutrients and climatic conditions [37] may play a role in their colonization on mine spoils. Many researchers have emphasized the significance of grasses as the first colonizers during the restoration of mine land [38–40]; [29]. Grassroots with their fibrous root systems, are said to help limit erosion, stabilize soil and conserve moisture [37]. Furthermore, the importance of grass species cover as nurse crops for later colonizers has been extensively documented [29, 40, 41]. Aside from the importance of species rich families of herbaceous species for restoration, measuring one of the key phytosociological attributes i.e. abundance of such species was considered as a tool or criteria to select the key species from the group of this plantlife form that can be successfully applied to the development of mining waste site restoration strategies. Analytical results on herbaceous species abundance in the mining forest area ranged from 1 to 9 with *Cyperus compressus* being the most abundant followed by *Chloris virgata*, *Dactyloctenium aegypticum* = *Digitaria marginata*, *Chloris barbata* = *Aristida setacea*, *Setaria verticillata* = *Isellema laxum* and so on. *Pennisetum* sp. on the other hand had the minimum (**Table 4**). Based on the abundance value and its rating the top sixteen herbaceous species from the mining forest region were selected for restoration activity (**Table 4**). As reported by [12]; [42] planting selected native herb species on the periphery of dumps or mine waste sites and streambeds can operate as a vegetative filter to reduce soil and water pollution in the surrounding areas. Herbs are preferably more successful than agroforestry crops at preventing runoff and erosion [34, 43]. As a result native herb species are recommended for the mine wast sites at the initial phase of restoration in this study. The slope gradient was one of the factors considered when selecting plant species for restoration. On the slopes, the herbaceous species named *Setaria verticillata, Themeda arundinaceae* and *Dactyloctenium aegyptium* were found abundant. Therefore, these plant species should be grown on mine waste slopes. As the soil physicochemical characters of mine waste sites were comparable to those of FA and P, and 70 cm of top soil was stored separately for spreading over dumps during resolution, the selected plant species will grow successfully on the mine waste sites or slag hips. These herbaceous species selected based on taxonomic and phytosociological attributes for the eco-restoration program may not only grow and spread in these locations but also provide food sources for local fauna and help to recover ecosystem services for local communities.

5. Conclusion

To restore the biological quality of the degraded areas of Jajang Iron and Manganese Ore Mine (JIMOM), revegetation with native or indigenous plant species selected from the mine forest area (FA) and plantation (P) constitutes the most effective, useful, and widely accepted way of ecological restoration of mining degraded lands to reduce soil erosion and protect the soils against degradation. Before revegetation, plant selection is very important for an effective restoration strategy. Plants need to be selected for restoration based on the study of their IVI, regeneration potential, economic rank, growth rate, productivity, relative index, abundance rank and their ability to survive and regenerate in the local, specific environment, and to stabilize the soil structure. Inhabitation of the land with different native or indigenous plant species enables the association of microorganisms which are fundamental to maintain soil quality through the decomposition of organic matter and nutrient cycle. The results of the study signify that the selective species of three different plant life forms such as trees (*Holarrhena antidysentrica, Mitragyna parviflora, Anogeissus latifolia, Adina cordifolia, Buchnania lanzan, Lannea coromandelica, Miliusa velutina, Xylia xylocarpa, Bridelia retusa,* etc. from mining forest area and *Samanea saman, Flindersia australis, Dalbergia sissoo, Albizia lebbeck, Peltophorum pterocarpum, Madhuca latifolia, Gmelina arborea, Delonix regia, Cassia siamea* from plantation), shrubs (*Woodfordia fruticosa, Helicteres isora, Nyctanthes arbor-tristis, Wendlandia exerta, Flacourtia indica* and *Cassia auriculata*) and herbs (*Cyperus compressus, Chloris virgata, Dactyloctenium aegypticum, Digitaria marginata, Chloris barbata, Aristida setacea, Setaria verticillata, Isellema laxum*, etc.) for plantation or afforestation can potentially enhance the recovery of mine degraded lands. This study not only provides an insight to restore the mining degraded lands of JIMOM but also facilitates the natural process of speciation and becomes a source of germplasm of various species. It improves all environmental conditions esthetically including economical aspects. Further, the ecorestoration approach described in this paper is also to be recommended for the environmental management of degraded mining lands. From a future restoration point of view and to strengthen the restoration practice in revegetated degraded mining lands of JIMOM monitoring of soil physicochemical parameters will be made at regular intervals to indicate the change in soil nutrient status of the restored area. In addition to this monitoring of vertebrate faunal communities and their association with plant life forms in restored areas may also be important in understanding the overall effects of restoration work and maintaining the biological diversity of the area for future prospects. Such scientific investigations will boost further restoration practice and also useful in a way to reduce high rates of forest destruction, energy shortages, and steps towards conservation of biological resources.

Acknowledgements

We thank Director, Jajang Iron and Manganese Ore Mine (JIOM), Keonjhar for providing permission and necessary support during the study.

Author details

Rabindra Kumar Mishra[1*], Barun Kumar Behera[2], Anita Dash[3] and Bidyut Kumar Patra[4]

1 Department of Wildlife and Biodiversity Conservation, Maharaja Sriram Chandra Bhanjadeo University, Baripada, Odisha, India

2 Jajang Iron and Manganese Ore Mines, Rungta Mines Limited, Keonjhar, Odisha, India

3 Department of Botany, Maharishi College of Natural Law, Bhubaneswar, India

4 Center for Envotech and Management Consultancy Pvt. Ltd., Nayapalli, Bhubaneswar, India

*Address all correspondence to: rabikumishra@gmail.com

References

[1] SERI. 2004. The SER International primer on ecological restoration. Society for Ecological Restoration International. Tucson: Arizona; USA. 2004.

[2] Anshumali. Ecological blueprint of plantation in mining sectors: an implication in biodiversity conservation and climate change. In: Soni P, Singh L. editors. Landscape Fragmentation and Restoration Researches in India. 1st ed. Heinrich: Lambert Academic Publishing; 2012. P.5-19. Ch1

[3] Bandyopadhyaya S, Maiti S K. Evaluation of ecological restoration success in mining-degraded lands. Environ Qual Manage. 2019: 1-12. DOI: doi.org/10.1002/tqem.21641

[4] Sonter L J, Ali H S, Watson E M J. Mining and biodiversity: key issues and research needs in conservation science. Proc. R. Soc. B. 2018:285: 1-9. DOI: doi.org./10.1098/rsbp. 2018.1926

[5] Pandey D N. Sustainability science for mine- spoil restoration. Current Science. 2002: 83:792-793.

[6] Cole R J, Holl K D, Zahawi R A. Seed rain under tree islands planted to restore degraded lands in a tropical agricultural landscape. 2010. Ecological Applications: 20: 1255-1269. DOI: doi. org/10.1890/09-0714.1

[7] Vibhash R , Sen P, Kumar D, Sarsawat A. A review on dump slope stabilization by revegetation with reference to indigenous plant. Ecological Processes. 2015: 4:1-14. DOI: doi.org/ 10.1186/s13717-015-0041-1

[8] Ahirwal J, Pandey V C. Ecological rehabilitation of mine-degraded land for sustainable environmental development in emerging nations. 2020: 1-5 RE-New (Opinion) Article. Doi: doi.org/10.1111/ rec.13268

[9] Mentis M. Environmental rehabilitation of damaged land. 2020. Forest Ecosystems. 2020:7-19. DOI: doi. org/10.1186/s40663-020-00233-4

[10] Jha AK, Singh A, Singh A N, Singh J S. Evolution of direct seeding of tree species as a means of re-vegetation of coal mine spoils. Indian Forester. 2000: 126 (11): 1217-1221.

[11] Dongmei L E I, Changqun D. Restoration potential of pioneer plants growing on land-zinc mine tailings in Lanping, south-west China. Journal of Environmental science. 2008. 20(10): 1202-1209. DOI: doi.org/10.1016/ s1001-0742(08)62210-x

[12] Sharma S D, Soni P, Chandra V. Amelioration of the overburden of iron ore mine for free establishment. Annals of forestry. 1998: 6 (2) : 239-244.

[13] Singh A N, Raghubanshi A S, Singh J S. Plantation as a tool for mine spoil restoration. Current Science.2002: 82 : 1436-1441.

[14] Sharma D, Sunderraj S F W. Species selection for improving disturbed habitats in western India. Current Science. 2005: 88(3): 462-467.

[15] Parrotta J A, Knowles O H. Restoration of tropical moist forests on bauxite mined lands in the Brazilian Amazon. Restoration Ecology.1999: 7: 103-116. DOI: doi.org/10.1046/ j.1526-100X.1999.72001.x.

[16] Kumar S S, Sharma B K, Gough L P. Richness, diversity and evenness of vegetation upon rehabilitation of gypsum mine spoiled lands in the Indian arid zone. Annals of Arid Zone. 1998: 37: 139-145.

[17] Jim CY. Ecological and landscape rehabilitation of a quarry site in Hong Kong. Restoration Ecology. 2001: 9:

85-94. DOI:doi.org/10.1046/j.1526-100x.2001.009001085.x

[18] Rao A V, Tak R. Growth of different tree species and their nutrient uptake in limestone mine spoil as influenced by arbuscular mycorrhizal (AM) fungi in India arid zone. Journal of Arid Environments. 2002: 51 : 113-119. DOI: doi.org/10.1006/jare.2001.0930.

[19] Singh A N, Raghubanshi A S, Singh J S. Impact of native tree plantations on mine spoil in a dry tropical environment. Forest Ecology and Management. 2004: 187: 49-60. DOI: doi.org/10.1016/S0378-1127(03)00309-8.

[20] Wong M H. Ecological restoration of mine degraded soils, with emphasis on metal contaminated soils. Chemosphere. 2003: 50: 775-780. DOI: doi.org/ 10.1016/s0045-6535(02)00232-1.

[21] Boyd E. The paradox of the CDM and sustainable development. International Forestry Review. 2002: 4: 77-80.

[22] Verma P, Verma R K. Species diversity of arbuscular mycorrhizal (AM) fungi in Dalli-Rajhara Iron Mine overburden dump of Chhattisgarh (Central India). International Journal of Current Microbiology and Applied Sciences. 2017: 6 (4): 2766-2781. DOI: doi.org/10.20546/ijcmas.2017.604.320.

[23] Paramasivam C R, Anbazhagan S. Soil fertility analysis in and around magnesite mines, Salem, India.Geology, Ecology and Landscapes. 2020: 4(2): 140-150. DOI:doi.org/10.1080/24749508.2019.1608407.

[24] Mueller D , Ellenberg H. Aims and Methods of Vegetation Ecology.1st ed. New York. 1st ed. New York: John Wiley and Sons; 1974. 547p.

[25] Kershaw K A. Quantitative and Dyamic Plant Ecology. 2nd ed. London : Edward Arnold Ltd.; 1973.308p.

[26] Mohanty R C, Mishra, R K, Bal S, Upadhyay V P. Plant diversity assessment of Shorea robusta dominated forest stands of Similipal biosphere reserve. Journal Indian Botanical Society.2005. 84: 21-29.

[27] Curtis J T, McIntosh R P. The interrelations of certain analytic and synthetic phytosociological characters. Ecology. 1950: 31: 434-455. DOI: doi.org/10.2307/1931497.

[28] Mishra R K, Parhi S, Biswal A K. Diversity of over storey plant communities of tropical forest covers of Balasore district, Odisha, India. Adv Plants Agric Res. 2018.8(1):20-26. DOI: doi.org/10.15406/apar.2018.08.00285.

[29] Mishra R K, Patra B K.Vegetation analysis: a tool for restoration of degraded habitats of Raikela Iron Ore Mines. Int J Environ Sci Nat Res. 2017.5 (5):161-166. DOI:doi.org/10.19080/IJESNR.2017.05.555674.

[30] Bremner L,Farley K A Does plantation forestry restore biodiversity or create green deserts? A synthesis of the effects of landuse transitions on plant species richness. Biodiversity Conservation. 2010:19:3893-3915.DOI: 10.1007/s 10531-010-9936-4.

[31] Maiti S K. Ecorestoration of the coalmine degraded lands. 1st ed. Springer New Delhi Heidelberg New York Dordrecht London. 2013. P. 1-357. ISBN: 978-81-322-0850-1. DOI: 10.1007/978-81-322-0851-8

[32] Useful Tropical Plants tropical.theferns.info

[33] Sayer J, Chokkalingam U, Poulsen J. The restoration of forest biodiversity and ecological value. Forest Ecological and Management. 2004: 201 : 3-14. DOI: doi.org/10.1016/j.foreco.2004.06.008.

[34] Sharma K D, Kumar P, Gough L P, Sanfilipo J R. Rehabilitation of a lignite

mine disturbed area in the Indian desert. Land Degradation and development.2004: 15 (2):163- 176. DOI: doi.org/10.1002/ldr.601

[35] Sekhar N U. Decentralized natural resource management: from state to co-management in India. Journal of Environmental Planning and Management. 2000: 43 : 123-138. DOI: d oi.org/10.1080/09640560010793.

[36] Sharma K D, Kumar S, Gough L. Rehabilitation of lands mined for limestone in the Indian desert. Land Degradation and Development. 2000: 11 : 563-574. DOI: doi.org/10.1002/ 1099-145X(200011/12)11:6<563::AID-LDR414>3.0.CO; 2-I.

[37] Tereza C G, Giulietti M, Raymond M, Harley I, Rodolfo J, Ronnie A, Carlos E, Nara F O, Caldeira Jr, Vera I, Imperatriz F, Antonio E, Furtini E. Siqueira O. Selecting plant species for practical restoration of degraded lands using a multiple-trait approach. Austral Ecology. 2016:2-12. DOI: doi:10.1111/aec.12470

[38] Nero B F. Structure, composition and diversity of restored forest ecosystems on mine-spoils in south-western Ghana. PLoS ONE. 2021: 16(6): 1-22. DOI: doi.org/10.1371/journal. pone.0252371.

[39] Nsa I Y, Oyebanji O O, Igbinigie E E, Odunsi A A. Floral distribution of a sub-bituminous coal dump site in Enugu, Nigeria. Frontiers in Ecology and Evolution. 2021: 9:1-10. DOI: doi: 10.3389/fevo.2021.649954

[40] Ekka N J, Behera N. Species composition and diversity of vegetation developing on an age series of coal mine spoil in an open cast coal field in Orissa, India. Tropical Ecology. 2011: 52(3): 337-343, 2011.

[41] Pratiwi N, Siregar C A, Turjaman M, Hidayat A, Rachmat H H, Mulyanto B, Suward I, Maharani R. Managing and reforesting degraded post-mining landscape in Indonesia: a review. Land. 2021: 10: 2-29. DOI: https://10.3390/ land10060658

[42] Chaubey O P, Jamaluddin O P, Ram Prakash R. Bio-reclamation of degraded ecosystem. International Journal of Bio-Science and Bio-Technology. 2014: 6(4): 145-154.DOI: doi.org/10.14257/ijbsb t.2014.6.4.14.

[43] Mensah A. Role of re-vegetation in restoring fertility of degraded mine soils in Ghana: a review. International Journal of Biodiversity and Conservation. 2015: 7(2): 57-80. doi.org/10.5897/ IJBC2014.0775.

Chapter 11

Integrating Ecological Site Descriptions with Soil Morphology to Optimize Forest Management: Three Missouri Case Studies

Michael Aide, Indi Braden and Christine Aide

Abstract

Academics and University Extension personnel have experience with soil mapping and providing soil suitability interpretations; however, a more efficient information conveyance to land custodians is desired to support informative land management applications. In the USA each state, in concert with the United States Department of Agriculture, has embarked on developing an online format linking soil survey with ecological site descriptions to provide information for forest and rangeland management to encourage soil protection - health and optimizing ecological services on individual land parcels. In this Missouri-based manuscript, we discuss three cases where soils and their associated ecological site descriptions provide land custodians information concerning their logical reference state vegetation community and detail land management decisions that transform the reference vegetation community to a different vegetation community. With each case, landscapes and their associated vegetations communities are potentially partitioned by soil, physiography, hydrology, and other attributes.

Keywords: ecological sites, forest management, Alfisols, Ultisols, soil mapping

1. Introduction

Alfisols are a soil order in USA "Keys of Soil Taxonomy" [1]. Alfisols are typically developed under mixed forests in temperate climates that maintain a low to moderate level of soil organic matter, a neutral to acidic pH and have a moderate degree of base saturation. One requirement of Alfisols is the presence of an argillic horizon, coupled with the requirement of having a base saturation greater than 35% in the argillic horizon control section [1]. In Missouri, Alfisols typically have aquic and udic moisture regimes and support deciduous forest vegetation [2]. Ultisols are a soil order in USA "Keys of Soil Taxonomy" that are similar to Alfisols with the exception that Ultisols have less than 35% base saturation in the control section [1].

The USDA-NRCS has developed the National Soils Information System based on a national soil survey composed of establishing soil characteristics using observations along soil delineation boundaries and determining map unit compositions

IntechOpen

by field transects [3]. Three different geographic databases have been established having different mapping intensities: (i) State Soil Geographic database (STATSGO at a scale of 1:250,000, (ii) Soil Survey Geographic (SSURGO) at a scale ranging from 1:12,000 to 1:63,360, and (iii) National Soil Geographic (NATSGO) at a scale of 1:7,500,000. The STATSGO database is well-suited to represent soil data relative to specified soil associations (a soil association represents two or more different soils that appear in a regularly repeating landscape pattern) and are well-suited for regional, multi-state, river basin and multi-county resource planning, management, and monitoring. The SSURGO database provides detailed information about individual soils and is well-suited for landowners, municipal, and county planners for more local and site-specific resource planning, management, and monitoring. The NATSGO database establishes information and the identification of the Major Land Resource Area (MLRA) map and associated attribute data. The MLRA is a land area having a clearly defined composition of geography, geology, soils, climate, physiographic features, potential natural vegetation, water resources and land practices.

Ecological classification is predicated on the separation of a landscape into discrete and repeatable land parcels, wherein the individual land parcels provide information to guide land management. An ecological site is defined as "a distinctive type of land based on recurring soil, landform, geological, and climate characteristics that differs from other kinds of land in its ability to produce distinctive kinds and amounts of vegetation and in its ability to respond similarly to management actions and natural disturbances" [4]. As such, ecological sites provide a framework for connecting soils and landscapes to vegetational communities; after which, thoughtful and knowledgeable natural resource management may proceed with a full understanding of potential beneficial and negative consequences [5]. Once established, ecosystem site descriptions may be assembled to provide land management ranging from a woodlot to a landscape to an ecosystem.

In Missouri, ecosystem site identification/isolation and subsequent descriptions are prepared by a multiagency cooperation involving diverse disciplines within the Missouri Department of Conservation and the United States Department Agriculture-Natural Resource and Conservation Service (USDA-NRCS). Literature utilized by this multiagency cooperative project includes materials produced by the Missouri Department of Conservation, USDA-NRCS and other entities [6–12]. Eight soil and ecological factors are identified that significantly influence vegetation and site productivity: (i) landform, (ii) parent material, (iii) root restrictions, (iv) base saturation, (v) soil drainage, (vi) soil texture, (vii) flooding, and (viii) ponding.

These soil and ecological factors have been previously characterized by a 50+ year county-based soil survey program, resulting in a national database. Subsequently, land parcels having a commonality of these soil factors were correlated with historical and potential vegetation communities. Ecological site names are based on soil/substrate, landform and the historic plant community, with one example being "Loess Fragipan Upland Flatwoods". Based on a verification process, ecological sites are initially termed "provisional ecological sites", then with further review and data acquisition, the ecological sites are eventually termed "correlated ecological sites". In addition to soil, climate, local hydrology, and physiographic information, the final product contains additional information on species composition, canopy cover, biomass estimates, and ground cover information.

Products available to the public are termed "ecological site descriptions (ESD's) and provide additional information: (i) ecological site extent maps, (ii) physiologic features, (iii) landscape block diagrams, (iv) soil descriptions and interpretations, (v) ecological dynamics with state and transition models, (vi) plant lists, and (vii) site interpretations for forestry and wildlife management.

Ecological site descriptions are not mapping units, rather they are taxonomic units. However, ecological site descriptions of an appropriate areal extent may be used as mapping units when the sites are highly patterned because of site topography, soil distribution, geology, and other attributes. The repeatable distribution of ecological sites provides for their useful application to manage land under the influence of livestock grazing, wildlife habitat, recreation, rural or urban development, forestry, and a multitude of other land uses. In general, we accept the definition proposed by Bestelmeyer et al. [13] and Briske et al. [14] to define an ecological site as landscape units that have similar characteristics of soil, topography, geological formations, and climate regimes that differ because of (i) the production and plant species composition under the disturbance of reference conditions associated with soil properties, the natural dynamics of vegetation and the ecosystem services provided, and (ii) the responses to management, processes of degradation, and restoration.

State and Transition Models attempt to explain how ecosystems transition from one state to another state. A state is a series of plant communities associated with specific soil properties that produce persistent attributes over time with structural and functional ecosystem characteristics [15]. The reference state is a state that provides the largest range of potential environmental services and typically is the "ideal" state. At its essence, researchers aim to understand how ecosystems function and respond to management or natural influences. Ecological resilience is the capacity to absorb and/or reorganize after a disturbance yet maintaining the site's structural integrity [15]. Thresholds are key biotic and abiotic factors and modified ecosystem functions that alter the ecosystem structure beyond the limits of ecological resilience resulting in a transition to a different state or limits recovery. Triggers are events, factors, processes and/or drivers that initiate a transition from one state to another.

The objectives of this project are to document the importance of combining soil survey information with ecological site descriptions to show relationships (i) between soil genesis-soil morphology with their resident plant communities, and (ii) and the actions of land management to alter the resident plant communities to a different plant community.

2. Materials and methods

2.1 Study areas

The study areas are all located in southeastern Missouri, USA. The study area containing the Knobtop, Taumsauk and Irondale Ultisol pedons is located at Taumsauk State Park and was selected because of its variable pedon depths and the presence of loess over igneous residuum/colluvium. The Knobtop (Fine-silty, mixed, active, mesic Aquic Hapludults) pedon is a moderately deep, moderately well-drained soil formed in loess overlying Precambrian rhyolite residuum. The pedon is located on a summit position having a 1 to 2 percent slope. The Irondale (Loamy-skeletal, mixed, active, mesic Typic Hapludults) pedon is moderately deep, well-drained, and moderately permeable soil formed in rhyolite residuum on a steep 35% slope supporting an oak forest. The Taumsauk (Loamy-skeletal, mixed, active, mesic Lithic Hapludults) pedon is a shallow, somewhat excessively-drained, moderately permeable soil formed in rhyolite colluvium. The Taumsauk pedon is located on a 10% convex slope and exhibits a mountain glade area.

The Caneyville and Hildebrecht pedons are in Sam A Baker State Park and were selected because the pedons were formed in loess over limestone residuum, which is a very common occurrence across east-central Missouri. The Caneyville (Fine, mixed, active, mesic Typic Hapludalfs) Alfisol pedon is a moderately deep, well-drained soil formed in a thin silty mantle overlying fine-textured limestone residuum. The Hildebrecht (Fine-silty, mixed, active, mesic Oxyaquic Fragiudalfs) Alfisol pedon is a very deep, moderately well-drained soil on a side slope. The pedon is formed in loess over weathered dolomitic residuum. Permeability is moderate above the fragipan and slow or very slow in the fragipan.

The study area containing the Amagon (Fine-silty, mixed, active, thermic Typic Endoaqualfs) and Calhoun (Fine-silty, mixed, active, thermic Typic Glossaqualfs) pedons are located in the Mingo National Wildlife Refuge. This study area was selected because these poorly-drained pedons were formed in alluvium, which is representative of the Mississippi River Embayment. The Amagon pedon is a very deep, poorly-drained, slowly permeable Alfisol that formed in loamy alluvium. The Calhoun pedon is a poorly-drained, slowly permeable Alfisol formed from loess-like material on a Pleistocene-age terrace.

The Knobtop, Taumsauk and Irondale study area and the Caneyville and Hildebrecht study area have a continental humid climate with winter having dry and cold air masses and summer having moist, warm air masses producing abundant rainfall events. The average annual precipitation 112 cm, whereas the average annual temperature is about 13°C [16]. The Amagon and Calhoun study area has a continental humid climate with an average rainfall of 126 cm. Mean winter temperatures are 4°C and mean summer temperature of 26°C, whereas the mean annual temperature is 13°C [17]. The The Knobtop, Taumsauk and Irondale study area and the Caneyville and Hildebrecht study area does not experience flooding, whereas the Amagon and Calhoun study area annually experiences either flooding or seasonal water saturation.

2.2 Methodology

Pedons were located, described, and sampled according to Soil Survey Division Staff [18] in undisturbed forest settings using excavated pits. Samples were oven-dried, lightly crushed, and sieved to remove materials larger than two mm. Soil pH using equal volumes of soil and water, the NH_4-acetate (pH 7.0) extraction of exchangeable bases, the total acidity by slow titration to pH 8.2, and the soil organic matter content (SOM) by loss on ignition were performed using standard methods [19]. The particle size distribution (mechanical analysis) was determined by Na-saturation of the exchange complex, dispersion in Na_2CO_3 (pH 9.0) and centrifuge fractionation to remove clay and wet sieving of the silt and sand separates [19].

The ecological site descriptions were obtained using the Ecosystem Dynamics Interpretive Tool (EDIT), which is an online information system for the sharing of ecological site descriptions [20] or ([https://edit.jornada.nmsu.edu/], verified February 2021).

3. Results and discussion

3.1 Knobtop Irondale Taumsauk Ultisol Assemblage

The Knobtop, Irondale and Taumsauk soils are Ultisols having fine silty or loamy-skeletal textures and exhibiting A-E-Bt-rhyolite rock horizon sequences. The Knobtop pedon resides on a summit position developed in a moderately thick loess mantle overlying rhyolitic residuum, whereas the Irondale and Taumsauk pedons occupy side and convex (shoulder) slope positions, respectively. The Irondale and Taumsauk pedons exhibit thin and very thin loess mantles overlying rhyolite colluvium, features attributed to erosion and mass-wasting during and subsequent to loess deposition.

The Knobtop (Aquic Hapludult), Taumsauk (Lithic Hapludult) and Irondale (Typic Hapludult) pedons reside in MLRA 116 in the St. Francois Knobs and Basins region. The Knobtop pedon exhibited a silt loam texture in the ochric epipedon and silty clay loam texture in the majority of the argillic horizon (**Table 1**). The Taumsauk pedon exhibited a very cobbly silt loam ochric epipedon (A horizon) and very cobbly silt loam (E horizon) transitioning to a very cobbly silty clay loam within the comparatively shallow-to-bedrock argillic horizon. Soil pH in the Knobtop and Taumsauk pedons are extremely acid, with a corresponding base saturation much less than 35% (**Table 2**). The exchangeable calcium concentration is very low, which is reflective of the very small Ca concentration of the analyzed rhyolite samples (rhyolite composition not shown). The Irondale pedon exhibits

Knobtop Horizon	Depth cm	Texture	Structure	Boundary	Color Matrix
A	3	Silt loam	1f&m gr	a,s	10YR5/2 grayish brown
E	13	Silt loam	1f sbk	a,s	10YR5/3 brown
Bt1	32	Silt loam	2 f&m sbk	c,s	10YR5/4 yellowish brown
Bt2	55	Silty clay loam	2 f&m sbk	c,s	10YR4/6 dark yellowish brown
Bt3	76	Silty clay loam	2 f&m sbk	c,s	10YR4/6 dark yellowish brown
2 BC	83	Silt loam	1 thick platy	a,s	10YR4/6 dark yellowish brown
R-rhyolite					
Taumsauk					
Horizon					
A	3	Silt loam	1f gr	a,s	10YR3/1 very dark gray
E	8	Silt loam	1f sbk	a,s	10YR4/3 brown
Bt1	25	Silt loam	2f&m sbk	c,s	10YR5/4 yellowish brown
Bt2	33	Silty clay loam	2f&m sbk	a,s	10YR5/6 yellowish brown
R-rhyolite					
Irondale					
Horizon					
A	8	Loam	1f&vf gr	a,s	10YR4/2 dark grayish brown
E	25	Silt loam	1f&vf gr	a,s	10YR 5/3 brown
Bt1	46	Silt loam	1f&vf sbk	c,s	5YR5/6 yellowish red
Bt2	56	Silt loam	1f sbk	c,s	7.5YR5/6 strong brown
R-Rhyolite					

Structure: 1 = weak, 2 = moderate, f = fine, m = medium, gr = spherical, sbk = subangular blocky.
Boundary: a = abrupt,, c = clear, s = smooth.

Table 1.
Morphological and physical properties of the Knobtop, Taumsauk, and Irondale pedons.

Horizon	pH	Total Acidity	SOM	Calcium	Magnesium	Potassium	Sodium	CEC	Base Saturation
Knobtop	**water**	**cmol/kg**	**%**	**cmol/kg**	**cmol/kg**	**cmol/kg**	**cmol/kg**	**cmol/kg**	**%**
A	4.1	19	12	0.83	0.67	0.35	0.15	20.8	9.6
E	4.1	12	1.6	0.25	0.2	0.15	0.11	12.6	5.6
Bt1	3.9	15.5	1.4	0.25	0.31	0.21	0.17	16.3	5.8
Bt2	3.9	19	1.7	0.25	0.66	0.32	0.15	20.2	6.8
Bt3	3.9	17	1.1	0.25	0.7	0.22	0.22	18.2	7.6
2 BC	3.9	15.5	0.7	0.25	1.03	0.16	0.22	16.9	9.8
Taumsauk									
A	4.7	17	16.5	2.85	1.98	0.52	0.15	22.4	24.6
E	4.2	16	3.4	0.25	0.56	0.21	0.14	17	6.8
Bt1	3.8	19.5	2.6	0.25	0.71	0.29	0.15	20.8	6.7
Bt2	3.8	19.5	2.5	0.25	0.63	0.27	0.16	20.6	6.4
Irondale									
Horizon									
A	4.4	5.8	6.1	1.5	0.13	0.24	0.26	7.9	27
E	4.4	5.5	2.9	1	0.08	0.28	0.25	7	22.2
Bt1	4.3	10.9	3.1	1.5	0.28	0.35	0.26	13.2	18.1
Bt2	4.3	6.3	3.3	1.3	0.34	0.28	0.39	8.6	26.8

SOM is soil organic matter, CEC is cation exchange capacity.

Table 2.
Chemical properties of the Knobtop, Taumsauk, and Irondale pedons.

a very acidic reaction, with a relatively greater base saturation; however, the base saturation remains less than 35% as required for the Ultisol order. The soil organic matter content is greatest in the A horizons and declines with increasing soil depth. Given the shallowness of these pedons, especially for the Taumsauk pedon, seasonal dryness during the summer and fall months is presumed to be a limiting factor for tree growth. The extreme soil acidity contributes to the reduced tree growth and limits the vegetational diversity.

For the Knobtop-Irondale-Taumsauk Ultisol assemblage, the corresponding provisional ecological site descriptions are (i) Dry Igneous Upland Woodland (F116CY003MO) having the Knobtop and Irondale soil series, (ii) the Dry Igneous Exposed Backslope Woodland (F116CY011MO) having the Irondale soil series, and (iii) the Shallow Igneous Knob Glade (R116CY006MO) having the Taumsauk soil series. For the Dry Igneous Exposed Backslope Woodland the dominant vegetation is post oak (*Quercus stellate*), black oak (*Quercus velutina*) with scattered blackjack oak (*Quercus marilandica*), northern red oak (*Quercus rubra*) and a ground flora of native grasses and shrubs (fragrant sumac (*Rhus aromatica*) and little bluestem (*Schizachyrium scorparium*)). For the Dry Igneous Upland Woodland, the vegetational community is similar, with exceptions including a slightly greater abundance of northern red oak (*Quercus rubra*) and a greater abundance of the herbaceous species *Danthonia spicata*. The Shallow Igneous Knob Glade has a few species of blackjack oak (*Quercus marilandica*) and the herbaceous species *Schizachyrium scorparium* and *Croton michauxil* var. ellipticus. Canopy closure varies with aspect and soil depth, ranging from 30 to 50% on exposed positions and shallower soil depths to 50–80% on protected positions and deeper soil depths. Fire, including controlled burning, has been present in these vegetational communities, reducing litter accumulation, stimulating grasses and forbs, and reducing the encroachment of woody species.

The Dry Igneous Upland Woodland has post oak (*Quercus stellate*) and northern red oak (*Quercus rubra*) as the dominant tree species in the reference state, with a fire-free interval of 10–15 years witnessing the encroachment of eastern red cedar (*Juniperus virginiana*). The reference state is in quasi-equilibrium with (i) the fire excluded mixed oak woodland state and the (ii) fire excluded and logged mixed oak woodland state based on the contrasting practices of long-term fire suppression and the opposing practice of forest stand improvement using prescribed burning with and without tree species removal. The Dry Igneous Exposed Backslope Woodland reference site and transition sites are similar to that of the Dry Igneous Upland Woodland, with differences attributed to subtle species compositions. The Shallow Igneous Knob Glade has a blackjack oak (*Quercus marilandica*) tree composition with little bluestem (*Schizachyrium scoparium*) and lichens with and associated reference state having eastern redcedar. Fire suppression transitions to a state with the addition of winged elm (*Ulmus alata*). The soil surface cover is variable, but typical estimates are tree basal cover (1%), shrub/vine/liana basal cover (1%), grass and grasslike basal cover (1%), forb basal cover (1%), non-vascular cover (5%), litter (30–50%) and surface fragments (10%).

3.2 Caneyville and Hildebrecht Alfisol Assemblage

The Caneyville and Hildebrecht soils are Alfisols having fine and fine-silty textures and exhibiting A-E-Bt and A-E-Bt-2Btx-3Bt horizon sequences, respectively (**Table 3**). The consensus of soil scientists who mapped these soils is that the Caneyville series developed in loess, whereas the Hildebrecht series developed in Peoria loess overlying a previous bisequal soil derived from older loess developed on limestone residuum.

Horizon	Depth	Texture	Structure	Clay	Sand	Color
	cm			%	%	
Caneyville						
A1	10	sandy loam	2f&mgr	3	60	10YR4/2
A2	18	silt loam	2f&mgr	7	36	10YR4/2
E	33	silt loam	1msbk	10	24	10YR5/4
Bt1	46	silt loam	2msbk	24	14	5YR4/6
Bt2	69	silty clay	2msbk	42	13	7.5YR5/6
Bt3	71	silty clay	2msbk	48	10	7.5YR5/6
Hildebrecht						
A	1	silt loam	2fgr	4	36	10YR3/2
E	3	silt loam	lmpl	9	23	10YR5/4
BE	6	silt loam	lfsbk	13	12	7.5YR5/4
Bt1	13	silty clay loam	2msbk	28	8	7.5YR4/4
Bt2	19	silty clay loam	2msbk	32	11	7.5YR4/4
2Ex	21	loam	l c prism	26	25	10YR5/4
2Btx1	30	loam	l c prism	16	45	10YR5/4
2Btx2	38	loam	l c prism	17	44	5YR5/4
3Bt3	60	clay	3msbk	56	29	2.5YR3/6

For the Hildebrecht pedon, the 2 Btxl to 3Bt3 horizons are very gravelly to extremely gravelly.
Structure; 1 is weak, 2 is moderate, f is fine, m is medium, gr is granular, sbk is subangular blocky.

Table 3.
Morphological and physical properties of the Caneyville and Hildebrecht pedons.

The Caneyville (Typic Hapludalf) pedon has sandy loam and silt loam textures in the ochric epipedon and silty clay loam in most of the argillic horizon. The pH is neutral to slightly acidic in the near surface horizons and strongly acid in the lower argillic horizons, with exchangeable Ca showing a gradual concentration reduction on transition to the deeper horizons (**Table 4**). The Hildebrecht (Oxyaquic Fragiudalf) pedon shows a silt loam texture in the eluvial horizons and a silty clay loam texture in the illuvial horizons. The fragipan has a loam texture which abruptly transitions to clay in the 3Bt3 horizon. The eluvial and argillic horizons appear to be developed in Peoria Loess, whereas the fragipan and 3Bt3 horizons are apparently developed in older Roxana Loess overlying limestone residuum, thus the Hildebrecht pedon appears to be a bisequal soil. The soil organic matter concentrations are greatest in the A horizons and decline upon soil profile transition.

For the Caneyville-Hildebrecht Alfisol assemblage the corresponding provisional ecological site descriptions are (i) the Fragipan Upland Woodland (F116AY004MO) containing the Hildebrecht soil series, and (ii) the Loamy Limestone/Dolomite Upland Woodlands (F115BY007MO) containing the Caneyville soil series. The dominant vegetation of the reference state of the Fragipan Upland Woodland is post oak (*Quercus stellata*) and black oak (*Quercus velutina*) with native grasses and legumes and other forbs in open canopy areas. Land management practices are related to (i) silvopasture to create a post oak (*Quercus stellata*) -shortleaf pine (*Pinus echinate*) state, (ii) clearcutting to create a

				Exchangeable Cations				
Horizon	pH	Acidity	SOM	Ca	Mg	K	Na	CEC
		cmol/kg	%			cmol/kg		
Caneyville								
A1	7.3	0	6.1	11.7	3.9	0.12	0.08	15.7
A2	7.4	0	2.9	6.7	2.7	0.08	0.08	9.6
E	6.9	0.5	1.1	4.3	2.0	0.11	0.04	6.9
Bt1	6.6	2.0	1.0	5.0	4.1	0.28	0.09	11.5
Bt2	6.4	3.0	1.4	5.7	9.1	0.50	0.11	18.4
Bt3	5.1	8.5	1.7	3.8	9.9	0.53	0.08	22.7
Hildebrecht								
A	4.8	1.6	8.4	5.2	2.2	0.21	0.41	9.6
E	4.7	2.0	2.9	1.3	0.6	0.19	0.55	4.6
BE	4.6	1.8	1.3	0.4	0.8	0.15	0.28	3.4
Bt1	4.5	2.7	1.7	1.9	2.0	0.20	0.22	7.0
Bt2	4.8	4.7	1.8	2.3	2.3	0.24	0.17	9.6
2Ex	4.0	3.1	1.4	1.0	2.0	0.17	0.27	6.5
2Btx1	4.0	2.2	0.9	0.5	2.0	0.14	0.34	5.2
2Btx2	4.1	2.0	0.9	0.6	2.0	0.12	0.29	5.0
3Bt3	4.5	1.2	1.2	9.6	2.6	0.10	0.38	13.9

CEC is the cation exchange capactiy, an estimate of the soil organic matter content.
Acidity is total acidity.

Table 4.
Chemical properties of the Caneyville and Hildebrecht pedons.

tall fescue (*Festuca arundinacea*) mixed pasture, and (iii) fire exclusion and logging to create a post oak (*Quercus stellata*), black oak (*Quercus velutina*), and black hickory (*Carya texana*) woodland. The dominant vegetation of the reference state of the Loamy Limestone/Dolomite Upland Woodlands is White Oak (*Quercus alba*), Chinkapin Oak (*Quercus muehlenbergii*) with Red Bud (*Cercis canadensis*), Aromatic Sumac (*Rhus aromatica*), Virginia Wildrye (*Elymus virginicus*) and Little Bluestem (*Schizachyrium scoparium*). Land management practices related to (i) a high graded and grazed woodland to establish a black oak (*Quercus velutina*), post oak (*Quercus stellata*), black hickory (*Carya texana*), (ii) logging creating a tall fescue (*Festuca arundinacea*) pasture, (iii) an even-aged managed woodland establishes a white oak (*Quercus alba*), chinkapin oak (*Quercus muehlenbergii*), and post oak (*Quercus stellata)* community and (iv) an uneven-aged managed woodland establishes a white oak (*Quercus alba*), black hickory (*Carya texana*), and northern red oak (*Quercus rubra*) community.

3.3 Amagon and Calhoun Alfisol Assemblage

The Amagon (Typic Endoaqualf) pedon and the Calhoun (Typic Glossaqualf) pedon possess A-E-Btg horizon sequences showing extensive redoximorphic features supportive of their poor-drained status (**Table 5**). These pedons have a relatively high cation exchange capacity, reflecting the abundance of smectite in the clay separate (X-ray diffraction data not presented). The near surface horizons have a very strongly acid or strongly acid reaction, transitioning to a slightly alkaline to neutral reactions in the argillic horizons (**Table 6**). The Amagon pedon also exhibits an elevated exchangeable sodium percentage in the argillic horizon.

Horizon Amagon	Depth cm	Texture	Structure	Matrix color
A	13	sandy loam	2f&vfsbk	10YR3/2
E	33	loam	2vfsbk and 1fgr	10YR5/3
Btg1	53	loam	2&3f&msbk	10YR5/1
Btg2	81	loam	2fsbk	10YR5/3
Btg3	107	loam	2f&msbk	10YR6/1
Btg4	137	sandy loam	2vf&fsbk	10YR3/4
BCg	193	loam	1 m&csbk	10YR6/2
Calhoun				
A	13	silt loam	2fsbk	10YR2/2
E	38	silt loam	3f&msbk	10YR4/2
Btg1	69	silty clay loam	2msbk	10YR4/1
Btg2	97	silty clay loam	2msbk	10YR5/1
Btg3	114	silt loam	2fsbk	10YR5/1
Cg	152	silt loam	2csbk	10YR5/1

Structure: 2 = common, 3 = many, f = fine, vf-very fine, m = medium, sbk = subangular blocky, gr = spherical.

Table 5.
Morphological and physical properties of the Amagon and Calhoun pedons.

Horizon	pH	Total Acidity	Ca	Mg	K	Na	CEC	ESP
Amagon		**cmol/kg**	**cmol/kg**	**cmol/kg**	**cmol/kg**	**cmol/kg**	**cmol/kg**	**%**
A	4.3	2	2.4	0.9	0.15	0.32	5.8	5.5
E	4.8	1.7	5.7	1.5	0.05	0.57	9.5	6
Btg1	7	0.1	10.7	5	0.1	2.22	18.1	12.3
Btg2	8.1	0	15.5	5.3	0.18	1.94	22.9	8.5
Btg3	8.1	0	14.8	5.9	0.14	1.01	21.8	4.6
Btg4	7.1	0.1	13	4.3	0.14	0.37	18	2.1
BCg	7	0.2	15.4	4.2	0.13	0.28	20.3	1.4
Calhoun								
A	4.9	1.4	13.9	4.8	0.14	0.27	20.5	1.3
E	4.6	1.6	14.6	4.7	0.11	0.37	21.4	1.8
Btg1	5.7	0.6	25.9	9.8	0.19	0.56	37	1.5
Btg2	6.8	0.5	22	8.4	0.22	0.61	31.7	1.9
Btg3	6.5	0.4	23.6	8.9	0.22	0.49	33.7	1.5
Cg	7.3	0.4	19.8	6.3	0.21	0.43	27.1	1.6

Ca, Mg, K, Na are exchangeable cations.

Table 6.
Chemical properties of the Amagon and Calhoun pedons.

For the Amagon-Calhoun assemblage the corresponding provisional ecological site descriptions are (i) the Wet Footslope Forest (F134XY014MO) for the Calhoun soil series and (ii) the Northern Wet Alluvial Flat (F134XY020AL) for the Amagon soil series. The reference state for the Wet Footslope Forest is a wet-Mesic Bottomland forest with an overstory dominated by bur oak (*Quercus macrocarpa*), cherrybark oak (*Quercus pagoda*), willow oak (*Quercus phellos*), sweetgum (*Liquidambar*), pin oak (*Quercus palustris*), nuttall oak (*Quercus texana*), water oak (*Quercus nigra*), American elm (*Ulmus americana*), sugarberry (*Celtis laevigata*), and green ash (*Fraxinus pennsylvanica*), an understory dominated by blue beech (*Carpinus caroliniana*), spicebush (*Lindera benzoin*), and Ohio buckeye (*Aesculus glabra*), and a rich herbaceous ground flora.

The Northern Wet Alluvial Flat ecological site description has mature tree stands consisting of overcup oak (*Quercus lyrate*), willow oak (*Quercus phellos*), water hickory (*Carya aquatica*), and occasional bald cypress (*Taxodium distichum*), and water tupelo (*Nyssa aquatica*) on the lowest and wettest land positions. The reference state is the wet bottom land forest dominated by overcup oak (*Quercus lyrate*) and water hickory (*Carya aquatica*). The altered or managed states include (i) post large scale disturbance with mixed species regrowth forest, (ii) timber management, usually involving overcup oak (*Quercus lyrate*) and water hickory (*Carya aquatica*), (iii) pastureland, and (iv) row-crop agriculture.

4. Value-adding to soil survey by employing ecological site descriptions

The intent of soil survey was to map soils based on observable diagnostic soil horizons and to provide soil interpretations. The linkage of soil spatial distributions with the spatial distribution of ecological sites as a digital product provides opportunities to (i) assist land owner decision making to improve ecosystem services and protect soil as a natural resource, (ii) empower land custodians to understand the ecosystem response and vegetational outcomes from land management applications, and (iii) understand behavior and changes to the soil resource because of land management applications. Each outcome of the soil survey linkage with ecological site descriptions is critical and each has a unique benefit to society.

The ability to assist land owner decision making to improve ecosystem services and protect soil as a natural resource has always been the central theme of the United States Department of Agriculture-Natural Resources and Conservation Service and the Missouri Department of Conservation. With the advent of online digital technologies, the likelihood that land custodians will seek these resources to guide land management is substantial, provided these digital online resources are comparative easy to navigate and conceptualize. The role of the soil scientist to understand behavior and changes to the soil resource because of land management applications was founded in the infancy of soil science when soil genesis was postulated to result from the five soil forming factors: (i) parent material, (ii) climate, (iii) organisms, (iv) topography (relief), and (v) time.

Essentially all five of the soil forming factors are evident and treated in the ecological site description. What is also intriguing are some of the potential benefits that may be realized in the near-term: (i) manage forests to sequester carbon, (ii) support selected sites for maintaining soil and vegetation to assist the recovery of endangered species, (iii) supporting land management application to protect highly erodible soils, and (iv) reducing fire threats to small rural communities.

Author details

Michael Aide*, Indi Braden and Christine Aide
Southeast Missouri State University, Cape Girardeau, Missouri, USA

*Address all correspondence to: mtaide@semo.edu

References

[1] Soil Survey Staff (2014) Keys to Soil Taxonomy, 12th ed. USDA-Natural Resources Conservation Service, Washington, DC.

[2] Buol SW, Southard RJ, Graham RC, and McDaniel PA (2003) Soil Genesis and Classification, Iowa State Press, Ames, IA.

[3] Fox HD, Kidwell MR, Lane LJ, Weltz MA. Major land resource areas and ecological site descriptions: potential databases for Multiple Objective Decision Support Systems. Proceedings of the 2nd International Conference on Multiple Object Decision Support Systems for Land, Water and Environment Management. 1999;1237:1-8

[4] Brown JR, Havstad KM. Using Ecological Site Information to Improve Landscape Management for Ecosystem Services. Rangelands. 2016;38:318-321

[5] USDA-NRCS: Ecological sites. [https://www.nrcs.usda.gov/wps/portal/nrcs/detail/national/landuse/rangepasture/?cid=stelprdb1068392].

[6] Missouri Department of Conservation, 2006. Missouri Forest and Woodland Community Profiles. Jefferson City, Missouri.

[7] National Vegetation Classification System Vegetation Association. 2010. http://www.natureserve.org/prodServices/ecomapping.jsp

[8] Natural Resources Conservation Service. 2002. Woodland Suitability Groups. Missouri FOTG, Section II, Soil Interpretations and Reports. 30 pgs.

[9] Nigh, T. A., and W. A. Schroeder. 2002. Atlas of Missouri Ecoregions. Missouri Department of Conservation, Jefferson City, Missouri. 212p.

[10] United States Department of Agriculture, Natural Resources Conservation Service. 2006. Land Resource Regions and Major Land Resource Areas of the United States, the Caribbean, and the Pacific Basin. U.S. Department of Agriculture Handbook 296.

[11] University of Missouri Climate Center – http://climate.missouri.edu/climate.php

[12] Soil Conservation Service (1961) Land-Capability Classification. USDA Handbook 210. U.S. Gov. Print. Office. Washington, DC. [(https://www.nrcs.usda.gov/Internet/FSE_DOCUMENTS/nrcs142p2_052290.pdf]

[13] Bestelmeye BT, Tugel AJ, Peacock GL, Robinett DG, Shaver PL, Brown JR, Herrick JE, Sanchez H, Havstad KM. State-and-transition models for heterogeneous landscapes: A strategy for development and application. Rangeland Ecol Management 2009;62:1-15.

[14] Briske DD, Bestelmeye BT, Stringham TK, Shaver PL. Recommendations for development of resilience-based state-and-transition models. Rangeland Ecol Management 2008;61:359-367.

[15] Peri PL, López DR, Rusch V, Rusch G, Rosas YM, Pastur GM. State and transition model approach in native forests of Southern Patagonia (Argentina): linking ecosystem services, thresholds and resilience. International Journal of Biodiversity Science, Ecosystem Services & Management. 2017;13;105-118

[16] Brown BL and Gregg KL. 1991. Soil Survey of Iron County, United States Department of Agriculture-Soil Conservation Service. https://www.nrcs.usda.gov/Internet/FSE_MANUSCRIPTS/missouri/MO093/0/iron_MO.pdf, verified 21 February 2021.

[17] Gurley PD. 1979. Soil Survey of Dunklin County, United States Department of Agriculture-Soil Conservation Service. https://www.blogs.nrcs.usda.gov/Internet/FSE_MANUSCRIPTS/missouri/MO069/0/dunklin_MO.pdf, verified 21 February 2021.

[18] Soil Survey Division Staff (1993) Soil survey manual. USDA Handbook 18. U.S. Gov. Print. Office. Washington, DC.

[19] Carter MR (1993) Soil sampling and methods of analysis. Lewis Publ. Boca Raton, Fl.

[20] Bestelmeye BT, Williamson JC, Talbot CJ, Cates, GW, Duniway MC, Brown JR. Improving the Effectiveness of Ecological Site Descriptions: General State-and-Transition Models and the Ecosystem Dynamics Interpretive Tool (EDIT). Rangelands. 2016;38:329-335 [https://doi.org/10.1016/j.rala.2016.10.001]

Chapter 12

Economic Value of Cultural Ecosystem Services in India: A Review

Muniyandi Balasubramanian

Abstract

Cultural ecosystem service (CES) is one of the important components in the ecosystem services framework which was designed by the Millennium Ecosystem Assessment. Cultural ecosystems services are the non-material benefits provides by various ecosystem services such as forest, wetland etc. CES is the vital contribution in the human well-being such as good physical and mental health. Further, CES is the major role in the Sustainable Development Goals (SDGs) for health and well-being. CES is still less primary investigation the economic literature especially in the Indian context link with the sustainable ecosystem management. Therefore, economic value of cultural ecosystem services is needed to study in the local level aspects. In the above mentioned context, this chapter is present the economic value of cultural ecosystem services in India. The main policy implication of the study is to design entry fee for many protected areas such as wildlife sanctuary, national park as well as sustainable environmental management for the present and future generation.

Keywords: Ecosystem Services, Travel Cost Method, Economics, India

1. Introduction

Cultural ecosystem services (CES) is non-material benefits provided by ecosystem services. Millennium Ecosystem Assessment [1–3] defined that "nonmaterial benefits people obtain from ecosystems through spiritual enrichment, cognitive development, cognitive development, reflection, recreation and aesthetic experiences". MEA has also classified such as cultural diversity, spiritual and religious values, knowledge systems, educational values, inspiration, aesthetic values, social relations, sense of place, cultural heritage value and recreation and ecotourism (See **Table 1**). Heretofore, most of the cultural ecosystem services have not been studied empirically at the local and national level. For example, there are a number of studies in tourism and recreational ecosystem services, Hermes et al., (2018), Fischer et al., (2018), Europe; Mayer et al., [4] Germany; Arslan et al. (2020), Turkey; Ribeiro et al., (2018), Brazil; Costanza et al. 1997, Global; Su, Li and Chen (2019); China. In India, there are a number of studies for example, Sinclair et al., (2018), tropical ramsar wetland; Balasubramanian [5] recreational value of two protected areas in Karnataka; Subramanian and Jana [6, 7] estimated the recreational value of some Indian

Cultural Ecosystem Services	Explanations
Cultural diversity	The diversity of ecosystems is one factor influencing the diversity of cultures
Spiritual and religious values	Many religions attach spiritual and religious values to ecosystems or their components
Knowledge systems	Ecosystems influence the types of knowledge systems developed by different cultures
Educational values	Ecosystems and their components and processes provide the basis for both formal and informal education in many societies
Inspiration	Ecosystems provide a rich source of inspiration for art, folklore, national symbols, architecture, and advertising
Aesthetic values	Many people find beauty or aesthetic value in various aspects of ecosystems, as reflected in the support for parks, "scenic drives" and the selection of housing locations.
Social relations	Ecosystems influence the types of social relations that are established in particular cultures.
Sense of place	Many people value the "sense of place" that is associated with recognized features of their environment, including aspects of the ecosystem.
Cultural heritage values	Many societies place high value on the maintenance of either historically important landscapes or culturally significant species
Recreation and ecotourism	People often choose where to spend their leisure time based in part on the characteristics of the natural or cultivated landscapes in a particular area.

Source: MEA [1].

Table 1.
Cultural ecosystem services and details.

cities; Badola et al. (2010) assessed the recreational value of Corbett tiger reserve, India; Ninan and Kontoleon (2016) estimated the value of recreational ecosystem services in the Nagarhole national park in Karnataka. Cultural ecosystem services have been vital role in the human well-being such as engagement with the nature positive physical and mental happiness (Bryce et al. 2016); cultural ecosystem services is the basic foundation for environment and human well-being [8]; CES has creative positive human well-being in the context of opportunity to express indigenous wish and needs [9]; cultural ecosystem services linking with human health and well-being [10]. Most of the cultural ecosystem services have been neglected from the day today decision making process [10]. A number of cultural ecosystem services have not been traded in the market, conceptual and methodological issues [11]. Although, CES is one of the most important ecosystem services protecting the ecosystem [12] through the religious and spiritual significance most the developing and developed countries [13]. The growing in attention in CES integrating into the decision making is an important for sustainable environmental management in the 21st century. Cultural ecosystem services are one of the important roles in the socio-economic and ecological aspects. CES is highlights three important aspects such as i) human well-being, ii) environmental or ecological decision making and iii) socio-ecological relation between human and nature [11]. CES is also reducing poverty through the engaging in the tourism and recreational services of many the developing countries, Bulte et al., (2008); Shuai et al., (2021); Gorden et al., (2010). CES is provide economic and employment opportunity to millions of people around the world.

1.1 Cultural ecosystem services and human well-being

CES is an important contribution to the human well-being through various aspects for example, Russell et al. [14–19] discussed cultural ecosystem services have been vital role to the human well-being such as learning capability, mental health, inspiration of imagination, subjective well-being, physical health and identity etc. in addition, there are strong relationship between human and nature through the four channels such as i) *knowing*, thinking about an ecosystem, ii) perceiving, remote interactions with ecosystem components; iii) interacting, physical, active, direct multisensory interactions with ecosystem component and iv) living within, everyday interactions with the ecosystem in which we live ([14]; 477). Generally, ecosystem services provide material and non-material benefits to human being. Further, provisioning ecosystem services has been strong association with human well-being, still cultural ecosystem services need more empirical analysis because benefits receiving as non-material (physical and mentally). Even though, there are number of studies has been investigated cultural ecosystem services and human well-being for example; Duraiappah [20]; Wang, Zhang and Chi [21]; Bryce et al., (2016); Leong et al., (2019); Bllock et al. (2018); Willis [22]; Yang et al. (2019); Kaltenborn et al. (2020). Environmental degradation has been highly impacts on human well-being through the various aspects for example land use and land cover changes; disservices has also impacts on marginalized group and indigenous people most of the developing countries [13]. Cultural ecosystem services are also one of the important tools for social relation in the world [20].

1.2 Economics of cultural ecosystem services

Provisioning ecosystem services has been highly studied and some services are traded in the market. Cultural ecosystem services have not been traded in the market because these services are not sold and bought in the market. However, cultural ecosystem services have been vital role in the context of generating income for local people, tourist guide, hospitality etc. through the outdoor recreation services. Cultural ecosystem services has been critical role in the day today economic activity of the millions of people for example **Figure 1** explained various type of CES changing in policy and behavior of local institution. For valuing CES could redesign parks entry fee for sustainable usage of recreational ecosystem services in the many developing and developed countries as well as behavioral changes for better environmental management at the local level. An improving economic well-being of the local, national and international level through the various aspects and finally valuing cultural ecosystem services has been one of the instruments of sustainable used of ecosystem goods and services for example, improving awareness among the various users of natural resources. There are a number of studies on valuing cultural ecosystem services especially recreational of parks, protected areas, wetlands and other ecosystem services at the local, national and international level. For example, value of cultural ecosystem services for various agriculture heritages in Chile was estimated at the US $ 40,361,120 through the contingent valuation method (Barrena et al. 2014); value of recreational ecosystem services was calculated at US $ 16.1–19.6 million for Popa Mountain National Park through the individual travel cost method (Zin et al. 2019). Recreational ecosystems services are one of the important components in the cultural ecosystem services. Most of the developing and developed countries have been much engaged in the tourism or recreational activities in their life. Heagney et al. (2010) calculated the value of tourism and recreational ecosystem services at AUD$ 3.3 billion per year of New South Wales in south-eastern Australia through the individual travel cost method.

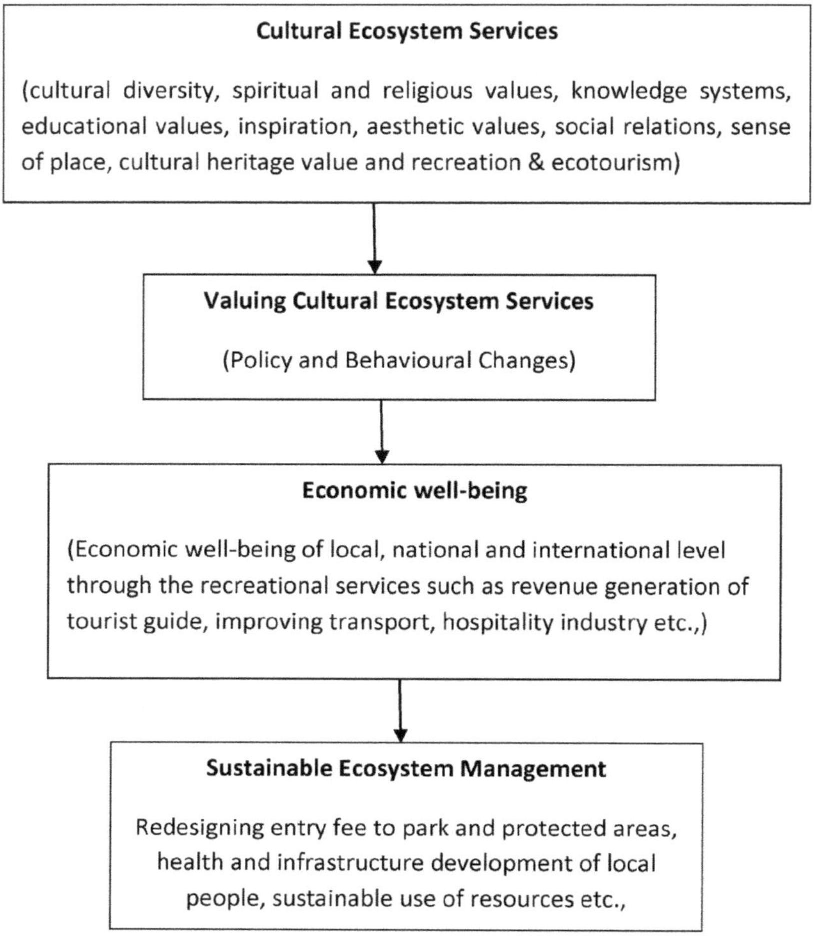

Figure 1.
Economic well-being of cultural ecosystem services. Source: Adapted from (Hirons et al., 2016).

Zandersen et al., (2009) estimated the value of recreational ecosystem services through meta-analysis of 26 studies from Europe. This study found that the consumer surplus were varied between euro 0.66 to 112 and the mean consumer surplus was calculated at 4.52 euro. Ezebilo [1] calculate the value of recreational ecosystem services for Sweden at US$16 per trip for forest areas. Nature based recreational ecosystem services of European Union was estimated at EUR 50 billion based on various environmental valuation method. Annual value of recreational ecosystem services provided by the Oku Aizu forest in Japan was calculated at US$ 27.07 million [23]. The value of recreational ecosystem services provided by urban green space at Santa Rosa, California was estimated at US$ 13.70 consumer surplus per trip to the site. Economic value of recreational ecosystem services provided by river Pajakkajoki had estimated at 40 to 144 euro per person annum. The value of recreation ecosystem services by national museum research centre of Altamira had estimated at 4.75 to 8 million euro per year based on individual travel cost method (Ortega et al., 2018). Estimated the value of recreational ecosystem services of national parks of Germany at 385.3 to 621.8 million euro per year [4].

National parks are vital contribution to economic well-being for example, total economic value of 11 Australian national parks had estimated at AUT $13.656 million [24]. Another study estimated by Neher et al. (2013) US$ 28.5 billion of 16 national parks in the US based on travel cost method. Therefore, recreational ecosystem service is the vital contribution to socio-economic and environmental well-being. However, the next section discuss about the economic value of recreational ecosystem services in India.

2. Economic value of recreational ecosystem services in India

According to Verma (2018) economic value of ecosystem services in India is emerging field of environmental economic subject. There are the number of studies has been investigated since 2000 in the various part of the country. Most of the studies have been focused on forest (68 studies), terrestrial wetlands (34 studies), marine, coastal wetland (19 studies) and other ecosystem services such as urban green space, agroecological ecosystem (25 studies). These figures are clearly shown that cultural ecosystem services are vital part in the economic valuation studies from various publications. Economic value of forest ecosystem services has been highly contribute compared than other ecosystem services for example Verma (2018) forest ecosystem services has contributed 1.7 percent in the total GDP in India. Cultural ecosystems services has been contributed nearly 26 percent in the total forest ecosystem services followed by 23 percent regulating and 15 percent supporting ecosystem services in Indian forest. Costal ecosystem services have been vital role in the economic and employment generation in India [25]. Valuation of cultural ecosystem services has been well recognized in India. Hence, there is lack of policy implication in the context of integrating in the state or national income accounts and designing entry fee for park, wildlife sanctuary and other protected areas in India. Most of the cultural services are free access or market failure due to poor environmental regulation. Therefore, degradation or environmental pollution is one of the important reasons for major environmental problem in India. However, there is lack of quantification of cultural ecosystem services at the local level due poor understanding among the local policy makers about the importance of cultural ecosystem services.

3. Materials and methods

The present study has developed a review of peer-reviewed journal articles on economic value of cultural ecosystem services. The recent review paper on cultural ecosystem services [13, 14, 20] provided a basic idea of the key terms. Reviews of literature were conducted during 1997 and 2021 using the web science core compilation of search term: 'ecosystem services' or 'cultural ecosystem services' or 'value of recreational services' or 'economic of cultural ecosystem services'. After title and abstract reading, 53 articles were considered this study, of which 22 were considered for data extraction after the full text reading. The categories of valuation methods, locations and authors with publication year were presented in the **Table 2**. Due to time constraints this paper has reviewed small number of research work on the value of cultural ecosystem services in India. In addition, due to heterogeneous literature based on various valuation methods and definition, a meta-analysis was not undertaken in the study.

Author and Year	Ecosystem Services	Location of the study area
Sinclair et al. 2018	Wetlands	Vembanad Lake, Kerala
[5]	Forest	Nandi Hills and Nagarhole National park
[6]	Green open space	Mumbai, Bangalore, Chennai
Ninan and Kontoeon	Forest	Nagarhole National Park
Sharma et al. 2020	Zoological park	New Delhi
Ghosh et al. 2016	Forest and wetland	Uttarakhand
[26]	Botanical Garden	Bangalore
[27]	Forest (tiger reserve)	Uttarakhand, Madhya Pradesh, Kerala, Assam, West Bengal and Rajasthan
Badola et al. 2010	Forest	Uttarakhand
[28]	Lake	Karnataka
Ramachandra et al. 2017	Forest	Karnataka
MoEFCC 2016	Forest	Karnataka
Gopal and Singh	Lake	Uttarakhand
IWRM	Lake	Uttarakhand
Rawat et al. 2005	Lake	Uttarakhand
Vengatachalam and Jayanthi 2015	Lake	Tamil Nadu
Costanza et al. 1997	Forest	Uttarakhand
Mukhopadhyay and da Costa 2015	Marine and costal	India
Gera et al. 2008	Forest	Uttarakhand
Kumar et al. 2018	Forest	Tamil Nadu
[29]	Forest	Karnataka
[26]	Forest	Karnataka

Table 2.
Details of the Ecosystem Services and study area.

4. Results and discussion

Of the 22 peer-reviewed articles included in this review on economic value of recreational ecosystem services in India; however there is the (12) studies on forest cultural ecosystem services various, (5) lake ecosystem services and each one from botanical garden, zoological park and marine ecosystem services parts of the country (**Figure 2**). While there is wide range of 9 states covered, the states with most publications are the Karnataka (9), Uttarakhand (8), Tamil Nadu (3) and Kerala (2). However, most the studies have used mixed methods both the qualitative and quantitative assessment for economic value of cultural ecosystem services in Karnataka. According to the Millennium Ecosystem Assessment [1] classified there are ten types of cultural ecosystem services see **Table 1**. Hence, most of the CES focused on recreational tourism ecosystem services in India. However, better understanding with cultural ecosystem services which is created good human

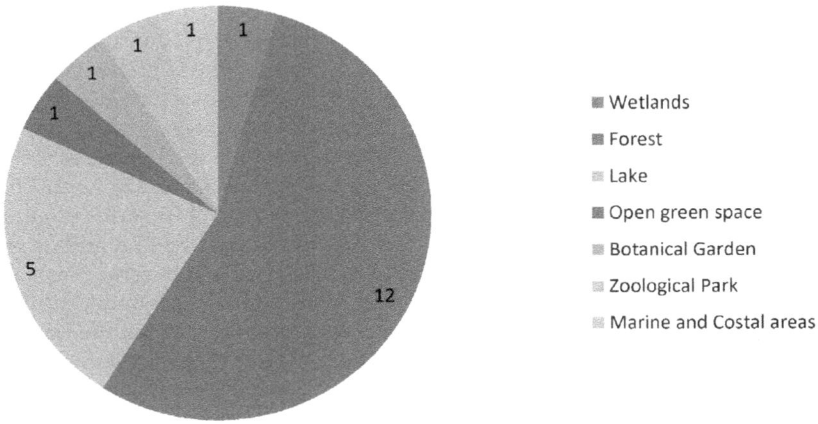

Figure 2.
Type of Ecosystem services and number of estimates. Source: Author estimates from various publications.

well-being [30, 31]. Therefore, need more studies on cultural value of ecosystem services. The present review is found that total economic value of 22 cultural ecosystem services at the US$ 1610 million in the 2020 (see **Figure 3**). Moreover, the value of forest related cultural ecosystems services is contributes more economic value at the US$ 657.51 million followed by marine and costal services US$ 720 and wetland land contribute US$205, open green space US$23 million and zoological park related cultural ecosystem services US$ 4.4 million (see **Figure 3**). Forest related cultural ecosystem services are vital role in the cultural ecosystems services for example, Karnataka has more than fifteen protected areas such as national park, wildlife sanctuary and tiger reserve. This present study is found that the value of recreational ecosystem services contribute at the US$ 434.6 million from Karnataka, US$ 6.705 million from Uttarakhand and Kerala US$ 205 million and other states have contributed few amounts in the total economic value of

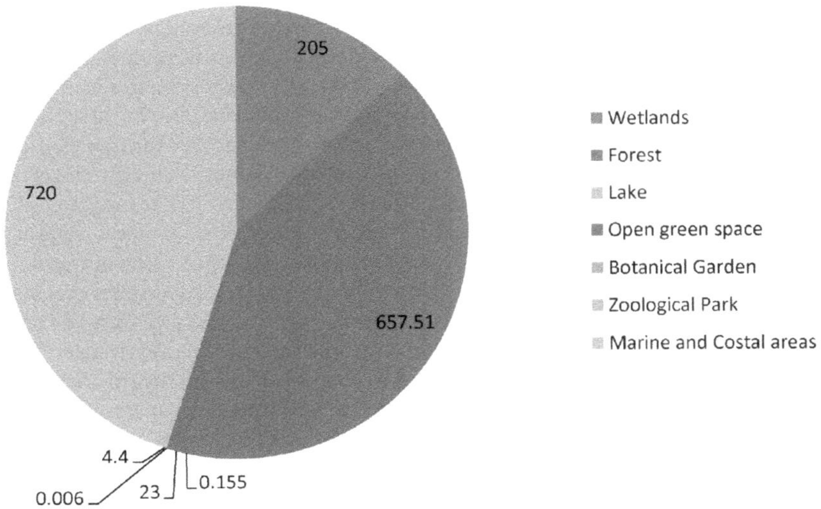

Figure 3.
Economic Value Recreational Ecosystem Services in India in US$ (2019--2020). Source: Author estimates from various publications.

cultural ecosystem services. Moreover, this study is found that the value of two global biological diversity such as Western Ghats and eastern Himalayas. The total value of recreational ecosystem services is contributed by the Himalayas at the US$ 14.5 million and the Western Ghats the US$ 1,595.5 million based on 22 publications. There are number of cultural ecosystem services has been investigated in the Himalayas, due to lack of literature collection this study is included very few publication from the particular region. There are only four articles has published in the *Ecosystem Services* journal for example, Verma et al. [27] the value of cultural ecosystem services provided by the five tiger reserves at the US$ 13.8 million from (Corbett Tiger Reserve, Kanha Tiger Reserve, Kaziranga Tiger Reserve, Periyar Tiger Reserve and Sundarbans Tiger Reserve), followed by Ninan and Kontoleon (2016) had estimated the value of recreational ecosystem services at the US$ 0.41 million by Nagarhole national park in Karnataka. A few articles has published in Springer published such as environmentalist for example, Badola et al. (2010) estimated the economic value of recreational ecosystem services at the US$ 1.6 million by Corbett tiger reserve in Uttarakhand followed by Ramachandra et al. (2017) assessed the value of tourism and recreational services work has published the journal of Biodiversity (Routledge Taylor & Francis Group). In addition two working paper by research institutes such as wetland ecosystem services, (Vengatachalam and Jayanthi, 2015) and marine and coastal Mukhopadhyay and de Costa [25], followed by other refereed journal such as Aarthika Charche FPI Journal of Economics and Governance, Government of Karnataka on valuation of ecosystem services two protected areas [29] and Monograph on Economic value of ecosystem services by urban botanical garden estimated by [32].

Ecosystem services are very critical role in the human life [33]. The recent economics of biodiversity review by [34] indicates that the current economic and population growth is degrading and over exploiting natural capital in this century. In addition, the current economic models of growth are inessential form especially non-renewable natural resources. Further, Balvanera et al. [29] argues demographic pressures, climate change and lack of governance are the main reasons for most of the environmental degradation or pollution. MEA [1] has estimated that 60% of the global ecosystem services including provisioning, regulating and cultural services are degraded due to various socio, economic and political reasons. There is increasing understand strategies on better and sustainable environmental management through the cultural ecosystem services. Therefore, the present review is one of the tool for better understand between economy and cultural ecosystem services in the Indian context. There are a number of review work has been done in the cultural ecosystem services for example, cultural ecosystem services and human well-being [10; 35–37]. Although, very few economic review on economics of cultural ecosystem services for example, Hirons et al., [11]; Fish et al., (2016); Plieninger et al., (2013). In India, lack of economic value of cultural ecosystem services in the aspects of meta-review. There is some few studies review of economics value of regulating ecosystem services [32] and a new study on value of marine and coastal ecosystem services by Mukhopadhyay and de Costa [25]. However, increasing number of studies on economic of provisioning ecosystem services for example, Verma et al. [27]; Ninan and Kontoleon (2016); Balasubramanian [5, 29, 38, 39]; Dhyani and Dhyani [34, 40–43] but lack of review on economic value of cultural ecosystem services. In addition, there are a less in interdisciplinary analysis in the research. Therefore, the current review work mainly focusing on economic value of cultural ecosystem services especially recreational perspective. Moreover, cultural ecosystem services how relating with the human-well being research is totally missing in the literature in India. The recent study evaluated the relationship between cultural ecosystem services and human well-being of the two indigenous communities in India [9].

The value of cultural ecosystem services may help to local and indigenous communities through the traditional health treatment based on purely natural medicine as well as income and environmental conservation at the local level [5, 33]. The value of cultural ecosystem services may help to local policy markers on various aspects such as designing urban green infrastructure, revising the entry fee for the many urban parks and protected areas, cultural ecosystem services into integrating into economic decision making at the local level, achieving sustainable development goals especially better environmental management.

5. Conclusion

The main aim of the review is to understand the value of cultural ecosystem services for better management of protected areas, urban parks, marine and coastal areas and other tourism and recreational sites is the one hand and cultural ecosystem services has been vital role in the physical and mental human well-being. The results of the review work indicate that the lack of understanding on the relationship between ecosystem services and economic decision making at the local level due to less research on this area. The current environmental crisis such as loss of biodiversity and ecosystem services, climate related events such as disaster, floods, and droughts are the main cause of degrading the area of cultural ecosystem services in India. Therefore, the local policy makers when designing the policy for ecosystem services, they should understand the value of ecosystem services such provisioning, regulating and cultural services. In addition, cultural ecosystem services are the main role of the human well-being, MEA [1, 5, 26, 33, 44, 45]. Finally, in the academics and policy decision should give equal priority to all ecosystem services in the context of creating economic value to the nature.

Author details

Muniyandi Balasubramanian
Centre for Ecological Economics and Natural Resources, Institute for Social and Economic Change, Bangalore, Karnataka, India

*Address all correspondence to: balasubramanian@isec.ac.in

References

[1] Ezebilo, Eugene E (2016) Economic Value of non-market ecosystem services: an application of the travel cost method to natural recreation in Sweden, International Journal of Biodiversity Science, Ecosystem Services & Management, 12(4), pp. 314-327.

[2] Milcu, A.I., Hanspach, J., Abson, D., Fischer, J., 2013. Cultural ecosystem services: A literature review and prospects for future research. Ecol. Soc. 18 (3).

[3] Millennium Ecosystem Assessment, 2005. Ecosystems and human well-being: Synthesis v. 1, 917.

[4] Mayer, M.; Woltering, M. Assessing and valuing the recreational ecosystem services of Germany's national parks using travel cost models. Ecosyst. Serv. 2018, 31, 371-386.

[5] Balasubramanian, M., 2021. Forest Ecosystem Services Contribution in the Sustainable Development Goals: A Case Study from the Western Ghats Region in Karnataka. Indian Forester, 147(4), pp.339-345.

[6] Subramanian, D. and Jana, A., 2019. Evaluating the cultural ecosystem services of India: Comparison of budget allocations to improve the use value of recreational open spaces. Ecosystem Services, 38, p.100960.

[7] Sun, R., Li, F. and Chen, L., 2019. A demand index for recreational ecosystem services associated with urban parks in Beijing, China. Journal of environmental management, 251, p.109612.

[8] Lohr, V.I. and Pearson-Mims, C.H., 2005. Children's active and passive interactions with plants influence their attitudes and actions toward trees and gardening as adults. *HortTechnology*, *15*(3), pp.472-476.

[9] Balasubramanian, M., 2019. Economic value of regulating ecosystem services: a comprehensive at the global level review. *Environmental monitoring and assessment*, *191*(10), pp.1-27.

[10] Chan, K.M., Guerry, A.D., Balvanera, P., Klain, S., Satterfield, T., Basurto, X., Bostrom, A., Chuenpagdee, R., Gould, R., Halpern, B.S. and Hannahs, N., 2012. Where are cultural and social in ecosystem services? A framework for constructive engagement. *BioScience*, *62*(8), pp.744-756.

[11] Hirons, Mark, Claudia Comberti and Robert Duford (2016) Valuing cultural ecosystem services, Annual Review of Environment and Resources, 41: 545-574.

[12] Gobster, P.H., Nassauer, J.I., Daniel, T.C., Fry, G., 2007. The shared landscape: what does aesthetics have to do with ecology? Landsc. Ecol. 22, 959-972.

[13] Daniel, T.C., Muhar, A., Arnberger, A., Aznar, O., Boyd, J.W., Chan, K.M.a., Costanza, R., Elmqvist, T., Flint, C.G., Gobster, P.H., Grêt-Regamey, A., Lave, R., Muhar, S.,Penker, M., Ribe, R.G., Schauppenlehner, T., Sikor, T., Soloviy, I., Spierenburg, M., Taczanowska, K., Tam, J., von der Dunk, A., 2012. Contributions of cultural services to the ecosystem services agenda. Proc. Natl. Acad. Sci. USA 109, 8812-8819. http://dx.doi.org/10.1073/pnas.1114773109.

[14] Fatoric, S. and Seekamp, E., 2017. Are cultural heritage and resources threatened by climate change? A systematic literature review. *Climatic change*, *142*(1-2), p.227.

[15] Russell, R., Guerry, A.D., Balvanera, P., Gould, R.K., Basurto, X., Chan, K.M.A., Klain, S., Levine, J., Tam, J., 2013a. Humans and nature: How knowing and experiencing nature affect well-being. Annu. Rev. Environ. Resour. 38, 473-502.

[16] Martin-Ortega, J. and Waylen, K.A., 2018. PES what a mess? An analysis of the position of environmental professionals in the conceptual debate on payments for ecosystem services. *Ecological Economics*, *154*, pp.218-237.

[17] Martín-López, B., Iniesta-Arandia, I., García-Llorente, M., Palomo, I., Casado-Arzuaga, I., Amo, D.G.D., Gómez-Baggethun, E., Oteros-Rozas, E., Palacios-Agundez, I., Willaarts, B. and González, J.A., 2012. Uncovering ecosystem service bundles through social preferences. *PLoS one*, *7*(6), p.e38970.

[18] Martínez Pastur, G., Peri, P.L., Lencinas, M.V., García-Llorente, M., Martín-López, B.,2016. Spatial patterns of cultural ecosystem services provision in Southern Patagonia. Landscape Ecol. 31 (2), 383-399.

[19] Russell, R., Guerry, A.D., Balvanera, P., Gould, R.K., Basurto, X., Chan, K.M.A., Klain, S., Levine, J., Tam, J., 2013b. Humans and nature: How knowing and experiencing nature affect well-being. Annu. Rev. Environ. Resour. 38, 473-502.

[20] Duraiappah, A.K., 2011. Ecosystem services and human well-being: do global findings make any sense?. *BioScience*, *61*(1), pp.7-8.

[21] Wang, L.J., Ma, S., Zhao, Y.G. and Zhang, J.C., 2021. Ecological restoration projects did not increase the value of all ecosystem services in Northeast China. *Forest Ecology and Management*, *495*, p.119340.

[22] Willis, C., 2015. The contribution of cultural ecosystem services to understanding the tourism–nature–wellbeing nexus. *Journal of Outdoor Recreation and Tourism*, *10*, pp.38-43.

[23] Ninan, K.N. and Inoue, M., 2014. Valuing forest ecosystem services: What we know and what we don't. *Valuing Ecosystem Services*.

[24] Ward, C., Stringer, L. and Holmes, G., 2018. Changing governance, changing inequalities: protected area co-management and access to forest ecosystem services: a Madagascar case study. *Ecosystem Services*, *30*, pp.137-148.

[25] Mukhopadhyay, P. and DaCosta, V., 2015. Recreational value of coastal and marine ecosystems in India: A partial estimate.

[26] Balasubramanian M. , 2020a. The Valuation of Ecosystem Services: A case study of BRTWLS in Karnataka. 56th Annual Conference of The Indian Econometric Society (TIES), organised by the School of Economics, Madurai Kamaraj University, Tamil Nadu: January 8th -10th 2020.

[27] Verma, M., Negandhi, D., Khanna, C., Edgaonkar, A., David, A., Kadekodi, G., Costanza, R., Gopal, R., Bonal, B.S., Yadav, S.P. and Kumar, S., 2017. Making the hidden visible: Economic valuation of tiger reserves in India. *Ecosystem services*, *26*, pp.236-244.

[28] Nandagiri, L., 2015. Evaluation of economic value of Pilikula Lake using travel cost and contingent valuation methods. *Aquatic Procedia*, *4*, pp.1315-1321.

[29] Balasubramanian M (2020) Valuation of Ecosystem Services and their impactions for Accounting for Natural Capital in Karnataka, Aarthika Charche:FPI Journal of Economics and Governance, Volume 5(1) pp:59-72

[30] Pascual, U., Balvanera, P., Díaz, S., Pataki, G., Roth, E., Stenseke, M., Watson, R.T., Dessane, E.B., Islar, M., Kelemen, E. and Maris, V., 2017a. Valuing nature's contributions to people: the IPBES approach. *Current Opinion in Environmental Sustainability*, *26*, pp.7-16.

[31] Pascual, U., Balvanera, P., Díaz, S., Pataki, G., Roth, E., Stenseke, M., Watson, R.T., Dessane, E.B., Islar, M., Kelemen, E. and Maris, V., 2017b.

Valuing nature's contributions to people: the IPBES approach. *Current Opinion in Environmental Sustainability*, *26*, pp.7-16.

[32] Balasubramanian M (2017) Economics of Urban Ecosystem Services: A Case Study of Bangalore, Institute for Social and Economic Change (ISEC) Monograph 53

[33] Balvanera, P., Pfaff, A., Viña, A., García Frapolli, E., Hussain, S.A., Merino, L., Akong Minang, P. and Nagabhatla, N., 2019. Status and Trends – Drivers of Change. In:IPBES (Editor), Global assessment report on biodiversity and ecosystem services of the Intergovernmental Science-Policy Platform on Biodiversity and Ecosystem Services. IPBES secretariat, Bonn.

[34] Dasgupta, P., 2021. *The Economics of Biodiversity: the Dasgupta Review*. HM Treasury.

[35] Dhyani, S. and Dhyani, D., 2016. Significance of provisioning ecosystem services from moist temperate forest ecosystems: lessons from upper Kedarnath valley, Garhwal, India. *Energy, Ecology and Environment*, *1*(2), pp.109-121.

[36] Howe, C., Suich, H., Vira, B. and Mace, G.M., 2014. Creating win-wins from trade-offs? Ecosystem services for human well-being: a meta-analysis of ecosystem service trade-offs and synergies in the real world. *Global Environmental Change*, *28*, pp.263-275.

[37] Shanahan, D.F., Franco, L., Lin, B.B., Gaston, K.J. and Fuller, R.A., 2016. The benefits of natural environments for physical activity. *Sports Medicine*, *46*(7), pp.989-995.

[38] Bherwani, H., Nair, M., Kapley, A. and Kumar, R., 2020. Valuation of ecosystem services and environmental damages: An imperative tool for decision making and sustainability. *European Journal of Sustainable Development Research*, *4*(4), p.em0133.

[39] Joshi, G. and Negi, G.C., 2011. Quantification and valuation of forest ecosystem services in the western Himalayan region of India. *International Journal of Biodiversity Science, Ecosystem Services & Management*, *7*(1), pp.2-11.

[40] Balasubramanian, M. and Sangha, K.K., 2021. Integrating Capabilities and Ecosystem Services Approaches to evaluate Indigenous connections with nature in a global biodiversity hotspot of Western Ghats, India. *Global Ecology and Conservation*, *27*, p.e01546.

[41] Keniger, L.E., Gaston, K.J., Irvine, K.N., Fuller, R.A., 2013. What are the Benefits of Interacting with Nature? Int. J. Environ. Res. Public Health 10 (3), 913-935.

[42] Kosanic, A. and Petzold, J., 2020. A systematic review of cultural ecosystem services and human wellbeing. *Ecosystem Services*, *45*, p.101168.

[43] Lakerveld, R.P., Lele, S., Crane, T.A., Fortuin, K.P.J. and Springate-Baginski, O., 2015. The social distribution of provisioning forest ecosystem services: Evidence and insights from Odisha, India. *Ecosystem Services*, *14*, pp.56-66.

[44] Díaz, S., Pascual, U., Stenseke, M., Martín-López, B., Watson, R.T., Molnár, Z., Hill, R., Chan, K.M.A., Baste, I.A., Brauman, K.A., Polasky, S., Church, A., Lonsdale, M.,Larigauderie, A., Leadley, P.W., van Oudenhoven, A.P.E., van der Plaat, F., Schröter, M., Lavorel, S., Aumeeruddy-Thomas, Y., Bukvareva, E., Davies, K., Demissew, S.,Erpul, G., Failler, P., Guerra, C.A., Hewitt, C.L., Keune, H., Lindley, S., Shirayama, Y.,2018. Assessing nature's contributions to people. Science 359 (6373), 270.

[45] IPBES, 2019. Summary for policymakers of the global assessment report on biodiversity and ecosystem services of the Intergovernmental Science-Policy Platform on Biodiversity and Ecosystem Services. IPBES secretariat, Bonn

Section 4

Sustainability

Chapter 13

The Challenges of Managing Water for Wetland Ecology, Flood Mitigation and Agriculture in the Upper Lunan Water, an Intensive Arable Catchment in Scotland

Andrew Vinten and Iain D.M. Gunn

Abstract

The "Water for All" project has aimed to develop a multi-disciplinary science case for adaptive management through a Payment for Ecosystem Services (PES) scheme in the Lunan Water, a lowland catchment in Scotland. Management needs for high and low flows, standing water levels and flow routing to/from high nature value mesotrophic wetlands were appraised. A key part has been the development of a real time hydrological-hydraulic model of the upper Lunan Water as an aid to management and scenario analysis especially with respect to existing and potential hydraulic structures. This provides better working knowledge and forecast-based simulations of high or low flow situations for catchment management planners, farmers, riparian owners and other local stakeholders. Engagement with local users and residents has included surveying Willingness To Pay (WTP) for hydraulic management as a function of governance mechanisms, development of a catchment management group, and interviews and workshops with riparian and other land-users. The work has highlighted the joys and sorrows of seeking to develop a PES approach and lessons to be learnt in project management, promotion of multiple benefits, catchment-scale water governance and the vices and virtues of "benign neglect".

Keywords: hydro-ecology, hydraulic modelling, Payment for Ecosystem Services, wetlands, water stakeholders

1. Introduction

Watershed or catchment management encompasses a complex tapestry of multi-stakeholder interests and water rights, cultural and historical norms, uncertainty of open system processes, and economic and environmental change [1, 2]. Moreover, the technical challenges to delivering across multiple objectives are significant. These include management of hydraulic structures, calibration of hydrological models of acceptable accuracy and precision, the need for real time or forecasted data streams and understanding of impacts of water management actions on ecosystems. A range of approaches has developed in recent years that aim to provide an integrated, consultative approach to natural resource management, among which

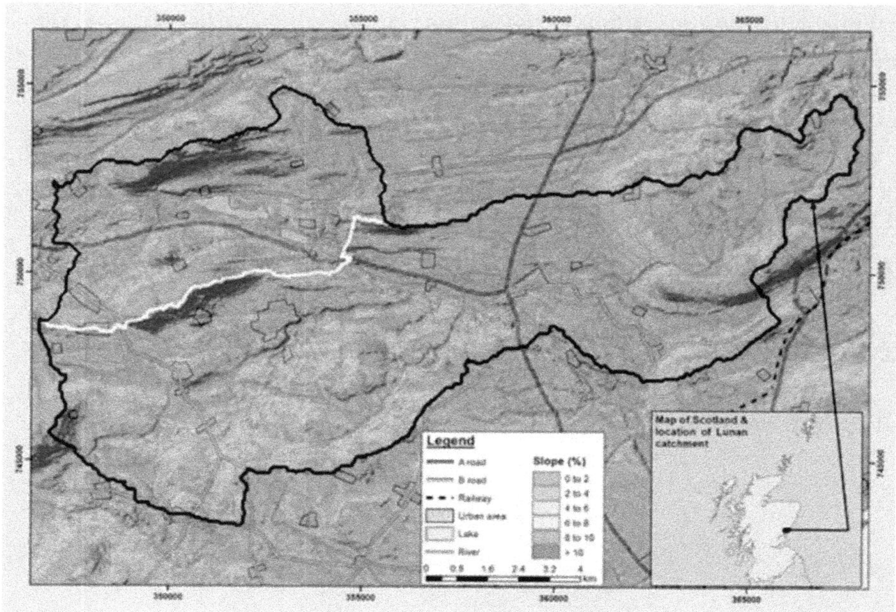

Figure 1.
Lunan water catchment. The upper catchment is delineated by the white line.

Payment for Ecosystem Services (PES) has emerged as a promising approach [3, 4]. PES schemes have been envisaged as an efficient way to ensure the provision of local public goods, such as water [5, 6]. Such schemes have the potential to increase the availability of ecosystem services for beneficiaries, whilst compensating the providers of such services. Examples of successful PES schemes with a focus on water include the Vittel water catchment area in France [7] and the "Upstream Thinking" scheme in SW England [5]. However, some aspects of catchment water management, such as the widely distributed and ill-defined benefits, and legacy issues, can undermine local participation and willingness to pay [3, 7].

This chapter outlines the evolution of an engineered water management strategy ("Water for All") for the Lunan Water catchment area, Angus, Scotland (see **Figure 1**). The project originally envisioned alleviation of winter flooding in the upper catchment, summer low flows and water shortages in the lower catchment, and nutrient/sediment pollution in wetland areas, to be managed as a PES scheme through local management and funding. The key engineered element was the introduction of remotely managed hydraulic controls (e.g. a tilting weir) to deliver the envisioned benefits.

Integrated analysis was made up of three main components:

- Hydrological analysis focused on deriving rainfall-runoff relationships for inflowing streams and a hydraulic model of the main channels and standing waters. This allowed simulation of upstream water levels and partitioning of flows as a function of existing or proposed management of hydraulic structures. It made use of long-term monitoring and survey data and the hydraulic modelling tool HECRAS 5.0.7;

- Ecological analysis considered the vegetation characteristics of the wetland using the UK National Vegetation Classification scheme [8], and the likely mixing behaviour of water from the river with other sources contributing to the wetlands, using End Member Mixing Analysis [9];

- Governance and stakeholder analysis focused on regular engagement through a stakeholder group (Lunan Catchment Management Group, which was set up at the start of the project in 2017), a survey of Willingness to Pay (WTP) for the tilting weir option, and interviews discussing the uncertainties and governance gaps that might impede implementation.

2. Ecosystem services provision potentially influenced by water management

At the start of the "Water for All" project, a workshop was run which compared the Lunan Water with the River Leven, another lowland catchment in eastern Scotland. Eight main elements of Ecosystem Services Provision that could be affected by water management in the two catchments were identified. These are summarised in **Table 1**. Of these, those marked as having a high potential for influence in the Lunan Water became the focus of attention for that catchment. A separate project [10] explored the potential of flushing for control of algal blooms in Loch Leven, on the River Leven, using the Lake algal model PROTECH [11].

The key risk factors considered for improved management were:

- Flood risk mitigation. A tilting weir, as a lateral structure on the common lade, could be used to modify flows from the upstream lakes to achieve a lower base level in the lakes prior to winter high flows, and provide managed release. Dredging of the mill lade might also be used to achieve this, but with less flexibility and greater potential for adverse impact;

- Risk of eutrophication of floodplain wetlands. Phosphorus, nitrogen and sediment discharge from the lakes displayed strong annual variation. Inflow of sediment/nutrient-rich waters can lead to loss of biodiversity in wetlands [12].

	Importance for two catchments in E. Scotland	
Influences of hydraulic management on Ecosystem Service Provision	Lunan Water	River Leven
a. The ecological response of changing water levels in wetlands associated with the standing waters.	H	M
b. Potential for management of water quality and pollutant loading into wetlands	H	M
c. The impact of flushing regimes, as determined by hydraulic structures, on aquatic ecology.	M	H
d. The management of fish passage and influence on ecology of fish	M	M
e. Opportunities and barriers for ecotourism	M	H
f. Governance needs for water level management.	M	H
g. Opportunities for hydro schemes	L	M
h. Upstream and downstream flood risk, as influenced by hydraulic management and other factors	H	M

Table 1.
Influences of hydraulic management on ecosystem service provision for two catchments in eastern Scotland. H = high, M = medium, L = low.

A tilting weir, as a lateral structure on the common lade, could help divert these sediment/nutrient rich waters away from floodplain wetlands at key times;

- Risk of low flows. This could cause damage to ecological status of the river and economic impact to downstream irrigators. An in-line tilting weir at the lake outlet to the common lade could act as a penning structure to facilitate retention of water in early summer in the lakes, to provide water for abstraction and maintain low flows. This element of the analysis was considered in detail elsewhere [13].

3. Hydrological analysis

The surface water sub-catchment areas for the upper Lunan Water have been separated, for water balance purposes, into the areas used for hydraulic modelling, which are shown in **Figure 2**. The areas of each of these sub-catchments were used to scale measured and modelled flows from monitored sub-catchments where water flow and water quality monitoring occurred. These are the Balgavies Burn sub-catchment, at Westerton (area = 4.4 km^2), which generates real time stage and flow data and the Baldardo Burn sub-catchment at Wemyss (area = 2.4 km^2), which generates water level data.

The "Water for All" project focused on the outlet zone of Balgavies Loch (**Figure 3**), where the Lunan Water discharges into a partially confined common channel (lade). This lade controls water delivery to a mill or returning to the river, controlled by an existing engineered gated weir, and water also flows from the river into to its lateral floodplain wetlands (Chapel Mires) via a non-engineered spillage zone, which replaced a now-blocked engineered spillway in the 1970's. The ecological value of these wetlands may be vulnerable due to ingress of sediment and

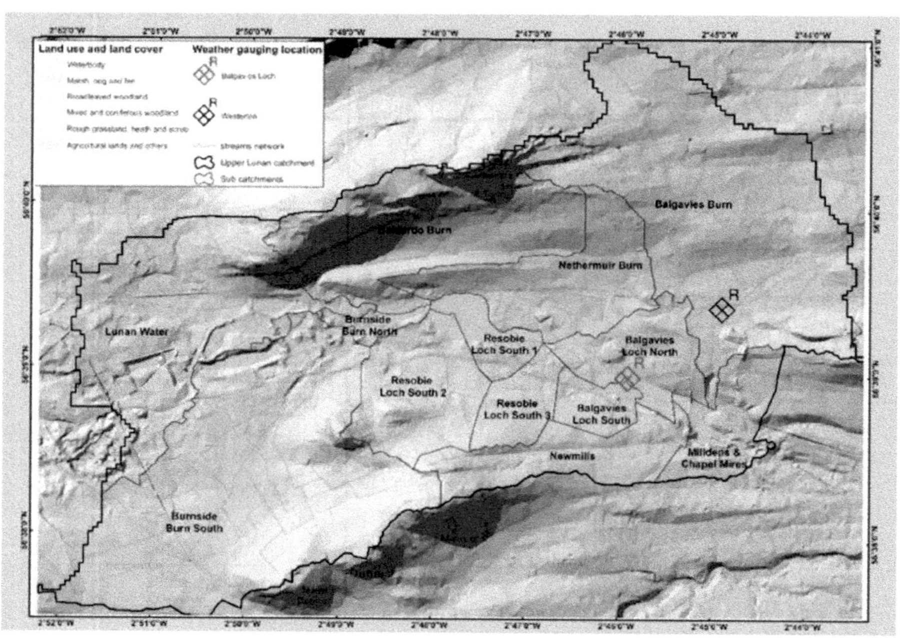

Figure 2.
Sub-catchments of upper Lunan water used in hydrological-hydraulic modelling.

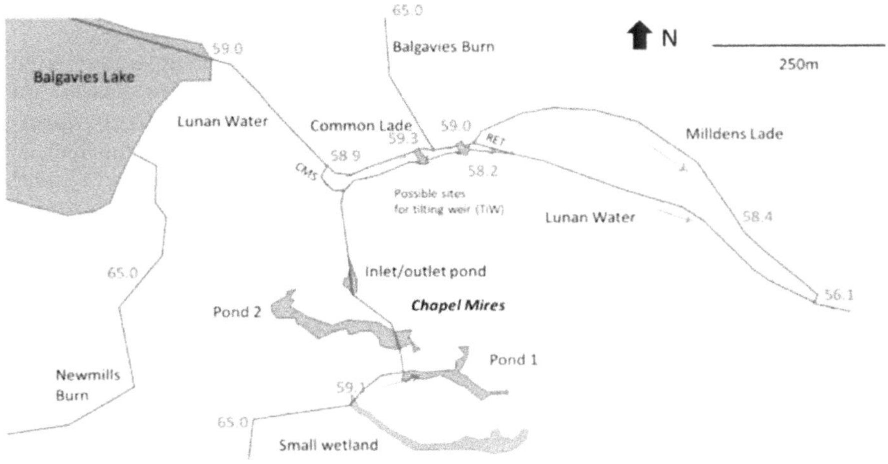

Figure 3.
Outlet structures of Balgavies loch to Lunan water. Bed levels shown in red in m above sea level. RET = return gate from common lade to Lunan water; CMS = existing chapel mires spillway; TIW1, TIW2 = possible sites for installation of tilting weir to manage flow routing and upstream water levels. Figures in red are elevation of bed level of stream above sea level in metres.

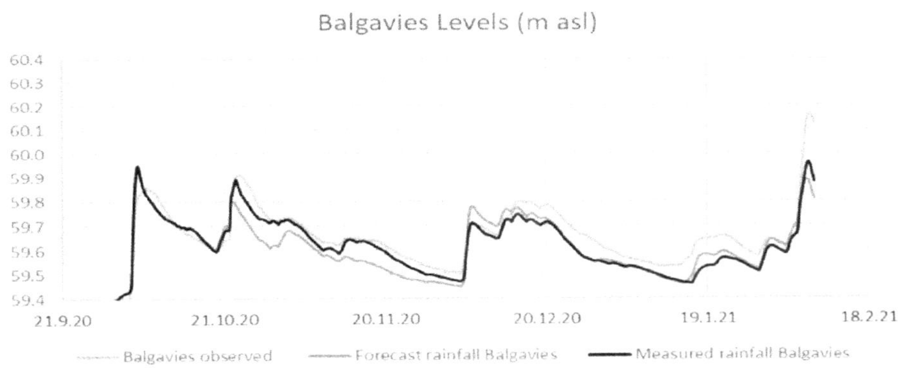

Figure 4.
Observed water levels in Balgavies loch over Oct 2020-Feb 2021 compared with results of simulations using the hydrological model with two alternative assumptions: a. using observed rainfall b. using rainfall from the 1d forecast on a 2x2km2 grid, updated daily from the UK meteorological office.

nutrients from the river [12, 14]. Hydro-ecological assessment involved developing a model of the upper Lunan Water and the operation of this outlet zone. The aim of the modelling is to generate a time series of historic, real-time and forecast based surface water and ground water flows and water levels in the upper Lunan Water catchment, whose area is defined by the surface water outlet at Milldens bridge (Grid Reference NO 354526 750566). These could then be used to provide triggers or other guidance for hydraulic management. This model is now running in a real time and forecasting mode.[1]

The hydrological-hydraulic model has the capability to simulate water levels in the upper Lunan Water lakes as illustrated in **Figure 4**, and flow routing between the Common Lade and the Lunan Water.

[1] https://www.hutton.ac.uk/research/projects/payments-ecosystem-services-lessons#waterforall

The model calibration provided the basis for some level of certainty about the impact of existing and potential hydraulic management. The scenario analysis pointed to the rather low impact of installation of a tilting weir on upstream water levels, whether this were to be installed either above or below the confluence of the Balgavies Burn and the Common Lade. However, it also pointed to a larger impact on water levels if dredging/vegetation management or other interventions that affect the Manning roughness coefficient downstream of Balgavies Loch are undertaken, in conjunction with tilting weir installation. It also shows that flow routing could be significantly impacted by a tilting weir, or by reinstatement of the blocked spillway downstream of the current spillway (see **Figure 3**), especially if combined with local dredging and/or vegetation management.

4. Ecological analysis

Rescobie and Balgavies Lochs, covering 1.78 km^2, support over 60 species of breeding birds and with their surrounds form a Site of Special Scientific Interest (SSSI). There are many aquatic species such as *Menyanthes trifoliata* (Bogbean) and *Utricularia australis* agg. (Bladderwort) that occur in shallow water and any significant change in water levels could affect them. In the area south of the Lunan Water (Chapel Mires – see **Figures 5** and **6**) there is a complex mosaic of open water, willow scrub and sedge-dominated fen vegetation including *Carex rostrata-Calliergon* mire, *Filipendula ulmaria –Angelica sylvetris* mire, *Phalaris* swamp, *Carex rostrata* swamp and *Carex rostrata–Equisetum fluviatile* sub-community occupying the lower lying areas. This has led to this area also being included in the Rescobie and Balgavies Lochs SSSI. The Nationally Scarce *Cicuta virosa* (Cowbane) and *Lysimachia thyrsiflora* (Tufted Loosestrife), could be threatened by changes in water levels or the input of sediment/nutrients as shown by [12].

Water sampling around Chapel Mires compared with the outlet of the Lunan Water at Bagavies Loch, and End Member Mixing Analysis (EMMA) confirmed the vegetation analysis and helped confirm the need to manage pollutant rich water inflow, especially if storm waters threaten the southern and eastern parts of the wetland, which are more pristine (see **Figure 7**).

Figure 5.
Chapel mires viewed from the SW. The line of the Lunan water is the trees between the arable (yellow) and grassland (green) field in the middle distance.

Figure 6.
Aerial view of chapel mires (red line shows SSSI boundary) and gradient of vegetation from (top right) Phalaris arundincea (reed canary-grass) and Sparganium erectum (branched bur-reed) rich (sediment tolerant) to (bottom right) Carex rostrata (bottle sedge) and Menyanthes trifoliata (Bogbean) rich (sediment intolerant) associations with distance from the Lunan water (located on northern boundary).

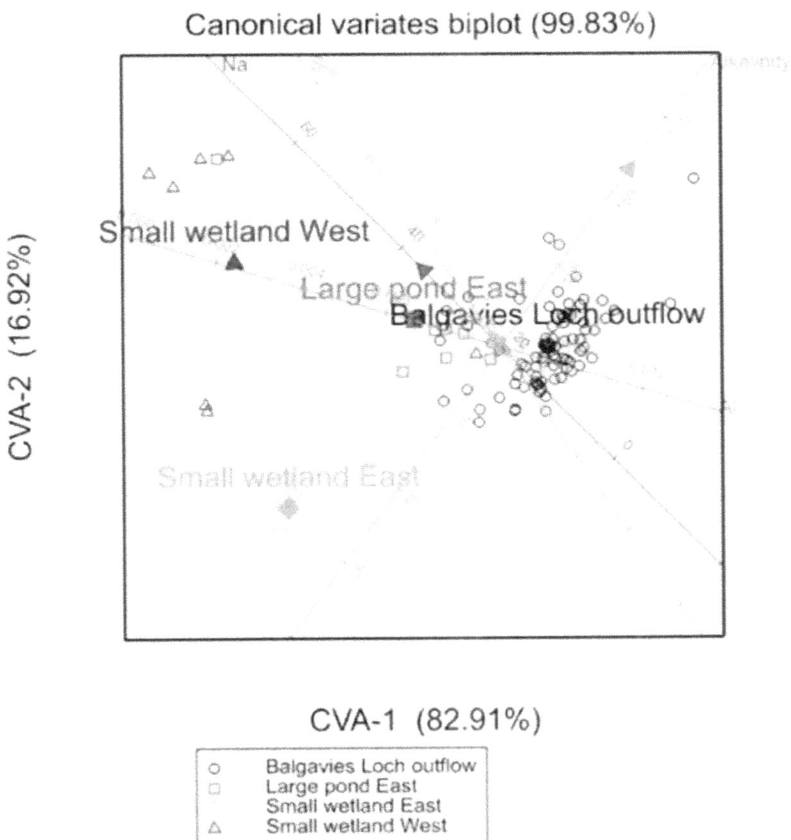

Figure 7.
Canonical variates biplot of water chemistry for the wetlands of chapel mires and the outflow of Balgavies loch, showing that the wetlands on the south eastern fringe of chapel mires are geochemically distinct.

5. Analysis of stakeholder engagement

Figure 8 summarises the conceptual framework for engaging with stakeholders. Detailed analyses of the results of a Willingness to Pay survey and interviews with riparian, other landowners and government agency stakeholders are reported elsewhere. Reports of the Lunan Catchment Management Group meetings can be found at the project website (see Footnote 1 above).

The following list summarises some key findings of this engagement process:

1. It is challenging to demonstrate technical feasibility

   The development and validation of the model to assess the impact of management scenarios on water levels and flow routing was a complex and time-consuming process. The project was set up with both technical and social science goals, which needed to run in parallel, yet each of which had uncertain outcomes;

2. Predicted benefits are quite thinly spread across users

   The multiple benefits of the scheme for flood risk, low flow risk, and ecological conservation was seen as a selling point for a Payment for Ecosystem Services scheme, but in practice it diluted the beneficial impact for each stakeholder and made the technical justification of the scheme based on robust evidence, more challenging;

3. The strongest concerns are for long-term management and legal issues

   The catchment has historically supported a series of working water mills for grain processing, and there is still historical memory of water disputes arising from these. While none of these mills are now operating commercially, there is still a recognition that active water management has the potential for dispute and legal challenge. A "benign neglect" approach, based on passive management, is therefore favoured by some. Governance systems to deal with such issues are generally weak in Scotland;

4. Among those in favour of "Water for All", there were no clear champions

   The multiple benefits aspects of the proposed scheme has meant that it has proved difficult to identify a single agency with sufficient interest to promote proposals. This has changed recently, with a more unified strategy to promote the benefits of the scheme for wetland ecological conservation;

5. The need to dedicate time and energy to pursuing approval for installation and management after installation

   The costs of demonstrating the proof-of-concept elements of the research project have detracted from the pursuit of management and governance planning post-installation and have led to adoption of a proposal that is more passive (reinstatement of blocked spillway) rather than active (management of a remotely operated tilting weir);

6. Insufficient or doubtful benefit to stakeholders

   The need for co-ordinated long-term planning and the existence of likely trade-offs (e.g. between up-and downstream interests; between wetland ecology and farming; between fisheries and irrigators; around issues of access to

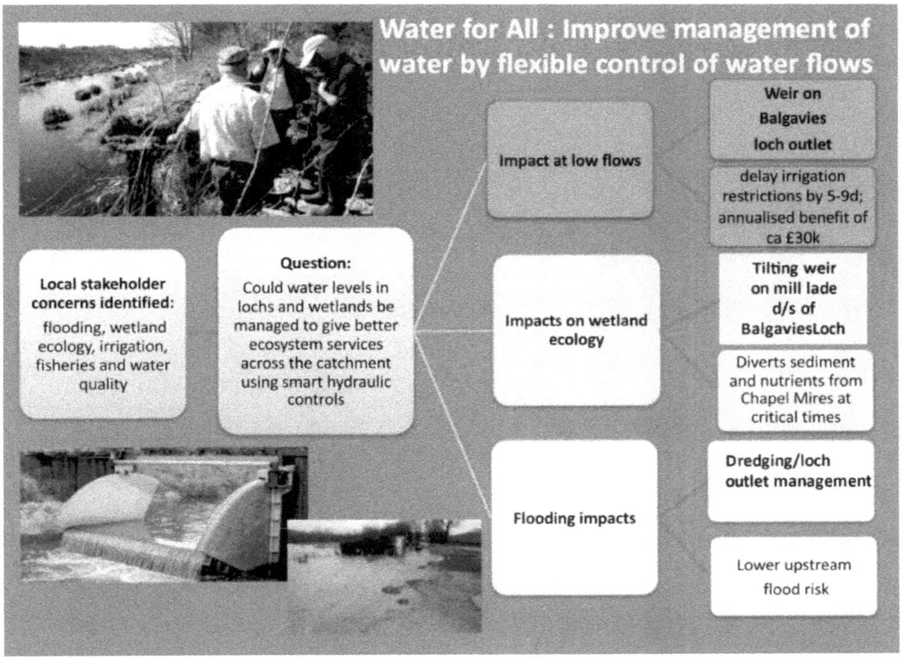

Figure 8.
Conceptual framework for engagement with agencies, land users and other stakeholders.

the environment) has led to some stakeholders considering the work required to achieve benefits is incommensurate. Few stakeholders have a comprehensive overview of benefits;

7. Lack of precedence

   Except on larger, well regulated catchments with strong fisheries, hydroelectric, water supply, navigation, abstraction or sewerage interests, such as the Tay, the Tweed, the Clyde, the Dee and the Forth, or on those designated for Priority Action under the Water Framework Directive, there is little precedence for local Catchment Management Groups and for use of hydraulic structures for integrated management;

8. Need for drainage boards in Scotland?

   Recent legal precedent elsewhere has led to a highlighting of the potential for drainage boards to be established in Scotland. The Pow of Inchaffray Drainage Board (River Earn catchment) and the North Glasgow Drainage scheme (River Kelvin and Scottish Union Canal) are recent examples where legally binding governance schemes have been established. The River Leven is also regulated by sluice gates on Loch Leven, but the governance of these gates is based on anachronistic rules developed in the context of obsolete industries downstream.

6. Deliberation and adaptation of objectives

In any integrated water management project of this kind, it is also vital to respond adaptively to stakeholder issues and barriers to implementation [15].

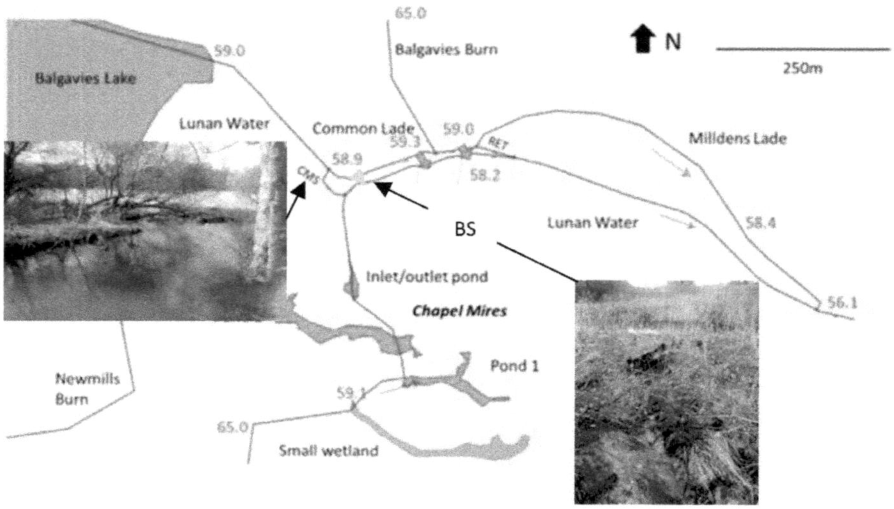

Figure 9.
Position of existing spillway separating the Lunan water from the common lade (CMS) and blocked spillway (BS), which was agreed with riparian owners and the Lunan catchment management group could be re-instated.

This project was one of a group of case studies that considered adaptive catchment management across Scotland[2].

Having considered the concerns listed above, a modified proposal was tabled to the Lunan Catchment Management Group and to riparian owners. This focused on re-instating a blocked spillway downstream of the existing spillway where the river and Common Lade separate (CMS in **Figures 3** and **9**). This blockage had been installed in the 1970's, to enhance the flow of water to the mill lade to feed a recently reinstated historic water mill. Modelling of scenarios of hydraulic management showed that this approach would provide one of the key benefits of the original scheme, namely the protection of Chapel Mires wetland ecology from sediment from Newmills Burn during peak runoff events. It would have a more passive approach to management and be in keeping with current river restoration policies aiming at returning to natural flow regimes, where possible. The modified proposals were agreed in principle by the local interest groups, opening the way for solicitation of funding for the re-instatement works required.

7. Conclusions

In any project of this kind, it is vital to respond adaptively to stakeholder issues and barriers to implementation. This chapter highlights key elements of an "action research" project to underpin Scottish Government science policy for sustainable management of water resources in Scotland. The paradigm of Payment for Ecosystem Services underpinned the approach taken and the aspiration was to see a pilot PES scheme developed and assessed within the original 5-year time. However, the combined challenges of demonstrating the technical benefits, adaptive response

[2] https://www.hutton.ac.uk/sites/default/files/files/research/srp2016-21/RESAS_srp143_aD1_ReportOnRelevantAdaptiveManagementApproachesForScotland_v0.8Final.pdf

to stakeholder concerns and lack of governance structures for water resources management at a catchment scale have slowed the process. The lessons learnt include:

1. Project management. Where technical challenges need to be met (i.e. development of a plausible hydraulic model), these may need to take precedence in the early part of project delivery, notwithstanding the need for co-operative development of project objectives;

2. Multiple Benefits. While the delivery of multiple benefits is a widely held aspiration, it may lead to a lack of championing of a proposal across different interest groups;

3. Governance. Weak, non-existent, vested or anachronistic governance mechanisms can be a barrier to implementation of water management projects, even at a relatively local scale. They may actually be more challenging at a small scale and on lower priority catchments where less leverage of regulation or funding occurs;

4. Passive vs. active water management. There is a tendency to descend to the lowest common denominator of "benign neglect" in management of water at a catchment scale. Cultural norms and perceptions tend to favour the status quo. It may be that such an approach is beneficial to overall ecosystem service delivery when economic as well as public goods are considered. However, any potential negative consequences of a new structure or intervention tend to be weighted more heavily in decision-making than the known negative consequences of the systems that we already have;

5. A way forward does now exist that has potential to deliver improvement of ecosystem services, but the payments mechanisms for works and ongoing monitoring and management are yet to be resolved.

Acknowledgements

We thank the Scottish Government for funding the PESLES project RD1.4.3d, through the RESAS Strategic Research Programme, 2016-2022.

Conflict of interest

The authors declare no conflict of interest.

Notes/thanks/other declarations

The authors wish to thank the following:

- The members of the Lunan Catchment Management Group, especially Janice Corrigan (Angus Council, chair), Peter McPhail, Gavin Clark and Deborah Spray (Nature Scotland); Alban Houghton (Balgavies Loch Reserve); Rab Potter (Scottish Wildlife Trust); Scott Leith (SEPA); Marshall Halliday and Craig Macintyre (Esk Rivers and Fisheries Trust);

- Lunan Riparian stakeholder associations, including the Rescobie Loch Development Association and Balgavies Loch committee;
- Individual riparian interests including Mr. Tom Sampson, Mr. James Osborne, Mr. Ian Guthrie for access permissions to instal water level recording equipment and carry out vegetation surveys and water management investigations;
- The Meteorological Office for provision of forecast rainfall data;
- UK National River Flow Archive for providing hydrometric records;
- David Riach, Helen Watson, Carol Taylor, Claire Abel and other support staff at James Hutton Institute;
- Remi Trenkmann, Marjorie Gabriel and Camille Hoang-Cong, intern students from ENGEES, Strasbourg, France.

Author details

Andrew Vinten[1*] and Iain D.M. Gunn[2]

1 James Hutton Institute, Aberdeen, UK

2 UK Centre for Ecology and Hydrology, Edinburgh, UK

*Address all correspondence to: andy.vinten@hutton.ac.uk

References

[1] Turner RK, van den Bergh JCJM, Söderqvist T, Barendregt A, van der Straaten J, Maltby E, et al. Ecological-economic analysis of wetlands: scientific integration for management and policy. Ecol Econ. 2000;35(1):7-23.

[2] Bizzi S, Pianosi F, Soncini-Sessa R. Valuing hydrological alteration in multi-objective water resources management. Journal of Hydrology. 2012;472-473:277-86.

[3] Waylen KA, Martin-Ortega J. Surveying views on Payments for Ecosystem Services: Implications for environmental management and research. Ecosystem Services. 2018;29:23-30.

[4] Schulz C, Ioris AAR, Martin-Ortega J, Glenk K. Prospects for Payments for Ecosystem Services in the Brazilian Pantanal: A Scenario Analysis. The Journal of Environment & Development. 2014;24(1):26-53.

[5] Matzdorf B, Biedermann C, Meyer C, Nicolaus K, Sattler C, Schomers S. Paying for Green? Payments for Ecosystem Services in Practice. Successful examples of PES from Germany, the United Kingdom and the United States2014.

[6] Ojea E, Martin-Ortega J. Understanding the economic value of water ecosystem services from tropical forests: A systematic review for South and Central America. Journal of Forest Economics. 2015;21(2):97-106.

[7] Perrot-Maître D. The Vittel Payments for Ecosystem Services: A "perfect" PES Case. 2006.

[8] Rodwell JSe. British Plant Communities. Volume 4. Aquatic communities, swamps and tall-herb fens. Cambridge University Press. 1995.

[9] Christophersen N, Hooper RP. Multivariate analysis of stream water chemical data: The use of principal components analysis for the end-member mixing problem. Water Resour Res. 1992;28(1):99-107.

[10] May L, Elliott, J.A. Can small changes in water retention time reduce the severity of algal blooms in lakes, providing mitigation of climate change impacts? A proof of concept using Loch Leven as a case study. Centre for Ecology and Hydrology Report for PESLES project. 2020:11.

[11] Elliott JA, Reynolds CS, Irish AE, Tett P. Exploring the potential of the PROTECH model to investigate phytoplankton community theory. Hydrobiologia. 1999;414(0):37-43.

[12] Werner KJ, Zedler JB. How sedge meadow soils, microtopography, and vegetation respond to sedimentation. Wetlands. 2002;22(3):451-66.

[13] Vinten A, Kuhfuss L, Shortall O, Stockan J, Ibiyemi A, Pohle I, et al. Water for all: Towards an integrated approach to wetland conservation and flood risk reduction in a lowland catchment in Scotland. J Environ Manage. 2019;246:881-96.

[14] Rojas IM, Zedler JB. An invasive exotic grass reduced sedge meadow species richness by half. Wetlands Ecology and Management. 2015;23(4):649-63.

[15] Engle NL, Johns OR, Lemos MC, Nelson DR. Integrated and Adaptive Management of Water Resources: Tensions, Legacies, and the Next Best Thing. Ecology and Society. 2011;16(1).

Chapter 14

Ensuring Water Availability in Future through Revival of Indian Traditional Water Culture

Yogranjan Singh, Sathak Pandey and Amit Kumar Goswami

Abstract

After the recurrent spells of weak monsoons, a big part of the country's population, are affected by a severe drought obliging India to walk towards a water-stressed future. The drought has dried up wells and other water reservoirs already stressed by overuse resulting into crop failure to a reasonable extent of more than 60 per cent. The current water management systems particularly in rural areas are poorly equipped to deal with the issue in significant part because they do not promote distributed water collection, water conservation, and water reuse. Providentially, a combination of often forgotten traditional water practices and more recent innovations in water use and management can help resolve this growing water crisis. These include rainwater capture, water recycling and reuse, and innovative technologies to purify water. India's history is witness to how well-planned cities of our ancient civilization were equipped with outstanding systems of water harvesting and drainage. These ancient structures synergized with well validated water practices were the strong support systems during the times when the modern infrastructural marvels did not exist, but they were more than efficient in managing the water resources even at the time. Today the traditional water practices and ancient but ignored water sources of the country are yearning to discharge the ancient traditions to revive the glorious history of their past for the dire need of the hour. If water strategists aim to spread the message of water conservation to the common people and want to ensure that every drop of water is conserved, then the proven and scientifically validated Indian traditional water culture will have to be revived. Coincidently, customary water bodies have always been subject of reverence for Indians, reviving these traditional water bodies by involving locals could be a strategy that every region needs to adopt. Stepping up these revival options will indispensably require change in legal and regulatory framework but will perceptibly offer policy makers a better chance to meet present demands and future needs in an increasingly water-constrained India.

Keywords: Water crisis, traditional water culture, water bodies, heritage, community approach

1. Introduction

India is endowed with rich biodiversity, natural beauty, and sound climatic as well as edaphic suitability. The country has a strange diversity of climatic regions, ranging from cold temperate and alpine in the Himalayan north to the hot and humid tropical in the south. The country also cherishes a rich history of water heritage. The tradition of water harvesting in India is centuries old, this shows how much respect people have for water since ancient times. Traditionally water was worshiped, stored and conserved. Although there was diversity in the water harvesting systems, but on a large scale, reservoirs were constructed on a coordinated basis, the main objective of which was to create a wide range of water storage systems. In spite of all these bounties, the unfortunate aspect is that presently, India has become a house of a huge proportion of the world's 'water poor' population. It holds only 4 per cent of the world's freshwater resources, but 18% of the global inhabitants [1]. Presently in the country, agitating climate variability, rapid urbanization, and competitive demand of water for agriculture, industry, energy production, and municipal supply puts tremendous pressure on underground reservoirs and is hence making it increasingly tough to meet the water challenges of the near future.

The chapter finds defects in the current water distribution and utilization systems which specifically aim at realizing immediate results without respecting ecological boundaries. Additionally, it argues that there is an urgent need to revive India's traditional water culture to better cope with the worsening water conditions prevalent across the country. The chapter also signifies that the shortcomings of current water system can be well addressed by regaining the old wisdom of traditional water culture, and by integrating it with current state of scientific methods and technologies. A blend of traditional water culture and advanced water technologies can lead to a transformation into a more relevant water infrastructure that integrates development within the sustainable water cycle.

2. The upcoming water crisis India faces and factors blamed

Water scarcity, like the entire world, has also become a common concern in India. Declining ground water levels and lack of adequate water resources to meet demands affects every state. No doubt that in view of increasing population and global climate change, the problem will increasingly amplify unless something instrumental is done. In a study conducted by central government in the year 2018, the country held 120th position on the list of 122 countries facing a water crisis [2, 3]. Four of the Indian cities [Chennai is first, Kolkata is second, Mumbai is at 11th and Delhi is at 15th position] are among the 400 cities in the world facing acute water crisis. The same study revealed that 21 cities of the country will reach zero ground water level as per the composite water management index. That is, these cities will not even have their own drinking water in near future. The major commercial metropolis like Bangalore, Chennai, Delhi and Hyderabad will be the worst affected, putting the lives of 100 million people at stake [4]. Water crisis in rural areas is the prime reason, the people are obliged to migrate to the cities already fighting with population pressure. Apart from this, the urban areas are already under numerous anthropogenic pressures, ranging from industrial development to desertification, pollution and loss of biodiversity. This fact itself necessitates an urgent action towards the conservation of the already scanty resources in rural areas, deprived of which the situation is bound to worsen day by day and will soon be out of control in the times to come.

The root cause behind tough scenario of water crisis is vital to be explored first in order to deal with it. It's not the delayed monsoon or the lack of rain as claimed by most of the people including media and policy makers. It is rather the consistent ignorance of the governments for years. Overlooking non-judicious distribution system, promoting dire habits and misusing the country's water resources are the core realities behind the current water crisis. These factors are more prominent ones in addition to unavoidable factors such as rapid urbanization, population growth and industrialization that can be held equally responsible for the upcoming crisis. Although factors like climate change have taken an unmanageable form, but various human activities are also responsible for its origin. Apart from this and above all, the situation of water crisis has become even more worse due to the gross neglect of the traditional water culture of India. Herein we review some of the major perpetrators as follow.

2.1 Irrational approach towards farming

Farming has always been the engine of the Indian economy; however, looking at it with full sensitivity and rational mindset, it is known that over the years, India has seen many changes in its cropping pattern and the approaches of irrigation. With the decreasing availability of water in reservoirs like canal, ponds and rivers along with the development of advanced techniques, there has been a vast change in the method of irrigation. The share of canal irrigated area in the total irrigable land has been continuously decreasing since last few decades. At present, the share of land irrigated by ground water has increased to more than half of the total land [5]. This misuse of groundwater resources in the north-western parts of the country is the biggest reason for the water crisis in the country. In addition, heavy water intensive crops such as paddy and sugarcane are cultivated in north-western parts of the country particularly in Punjab, Uttar Pradesh and Maharashtra. Rice is the most important staple grain of the country. It takes 3500 liters of water to grow one Kg of rice [6]. The Punjab is entirely dependent on ground water for rice cultivation. Although in terms of rice productivity, performance of this state is exceptionally good, but it is far behind the states of the Northeast in terms of better use of water. Punjab uses two to three times more water in comparison to Bihar and West Bengal to produce one Kg of rice [7]. Farmers in Punjab have the privilege of cheap electricity and input subsidy. Besides, the government also implements favorable policies to procure farmers' crops. In such a situation, rice cultivation becomes very beneficial for the farmers of Punjab. On the other hand, farmers of the north east states such as Assam, Tripura, Bengal and Bihar do not get such facilities. Similar is the story of sugarcane, which again demands a lot of water. Sugarcane is primarily grown as cash crop that demands 1500–3000 liters of water to produce a kg of sugarcane [8]. Farmers in Maharashtra state cultivate sugarcane on a large scale and use ground water for its irrigation. Farmers take the advantages of having sugar mills of the state which buy their fresh produce. At the same time, where Bihar extends quite favorable environment for sugarcane cultivation, ironically, only 4% of the total sugarcane production of the country is produced.

The methods of irrigation which are commonly adopted in the country are as well not judicious. Despite being numerous demerits of flood irrigation like water wastage, nutrient leaching, and weed growth, majority of farmers in India still prefer it over other water saving methods. A big reason for this natural selection is that more than 80% of the farming community falls under the marginal and small farmers' category. They do not have the money to afford the cost of equipments required to install drips or sprinklers in their fields. Moreover, they own considerably small pieces of farmland which are more suitable for subsistence farming rather than commercial farming.

2.2 Explosive population growth

When the population reaches an explosive state in any country, it starts growing disproportionately with the resources, and so is the case with ground water. The population of India in 2019 was reported to be 13.4 billion with an annual growth rate of 1% [9]. Owing to this explosive growth, the biggest impact has been on groundwater in terms of its indiscriminate exploitation. Many states in India have either enacted or are about to enact laws regarding underground water harvesting to deal with the emergent problem. But it is quite unfortunate that even if laws are in force, they themselves have become the victims of ignorance. As a matter of fact, the total requirement of ground water was 252 billion cubic meters [BCM] in 2010 and is projected to be 282 BCM in 2025 and 428 BCM in 2050 [10]. The total domestic and public need for water includes the water requirement of animals, for irrigation, domestic and public use, industry, power generation, inland shipping and ecological purposes. An unruly population growth near urban areas has put a bonus pressure on groundwater resources. Given the growing imbalance between demand and supply, indiscriminate and excessive use of ground water requires urgent attention.

2.3 Rapid urbanization

Over the years, the increasing population has directly impacted the demography of urban India [11]. According to the census released in the year 2001, urban population was 26.75 per cent, which after ten years i.e. in 2011, increased to a tune of 30 per cent at the annual growth rate of 3.35 per cent [12]. It is anticipated that by the year 2030, Indian cities will have 40 per cent of total country's population. Thinking on the number of people having access of clean water by then is quite panicky. With the expansion of cities, there has been an unprecedented increase in buildings, roads and other construction works. Most parts of the metropolitan cities are either residential areas or commercial spaces. It is hence very hard to find open, fallow land in the cities. Almost the entire ground surface is covered with asphalt roads and that too at the cost of massive deforestation. There is an inextricable relationship between forest and rain, due to which the water storage areas do not irrigate the underground aquifers and create conditions like drought in summer and flood in monsoon. These conditions make it almost impossible for the rainwater to percolate into the soil and recharge the groundwater tables. Furthermore, most of the metropolitan cities of India majorly depend on groundwater reserves as their primary source of water. This juxtaposition of ignorance and reality is the key reason why most of these cities now have to confront a tough predicament.

2.4 Over and non-judicious use of water resources

Wastage of water does not only mean using it more than what we require when it is scarce, rather it encompasses failing to conserve it when it is in abundance. Lack of awareness and poor infrastructure towards water conservation is the foremost driver behind the water wastage problem. It's pretty regrettable that despite realizing the horrific situation of water crisis in the future, man has not stopped using the available ground water indiscriminately. The crisis seems even more daunting when the numbers related to the wastage of water are shockingly high. Inside the 1.3 billion tons of food wasted every year worldwide involves 45 trillion gallons of water [13]. This fairly represents a staggering 24 per cent of all water used for agriculture. For a majority of the countries, the primary source of irrigation is groundwater, India being one of them. Sadly for India, the picture is not a happy one, as far as groundwater resources are concerned and the data speak more eloquently and loudly than words. In fact, groundwater is being exhausted at a mean rate of $4.0 \pm 1.0\,cm\,yr.^{-1}$, that implies an equivalent height of water [$17.7 \pm 4.5\,km3\,yr.^{-1}$] is being depleted every year across the Indian states of Rajasthan, Punjab and Haryana [including Delhi] [14]. The study revealed that the lessening of groundwater in a period of August 2002 to October 2008 was equivalent to a net loss of 109 km^3 of water, which in fact, is double of the capacity of India's largest surface-water pool. Additionally, bitter competition between rural and urban consumers is increasing and at some places even conflict has come to the fore. This problem is more severe in areas where the rocks are hard or the level of recharge is very low. Poor farmers are deprived of irrigation sources, while rich farmers are successful in drilling deep wells. Massively falling water table increases energy consumption as more energy is expended in pumping water from higher down. Roughly 30.5 per cent of India's electricity generation is currently spent on pumping groundwater [15].

The efforts of the government are also proving to be insufficient and short-sighted in this direction. Instead of meeting the needs of the agricultural sectors, water is being brought through intensive pipelines from various water sources not only for the population of the city but also for industrial need. For example; water is being carried to the capital Delhi from Tehri dam in Uttarakhand that is 300 km away. Water is being supplied to Hyderabad; the IT hub of India from NagarjunaSagar Dam of Krishna river built at a distance of 116 km. Whereas the Kaveri river is supplying water to Bengaluru that is 100 km away. In this way, water needs are being met in the expanding city and industrial areas that otherwise were ought to be for farming.

2.5 The broken water management systems of rural India

The rural India has proven to be resilient even in the hardest of times like the pandemic of 2020. Unlike their urban counterparts, people of rural India were able to contain the spread of the virus, during the first wave of the pandemic. Such response was made possible by the cooperative efforts of the villagers. With only a little help from the administration, the residents took steps like sealing their respective villages as and when cases rose, forbidding non-residents from entering their village, setting up makeshift quarantine centers for taking care of residents developing symptoms of illness. As a result, the death toll in villages was remarkably less than what it was in the metropolitan cities. These incidents are evidence that rural India is not a setup that should be mistaken as a group of people with little knowledge of worldly affairs. However, the anatomy of Indian villages is anything but that simple. During times of crisis, they proactively work together as a unit with a common goal for the mutual benefit of their village. This is just one among the many examples wherein the villages have faced a great calamity on the strength of cooperatives and traditions. Similarly, water management had a rural style of its own, which, till a few decades ago, defied any likelihood of water crisis in rural arena, however, in the recent past, the water management systems of a sizable chunk of rural India appears to be perpetually broken. Modern systems, in fact based on market principles have broken communities and have proved to be cruel and biased on the distribution front.

Rural India cherishes a long history of water resources management. The collective style of water use and its conservation used to be an integral part of it. A variety of structures were also built for diverse uses of water including domestic purposes and irrigation. Since ancient times, the Indian priests [locally known as Bhagiraths], along with the development of civilization and culture, took into account the climate, soil nature and other variations for maximally utilizing and conserving the rain water, rivers, streams and underground water resources. This approach was suitable for the specific and local conditions of the north-eastern region from snow-capped Laddakh to the plateau in the south and the arid desert of Thar to the high rainfall for most of the year. Keeping in view the climate and availability of water or ice at all these places, methods of water harvesting, its disposal and use in irrigation were discovered and time-tested methods were developed. Strong evidence of these achievements is available in every nook and corner of the country. In fact, these evidences reflect the advanced knowledge, vision and excellent understanding of the circumstances of the ancient rural Indians and are also relevant in the present context. The systematic approach of ancient people is well exemplified by the practices that were followed during the rule of several rulers of ancient and medieval India. Being well versed in the knowledge related to hydrology and water management, the society also carried out the work of building, running and maintaining the structures. The function of the ruler or king of that period was to help in running the system smoothly. The rural peasants were also well acquainted with the work of flood control [some examples are cited in the coming section]. They built interconnected structures of canals and ponds to avoid the floods of the over floating rivers.

2.6 Climate unpredictability

The critical levels of climate change are alarming. The changes in weather over the years have been very apparently noticed in the form of dryer summers and recurrent droughts. Then comes dripping winters too that cause flooding. The dryer and hotter summers simply mean a greater amount of water evaporating back into the atmosphere leading to lesser availability of ground water for abstraction when it is urgently required, particularly in times of drought. Unpredictable and sudden heavy rainfalls cause flooding that lakes, rivers and reservoirs cannot cope with and thus affecting all forms of human activities directly including structural and environmental damage. The unpredicted rainfall, abrupt drought or heat waves makes it quite difficult to plan for water availability on one hand, while on the other lower or scanty rainfall reduces water levels in rivers, ponds and reservoirs across the country. During the first half of year 2018, a total of 91 major reservoirs in India recorded 32% drop in their water capacity [16]. These all scenarios indicate the need to understand potential impacts of climate unpredictability on water dynamics.

3. Risks envisaged: apprehension of appalling future

The situation of water emergency is that approximately 2 lakh people die every year in India due to consumption of inadequate and polluted water [17]. The threats looming overhead due to water scarcity are not only confined to the human race. Depleting water levels coupled with many anthropogenic activities has put our biodiversity in an extremely vulnerable position. Almost everywhere, watersheds appear to be dying and shrinking because of their reduced rainwater harvesting capabilities. The storage areas of the catchments were either diverted to other uses or became deforested. As a consequence, the situation is getting tough day by day. In those areas of the country which are facing the dire situation of water crisis, the cost of a pitcher of water is more than the life of a person or human being. During the summer, women in several parts of Rajasthan, Maharashtra and Bundelkhand start arranging water from very early morning. Last year, drinking water was transported by train to the people of drought-hit Latur district of Maharashtra and Bundelkhand region of Uttar Pradesh. These days, the news of water disputes at various locations has become quite common. This crisis may increase further in the coming times. Analysts have been expressing apprehension that the use of water in the form of a weapon is also possible in the near future. Some time ago, due to tension with Pakistan, India had threatened to disrupt the availability of water by stopping the flow of the Indus River. In this section we will discuss the potential dangers arising out of water crisis.

3.1 Agriculture at the center of the crisis

Agriculture is a major contributor in the country's economy, where out of total available land, 51 per cent is agricultural, 4 per cent is pasture, 21 per cent is forested and 24 per cent is barren. The livelihood of 52 per cent of the country is dependent on agriculture and allied industries. The share of agriculture sector in total water use is more than other sectors. The agriculture sector alone consumes 80 per cent of water resources in India and is responsible for almost 90 per cent of groundwater withdrawals. Tube Wells and canals are the most common modes of irrigation throughout India. These methods have allowed the farmers to conveniently extract water on a large scale and flood their fields with all the water they can get. Subsidy is also provisioned by the government for boring in the fields by the farmers. Massive abstraction of ground water very clearly reflected into drying up in many parts of the country. The problem of water crisis in Bundelkhand, Rajasthan, Maharashtra and Karnataka are now very recurrent. At some places, the problem is so severe that the prevailing conditions coerced the farmers to give up farming.

The problem is aggravated by climate unpredictability. Due to the spatial–temporal variation of rainfall most of the country remains rainless and drought prone. North-Western India and the Deccan Plateau are the most affected. Besides, in most parts of the country, more or less dryness is found in winter and summer, so it is difficult to cultivate without irrigation in dry seasons. On the other hand, in areas with sufficient rainfall, such as West Bengal and Bihar, segmental rainfall during the monsoon season creates a drought-like situation, which is harmful to agriculture. The scarcity of water makes irrigation necessary for some crops. For example, rice, sugarcane, jute etc. require a lot of water which is possible only through irrigation. Secondly, regular moisture supply is necessary for high yielding varieties of crops which is again dependent on developed irrigation system. In Punjab, Haryana and western Uttar Pradesh, 85 per cent of the net sown area is under irrigation [18]. Wheat and rice are mainly grown in these states with the help of irrigation. In Punjab, 76 per cent of the net irrigated area and 51 per cent in Haryana, is irrigated by wells and tube wells [19]. In fact, in some states, such as Rajasthan and Maharashtra, the concentration of fluoride in ground water has increased due to excess water withdrawal and this has led to an adverse impact on agriculture as well on human health.

3.2 Deteriorated drinking water quality and health concern

The falling groundwater levels are not the only red flag that we see today. Rather, the issue of quality of drinking water is also a big concern. Approximately 785 million people lack even a basic drinking-water service, including 144 million people who are dependent on surface water [20]. Cases related to water borne diseases like typhoid, cholera and jaundice have been on the rise in recent years in developing nations. Contaminated drinking water is estimated to cause 485 000 diarrhoeal deaths each year [21]. For a developing nation like India, the challenge of supplying clean drinking water is even bigger due to the vastness of the population. What fuels the apprehensions is an unfortunate truth that despite the increased awareness regarding water safety, sheer negligence towards contamination of water bodies does not seem to take a toll. Farmers across India unmindfully carry on with their habit of applying heavy doses of chemicals to ensure a good yield from their crop.

Little do they realize that these very chemicals get washed away and canals and rivers gets contaminated by lethal chemicals. These reservoirs are not only used by humans as a source of drinking water but also by the animals and livestock of that area. As a result, we end up consuming not just unhealthy water, but also unhealthy food, milk, eggs and meat, all grown using the very same toxic water.

3.3 The rising cost of water

In view of tough situation, an extensive and quite expensive infrastructure is needed to ensure water availability to the common people may it be for digging very deep or supplying water from a long distance to a big city through an extensive pipeline. Although due to the fundamental right of the people to access free water and some political obligations, the tax on water cannot be increased directly. Policy makers around the country face a tight situation in recovering the expenses incurred in the development of infrastructure. Government recovers the expenses either in the form of inflation of other essential commodities or heavy taxes are imposed by the Municipal Corporation. People are expected to pay as the infrastructure development fees. In some states, separate tax provisions have been made for the supply of drinking water and water for other uses. In this way, low- and middle-income families carry most of the load of the mounting expanses indirectly.

4. Management through harnessing traditional water heritage

The practice of water harvesting and management in India is incredibly old. Traditional systems are a characteristic hybrid of the ecology and culture of the region in which they develop. They have not only stood the test of time, but also met the local needs keeping in sync with the environment. Unlike modern systems that exploit the environment, these ancient systems emphasize on ecological conservation. Traditional systems have been benefiting from shared human experiences since time immemorial and this is their greatest strength. Traditional systems based on community also emphasize social harmony and self-reliance. In these, decision-making authority was often given to individuals, groups or local communities, who were working together. This increased economic independence and made full use of local resources at the lower level.

Historical and archeological evidences show that since the 400 BC, small communities in many areas of the country have been making effective arrangements for water harvesting and distribution. The Nanda rulers [363–321 BC] built canals and community-dependent irrigation systems. The Gaur rulers [600–1303 AD] of central India not only created better systems of irrigation and water supply, but also developed necessary social and administrative arrangements for their maintenance. It is noteworthy that all the traditional systems built by these rulers were not small. Large systems were also constructed to meet the needs of the cities but they were coordinated with smaller systems, as observed in the Chola period [848–1279 AD] and the medieval Vijayanagara period [1336–1646 AD]. These systems used contemptible but simple technology that the local people could easily maintain. These systems are also important because they have given life to communities even during long periods of drought or famine. Although, sometimes smaller systems would fail when there was no rain for years. This would have created the need for larger systems, but the balance between small and large systems was carefully maintained. This cannot happen unless both rural and urban communities participate in the planning and implementation of systems. In this way, without glorifying antiquity, it can be said that traditional systems were more effective then and still are in terms of water supply and return on capital.

4.1 Indian water bodies: a precious estate

India is endowed with extraordinarily diverse and distinctive traditional water-bodies known by their different names in different parts of the country, such as Khadin and Baolis [Rajasthan], Dung or Jumpois [Jalpaiguri district, West Bengal] Bhandaras [Maharashtra], Vavdi [Gujarat], AharPynes [Bihar] and Zing [Ladakh, Kashmir]. These water bodies are vital for sustenance to Indian agriculture and have been playing important role in the overall management of water resources of the country. Religious significance are also adhered with the water bodies. Several Indian lakes such as Gurudongmar in Sikkim and Pushkar in Rajasthan are renowned for their religious magnitude. These lakes provide an adequate water in the form of large storage tanks to the monsoon-dependent areas of the country where there exist quite a short spell of rainfall and a long dry period with very high deviation of annual rainfall. The small storage tanks are called ponds or locally bundhis which, as a rule, are community owned, while on the other, the large storage tanks with command areas from 20 to 2000 hectares were usually built by the regional rulers. These water bodies reflect the regional style of construction and typically were based on the provincial demand of water. Some key examples of classical water bodies are presented as follow:

i. In the mountain areas, a diverse pattern of natural depressions are used for rainwater harvesting. The most familiar examples are chaals or lakes. Chaals are the depression found in the saddle between two adjacent crests along mountain ridge tops. It can store several thousand cubic meters of water. They were believed to be formed by the glacial action of snowmelt in the past, leading to the formation of small lakes with a relatively thick soil bed.

ii. Chappris, in Himachal Pradesh, are usually shallow dug ponds without any masonry work and located on the hill sides where the slope tends to flatten out.

iii. Simars are water-logged flat lands found in the high-altitude areas of Uttarakhand.

iv. Canals in western Himalayan regions were built with contours to draw water from hill streams or springs. These canals may vary in length from 1 to 15 km.

v. Ponds are fairly common in the Jammu region. They serve the purpose of livestock and irrigation need.

vi. Tanks of variable sizes with depth not more than five to six metres were also built in plateau region.

vii. Other sources of irrigation were dams that were built across a river, a stream, or an estuary to hold water. Kallanai dam is particularly interesting that was built during the second century AD by Karikalan, a king of southern India's old Chola Dynasty. It is one of the oldest irrigation systems in the world that is still in use [22]. The dam has been built with uneven stones and is 329 m long and 20 m wide (**Figure 1**). The purpose of the dam was to divert the waters of the Kaveri across the fertile Thanjavur delta region for irrigation via canals.

After independence, the government has taken control over these water bodies and making structural changes as needed. However, since last few decades, water bodies have been under continuous and unrelenting stress, caused primarily by unplanned growth and rapid urbanization.

4.2 Traditional water culture: lessons from the past

The first evidence of water management was found during excavations in the Indus Valley [23]. A good quality arrangement was made for the drainage of flood water in this area. Similarly, the art of making wells also developed during the Harappan period [2600 to 1900 BCE] [24]. It is known from the excavations and surveys in this area that there was a well in every third house. About 300 BC, the people of Kutch and Balochistan [now in Pakistan] were familiar with the art of building dams. They built very strong dams with the help of pebbles and stones and stored rainwater in them. This water stored in dams was used to meet drinking water and irrigation needs and people were skilled in managing the water collected in the dam. The systematic approach of ancient people is also well exemplified by the practices followed during the reign of Chandragupta Maurya [321–297 years BCE]. During this tenure, the Indian farmer was not only familiar with the means of irrigation, such as ponds, dams, etc.

4.2.1 Regional diversity in traditional water culture

Diverse ranges of approaches for water conservation have been developed in different regions of India that is mainly divided into five parts on the basis of climatic and physical characteristics.

Figure 1.
Kallanai dam.

4.2.1.1 Himalayan Mountains

The states of Jammu and Kashmir, Himachal Pradesh, Uttarakhand, Sikkim, Arunachal Pradesh, Assam, Nagaland, Meghalaya, Manipur and Tripura are included in the Himalayan mountain region. These states have different types of water practices as per the different geographical conditions and water availability. The canal system has been developed in these areas since ancient times. These mountain streams are up to 15 km long. The canals are connected to uncooked drains locally called Mogha. Through this system, the melt water of the glacier flows and is stored in the ponds, it flows at a fast speed during the snowfall and less amount of water comes in it during the cold season. The system was depended on mutual cooperation and partnership for water distribution. The construction of canals and Mogha in ancient times was the responsibility of merchants and upper class of the society. Similar systems were developed in Lahol and Sfiti regions through which the snow melts and reaches the villages in the form of water. Their main part of the system is the glacial estuary where water is preserved. Stones were laid on the sides and floor to prevent the leakage of water on its way. In many places, the local administration is also getting them repaired, but their appearance is becoming modern.

In the state of Uttar Pradesh, ancient ponds and other small wells, called Naula used to be a suitable system of traditional water harvesting of the region. Religious organizations have also been considered to contribute in their construction. Presently, massive plantation is being done on both sides of these just to reduce the evaporation loss.

The Darjeeling, Arunachal Pradesh and Meghalay region in the eastern Himalayas is traditionally irrigated by springs. Here, water is carried through bamboo pipes to the terraced fields. This system is similar to the current drip irrigation system. These drains release 18 to 20 liters of water per minute. Bamboos of different diameters are used to make waterways. Before making this system, the bamboo is peeled and thinned and the knots formed in the middle are removed. After this, small drains are used to carry and distribute water from the main road to different places. This system is prevalent in Gara, War and Khasi areas. This method has been kept alive by the local tribes like Lepya, Bhotia and Gurung people. In Subansiri district of Arunachal Pradesh, traditional dams have been built by Apatanitribals on Banana River to conserve water of the springs as well as for fish farming. A unique point here is that the Apatani people make water harvesting routes near the village so that the sewage and urine of humans and animals mix with this irrigation water to convert it into manure.

4.2.1.2 Ganges-Brahmaputra plain

The Gangetic plain in India is a vast area of small rivers. In Punjab, canals, wells and skirts are prominent in the traditional systems. Skirts are wide wells with less depth. It has been a tradition to draw water and irrigate with the help of pulleys and ropes. In Haryana, apart from wells and canals, water is stored in the abyss. Abyss is a type of pond in which rainwater is stored. Delhi's Surajkund is also a classical example of traditional water harvesting, in which water comes from the northern part of the Aravalli. Similar water harvesting is done in the Shamsi lake near the capital Delhi.

The Ahar-Pin system of Bihar is also an excellent example of traditional water harvesting. Ahar is rectangular in shape surrounded by water on three sides from which water is carried to the fields by pine. Earlier, people used to exploit it together, but due to continuous floods, their ancient form has distorted. In the high mountainous regions of Assam, puddles were built by the tribes called Dogs. Water is stored in the Brahmaputra plain by the Jampoi method. In the Jampoi method, small drains called Doong are made to store water. Owing to the excessive deforestation led recurrent floods, their shape is altering.

4.2.1.3 Plateau regions

The Haveli system of Madhya Pradesh and the Kere system of Karnataka are prominent in the plateau parts. The arrangement of water management during the Mughal period [1526–1761 AD] is found in Madhya Pradesh. In Jabalpur, high dams were constructed to carry rain water, which remains in the fields till the crop is sown. To prevent this, a ridge called Bandhare is built around the fields. Phad system in Maharashtra is a suitable system of water harvesting in the traditional way. Its history is 300 to 400 years old, when they were first developed in northwest region of Maharashtra.

4.2.1.4 Coastal Plains and Islands

In the western coastal parts of Gujarat in the Kathiawar region, the groundwater is very high and here for water harvesting stepwells are made which are called vavs. Many ponds were built in the 15th century in Gujarat, most of which were built by Sultan Qutbuddin [1150–1210]. The Mansar lake spread in 6 hectares is famous, in which water remains throughout the year. A number of rivers namely Vaitarni, Ulhas, Tasan, Savitri and Vashishti flow across the vast plains of Maharashtra, originating from the Western Ghats. Apart from these, they also collect rainwater in ponds and lakes. Here, by making bunds of the fields, they stop the water of the years in the traditional way. There are many reservoirs in Konkan, which were built by Hindu rulers and philanthropists, among them Borala, Pathardi, Nageshwar and Kashar reservoirs are famous. In Thane and Colaba in Maharashtra, water from sea tides was stored in dams to irrigate the fields.

In Karnataka Kasam system prevails. The Kasam is a long pond, which is built below the river bed. In which the water of the river seeps and gets stored. In this river basin, people have made arrangements for many types of water harvesting. In which Revu, Don, Odu, Gokutan, Kutan and Cheruvu are the main ones. Revu system was a system of collecting water from springs which were made of stone, mud and grass.

The traditional water harvesting techniques of Tamil Nadu are found in ponds. 35 per cent of Tamil Nadu is irrigated by ponds locally knows as Erie. The control of floods through the construction of the Erie prevents soil erosion and collects waste rainwater, which has raised the groundwater reserves. Historical data reveals that 20th of the total production of each village was engaged for the maintenance and irrigation of Erie. Over time, these traditional water sources started to decline.

The tribes of the Andaman and Nicobar Islands are skilled in preserving the traditional water harvesting methods, where the Sopan and Jarawa tribes collect water by ripping bamboo and using it. The bamboo is cut and placed at low places according to the slope, through which the scattered rain water gets stored in shallow pits, which are called 'Jackwells'. Torn bamboos are also laid under the trees to store water from the leaves. Jackwells stay connected to each other. In which filling one pit keeps burning in the other and finally gets deposited in the big jackwell. In addition to the bamboo technique, water harvesting is also done by placing pots or pots under coconut trees.

It is clear from the above examples that the traditional water harvesting systems have stood the test of time. These systems have emerged in their effective form due to various social, economic and political conditions. These systems developed in different regions of India have emerged in their own special form, in whose development the influence of various geographical factors along with historical elements is prominent.

4.2.2 Water culture: temporal diversity

Today, the center of the definition of big cities in the country is its population, business and industry, whereas in ancient Indian tradition, the definition of a big city or village included its ponds. The size of the population, volume of the business and industrial presence was never asked, rather how many ponds a village or a city had used to be in the core of identity. A comprehensive study of various Indian traditions tells us the integral linkage of ancient Indians with water resources.

In the Madhubani area of Bihar, in the sixth century, the villagers altogether had made 63 ponds in the entire area. It thrills us to think that how big an organization that too of people from diverse communities would have been formed and how many resources would have been mobilized to complete such a big but social project. These ponds in Madhubani are still alive and people keep on remembering them with gratitude. The only secret of the long life of all these ponds was the importance of these ponds in the minds of the people and a kind of family attachment.

The story of the creation of ponds in the tribal-dominated areas of Madhya Pradesh, Chhattisgarh and Orissa is linked to the judicial system prevailing in that era. Somewhere in villages, a pond was made as a reward of timely payment of taxes, while in some cases, the reward for constructing a pond was extended by the Gond kings [From the 14th to the 18th century] in the state of Madhya Pradesh, in addition, the land below the newly built pond did not have to be rented, this practice was especially observed in the Narmada region of Madhya Pradesh, the entire Chhattisgarh and Sambalpur region of Orissa.

Similarly, construction of a pond used to be a part of the penal legislation in certain areas of central India. In Bundelkhand region, when the community panchayats used to punish for the unforgivable mistake of one of their members, they had often asked them to build a pond in the residential area. There has been another interesting tradition; it was believed that everyone has to undertake a pilgrimage in their life. Those who could not go on pilgrimage due to any compulsion, they can do religious work by making a pond near their house. The people who put their resources and energy for the construction of pond were regarded as a virtuous soul. The person who raised resources and labor for the ponds in the society was looked upon with respect and counted in the category of a priest.

It has been a tradition in Chhattisgarh that out of the 13 full moons of the year, 11 were kept for collective labor work by the community people, but on the full moon of the month of Pauṣa [a month of the Hindu calendar that corresponds to December/January], there was a tradition of collecting paddy or in turn money for the pond. It has been a tradition to celebrate an annual festival in this month with the spirit of paying an honor to preceding rainy season. In this festival, groups of people used to go out, sing songs and collect money from individuals. The funds deposited in this way were kept in the village fund. From this fund, repairs and new works of ponds and other public places were completed. In this area, there was a unique tradition related to the respect of ponds. Ponds were also married with complete rituals. This practice continues in Chhattisgarh even today. The pond could not have been used before the said marriage, neither to drain it nor to cross it. People used to bring the soil of all the surrounding temples of the area, water from other five or seven ponds nearby and holy Ganges water on this ceremonial day. The marriage was said to be completed by mixing all these water and soil. At some places, the people used to arrange dowry according to their ability, the annual anniversary of marriage was also celebrated on the pond. Much later, when the pond was cleaned and excavated again, there was a tradition of erecting pillars in memory of that ceremony.

This tradition is still being carried out on a large scale in some areas of India. In BinduSagar, near the famous JagannathPuri temple of Orissa, water from every water source across the country has been piously mixed, even from far and wide. Devotees who come to the temple of JagannathPuri from different directions bring some water from their area with them and offer it to Bindusagar. BinduSagar is a symbol of the unity of the whole of India.

In northern, Bihar, there was a custom to build a pond by the rich people of the society after the acquisition of education. This tradition continued for a long time in Madhubani and Darbhanga regions of the state. There also existed a system of nomenclature of these ponds which were scripted on the copper plate, on which the complete details of the pond were also engraved.

In Gujrat, the full filling of the pond was not only considered an event, but was also considered an indicator of happiness and good luck. It came under the category of a festival. An elephant statue built in the Ghat of Hamirsar, the largest pond in Bhuj or Kutch of Gujarat used to represent the level of water. When the water touched this idol, news spread throughout the city and the townspeople would gather at the ghats of the pond. This event was celebrated as a festival, the kings of Bhuj would come to the ghat and worship the pond in the presence of the whole city and return with the blessings of the full tank.

5. Community approach of the day towards water management: illustrations of grassroots practices

India and Indians have always taken pride in coming up with unconventional and innovative approaches towards problem-solving. For example; the will and determination of the tribal population of India is apparently seen in their efforts towards water management and sustainability. One interesting example of collective effort is "Halma", which is commonly practiced in the Jhabua district of Madhya Pradesh. Halma is a traditional yet sustainable approach towards water harvesting that was initiated by the people of the Bhil community many years back wherein a day or two were marked each year when every member of the community [including women and children] would come together with spades, shovels and pickaxes to deepen the contours of their village trenches and ponds or dig new ones if necessary. The spirit of this joint operation was that since all residents of the village utilized water from the pond throughout the year, then it was their moral obligation towards the pond to contribute at least a single day in reviving it. This practice was vastly adopted across the whole district of Jhabua so much so that in 2018, approximately 12000 people or more from almost 400 villages across Jhabua participated at the Halma. A big share of the credit for getting such a massive response from the people of Jhabua goes to the ShivgangaSamagraGramvikasParishad, which is an NGO that motivates the people through the mythological tale of river Ganga arriving on earth through lord Shiva's Jata [hair locks] after King Bhagirath prayed to him.

A parallel example is of NGO namely the Tarun Bharat Sangh, that has been actively working by restoring and reviving the water conservation structures across many water-stressed states of India for more than two decades now. It is due to their efforts that the Arvari river in the Alwar district of Rajasthan was revived and now is a reliable source of irrigation for the people living in its vicinity. The Tarun

Bharat Sangh, in two decades, has built 402 structures over an area of 500 square kilometers to revive the Arvari river. As a result, water availability through wells and tube wells has increased substantially in the nearby villages that have now shifted from subsistence to commercial farming. The ecosystem of the area has also been rejuvenated through these efforts. The NGO is actively working in other states like Uttar Pradesh, Bihar, Jharkhand and Uttarakhand along the same lines. It is through the efforts of groups of like-minded people like these that sustainable approaches towards water conservation can be used as weapons to combat the upcoming water crisis. Similarly, in many areas of the country, many social and religious organizations are running intensive programs of public awareness for water conservation.

Another inspirational example comes from the Lapodiya village, which is two hours away from Jaipur, the capital of Rajasthan. Prior to 1977, the place was known to be an arid region with acute water shortage in summer seasons. Agriculture and cattle rearing had started to diminish due to a lack of water. The rainfall pattern was so erratic that food and fodder for cattle had to be bought from the market. But thanks to the initiative of a few villagers, the 300-household strong Lapodiya has now turned into a green oasis. A joint operation carried out with coordinated efforts from all the villagers has enabled the village to construct three major community ponds that serve their domestic as well as agricultural requirements throughout the year. Suitable slopes and systematic drains have been constructed in the entire village so that the rain water is stored in the pond itself. There is no more shortage of green fodder in the village as grazing land is now available for the cattle in the village itself. The ponds have recharged the water table and water shortage in the village has now become a thing of the past. During the time of good rains, the water is stored in the ponds and then reused for subsequent seasons. This stored water lasts for up to three whole years and protects the villagers against distress arising from scanty or no rainfall at all. The efficient water management system of Lapodiya has earned for itself the recognition of a model village for rainwater harvesting by the authorities. Several villages in diverse parts of country too have demonstrated similar examples.

6. Water policy and social change

India is traditionally an agrarian economy, therefore, since the very first Five Year Plans; a high priority has been given to the development of irrigation facilities to increase agricultural production. Several multipurpose river valley projects such as Bhakra Nangal, Hirakud, Damodar Valley, NagarjunaSagar, Indira Gandhi Canal Project etc. have been started. All these measures take credit for the fact that today the share of agriculture sector in total water use is more than other sectors. Nevertheless, the use of water in the industrial and domestic sectors in the country is likely to continue to increase with the growth in future. In view of the dire situation of water crisis, emphasis of the government is also on water conservation and many steps have been taken in this direction in the last few decades. The initiative of the Jal Shakti Abhiyan, a time-bound, water conservation movement under the ministry of water resources of government of India is a convivial step focusing on rainwater conservation, rejuvenation of water bodies, reuse of wastewater after proper treatment, and serious afforestation. It is extremely important for us to meet the rising demand for water expansion, civilizing the health of water bodies as they are required to manage microclimate, biodiversity and nutrient cycling. Besides, Wetlands Authority is being established in many states for notifying and conserving natural water bodies.

Undoubtedly all these are welcoming steps, but apart from this, there are some common expectations from the government. As described earlier the heavy water intensive crops are irrationally grown in the water scarce state, the state governments should promote the cultivation of less water consuming crops like pulses, jowar-millet and oilseeds. Rice and sugarcane cultivation should be allowed only in those areas where water is available in plenty. The government should also take immediate steps to encourage the efforts being made at various levels for water conservation and to set strict legal provisions on its misuse.

7. Conclusion

The water crisis is pushing the entire human race to such a corner, from where it is difficult to return. Nature gives warnings from time to time, but we are deaf in the noise of modernity. It is very complicated to convey a message to the people is the inevitability to take measures that seem to ask people to adopt old customs. We need to understand that the current technology backed system alone cannot provide us the solution. Depending on the purpose, ecological services, livelihood and socio-cultural practices, an integration of modern technology synergized with traditional culture can ensure the return of water to the water bodies. Any effort for revival of water bodies has to be made on the social front by motivating local people specially youths to collaborate with other stakeholders to efficiently utilize resources for protection and conservation of traditional water bodies. Customarily, water was considered as a social responsibility and the people cooperatively took the responsibility of building and maintaining the water bodies. This trend needs to be brought back into the system today. Thus, an incorporated approach for the revival of Indian traditional water culture with long-term sustainability is inevitably required.

Author details

Yogranjan Singh[1*], Sathak Pandey[2] and Amit Kumar Goswami[3]

1 JNKVV, College of Agriculture, Tikamgarh, India

2 JNKVV, College of Agriculture, Jabalpur, India

3 ICAR-Indian Agricultural Research Institute, New Delhi, India

*Address all correspondence to: yogranjan@gmail.com

References

[1] Dharminder R K S, Kumar V, Devedee A K, Mruthyunjaya M, Bhardwaj R. The clean water: The basic need of human and agriculture. IJCS. 2019; 7(2): 1994-1998.E-ISSN: 2321-4902

[2] NitiAayog. Composite water management index. National Institution for Transforming India, Government of India 2018. pp. 239. http://social.niti.gov.in/uploads/sample/water_index_report2.pdf

[3] NitiAayog, (2018). Composite Water Management Index: a tool for water management.http://social.niti.gov.in/uploads/sample/water_index_report2.pdf

[4] Chatterjee A, Chattopadhyay R N. Metropolitan Regions of India: Rapid Growth, Changing Landuse and Challenges. In: Satellite Towns in Neo-metropolitan Development in India. Springer; 2020. p. 87-100. DOI: 10.1007/978-981-15-1502-6_4

[5] Fishman R. Groundwater depletion limits the scope for adaptation to increased rainfall variability in India. Climatic change, 2018. 147(1): 195-209. DOI:10.1007/s10584-018-2146-x

[6] Mahajan G, Kumar V, Chauhan B S. Rice production in India. In: Chauhan B S,Jabran, K, Mahajan G, editors. Rice production worldwide. Springer, Cham. 2017. p. 53-91.DOI:10.1007/978-3-319-47516-5

[7] Kaur J. Rice production in Punjab: Depletion of water resourced environmental problems. Indian Journal of Economics and Development, 2020. 16(2s): 294-299.Article DOI: 10.35716/ijed/NS20-007

[8] Etienne G. EKSAL. In Studies in Indian Agriculture. University of California Press.2020. P. 241-255. ISBN: 9780520323780

[9] Srivastav A. Energy Dynamics and Climate Mitigation: An Indian Perspective. 1st ed. Springer Nature, 2020. P 194. ISBN: 978-981-15-8940-9

[10] Reddy K Y, Reddy L N. Incentivizing Water Use Efficiency-Virtual Water Approach. IWRA (India) Journal (Half Yearly Technical Journal of Indian Geographical Committee of IWRA) 2017. 6(1): 35-42.ISSN: 2277-1301

[11] Jiang L, O'Neill B C. Determinants of urban growth during demographic and mobility transitions: Evidence from India, Mexico, and the US. Population and development review. 2018. 44(2): 363-389. https://doi.org/10.1111/padr.12150

[12] Kundu D, Pandey A, Sharma P, Bhusan S, Mondal B, Lahiri B, Sharma T C, Vijh S. India: National Urban Policies and City Profiles for Delhi and Madurai. GCRF SHLC. 186 p. 2018.

[13] Ebikade E, Athaley A, Fisher B, Yang K, Wu C, Ierapetritou M G, Vlachos D G. The future is garbage: repurposing of food waste to an integrated biorefinery. ACS Sustainable Chemistry and Engineering. 2020. 8(22): 8124-8136. doi/10.1021/acssuschemeng.9b07479.

[14] Bhanja S N, Mukherjee A, Rodell M, Wada Y, Chattopadhyay S, Velicogna I, Pangaluru K, Famiglietti J S. Groundwater rejuvenation in parts of India influenced by water-policy change implementation. Scientific reports. 2017. 7(1) :1-7.DOI: 10.1038/s41598-017-07058-2

[15] Singh Y, Sidana B K. Water and Energy Use Efficiency of Maize vis-à-vis Paddy Crop in Punjab Agriculture: A Move towards CropDiversification. Indian Journal of Economics and Development. 2018. 14(1a): 87-95.DOI: 10.5958/2322-0430.2018.00041.0

[16] Sharma P J, Patel P L, Jothiprakash V. Impact of rainfall variability and anthropogenic activities on streamflow changes and water stress conditions across Tapi Basin in India. Science of the total environment. 2019. 687: 885-897.DOI: 10.1016/j.scitotenv.2019.06.097

[17] Pradhan P, Irshad N. Media coverage of swachhbharatabhiyan in mainstream dailies of India. Mass Communicator: International Journal of Communication Studies. 2018. 12(2): 14-21. DOI: 10.5958/0973-967X.2018.00010.8

[18] Shiksha, Mittal P. A Study of the Impact of Production Variables on Indian Food Grains Productivity. Pacific Business Review International. 2017A 9(12):1-6.

[19] Kasana A, Singh O. Groundwater irrigation economy of Haryana: A glimpse into spread, extent and issues. Journal of Rural Development. 2017. 36(4): 531-555.DOI: 10.25175/jrd/2017/v36/i4/120624

[20] Ekumah B, Armah F A, Yawson D O, Quansah R, Nyieku F E, Owusu S A, Odoi J O, Afitiri A R. Disparate on-site access to water, sanitation, and food storage heighten the risk of COVID-19 spread in Sub-Saharan Africa. Environmental research. 2020. 189: 109936.DOI: 10.1016/j.envres.2020.109936

[21] Nischal P M. Billions of people still lack safe drinking water, sanitation facilities and basic hygiene. The National Medical Journal of India. 2019. 32(4): 255-256.DOI: 10.4103/0970-258X.291311

[22] Agoramoorthy G, Hsu M J. Small size, big potential: Check dams for sustainable development. Environment: Science and Policy for Sustainable Development. 2008. 50(4): 22-35.DOI: 10.3200/ENVT.50.4.22-35

[23] Khan S, Dialynas E, Kasaraneni V K, Angelakis A N. 2020. Similarities of Minoan and Indus Valley hydro-technologies. Sustainability. 2020. 12(12): 4897.DOI: 10.3390/su12124897

[24] Voudouris K, Valipour M, Kaiafa A, Zheng X Y, Kumar R, Zanier K, Kolokytha E, Angelakis A. Evolution of water wells focusing on Balkan and Asian civilizations. Water Supply. 2019. 19(2): 347-364.DOI: 10.2166/ws.2018.114

Chapter 15

Necessity, Principle and Technique of Evaluation Model to Assess Sustainability of Oil Palm Plantation in Indonesia

Latief Mahir Rachman

Abstract

Indonesia should have a scientific-based approach and evaluation system to counteract negative accusations and allegations that Oil Palm Plantations (OPP) in Indonesia are not environmentally friendly, unsustainable, and destroy forests and peatlands. The proposed evaluation instrument basically to assess the OPP sustainability and current productivity also the limiting factors for oil palm production which are useful to determine management recommendations for increasing the productivity of each type of OPP. Basically, the evaluation model assessed recent soil-land and environment conditions/quality and linked it to productivity, and then compared it with soil-land and environment conditions/quality before the land was converted into OPP. After comparing soil-land and environment qualities before and after converted into OPP, hence the balance derived from the increase or decrease in the quality of soil-land and the environment from all OPP types can be calculated as a result of the development of OPPs throughout Indonesia.

Keywords: environment degradation, evaluation model, oil palm productivity, soil-land quality, sustainability

1. Introduction

Indonesia is the biggest producer of palm oil in the world. Palm oil is an important commodity for various products, such as cooking oil, margarine, cosmetics, and biofuel. Until now, the Indonesian palm oil industry has played a very strategic role and has made a real contribution to Indonesia's economic development and has become a mainstay in achieving the Sustainable Development Goals (SDGs).

Nowadays, however, Indonesia was accused and deemed to have developed oil palm plantation (OPP) with high risk to the environment by the European Union (EU) based on the Renewable Energy Directive (RED) II and its technical regulations (delegated art). As a consequence, Indonesian palm oil products will be gradually restricted and removed from the EU biofuel market. The EU's decision to exclude palm oil as renewable energy in the RED II faced critics and protest from Indonesia. It finally creates EU-Indonesia palm oil dispute since this action threatens the 12% share of Indonesia's palm oil exports, particularly exports destined for the EU.

The EU's views and allegations need to be scientifically and proportionally responded to, especially to the main issues that were raised. The EU argued that the expansion of palm oil has direct link with deforestation and degradation of forest, peat land degradation and emissions escalation [1, 2]. Another hot issue is loss of biodiversity, saving peat lands, and disturbing the balance of the ecosystem. Indonesian government is considered not serious in implementing sustainable land-use policies that enabled palm oil corporation harming forest and its biodiversity [3].

In fact, many palm oil companies in Indonesia have considered and counted environmental and sustainability factors into their business development concept. The 3-P (Planet-People-Profit) concept has been widely used as a guideline in the management of the palm oil industry in Indonesia. In addition, efforts to achieve sustainability, particularly regarding oil palm plantation sustainability (OPPS) have been implemented through ISPO (Indonesian Sustainable Palm Oil) and RSPO (Roundtable Sustainable Palm Oil) certification [4, 5]. However, in reality, these efforts have not been deemed sufficient to be considered as producing a sustainable palm oil industry, not causing damage or degradation of soil-land-environment (S-L-E). Indonesia should have a scientific-based approach and evaluation system to counteract negative accusations and allegations that the OPP in Indonesia is not environmentally friendly, unsustainable and destroy forests and peat-lands. For this reason, more concrete efforts are needed in the form of a system supported by tools that can be used to evaluate the effects of OPP in Indonesia objectively, rationally, scientifically, measurably, proportionally, quantitatively and accurately to the quality of S-L-E in Indonesia which can also be used to increase productivity. and help design management to prevent S-L-E degradation.

2. Principle of oil palm plantation sustainability (OPPS) evaluation

There are at least three principles that can be used as guidelines for assessing OPP in Indonesia. First, the evaluation of the oil palm industry effect, especially OPP, on S-L-E should not be generalized, but evaluated objectively and proportionally, particularly based on the origin of the OPP. In reality, OPP in Indonesia is very diverse, both from the type of land, climate, topography, age and plantation management, as well as the origin of the OPP. OPP in Indonesia is scattered on mineral and peat soils with very varied characteristics, with very varied slopes and climates, etc. Not all OPP comes from forest clearing, many also come from the conversion of rubber, cocoa or other plantation crops, moor or grassland, mixed gardens and even rice fields, shrubs, *Imperata cylindrica* grass fields, idle or abandoned land, former illegal logging, critical land, etc. OPP management differences also have different effects on S-L-E conditions. Thus, data on the origin of an OPP is important and crucial to be traced and identified.

Second, OPP in Indonesia is mostly planted on suboptimal land. Suboptimal land has marginal land quality [6–9]. Facts in the field show that oil palm plants are able to adapt and be cultivated on suboptimal land. In fact, the OPP was deemed able to apply regional ecological principles based on the optimization and preservation of resources, especially on suboptimal land. In other words, OPP is not always associated with a decrease in soil quality, land quality and environmental quality. In fact, in some places, OPP planted on marginal lands is believed to be able to improve soil quality, land quality and environmental quality.

Third, to resolve disagreements and polemics about OPP in Indonesia, an objective evaluation system is needed as a platform or indicator that can assess OPP in an empirical, measurable, quantitative, accurate and standardized manner. The reliable evaluation model system is also expected to be able to evaluate and provide information about the quality of S-L-E; palm oil productivity; constraining factors for the growth and production of oil palm; as well as directions for management recommendations to increase the productivity and quality of S-L-E and prevent land damage and degradation. The evaluation system needs to be supported by the Plant Potential Productivity Index (PPPI), Soil Quality Index (SQI), Land Quality Index (LQI) and Environmental Quality Index (EQI).

3. Fundamental technique for assessing OPPS

A technique used for assessing OPPS should be based on agroecosystem principles. In Ref. [10], there are 4 principle components of sustainable agroecosystem: productivity, stability, sustainability, and equitability.

The assessment of OPPS requires evaluation of aspects of plant productivity and S-L-E quality as well as changes in these aspects compared to their original use and/or previous conditions. Plant productivity is compiled from data and production potential. Soil quality score and land quality score could be determined in the representative area where the OPP are planted. Environmental quality is compiled in a similar way to the soil quality and land quality by selecting key environmental parameters. OPPS can be analyzed from changes or differences in the productivity value of plants, soil quality score, land quality score, and environmental quality score as compared to the original land use before planted by oil palm crop. All of these would be presented as the Plant Potential Productivity Index (PPPI), Soil Quality Index (SQI), Land Quality Index (LQI) and Environmental Quality Index (EQI).

In fact, not all OPP originate from forest clearing. Majority of OPPs do not come from forests, even from abandoned land ex-illegal logging, grasslands, shrubs, gardens that are not or less productive, etc. so that the effects of OPP on S-L-E quality and S-L-E degradation vary widely. The effect is strongly influenced by the origin or history before the OPP was created [11, 12], soil type, topography (especially slopes), climate (especially rainfall and climate type), applied management [13], both during land clearing and after planting, plant age, especially related plant factors and their influence on production, surface water absorption (infiltration), surface runoff and erosion and oil palm plantation management [14, 15]. It is necessary to study the effect of OPP on the degradation and improvement of S-L-E. The study especially needs to focus on the main issues that are accused of causing effects on S-L-E, including: 1) groundwater, 2) infiltration, 3) surface and river discharge, 4) soil erosion and sedimentation, 5) gas emissions and absorption greenhouse or carbon dioxide (CO2), 6) forest area, 7) biodiversity, and 8) degradation of peat lands.

All of sustainability evaluation of OPP effects would be presented as the PPPI, SQI, LQI and EQI. SQI and LQI could be developed to provide information about: 1) soil and land quality scores, 2) quality levels (very bad to very good), 3) growth inhibiting factors and crop production that needs to be addressed by soil-land management. If this information is correlated with production data, it can produce PPPI. SQI, LQI as well as EQI score is compiled by selecting key parameters, determining the weights and assigning a score to each parameter. Supported by PPPI together with SQI, LQI and EQI of all types of OPP with their area and their originate use area, an evaluation system could be developed which is very useful for S-L-E assessments to support OPPS in Indonesia.

The need and support to be able to evaluate empirically, measurably, objectively, quantitatively, accurately and periodically is increasing. Technological advances are increasingly supporting the implementation of Agriculture 3.0 which is characterized by smart farming and precision farming and Agriculture 4.0 which is characterized by agricultural digitization. Support for quantitative land data is needed [16–18]. Software models are very helpful in simulating and predicting surface runoff, discharge, sediment loads, other environmental pollutants and helping to prepare recommendations for planning techniques for soil conservation and water improvement for SLE [19–23].

4. Basic configuration and structure of model for assessing OPPS

4.1 Identification, goals, and boundaries

A model can be set up and operated to assess or evaluate sustainability of OPP in Indonesia empirically, objectively, measurably, quantitatively, and accurately to measure the effects of OPP on quality of S-L-E. This model is targeted to be able to produce information on: 1) evaluation on S-L-E qualities, 2) potential productivity of oil palm, 3) factors that are constraining to the growth and production of oil palm, and 4) direction for management recommendations to increase productivity, maintain and improve the quality of S-L-E and preventing the damage and degradation of S-L-E.

The issue that the model hopes to address is doubts about sustainability of OPP regarding the degradation of S-L-E. Regarding the limitation of this model, this model is only to assess the sustainability of OPP in terms of physical and environmental resources, not to assess sustainability of the economic and social aspects.

4.2 Conceptualization of model

The model is built using an input - process - output model (see **Figure 1**).

Input consists of controllable input and uncontrollable input. Meanwhile, the output consists of the desirable output and the undesirable output. Feedback will also be analyzed thoroughly. To facilitate organization, the model will be divided into several sub-models, each sub-model will be further divided into several sub sub-models.

The model consists of 5 subsystems: 1) Plant (Crop), 2) Soil, 3) Land, 4) Environment, and 5) OPPS. The interaction of the five subsystems is presented in **Figure 2**.

Model input – proses - output will be applied. Input of this model consists of all parameters related to the all components (see **Table 1**). While output this model involves both expected outputs and unexpected output.

The model that has been developed, validated and mutually agreed upon will then be used to assess aspects of crop productivity, soil quality, land and environment as well as OPPS in various types of oil palm plantations in Indonesia.

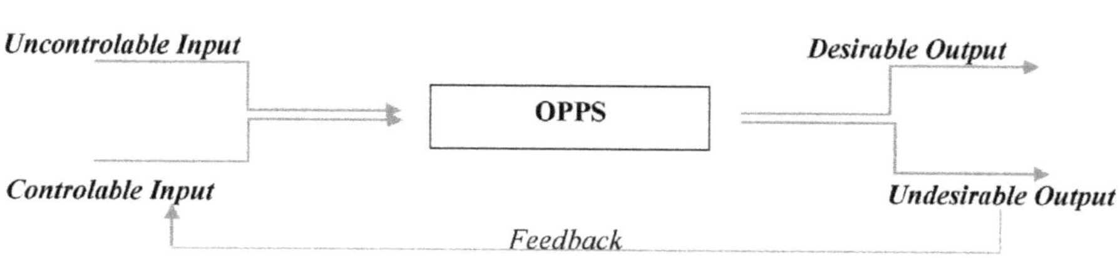

Figure 1.
Model input – Proses – Output of OPPS model.

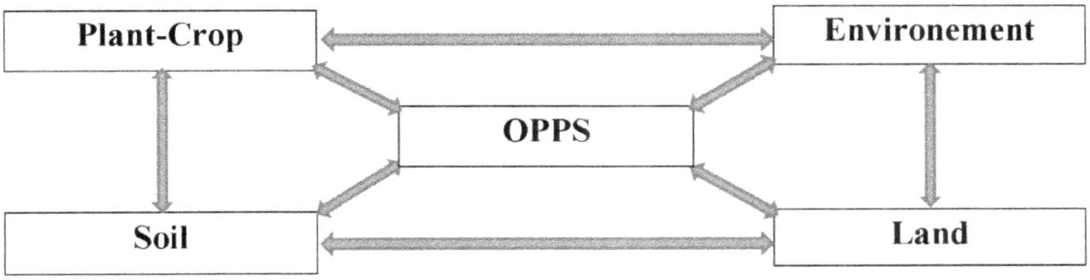

Figure 2.
Subsystem components of oil palm plantation system and their interactions.

Subsystem	Parameters Component	Parameters Management
Plant-Crop	Production, Productivity, Land cover, Biomass, Plant-Crop (CN) factors*, Emissions and Carbon sequestration	Types and sources of seeds, foliar fertilizers, Use of PHF**, Pest-Disease Control
Soil	Physical, chemical, biological properties of soil	Inorganic and organic fertilization, liming, soil amendment, soil and water conservation
Land	Soil, topography, climate, erosion, subsidence, flood, surface, rock	Micro reservoir, irrigation, drainage, erosion prevention
Environment	Land fires, air quality, Greenhouse Gas Effects, biodiversity, discharge, runoff, drought, infiltration, water balance, ground water level, water quality, industrial and agrochemical waste pollution	ISPO and RSPO certification, High Conservation Value Area, Wastewater Treatment Plant, Land Fire Task Force, Zero Waste Program, Environmental Impact Analysis Reporting
OPPS	Change and / or trend of productivity, quality of S-L-E (increased, fixed or decreased)	Planning, management recommendations for productivity improvement, preventing degradation to achieve OPPS

**Information: To predict erosion (USLE).*
***Pesticides, Herbicides and Fungicides.*

Table 1.
Component variables and management of each sub-system.

4.3 Specification of model

The model consists of 5 sub models, plants, soil, land, environment and OPPS.

a. The crop sub-model assesses aspects of production/productivity and crop management.

b. Soil sub-models to assess soil quality, soil factors that inhibit oil palm growth and production, and soil management. This sub-model will be based on the SQI.

c. Land sub-model to assess land quality, land factors that inhibit oil palm growth and production, and land management. This sub-model will be based on the LQI.

d. Environmental sub-model to assess environmental quality, environmental factors causing environmental damage or degradation and environmental management.

e. Meanwhile, the OPPS sub-model assesses the aspects of S-L-E damage, S-L-E degradation as well as the concepts and management needed to increase the productivity of oil palm plants and prevent S-L-E degradation.

At this stage, the meaning of each conceptual model relation is also carried out. Followed by quantification of the sub-model and use of numerical equations and formulas as required and determining the software selected and used.

4.4 Model evaluation and validation

Basically, at this stage, testing or validation is carried out about has the model produced logical outputs in common sense and is in line with the real world or existing facts, are the existing relationships are logical, are the model's behavior is in accordance with expectations or goals. Model design, are the model outputs appropriate or very close to the field data, and so on. Some of the references that will be used are OPP references that have received ISPO and/or RSPO certification, as well as for OPP which are considered to be reference plantations that are very well managed.

5. Type of OPP as target of evaluation of OPPS

Evaluation or assessment of the sustainability of oil palm plantations needs to be carried out in various regions throughout Indonesia, in order to represent the various types of oil palm plantations that exist today (see **Table 2**).

Type of Land	Type of OPP	Variation Garden
Mineral	Flat, low rainfall	With variations in the age of the oil palm; plantation management (managed by companies and smallholder oil palm plantations); as well as the origin of land use / cover before it was converted into oil palm plantations
	Flat, moderate rainfall	
	Flat, high rainfall	
	Medium slope, low rainfall	
	Medium slope, moderate rainfall	
	Medium slope, high rainfall	
	High slope, low rainfall	
	High slope, moderate rainfall	
	High slope, high rainfall	
Peat	Thin peat, less rainfall	With variations of peat in tidal, non-tidal, lowland areas; peat maturity level; age of oil palm; variations in plantation management (managed by companies and smallholder oil palm plantations); as well as the origin of land use / cover before it was converted into oil palm plantations
	Thin peat, moderate rainfall	
	Thin peat, high rainfall	
	Medium peat, less rainfall	
	Medium peat, moderate rainfall	
	Medium peat, high rainfall	
	Deep peat, less rainfall	
	Deep peat, moderate rainfall	
	Deep peat, high rainfall	
	Marine peat	
	Brackish peat	

Table 2.
Several types of oil palm plantations (OPPs) that are targeted by the palm oil palm plantation sustainability (OPPS) evaluation system.

The validated OPPS model is used to evaluate several types of OPP in Indonesia. Basically, the types of OPP can be divided into those cultivated on mineral soils and peat lands with the following variations:

a. Mineral soils: on land with various variations in topography, climate, age of oil palm; plantation management (companies and smallholder oil palm plantations); as well as the origin of land use/cover before it was turned into oil palm plantations, etc.

b. Peat land: on peat with varying levels of depth and maturity of peat, topography/physiography (coastal peat /marine peat, transitional peat/brackish peat), climate, age of oil palm; plantation management (companies and smallholder oil palm plantations); as well as the origin of land use/cover before it was converted into oil palm plantations, tidal and non-tidal areas, swamps, etc.

6. Methodology

6.1 Method

The methods used to measure, determine or obtain data for each parameter are presented in **Table 3**.

6.2 Processing and data analysis

Some of the main analysis methods that are needed in order to build the evaluation model are: 1) regression-correlation analysis and multi-variate analysis, 2) continuity analysis using Multi-Dimensional Scaling (MDS), 3) Interpretative Structural Modeling to select key parameters in order to determine the SQI, LQI and EQI, 4) Analytical Hierarchy Process to weight each key parameter in determining the SQI, LQI and EQI, 5) SWOT analysis (Strength, Weaknesses, Opportunity and Threat) to strengthen the formulation of management improvement strategies to achieve OPPS.

6.3 Determination of the OPPS index and the index and Categorization of degradation or improvement

6.3.1 PPPI calculation

- Select and define key plant parameters to get SQI
- Set the weights of each of the key plant parameters
- Defining criteria and scoring for each of the key crop parameters
- Calculating the PPPI score by adding the multiplication of the score and weight for each key plant parameter.
- PPPI scores are then categorized into very bad, very bad, bad, moderate, moderate, good and very good levels.

Sub System Parameters	Method used
1. Plant/Crop	
Production and productivity	Interview and secondary data
Land cover	Field observations, secondary data
Biomass	Field observations, secondary data
Plant Factors (CN)*	Field observations, secondary data
Carbon emissions and sequestration	Field observations, secondary data
Types and sources of seeds	Interview and secondary data
Foliar fertilizer	Interview and secondary data
Use of PHF**	Interview and secondary data
Pest-Disease Control	Interview and secondary data
2. Soil	
Physical, Chemical, Biological Properties	Field observation and lab analysis
Inorganic fertilization	Interview and secondary data
Soil Conservation	Field observation
Liming, *soil amandment*	Interview and secondary data
Provision of organic material (biological)	Interview and secondary data
3. Land	
Soil	Field observation and lab analysis
Topography (slopes)	Field observations, secondary data
Climate (rainfall and climate type)	Secondary data processing
Runoff, discharge, flood	CIA: Model Mock; Weibull, dll.
Erosion Hazard Level	*Universal Soil Loss Equation*
Subsidence	Secondary data, field observations
Surface rock	Field observations, secondary data
Micro reservoir, irrigation	Field observations, secondary data
Drainage	Field observations, secondary data
Erosion prevention	Interview and secondary data
4. Environment	
Land fires	Field observations, secondary data
Air quality	Field observations, secondary data
Surface flow, discharge	Field observations, secondary data
Greenhouse Gas Effect	Field observations, secondary data
Drought and water balance	Interviews, secondary data, and the Thornthwaite and Mather Model, etc.
Biodiversity	Field observations, secondary data
Infiltration	Field observations, secondary data
Factory waste pollution	Lab analysis and secondary data
Agrochemical contamination	Lab analysis and secondary data
Ground water level	Field observations, secondary data
High Conservation Value Area	Interview and secondary data
Water quality	Lab analysis and secondary data

Sub System Parameters	Method used
ISPO*** and / or RSPO**** certification	Interview and secondary data
Wastewater Treatment Plant	Interview and secondary data
Land Fire Task Force	Interview and secondary data
Zero Waste Program	Field observations and interviews
Environment Analysis Impact Reporting	Interview and secondary data

*For volume and peak discharge calculations.
**PHF = Pesticides, Herbicides, Fungicides.
***Indonesian Sustaianable Palm Oil.
****Roundtable Sustainable Palm Oil.

Table 3.
Main parameters of each subsystem and the methods used.

6.3.2 SQI calculation and categorization

- Select and define land key parameters to get SQI
- Set the weights of each of the key soil parameters
- Establish criteria and score for each key soil parameter
- Calculating the SQI score by adding the multiplication of the score and weight for each key parameter.
- The SQI scores are then categorized into very bad, very bad, bad, moderate, moderately good, good and very good levels.

6.3.3 LQI calculation and categorization

- Select and define key land parameters to get LQI
- Set the weight for each of the key land parameters
- Establish criteria and score for each key field parameter
- Calculating the LQI score by adding the multiplication of the score and weight for each key parameter.
- The LQI scores are then categorized into very bad, very bad, bad, moderate, moderately good, good and very good levels.

6.3.4 EQI calculation and categorization

- Select and define key parameters to get EQI
- Set the weight for each of the EQI key parameters
- Defining criteria and scoring for each key environmental parameter
- Calculating the EQI score by adding the multiplication result of the score and the weight of each key parameter.

- The EQI scores are then categorized into levels of no degradation, very bad, bad, moderate, moderate, moderately good, good and very good.

6.3.5 OPPS score calculation and categorization

- Determine the weights of PPPI, SQI, LQI and EQI
- Calculating the OPPS score by adding the multiplication results of the scores and weights of each PPPI, SQI, LQI and EQI
- The KIS scores are then categorized into very bad, very bad, bad, moderate, moderately good, good and very good levels.

6.3.6 Calculation of the Index of degradation (ID) or index of improvement (IP)

- Calculating the ID or IP by calculating the difference between subtracting the OPPS scores from the OPPS score for land use before the OPP was made or the original OPP score with the OPPS score after a certain period, then converted into a percent. If the OPPS score of OPP score is lower, then a negative score is generated and an ID is obtained. Conversely, if the OPPS score of OPP score is greater than a positive value will be generated, then an IP is generated.
- ID and IP are then categorized into levels of no degradation, very low, low, medium, high, very high and very high.

7. Summary and outlook

In order to respond negative accusations and allegations that the OPP in Indonesia is not environmentally friendly, unsustainable and destroy forests and peat-lands, Indonesia should have an evaluation system that is based on a scientific approach. In order to achieve this aims, concrete efforts are needed in the form of a system supported by tools that can be used to evaluate the effects of OPP in Indonesia objectively, rationally, scientifically, measurably, proportionally, quantitatively and accurately to the quality of S-L-E in Indonesia which can also be used to increase productivity and to help design management to prevent S-L-E degradation. The evaluation system needs to be supported by the Plant Potential Productivity Index (PPPI), Soil Quality Index (SQI), Land Quality Index (LQI) and Environmental Quality Index (EQI). By having the evaluation system, the effect of OPP on the natural resources and environment can be determined, whether OPP produces degradation or improvement on certain area as well as for a national scale.

Author details

Latief Mahir Rachman
Department of Soil Science and Land Resource, IPB University, Bogor, Indonesia

*Address all correspondence to: latiefra@apps.ipb.ac.id

References

[1] Reuters. EU to phase out palm oil from transport fuel by 2030 [Internet]. 2018. Available from: https://www.reuters.com/article/us-eu-climatechange-palmoil/eu-to-phase-out-palm-oil-from-trasport-fuel-by-2030-idUSKBN1JA21F [Accessed: 2018-06-14]

[2] Robertua V. Environmental diplomacy: Case study of the EU-Indonesia palm oil dispute. MANDALA Jurnal Hubungan Internasional. 2019; 2(1): 1-21.

[3] Larsen RK, Jiwan N, Rompas A, Jenito J, Osbeck M, Tarigan A. Towards 'hybrid accountability' in EU biofuels policy? Community grievances and competing water claims in the Central Kalimantan oil palm sector. Geoforum. 2014; 295-305.

[4] Kospa HSD. Konsep perkebunan kelapa sawit berkelanjutan. Jurnal Tekno Global. 2016; 5(1).

[5] Indrapraja FM. Analisis terhadap sertifikasi minyak kelapa sawit berkelanjutan sebagai instrumen penataan hukum lingkungan. Jurnal Hukum Lingkungan. 2018; 4(2).

[6] Laz I, Mulyani A. Sumberdaya lahan potensial tersedia untuk mendukung ketahanan pangan dan energi. In: Proseding Nasional Strategi Penanganan Krisis Sumberdaya Lahan untuk Mendukung Kedaulatan Pangan dan Energi. Departemen Ilmu Tanah dan Sumberdaya Lahan. Fakultas Pertanian. IPB; 2005; Bogor.

[7] Rachman LM. Karakteristik dan variabilitas sifat–sifat fisik tanah dan evaluasi kualitas fisik tanah pada lahan suboptimal. In: Prosiding Seminar Nasional Lahan Suboptimal; 4-5 September 2019; Palembang. p. 111 – 120.

[8] Rachman LM, Baskoro DPT, Wahjunie ED, Nurmilah A, Astriani T, Dewi NM. Evaluasi sifat fisik tanah pengendali kemampuan tanah memegang air dan memasok air bagi tanaman serta kaitannya dengan manajemen pertanian pada lahan suboptimal. In: Prosiding Seminar Nasional Lahan Suboptimal; 4-5 September 2019; Palembang. p. 111 – 120.

[9] Rachman LM, Hazra F, Anisa R. Penilaian terhadap sifat-sifat fisika dan kimia tanah serta kualitasnya pada lahan sawah marjinal. Jurnal Tanah dan Sumberdaya Lahan. 2020; 7(2): 225-236.

[10] Conway GR. Agroecsystem Analysis for Research and Development. Bangkok: Winrock International; 1986.

[11] Dislich C, Keyel AC, Selecker J, Kisel YT, Meyer KM, Tarigan, S. A review of the ecosystem functions in oil palm plantation using forest as reference system. Biol. Rev. Camb. Philos. Soc. 2017; 92(3):1539-1569.

[12] Dislich C. Hettig E, Selecker J, Heinonen J, Lay J, Meyer KM, Tarigan, S. Land use change in oil palm dominated tropical landscape–an agent-based model to explore ecological and socio-economic trade-offs. PLoS ONE. 2018; 13(1). DOI: http://doi.org/10.1371/journal pone 0190506.

[13] Darras K. Corre MD, Formaglio G, Aiyen T, Potapov A, Tarigan, S. Reducing fertilizer and avoiding herbicides in oil palm plantation-ecological and economic valuations. Front For. Glob. Change. 2019. DOI: http://doi.org/10.3389/ ffgc.00065.

[14] Sarjono A, Guntoro, D, Supijatno. The role of Biomulch Arachis pintol in increasing soil infiltration rate on sloping land of oil palm plantation. Journal of Tropic Crops. Science. 2018.

[15] Sudrajat, Purwanto OD, Faustina E, Shintarika F, Supijatno. Role and

optimation rate of potassium fertilizer for immature oil palm on an Ultisol Soil in Indonesia. Journal of Agriculture and Rural Development in Tropic and Subtropic. 2018.

[16] Rachman LM. Essence, necessity, and principle of assessing soil health. In: Proceeding of International Conference on Challenge and Opportunities Sustainable Environmental Development: EAI Publisher. 2019.

[17] Rachman LM. Development of technique to determine soil quality index for assessing soil condition. In: IOP Proceeding: Journal of Physic: Conf. Series. 2019; 1375(1).

[18] Rachman LM. Using Soil Quality Index Plus to assess soil conditions and limiting factors for dryland farming. Sains Tanah-Journal of Soil Science and Agroclimatology. 2020; 17(2), 100 – 107.

[19] Radcliffe DE, Simunet JIH. Soil Physics with Hydrus. Modelling and Applications. London: New York: CRC Press. Taylor & Francis Group. 2010.

[20] Tarigan S, Sunarti, Wiegang K, Dislich K, Slamet B, Heinonen J, Meyer K. Mitigation options for improving the ecosystem function of water flow regulation in a watershed with rapid expansion of oil palm plantations. Sustain Water Qual. Ecol. 2016; 8: 4-13. http://dx.dol.org/10.1016/j.swage.2016.05 11.

[21] Rachman LM, Hidayat Y, Baskoro DPT, Noywuli N. Simulasi pengendalian debit DAS Ciliwung hulu dengan menggunakan model SWAT. In: prosiding seminar nasional pengelolaan daerah aliran sungai secara terpadu. 2018. 291-304

[22] Tarigan S. Stiegler C, Wiegang K, Knohl A, Murtilaksono K. Relative contribution of evapotranspiration and soil compaction to the fluctuation of catchment discharge: case study from a plantation landscape. Hydrological Sciences Journal. 2020; 65 (7). 1239-1248. DOI: 10.1080/02626667.2020.1739287.

[23] Rachman LM, Nursari E, Baskoro DPT. Application of SWAT in selecting soil and water conservation techniques for preparing management recommendation of Cilemer Watershed, Banten, Indonesia. In: IOP Conference Series; earth and Environmental Science, 622. 2021.

Chapter 16

The Increasing Importance of Environmental, Social and Governance (ESG) Investing in Combating Climate Change

Percy Jinga

Abstract

The current climate change is significantly caused by anthropogenic greenhouse gases, particularly CO_2 released by burning of fossil fuels. Climate change is predicted to disrupt production systems and supply chains of businesses, potentially affecting their financial performance. ESG investing, the consideration of environmental, social and governance factors by asset managers will likely play a crucial role in combating climate change. To attract ESG funds, companies will have to reduce their carbon footprint, among other actions. When companies reduce scope emissions, they help achieve a goal of the Paris Agreement of limiting average global temperature increase to below 2°C above pre-industrial level. The aim is to identify factors that are likely to increase uptake of ESG investing. The increase in number of ESG investors and their assets, higher financial performance of ESG-linked investments, and increasing regulatory and investor initiatives are likely to increase the impact of ESG investing in reducing greenhouse gas emissions. In addition, investors are becoming more environmentally conscious when making investment decisions. Although some challenges persist, including inconsistency in terminology, huge amount of data to analyze and heterogenous rating standards, ESG investing is likely to play an important role in influencing entities to reduce their carbon footprint.

Keywords: Biodiversity, Climate change, ESG rating, ESG strategy, Financial performance, Greenhouse gas, Scope emission

1. Introduction

Climate change is the shift in the state of climate that can be observed through variability of its components and lasts for a relatively long period of time, typically decades [1]. Long-term changes in climate are caused by natural factors, such as modulations of the solar cycle, as well as human factors. The current climate change is largely attributed to the high concentration of anthropogenically generated CO_2 in the atmosphere. As at September 2020, the atmospheric CO_2 concentration was around 414 ppm, a concentration way above a historic maximum of 300 ppm estimated at around 300 000 years ago [2]. The burning of fossil fuels and deforestation have accelerated the concentration of CO_2 and other greenhouse gases in the atmosphere. The increasing human population may result in more deforestation to establish farmland and human settlements. In the near term, the concentration of atmospheric CO_2 is expected to continue rising, together with the resultant consequences of climate change.

A warming climate has undesirable consequences for biodiversity in many ecosystems and negatively impacts livelihoods, especially in developing countries with less resilient systems. Polar ice is melting at a rapid rate, increasing sea level that threatens to flood coastal communities and small islands. In the Arctic, summer sea ice extent has declined by 45% over the last 30 years, glaciers have lost their protective cap of perennial ice, permafrost is thawing rapidly and coastlines are experiencing high wave action and erosion [3]. Climate change may increase frequency and severity of pest and disease outbreaks [4]. Extreme weather events, such as floods, storms, hurricanes, droughts, wild fires and heatwaves are being frequently experienced with devastating consequences on livelihoods and ecosystems [5]. Severe and more frequent droughts in Zimbabwe and the increasing incidences of malaria, a disease that affects about 50% of the world's population, have all been attributed to climate change [5, 6]. In addition to impacting livelihoods at personal, family and community levels, climate change also impacts business activities.

International, regional and national actions, conventions, agreements and policies have been drafted to reverse and mitigate risks and impacts of climate change. Over 180 countries which form parties of the United Nations Convention on Climate Change (UNCCC) drafted the Paris Agreement in 2015 to tackle climate change. One of the objectives of the Paris Agreement is to hold the increase in global average temperature below 2°C above preindustrial levels [7]. All parties agreed to determine national contributions to reduce emission of greenhouse gases that will help achieve the objective. The nationally and voluntarily determined targets are renewed incrementally after five years. Limiting global average temperature increase to below 2°C above preindustrial level is strongly predicted to significantly reduce risks and impacts of climate change.

Regionally, under the EU's European green deal, the European climate law sets a goal of achieving carbon neutrality by 2050. The European climate pact encourages governments and local authorities to engage all citizens in climate change action, while the 2030 target plan aims to reduce greenhouse gas emissions by at least 55% by 2030 [8]. Other regional and continental organizations, such as the African Union, the Arab states and the Organization of American States, have similar plans to curb emission of greenhouse gases [9–11]. Nationally, governments are implementing different measures, including giving tax credits to companies that switch to clean energy, such as wind and solar energy. Countries are also tightening regulations on deforestation and vehicle fuel standards. International, regional and national not-for-profit organizations and civil society groups are aggressively involved in diverse activities to combat climate change, including advocacy, education and litigation.

Socially responsible investing (SRI) is a theme that advances investor morals and values. SRI is not necessarily a new theme as it can be traced back centuries ago. SRI is integrating personal values and societal concerns with investment decisions [12–14]. Restrictions to investing, called negative screening, in companies linked to weapons, tobacco, alcohol, gambling and slavery imposed by the church during the middle ages marked the early roots of SRI [15]. Under SRI, an investor intentionally invests to effect desirable social change. In recent history, investment restrictions were imposed on companies linked to colonialism, the Vietnam war, ponography and racism, among other issues [16]. It is emerging, though, that although negative screening can be useful to express ethical, religious or moral values of investors through their investment portfolios, for many, it may prove to be too restrictive [17].

Closely aligned with SRI is environmental, social and governance (ESG) investing, which involves integrating environmental, social and governance factors into fundamental investment analysis with the belief that the factors are material to financial performance. ESG investing takes a broader view than SRI by examining whether environmental, social and governance factors are important to performance, and therefore to the investment performance of a long-term portfolio [17]. In 1996, after recognizing the importance of ESG investing, the UN launched the United Nations Principles for Responsible Investment (UNPRI). The UNPRI is an investor led initiative to support investors when incorporating environmental, social and governance (ESG) factors into their investment decisions [18].

The aim of the chapter is to describe factors that are likely to elevate ESG investing in reducing greenhouse gas emissions. Due to its growing acceptance among investors, ESG investing should be recognized, just like international, regional and national initiatives, as vital to reduce risks and impacts of climate change. The objectives of the chapter are to (i) describe the concept of ESG investing, (ii) describe factors increasing the contribution of ESG investing in reducing emission of greenhouse gases, and (iii) discuss challenges of ESG investing. With rising consumer activism among a world population that is getting increasingly younger on average and more environmentally conscious, investors are likely to be under growing pressure to invest responsibly.

2. What is ESG investing?

ESG investing is the consideration of environmental, social and governance factors (**Table 1**), alongside financial factors, when evaluating risks, opportunities and sustainability of investments [20, 21]. ESG investors believe that ESG factors are drivers of a company's long-term value, risk and return, and the factors indicate long-term sustainability [21].

Environmental	Social	Governance
Air emissions	Adequate housing	Antitrust violations
Air quality	Abortion services	Auditor independence
Biodiversity protection	Child labor	Board independence
Community health	Consumer privacy	Board diversity
Community safety	Minorities employment	Disclosure of risk
Community security	Human rights	Executive compensation
Energy conservation	Indigenous people rights	Oversight strategy
Fossil fuels	Income equality	Reporting transparency
Hazardous materials use	Slavery	Voting rights
Land contamination	Unionism	
Natural resources use		
Renewable energy use		
Waste generation		
Waste recycling		

Table 1.
List of potential environmental, social and governance (ESG) factors considered under ESG investing [19].

2.1 Environmental factors

The "E" in ESG investing considers how a company takes care of the natural or physical environment. Environmental factors (**Table 1**) consider a company's utilization of natural resources and impacts of its direct operations and supply chains on the environment. The environmental factors examine a company's environmental disclosure, impact and efforts to reduce carbon emissions, issues which represent risks and opportunities for a company [22]. Conservation of biodiversity, pollution, waste generation and community health are common environmental factors that pose risks and opportunities. For example, companies that violate waste disposal regulations are prone to costly litigation and criminal prosecution while those implicated in biodiversity loss may experience negative publicity and customer backlash. The 2010 BP oil spill in the Gulf of Mexico brought a record fine and furious negative publicity to the company. Investors may choose to avoid oil and gas companies altogether because of such environmental risks associated with their operations.

Reduction of greenhouse gas emissions is becoming a significant positive screening environmental factor in light of the current climate change. Climate change is expected to increase the occurrence of catastrophic events and, therefore, it imposes a realistic financial risk, especially to companies that are inadequately prepared and poorly resourced [22]. Carbon emissions have been categorized into scopes 1–3. Scope 1 are carbon emissions directly linked to the activities of a company and they mostly occur at premises of the company [23]. For example, carbon emissions resulting from baking of bread at a bakery or burning of coal at a power plant constitute scope 1 emissions for the bakery and power plant. Emissions associated with the supply of electricity are scope 2. All other indirect emissions not associated with electricity constitute scope 3 [23]. Scope 3 may emanate from downstream (consumers) and or upstream activities (suppliers). Since on average more than 75% of an industry sector's carbon footprint is from scope 3 sources, companies are now being encouraged to target this scope across their supply chain [24]. Overall, a company's strategy to reduce carbon emission depends on the targeted scope.

2.2 Social factors

Social factors (**Table 1**) relate to how a company manages relationships with its workforce, suppliers, customers, communities and political environment it operates under. Human rights, community outreach, diversity policies, modern slavery, child labor, working conditions and racial disparities are some of the social factors important to a company's long-term performance [25]. Investors may be influenced by whether a company provides safe and healthy working conditions, or if it donates time, money or other resources to communities where it operates. Unsafe working conditions or a disregard for community or customer concerns are potential grave financial risks. In contrast, companies that treat employees well and donate to communities are judged as less risky and they can benefit from higher productivity and attraction of top talent.

The UN's International Bill of Human Rights (IBHR) and the International Labor Organization (ILO) Core Conventions set out social factors that are important for long-term financial performance. The United Nations Declaration on the Rights of Indigenous Peoples (UNDRIP) helps companies to avoid conflict with indigenous populations. The seemingly unending birth pangs of the Keystone XL pipeline in the US and the incessant negative publicity directed at Rio Tinto after the company blew up ancient caves in western Australia despite opposition from Aboriginal communities may be consequences of overlooking indigenous peoples' rights. Such disregard of social factors may turn out to be financially costly to investors.

2.3 Governance factors

Governance factors (**Table 1**) are concerned with a company's decision-making, from policymaking to the distribution of rights and responsibilities among different participants, including the board of directors, managers and shareholders. Governance factors indicate the rules and procedures for companies, and allow investors to screen for appropriate governance practices as they would for environmental and social factors. A corporation's purpose, the role and makeup of boards of directors, shareholder rights and how corporate performance is measured are core elements of corporate governance structures [26]. Gender diversity and equity are becoming important to investors who are increasingly demanding better representation of women and people of color on corporate boards and in executive ranks, as well as equal compensation and promotion prospects.

A company that has robust governance structures is transparent and fair, and it operates within regulations and policies. Good governance mitigates risks of mismanagement, corruption and regulatory penalties. The Volkswagen emission cheating scandal that was revealed in 2015 in the US may be a result of governance failure. Volkswagen installed a software that was programmed to allow their vehicles to pass testing performed by the Environmental Protection Agency (EPA) but pollute up to 40x the federal maximum when on the road [27]. The governance failure of the company potentially had a negative effect on its stock price and financial performance, on top of reputational damage [28].

3. ESG strategies

Investors and asset managers use seven strategies to integrate ESG factors in their investments. Selection of the strategies is influenced by investor objectives. The strategies are Best-in-class, Exclusions, ESG integration, Impact investing, Norms-based screening, Sustainability-themed and Engagement and voting [29]. Descriptions of the strategies below are largely according to [29], although there are other bodies that use slightly different nomenclature.

3.1 Best-in-class

Best-in-class involves the selection of companies with the best ESG practices. The best companies are identified by ESG analysis, and they are usually selected by comparing ESG ratings provided by different rating agencies. Asset managers invest in companies with the best ESG ratings.

3.2 Exclusions

This is an approach where companies are excluded based on the values of an investor. Companies engaging in activities deemed negative to society are excluded. Activities and or products that may result in exclusion include controversial weapons, pornography, tobacco and alcohol, fossil fuel extraction and nuclear energy. In the past, there were divestment from companies involved in the Vietnam war, colonialism, slavery, apartheid as well as those that were complicit in racism.

3.3 ESG integration

ESG integration in the sense of ESG strategies is the consideration of ESG factors alongside financial factors, in the analysis of investments. The integration process is influenced by the potential impact of ESG factors on financial performance. The investor believes that a company will have good financial returns if it has high ESG ratings.

3.4 Impact investing

Impact investments are made into companies with a clear intention to generate an ESG impact alongside a financial return. A major characteristic is the intention of the investor to have measurable ESG impacts from the investment. The financial return ranges from below-market to market rate.

3.5 Norms-based screening

Norms-based screening is an approach that involves excluding companies that violate international norms and conventions. These norms and conventions are defined by international organizations. They include the UN Global Compact Principles, the Universal Declaration of Human Rights, ILO Declaration on Fundamental Principles and Rights at Work, and the United Nations Convention against Corruption.

3.6 Sustainability-themed

Themed investing is the selection of companies involved in sustainable development challenges. Sustainability themes include renewable energy, waste recycling, clean water provision and human health.

3.7 Engagement and voting

Engagement refers to all interactions between an investor and investee to address ESG issues and business strategy. The objective of engagement is to exert influence on ESG issues. Voting is the investor's practice of exerting voting rights at annual general meetings, where commonly ESG issues are taken into consideration. Engagement and voting is a long-term strategy seeking to influence corporate culture and increase disclosure.

4. ESG investing in combating climate change

ESG investing is likely to contribute significantly to steering companies to reduce their carbon footprint. There is increasing evidence that companies which incorporate ESG factors are likely to have higher financial performance, climate change issues are becoming popular among younger investors, the number of investors pledging to evaluate ESG factors when making investment decisions is increasing, and investor and regulatory ESG promoting initiatives are increasing. Taken collectively, these observations are likely to elevate the impact of ESG investing in combating climate change.

4.1 ESG investing and financial performance

There are competing views on the impact of ESG investing on financial performance. One view is that companies incur costs from socially responsible actions that put them at an economic disadvantage compared to other firms that are less socially responsible. A second, contrasting view is that costs associated with ESG factors are necessary because companies overall benefit through high employee morale and productivity [30]. The pioneering studies of the impact of ESG investing, then

SRI, on financial performance can be traced to [31]. In the study by [31], fourteen companies were selected based on their social responsibility credentials, and the rate of their return on common stock was calculated [31]. The stocks of the selected companies appreciated at a higher rate compared to major market indices [32]. This difference in performance was attributed to responsible investing [32]. A number of subsequent studies have validated the positive correlation between social responsibility and financial performance.

In a review of 2 200 studies on effect of ESG investing on corporate financial performance, 90% concluded a positive correlation [33]. The positive correlation was observed to be stable over time, especially in North America and emerging markets [33]. Age of a company is an important variable since old equipment and buildings might incur more expenses in making them environmentally and socially compatible with modern regulatory standards. After correcting for age of a company, a positive relationship was observed between social responsibility and financial performance [34]. When a Morgan Stanley Capital International (MSCI) ESG rating was applied to study corporate returns over a 10-year period, 2007–2017, it was observed that ESG-rated companies paid higher dividends and showed higher valuation levels [21, 35]. Among 100 American companies, employee satisfaction was associated with positive risk-adjusted returns at a statistically significant level [36]. Similarly, an evaluation of two equity portfolios that differed in eco-efficiency showed that the high-ranked portfolio provided substantially higher average returns than its low-ranked counterpart over the 1995–2003 period [37].

Although there are also some studies refuting the non-negative correlation between ESG investing and financial performance [38–40], orientation towards long-term ESG investing is important for investors to fulfill their fiduciary duties and achieving objectives of society [41]. Companies can build goodwill through ESG investing which can protect against reputational damage from catastrophic occurrences. The widely reported positive financial performance will likely influence more asset managers and investors to consider ESG factors, thereby becoming material in combating climate change.

4.2 Investor participation in ESG investing

Companies are under pressure from shareholders to maximize productivity, and from consumers, workers and communities at large to consider ESG factors [39]. Consumers are increasingly becoming conscious of environmental issues, and are showing preferences for environmentally friendly products. Companies are, therefore, not only concerned about financial performance, but also impact of their activities on the environment, social wellbeing of workers and the broader community. The concern is reflected by the increasing number of companies that are publicly declaring their commitment to ESG investing [16]. In 2019, ESG-themed mutual funds had a net inflow of US $20 billion, an increase from the previous year by a factor of four [42]. Since the formation of UNPRI, the number of signatories has increased to over 3 000 at the end of 2020, with their assets under management at US $103.4 trillion (**Figure 1**).

As at January 2021, 61 large companies from diverse sectors had committed to stakeholder capitalism metrics (SCI), a set of environmental, social and governance metrics and disclosures released by the World Economic Forum (WFP) and its international business council (IBC) that measure long-term value creation for stakeholders [43, 44]. In making these commitments, influential companies signaled that ESG factors are increasingly becoming important to success and long-term viability. The commitments to SCI and UNPRI represent the intent of leading global companies to integrate ESG factors into their core strategy and operations

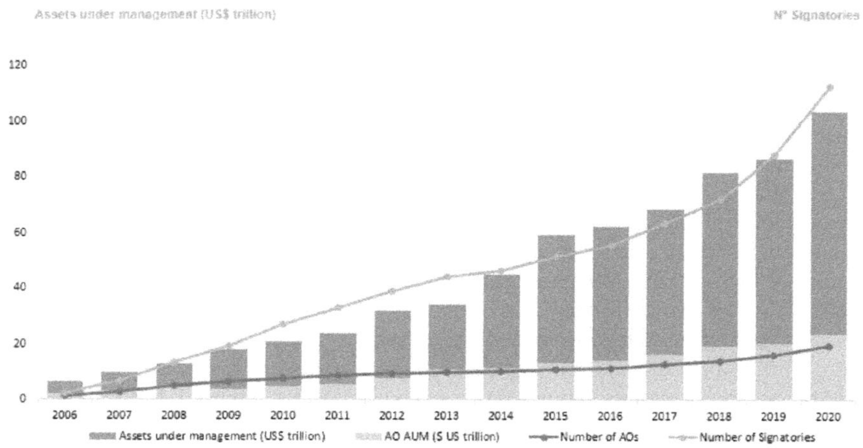

Figure 1.
Increase in number of signatories to the United Nations principles for responsible investment (UNPRI) and assets under management (source: UNPRI).

which is likely to result in tangible action towards reduction of their carbon footprint.

4.3 Regulatory initiatives

The number of policy initiatives to encourage ESG investing has also increased in tandem with the number of investors and assets. For example, the sustainable banking network (SBN) was formed in 2012 by financial sector regulatory agencies and banks in emerging market economies (EME). The aims of the SBN are to support companies to adapt to environmental and social sustainability and to contribute to national development goals [21]. In 2015, the taskforce on climate-related financial disclosures (TCFD) was formed by the G20. The task of TCFD is to identify information needed by investors to asses climate-related risks, among other sustainability issues. The TCFD drafted recommendations on climate-related financial disclosures which have been widely adopted [45]. The high-level expert group (HLEG) on sustainable finance was formed by the European Commission in 2016 to channel public and private capital flows towards sustainable investments and to protect stability of financial systems from climate change related risks [21]. These and other policy initiatives are likely to influence more asset managers and investors towards ESG investing.

4.4 Popularity of environmental factors among investors

Environmental factors topped the list of individual investors as far back as 1991 [46]. A 1991 survey of 4 000 individual investors in two mutual funds that incorporate ESG factors in investment decisions established that environmental and labor issues were a top priority [46]. The majority of the investors were generally young (below 44 years of age) and better educated, with at least a college degree. In a similar study among members of the American Association of Individual Investors (AAII), it was observed that environmental factors dominate in their decision making [14]. A company's environmental performance and the environmental impacts of its products are important considerations for ESG investors. With the continued increase in the concentration of atmospheric greenhouse gases, environmental factors, particularly climate change, are likely to attract most investor concern [47, 48].

Climate change activism, especially among the younger population, is making international headlines. Climate change threatens both financial performance of companies and social well-being of communities. Rising sea level will impact nearly 40% of the US population and other coastal communities around the world [48]. Hurricanes, storms, heat waves and floods will disrupt company activities and community cohesion. Investors and asset managers are likely to continue reducing climate change risk in their portfolios, especially with carbon-intensive companies [48].

4.5 Investor initiatives

Investors worried about impacts of climate change are taking their own initiatives to reduce greenhouse gas emissions. Climate Action 100+ is an investor-led initiative to ensure the world's largest corporate greenhouse gas emitters take necessary actions to reduce emissions. The Investor Agenda aims to accelerate actions that are critical to tackling climate change and achieving goals of the Paris Agreement. The Investor Agenda encourages investors to set science-based portfolio emissions reduction targets that allow global net-zero emissions by 2050 or sooner, with credible intermediate targets. It provides actions to meet the emissions reduction targets that align with the goals of the Paris Agreement. The investor led initiatives and the resultant decarbonation actions by companies are vital in reducing climate change risks and exposure.

5. Challenges of ESG investing

ESG investing has been fraught with challenges since its early days. The lack of common terms, huge volumes of data to be processed from company reports and other sources, and heterogeneity of rating methods are noteworthy drawbacks.

5.1 Terminology variability

The variety of terms that are used under ESG investing may create confusion among investors. For example, the term "environment" to describe a fund with positive environmental impact may alternatively be substituted with "sustainable", "green" and "eco" [16]. There are also terms that are sometimes used interchangeably with ESG investing, such as SRI, responsible investment, sustainable investment, impact investing and ethical investing [16]. There is need to resolve such terminology variability so that evaluation can be more consistent. Apart from terminology ambiguities, scoring some ESG factors may be highly influenced by context. For example, a company that accords its workers a worshipping hour may score highly under social factors in a predominantly religious society than in an atheistic one. A company may be negatively screened in one community while positively screened in another due to cultural, religious, ideological and ethical differences.

5.2 Huge volume of data

To score ESG factors, huge volume of data needs to be processed. These data may be mined from company reports, regulatory agencies' reports and other mandatory and or non-obligatory disclosures, a very laborious and cumbersome process for investors. Scoring of factors is to some extent subjective. Some investors may score environmental factors highly compared to social factors while others score vice versa. An environmentally-friendly company could mistreat workers [42], and thus it is challenging to balance such factors when evaluating the company. There is also a risk of evaluating greenwashed and impact-washed data. Greenwashing is a false claim to deceive consumers into believing that a company's products and actions are environmentally friendly [48]. Impact washing is promoting the positive impact of a company to society while it engages in other damaging activities [48]. For example, a mining company may tout how its solar power plant will result in decarbonation, while simultaneously the company will be releasing toxic chemicals that cause deforestation. To circumvent the problem of scouring over enormous amount of data, asset managers and investors usually rely on ESG indices prepared by vendors. There is a possibility in future of using artificial intelligence and machine learning methods to score the huge volume of ESG data [48].

5.3 Heterogeneity of ESG rating methods

ESG rating agencies analyze publicly available data reported by a company, sector-specific NGOs, government agencies, trade unions and other sources to produce an ESG rating for a company. The rating agencies are paid by investors who use the ratings to evaluate investment decisions. Leading international ESG rating agencies include Vigeo Eiris, MSCI, ISS-oekom, Inrate and Sustainalytics. The rating criteria, however, differ among agencies and business sectors. As no common standard exists for ESG rating, each agency develops its own method, and as a result, ratings from different agencies sometimes disagree [42]. ESG investing is a rapidly evolving field, and rating agencies are adapting to the evolution by making continuous improvements and changes to their rating criteria.

There are ongoing efforts to create standards in ESG investing in order to have consistence and reliability. In Europe, the EU taxonomy was drafted to provide a list of environmentally sustainable economic activities. It is a classification system that enables grouping of economic activities that are crucial in climate change mitigation and adaptation [49]. The EU taxonomy is crucial in scaling up sustainable investment and implementation of the European green deal. It provides appropriate definitions to companies, investors and policymakers on which economic activities can be considered environmentally sustainable. It is, therefore, expected to protect investors from greenwashing and impact washing, help companies to transition to decarbonation, and move investments where they are most needed [49]. Internationally, the SCI is another important endeavor to create universal standards in ESG investing. The SCI are a set of 21 universal, comparable disclosures that were derived from voluntary standards and are focused on people, planet, prosperity and principles of governance that companies can report on regardless of sector or region [43, 44]. The regional and international standardization efforts will likely lead to convergence of ESG rating methods.

6. Conclusions

Environmental, social and governance factors are becoming vital determinants of investment decisions. It is apparent that environmental factors, especially climate change, pose a substantial financial risk to companies. Increasing frequency of extreme events, rising sea level and destruction of biodiversity are some consequences of climate change that impact financial performance. ESG investing is likely to influence more companies to implement strategies to reduce their carbon footprint. Reduction of scope emissions will contribute to holding the increase in average global temperatures to below 2°C above preindustrial levels, a goal of the Paris Agreement. Reduction of scope emissions will also help to achieve net carbon neutrality by 2050, a target considered crucial to combat the current climate change. The high financial performance of ESG investing, increase in the number of ESG investors and financial assets, environmental consciousness among younger investors, and regulatory and investor ESG promoting initiatives are likely to influence more companies to implement strategies towards carbon neutrality. The lack of ESG scoring standards, terminology variability and enormous amount of data to process are some challenges of ESG investing. There are initiatives, however, to have standards in ESG rating, and attempts are also being made at using artificial intelligence to process huge volumes of data. Despite the challenges, and going forward, ESG investing is likely to play an important role in combating climate change.

Acknowledgements

Appreciation goes to Grim, D.M. of The Vanguard Group, and Barrett, J. of UNPRI for providing updated information and statistics.

Conflict of interest

The author declares no conflict of interest.

Author details

Percy Jinga[1,2]

1 Swiss Federal Institute for Forest, Snow and Landscape Research WSL, Dynamic Macroecology Group, Birmensdorf, Switzerland

2 Biological Sciences Department, Bindura University of Science Education, Bindura, Zimbabwe

*Address all correspondence to: percy.jinga@fulbrightmail.org

References

[1] IPCC. Annex I: Glossary. In: Masson-Delmotte V, Zhai P, Portner H-O, Roberts D, Skea J, Shukla PR, Pirani A, Moufouma-Okia W, Pean C, Pidcock R, Connors S, Matthews JBR, Chen Y, Zhou X, Gomis MI, Lonnoy E, Maycock T, Tignor M, Waterfield T, editors. Global warming of 1.5°C. An IPCC Special Report on the impacts of global warming of 1.5°C above pre-industrial levels and related global greenhouse gas emission pathways, in the context of strengthening the global response to the threat of climate change, sustainable development, and efforts to eradicate poverty Geneva: United Nations; 2018. p. 539-562

[2] National Oceanic and Atmospheric Administration [Internet]. 2021. Available from: https://www.climate.gov [Accessed: 2021-01-23]

[3] Vincent WF. Arctic climate change: Local impacts, global consequences, and policy implications. In: Coates K, Holroyd C, editors. The Palgrave Handbook of Arctic Policy and Politics. Cham: Palgrave Macmillan; 2020. p. 507-526. DOI: 10.1007/978-3-030-20557-7_31

[4] Cilas C, Bastide P. Challenges to cocoa production in the face of climate change and the spread of pests and diseases. Agronomy. 2020; 10: 1232. DOI: 10.3390/agronomy10091232

[5] Huckelba AL, Van Lange PAM. The silent killer: consequences of climate change and how to survive past the year 2050. Sustainability. 2020; 12: 3757. DOI: 10.3390/su12093757

[6] Bartlett S. Climate change and urban children: Impacts and implications for adaptation in low- and middle-income countries. Environment and Urbanization. 2008; 20: 501-519. DOI: 10.1177/0956247808096125

[7] United Nations Framework Convention on Climate Change. Paris Agreement. Bonn: United Nations; 2015.

[8] The European Commission [Internet]. 2021. EU climate action and the European Green Deal. Available from: https://ec.europa.eu/clima/policies/eu-climate-action_en [Accessed: 2021-02-05]

[9] The African Union [Internet]. 2021. Agriculture and environmental management treaties. Available from: https://au.int/en/treaties/1160 [Accessed: 2021-01-25]

[10] United Nations Development Programme. Climate change adaptation in the Arab states: Best practices and lessons learned. Bangkok: United Nations; 2018

[11] Organization of American States [Internet]. 2021. Environment: Climate change. Available from: http://www.summit-americas.org/sisca/env_climate.html [Accessed: 2021-01-25]

[12] Schueth S. Socially responsible investing in the United States. Journal of Business Ethics. 2003; 43: 189-194. DOI: 10.1023/A:1022981828869

[13] Shank TM, Manullang DK, Hill RP. Is it better to be naughty or nice? Journal of Investing. 2005; 14: 82-88. DOI: 10.3905/joi.2005.580553

[14] Berry TC, Junkus JC. Socially responsible investing: an investor perspective. Journal of Business Ethics. 2013; 112: 707-720. DOI: 10.1007/s10551-012-1567-0

[15] Schwartz MS. The 'ethics' of ethical investing. Journal of Business Ethics. 2003; 43: 195-213. DOI: 10.1023/A:1022933912939

[16] Daugaard D. Emerging new themes in environmental, social and governance investing: a systematic literature review. Accounting and Finance. 2020; 60: 1501-1530. DOI: 10.1111/acfi.12479

[17] Caplan L, Griswold JS, Jarvis WF. From SRI to ESG: the changing world of responsible investing. Wilton CT: Commonfund Institute; 2013

[18] Sandberg JM, Juravle C, Hedesström TM, Hamilton I. The heterogeneity of socially responsible investment. Journal of Business Ethics. 2009; 87: 519-533. DOI: 10.1007/s10551-008-9956-0

[19] Grim DM, Berkowitz DB. ESG, SRI, and impact investing: A primer for decision-making. The Journal of Impact and ESG Investing. 2020; 1: 1-19. DOI: 10.3905/jesg.2020.1.1.047

[20] van Duuren E, Plantinga A, Scholtens B. ESG integration and the investment management process: fundamental investing reinvented. Journal of Business Ethics. 2016; 138: 525-533. DOI: 10.1007/s10551-015-2610-8

[21] Elsenhuber U, Skenderasi A. ESG investing: the role of public investors in sustainable investing. Evolving Practices in Public Asset Management. In: Proceedings of the Seventh Public Investors Conference; 22-23 October 2018; Rome: p. 45-56

[22] S&P Global [Internet]. 2019. Understanding the "E" in ESG. Available from: https://www.spglobal.com/en/research-insights/articles/understanding-the-e-in-esg [Accessed: 2021-01-27]

[23] Hertwich EG, Wood R. The growing importance of scope 3 gas emissions from industry. Environmental Research Letters. 2018; 13: 104013. DOI: 10.1088/1748-9326/aae19a

[24] Huang YA, Weber CL, Matthews HS. Categorization of scope 3 emissions for streamlined enterprise carbon footprinting. Environmental Science and Technology. 2009; 43: 8509-8515. DOI: 10.1021/es901643a

[25] S&P Global [Internet]. 2020. What is the "S" in ESG? Available from: https://www.spglobal.com/en/research-insights/articles/what-is-the-s-in-esg [Accessed: 2021-01-27]

[26] S&P Global [Internet]. 2020. What is the "G" in ESG? Available from: https://www.spglobal.com/en/research-insights/articles/what-is-the-g-in-esg [Accessed: 2021-01-27]

[27] Mačaitytė I, Virbašiūtė G. Volkswagen emission scandal and corporate social responsibility– A case study. Business Ethics and Leadership. 2018; 2: 6-13. DOI: 10.21272/bel.2(1).6-13.2018

[28] Jung JC, Sharon E. The Volkswagen emissions scandal and its aftermath. Global Business and Organizational Excellence. 2019; 38: 6-15. DOI: 10.1002/joe.21930

[29] Eurosif. [Internet]. 2021. Responsible investment strategies. Available from: http://www.eurosif.org/responsile-investment-strategies/ [Accessed: 2021-04-02]

[30] McGuire JB, Sundgren A, Scheneeweis A. Corporate social responsibility and firm financial performance. Academy of Management Journal. 1988; 31: 854-872. DOI: 10.5465/256342

[31] Moskowitz MR. Choosing socially responsible stocks. Business and Society Review. 1972; 1: 71-75

[32] Alexander GJ, Buchholz RS. Corporate social responsibility and stock market performance. Academy of Management Journal. 1978; 21: 479-486

[33] Friede G, Busch T, Bassen A. ESG and financial performance: aggregated evidence from more than 2000 empirical studies, Journal of Sustainable Finance and Investment. 2015; 5: 210-233. DOI: 10.1080/20430795.2015.1118917

[34] Cochran PL, Wood RA. Corporate social responsibility and financial performance. Academy of Management Journal. 1984; 27: 42-56

[35] Giese G, Lee L-E, Melas D, Nagy Z, Nishikawa L. Foundations of ESG investing: how ESG affects equity valuation, risk and performance. The Journal of Portfolio Management. 2019; 45: 69-83. DOI: 10.3905/jpm.2019.45.5.069

[36] Edmans A. Does stock market fully value tangibles? Employee satisfaction and equity prices. Journal of Financial Economics. 2011; 101: 621-640. DOI: 10.1016/j.jfineco.2011.03.021

[37] Derwall J, Guenster N, Bauer R, Koedijk K. The eco-efficiency premium puzzle. Financial Analysts Journal. 2005; 61: 51-63. DOI: 10.2469/faj.v61.n2.2716

[38] Atan R, Alam MM, Said J, Zamri M. The impacts of environmental, social and governance factors on firm performance: panel study of Malaysian companies. Management of Environmental Quality. 2018; 29: 182-194. DOI: 10.1108/MEQ-03-2017-0033

[39] Duque-Grisales E, Aguilera-Caracuel J. Environmental, social and governance (ESG) scores and financial performance of multilatinas: moderating effects of geographic international diversification and financial slack. Journal of Business Ethics. 2021; 168: 315-334. DOI: 10.1007/s10551-019-04177-w

[40] Torre ML, Mango F, Cafaro A, Leo S. Does the ESG index affect stock return? Evidence from the Eurostoxx50. Sustainability. 2020; 12: 6387. DOI: 10.3390/su12166387

[41] Khan MN, Serafeim G, Yoon A. Corporate sustainability: first evidence on materiality. Harvard Business School Working Paper No. 15-073. Boston: Harvard Business School; 2015

[42] Schanzenbach MM, Sitkoff RH. ESG investing: Theory, evidence and fiduciary principles. Journal of Financial Planning. 2020; 42-50

[43] Modern Diplomacy [Internet]. 2021. Global business leaders committing to stakeholder capitalism metrics. Available from: https://moderndiplomacy.eu/2021/01/27/global-business-leaders-committing-to-stakeholder-capitalism-metrics/ [Accessed: 2021-01-30]

[44] World Economic Forum [Internet]. 2020. Measuring stakeholder capitalism: Towards common metrics and consistent reporting of sustainable value creation. Available from: https://www.weforum.org/reports/measuring-stakeholder-capitalism-towards-common-metrics-and-consistent-reporting-of-sustainable-value-creation [Accessed: 2021-01-30]

[45] TCFD [Internet]. 2017. Recommendations of the task force on climate-related financial disclosures. Final Report. Available from: https://www.fsb-tcfd.org/recommendations/ [Accessed:2021-01-30]

[46] Rosen BN, Sandler DM, Shani D. Social issues and socially responsible investment behavior: A preliminary empirical investigation. The Journal of Consumer Affairs. 1991; 25: 221-234. DOI: 10.1111/j.1745-6606.1991.tb00003.x

[47] Reynolds F [Internet]. 2019. Climate change tops the list of ESG concerns for investors in 2019. Principles of Responsible Investment. Available from: https://www.unpri.org/pri-blogs/climate-change-tops-the-list-of-esg-concerns-for-investors-in-2019/4163.article [Accessed: 2021-02-02]

[48] Mascotto G [Internet]. 2020. ESG outlook: Five key trends are driving momentum in 2020. American Century Investments. Available from: https://ipro.americancentury.com/content/ipro/en/insights/key-topics/esg-sustainable-investing/esg-outlook.html [Accessed: 2021-02-02]

[49] European Commission [Internet]. 2020. EU taxonomy for sustainable activities. Available from: https://ec.europa.eu/info/business-economy-euro/banking-and-finance/sustainable-finance/eu-taxonomy-sustainable-activities_en [Accessed: 2021-02-04]

CPSIA information can be obtained
at www.ICGtesting.com
Printed in the USA
LVHW060758130422
716078LV00006B/226

9 781839 625466